*For all those
extraordinary men, who, for
more than 1,200 years
have cherished
Mount Athos
and kept it
Holy*

Thirty Years of the Friends of Mount Athos

Encounters on the Holy Mountain
Stories from Mount Athos

Compiled and edited by
Peter Howorth FRGS *&* Christopher Thomas FRGS

Photographs by
Roland Baetens

With a Foreword by
HRH The Prince of Wales

BREPOLS

ISBN 978-2-503-58911-4
D/2020/0095/262

Designed by Paul van Calster

Printed in the EU on acid-free paper.

Publications by the Friends of Mount Athos

The Life of Prayer on Mount Athos
Edited by Douglas Dales and Graham Speake, 2020

A Pilgrim's Guide to Mount Athos
Sixth Edition, 2020

The Friends of Mount Athos 1990–2020
A Very Short History
By Graham Speake et al., 2020

A History of the Athonite Commonwealth
The Spiritual and Cultural Diaspora of Mount Athos
By Graham Speake, 2018

Mount Athos and Russia 1016–2016
Edited by Nicholas Fennell and Graham Speake, 2018

Rightly Dividing the Word of Truth
Studies in Honour of Metropolitan Kallistos of Diokleia
Edited by Andreas Andreopoulos and Graham Speake, 2016

Spiritual Guidance on Mount Athos
Edited by Graham Speake and Metropolitan Kallistos Ware, 2015

Mount Athos: Renewal in Paradise
By Graham Speake. Second Edition, 2014

Mount Athos: Microcosm of the Christian East
Edited by Graham Speake and Metropolitan Kallistos Ware, 2012

Monk Sáva of Hilandar: A Scholar
By Petr Balcárek, 2012

The Monastic Magnet. Roads to and from Mount Athos
Edited by René Gothóni and Graham Speake, 2008

Mount Athos the Sacred Bridge
The Spirituality of the Holy Mountain
Edited by Dimitri Conomos and Graham Speake, 2005

Here, in lush valleys, teem bees, figs, and olives.
The inmates of the monasteries weave cloth, stitch shoes,
and make nets. One turns the spindle of a hand-loom through the wool;
another twists a basket of twigs. From time to time, at stated hours, all essay
to praise God, and peace reigns among them, always and for ever.

—Cristoforo Buondelmonti (1386–1430), Traveller in the East, 1420

Cristoforo Buondelmonti, Liber Insularum Archipelagi (1420), Mount Athos

Table of Contents

Acknowledgements

It goes without saying that this book would not exist without contributions
from so many distinguished, enthusiastic and knowledgable people.
We had no idea what would be submitted and we have been
stunned by what we have received – the quality
has significantly exceeded our expectations.
So thank you!

Beyond that, there is a group of individuals whose contribution is either
not acknowledged elsewhere or whose efforts need an additional thank you including:

Graham Speake
The Friends of Mount Athos Committee
SETE Group (Latsis Foundation)
Andrew Maskall
Dave Powell
Bart Janssens
Gavin Agamemnon
James Barnes

Two gentlemen deserve to be placed on a higher pedestal:

Trevor Curnow brought much needed discipline and
expertise to the task of editing. His experience was invaluable and without it,
this book would not be the polished volume it has become.

Johan Van der Beke is our wonderful publisher from Brepols –
he and his team took our extremely raw text and images and magically turned it
into this beautiful book. We are amazed and delighted.

And finally, we wish to honour the memory of Theoclis Chrysanthou,
a great man we did not have the privilege to get to know.

Foreword by HRH The Prince of Wales

CLARENCE HOUSE

Mount Athos, the spiritual heart of the Orthodox Church, offers its gifts to those who take the time to listen – young and old, men and women, Orthodox and non-Orthodox. For the past thirty years, the Friends of Mount Athos have, by means of their many activities, encouraged people to receive those gifts and to hear the Mountain's timeless message.

For my part, I can only say what great pleasure it has given me, as Patron, to support the activities of the Friends of Mount Athos over these past decades. The Society's original aims to study and promulgate knowledge of the history, arts, architecture, natural history and literature of the Orthodox monasteries of Mount Athos have been so marvellously delivered through fundraising events, pilgrimages and practical endeavours such as path-clearing and map-making.

I dearly hope that this beautiful book, and its wonderful collection of stories, encounters, pictures and experiences, might bring the Mountain not just to those who know it, but also to those who do not. The stories in this book are often a reflection of the joy that pilgrims have attained, and of the many ways in which friendship with the monks of Mount Athos has enriched their lives and provided them with new insights into a different, sacred engagement with the world around them.

Life on the Holy Mountain gives all visitors an example of a more holistic, kinder and less invasive way of life. I hope that this book might bring a taste of that very special experience to even more people.

Introduction

PETER HOWORTH & CHRIS THOMAS

We are writing this at the beginning of May 2020 from opposite sides of a planet shattered by the coronavirus pandemic. In New Zealand, the impact has, thankfully, been modest and there are hopes that the effects will be minimal. The same cannot be said for the United Kingdom with more than one thousand people dying each day. Somewhere between the two, Greece and our beloved Mount Athos are slowly beginning to emerge from the nightmare. Northern Greece, including Mount Athos, has had to contend additionally with extreme weather which has affected roads and other infrastructure. The main road between the Holy Mountain's only port (Daphne) and only settlement and administrative centre (Karyes) is no longer usable – Mount Athos is officially under a state of emergency and for the first time in a very long time, there are no pilgrims on the mountain. If ever there was a moment to pause and take stock, it is now.

It's appropriate that the pause be broken by Peter's characteristic Kiwi bluntness. 'It is ridiculous to hope that we will return to the previous way of life – one does not undergo treatment for lung cancer so that one can take up smoking again', he says in both hope and expectation that we will not react to this crisis by simply returning to the way things were.

So many stories in this book are about discomfort, sacrifice, spiritual discovery and recognition of how the earth would really like us to treat it, and we hope you will find these reflections and recollections all the more powerful and poignant in light of recent events.

When the two of us began talking about this book a year or so ago, the main idea was to provide a volume that would explain the lure of the Holy Mountain to people who could not experience this for themselves. This place, Mount Athos, is the centre of Orthodox spirituality. It is forbidden to women and has been the home of monks for more than 1,200 years. This is quite difficult for non-Orthodox as well as women to imagine. So why do we want to return there again and again?

We have tried to answer that by creating a grand metaphor for a pilgrimage to the Holy Mountain. And each story within is a metaphor in itself. It is a bit like what one pilgrim said after he'd bought the map, visited and come back 'Before I went, I looked at life and thought, is this all there is? Now I know that the answer is no!'

Pilgrimage is an approach to life that is grounded in the present and moves along an open-hearted journey of transformation. Pilgrimage begins with a few incremental, ordinary steps, and sometimes becomes a momentous journey, that integrates body and soul. Pilgrimage trains the eye of the soul to see God daily, everywhere. When you set out on your own pilgrimage, you discover yourself and the Divine presence in a whole new way.

Today's technology is cocooning us, allowing us to forget our natural aptitudes and abilities. We no longer need to use our vast natural reservoir of skills in order to engage with our surroundings. As humans we have been blessed with extraordinary abilities of sight and hearing and navigation, however, modern technology means that these abilities are no longer essential. Pilgrims who visit the Holy Mountain often find that the cocoon of technology that has sheltered them is no longer there. This means that for the first time for many years, nature and people in all their complexity and clarity are encountered. The richness of this encounter is, for most, extraordinary. It can seem as if it is perhaps the first time they have truly engaged with the world. And then, of course, once one has engaged with something, one can never be indifferent to it. We find that after the first engagement with the Holy Mountain, it becomes a permanent presence in our consciousness.

While discussing photography with a professional photographer recently, we stumbled on a thought that was unexpectedly profound. He told us that the new technology of High Dynamic Range (HDR) television was creating in people a new way of looking at things. Because HDR technology produces such an intensely heightened image of reality, people discount normal landscape and colours regarding them as insipid, and of no importance. So now when people look at landscapes, and see what they expect to see, they look no deeper. The net effect of this is that people do not actually see what they are looking at.

In addition, there are problems with communication, as many people communicate by text or email. The majority of their interaction therefore is only one-dimensional. People do not use pencils and pens, and thus they have lost the joy of the brain-hand connection. Many people prefer to use GPS rather than maps, and so all our natural way-finding abilities are not being developed.

Nothing about the Holy Mountain is familiar; there are none of the crutches or comforts of home. You are forced to reach out to fellow pilgrims or monks. In losing the familiar, you find yourself. You shed the cocoon and become just you. No profession, barbecue, lawnmower, credit card or fishing rod to be used as a crutch. The naked you then discovers he can communicate and rediscover the person he always was. After that, you are never the same.

While we were musing on this, we came across a wonderful quotation from Rachel Carson:

Mankind has gone very far into an artificial world of his own creation. He has sought to insulate himself, in his cities of steel and concrete, from the realities of earth and water and the growing seed. Intoxicated with a sense of his own power, he seems to be going farther and farther into more experiments for the destruction of himself and his world. There is certainly no single remedy for this condition and I am offering no panacea. But it seems reasonable to believe – and I do believe – that the more clearly we can focus our attention on the wonders and realities of the universe about us the less taste we shall have for the destruction of our race. Wonder and humility are wholesome emotions, and they do not exist side by side with a lust for destruction.'

—*Lost Woods: The Discovered Writing of Rachel Carson* (1999) edited by Linda Lear

So, what do we have here in this book? People have been exceptionally open with themselves, disclosing many different aspects of their inner selves, and, in so doing, help the rest of us to recognise some of what is going on inside us. These contributions are extraordinary in their scope, all from authors doing interesting things, but affected in some way by the enduring grace of Mount Athos, the Holy Mountain.

Organising these many submissions had the makings of a huge challenge – different eras, different perspectives and a huge diversity of subject matter – but the sections with which we have sought to bring some semblance of structure and organisation came to us easily and every contribution we received thereafter slotted in perfectly, as if by divine predestination.

The end-product is a book which we hope brings to life the richness, colour, holiness and allure of the Holy Mountain through its extraordinary history stretching over a millennium. We use the word 'history' in its broadest possible sense – this book is about faith, landscape, architecture, iconography, ecology, humanity, pilgrimage, food, medicine and so much more. Our goal was to do justice to our contributors by packaging it in a way that is accessible and uplifting.

A significant section of the book is devoted to path-clearing and we feel that this does require some additional context. Clearing footpaths on the Holy Mountain is how we first encountered the power and beauty of the mountain, it is how the two of us met and it is how we were inspired to bring our good fortune to a wider audience through this book.

Events that took place in the life of one of our fellow path-clearers while we worked to bring this book to fruition inspired us further – he, the friend, had just been through the toughest of journeys – the loss of his wife. The loss was made easier to bear by the presence of the Holy Mountain throughout the difficult months that had just passed. Our friend moved us almost to tears as he related to Peter his views on the permanence and the pervasiveness of the aroma of grace that binds us all together, the shared understanding, faith and love that is just below the surface.

This is our gift for you.

NOTE – *The monks do not regard the Holy Mountain as part of 'The World', and seek to retain their privacy and peace. Thus living monks are only identified by an initial.*

Part One

Before

Apparently the Gods dropped a huge rock on the Aegean Sea that landed on a giant called Athos. This is said to be the origin of the peninsula and the mountain. In ancient times there were about five cities there, and by the second and third centuries it was under the rule of the Macedonians and King Philip, and later Alexander the Great. Alexander's architect made a proposal to carve the mountain into a likeness of Alexander, but he refused, saying that one of his predecessors displayed enough arrogance by building the canal of Xerxes.

In the fourth century the first monks arrived, as the land was uninhabited. Monks from the peninsula were recorded at the Nicene Council of AD 787, and from about AD 860 various settlements were formally founded. Emperor Basil declared the Peninsula a haven for monks, and no laymen or cattle breeders were allowed to live there. The first administrative structure was recorded in AD 908, in AD 943 the boundaries were properly mapped, and in AD 972 the first Charter of Mount Athos was established.

AD 963 is generally regarded as the completion date of the oldest monastery, the Great Lavra. By the end of the eleventh century most of the 20 monasteries were established, and so were many cells.

The Fourth Crusade meant that the Catholic Church became involved, and the monks complained to the Pope when the financial demands got too heavy.

In the fifteenth century the Byzantine Empire collapsed and the Ottoman Empire took its place. When Murad II conquered Thessaloniki, the monks of the Holy Mountain immediately pledged allegiance to him to avoid interference or destruction. Murad recognized the monasteries' property, and this was later formally ratified by his successor after the fall of Constantinople in 1453.

By the end of the fifteenth century, the roots of Athonite pan-Orthodoxy were clearly evident, paralleling the breadth of Christianity itself, with monasteries reflecting this diversity of occupation: these included Iviron by Georgians, Panteleimon by Russians, Chilandar, Grigoriou, and St Paul by Serbs, and Zografou, Filotheou and Simonos Petras by Bulgarians. These were prosperous times for the Holy Mountain, but could also be at times tumultuous, as Hagiorite fathers of very different ethnic and cultural backgrounds had to learn how to respect and live with each other. The final monastery, Stavronikita, was completed. Tsars and Princes helped with large donations. Then the numbers slowly shrank; by the beginning of the nineteenth century, the only Slav monasteries were Chilandar, Zografou, St Paul and Xenophontos.

The monasteries were mainly left on their own, but the Ottomans taxed them and took land from them, creating an economic crisis in the seventeenth century. This led to the spread of the so-called 'idiorrhythmic' lifestyle by a few monasteries at first and later, by all. The monasteries' abbots were replaced by committees and at Karyes the Protos was replaced by a four-member committee.

During the Greek War of Independence the monasteries were occupied by the Ottoman Turks. Three garrisons were established. The population of monks and their wealth partially were revitalized during the nineteenth century, particularly by the patronage of the Russian government. Russian monks took over the monastery of Panteleimon, elected their own abbot and spread further to numerous cells and sketes as their number was growing continuously, until eventually there were five thousand Russian monks against four thousand Greek monks.

During the First Balkan War, the Ottomans were forced out by the Greek Navy. Greece claimed the peninsula. After a false start, peace was agreed at the Treaty of Bucharest on 10 August 1913.

In June 1913, a small Russian fleet, consisting of the gunboat Donets and the transport ships Tsar and Kherson, delivered the Archbishop of Vologda and a number of troops to Mount Athos to intervene in a theological controversy. After unsuccessful talks, the troops stormed the St Panteleimon Monastery. After this, the monks from the Skete of St Andrew surrendered voluntarily. The military transport Kherson was converted into a prison ship and more than a thousand monks were sent to Odessa where they were excommunicated and dispersed throughout Russia.

After a brief diplomatic conflict, the peninsula formally came under Greek sovereignty after World War I. In 1924 a five-member committee of eminent Athonites prepared the 'Charter for the Holy Mountain of Athos', which codified regulations and administrative dispositions stemming not only from written sources, but also from tradition and customary usage. This Charter was approved that same year by the Athonite Assembly known as the 'double Synaxis'.

On the basis of this official text the Greek state drafted a Legislative Decree, which the Greek Parliament passed into law in 1926. At the same time, the 1927 Greek Constitution contained special articles (included in each subsequent constitution) on the general principles governing the status of Mount Athos.

These were the official documents defining the peninsula's relations with Greece and with the Church, as well as the competence of its administrative institutions, the Holy Community and the Holy Epistasia.

During World War II, the executive committee, prompted and guided by the local German Commander, formally sought and obtained Hitler's protection of the Athonite Peninsula from the threatened raids by Balkan groups that had arisen since the German invasion of northern Greece.

The 1000th anniversary of the Holy Mountain in 1963 was attended by all heads of the Eastern Orthodox Churches.

Simopetra (Simonos Petras)

ROBERT BYRON

This extract is from The Station *by Robert Byron (1927), a book about a visit to the Holy Mountain
by three friends: Robert Byron, David Talbot Rice, and Mark Ogilvie Grant.
Elsewhere in this book you will find a story about a contemporary
'reunion' visit made by Nicky Talbot Rice, David's son,
to Simonos Petras and other places.*

The journey from Grigoriou to Simonos Petras' arsenal occupied twenty minutes, the boatman boasting his knowledge of Africa, where he had peddled unspecified wares also in Bulawayo. He told us that the Greek for prickly pear, which we saw growing on the shore, was 'Frankish fig' – a poor compliment to the other side of our continent. Arrived, we disembarked at a little quay, to be greeted by a monk of immeasurable girth, who ushered us to his house and fed us with grapes taut and sweet as himself. These we ate upon the verandah over which they grew, perched on struts above the water like a Samoan village in an instructional film. The heat was intense. Anxious to forget the climb that lay ahead, we sat in motionless content beneath the vine. And our host was enquiring after the others in whose company I had first met him, when a fleet of mules clattered past a door visible at the other end of the passage. He hailed them. And, loth to lose this chance of a ride, we gained the muleteer's approval with a present of cigarettes, and mounted. Our luggage remained below.

To portray a building whose dissimilarity from its fellows on this globe robs metaphor of its natural function is best left to other means than words. Yet, in the case of this building, the action of its changing aspects is invisible to the stationary beholder. A film might suffice. Unfortunately, this is a book.

Approaching, hypothetically winged, from the southern point of Longos, there is disclosed, as the promontory resolves into detail, a plain white mark high upon the ridge. Other patches, scattered along the shore, proclaim by their innumerable roofs and walls other monasteries: Grigoriou, Russico, Dochiariou. This, on proximity, consists, unlike them, of three tall blocks, towering backward on a crag, white against a mountain slope half as high again as the distance beneath. Their brilliance is accented by a deep shadow, cast westwards in the morning light from wall and rock alike. Far below, at the water's edge, a tower and house, white specks, denote the monastery's port.

The hills close round, shutting out the summit, and the other valleys and other monasteries, till they form a shallow bay. The tower at the edge reveals a new dignity in reflection. Above, the building, risen, now that we are underneath, to the skyline, thrusts its triple clump aloft, each incredible facade exaggerating its own perspective to the call of some invisible scene-shifter behind the imminent cerulean canvas. Trenched inward from the contour of the bay and the spreading hills, a wooded ravine of perpetual shadow rises perpendicular some 900 feet. Until, from its womb, leaps to the light a pedestal of twisted, golden rock; and from it, gathering to itself the shadowed, shrub-grown ledges, Simonos Petras, the monastery, 'Rock of Simon'.

The path, topping the tower, twists up one side of the indentation, among precarious olive-groves. At first the building is invisible; until, upon a corner, it reappears, expanded, astounding. With every zigzag of the road it swells; new planes revealed, new lines composed. For the three blocks, each built back one behind the other as the rock demands, are not set square. The middle meets

FIG. 2 *Simonos Petras and Osiou Grigoriou*

the foremost at a greater than a right-angle, the hinder the middle at a lesser. From no two positions, therefore, is the building consistent with its former self. As the blocks rise, unadorned save for the encircling stripes of wooden balconies, they narrow. Or, more accurately, the foundations diverge, that of the most prominent resting on a gigantic buttress sloping down the rock to a terraced foothold. And below it, from the curving beds of beans and tomatoes hanging nervously fifteen feet above each other, dark cypresses also engage in the festivity of line, urge up and on, till the human eye, unused to these dynamic harmonies, must slip its socket. With their perpetual variation and impatience of gravity, the three striped torsos resemble a group of footballers in that instant before the ball descends. Thus, petrified in colour, feet hidden in the cleft, knees of golden rock, white linen shorts and striped jerseys, they stand everlasting.

And the ball does not descend.

We dismounted at the long, upward-sloping tunnel that gives entrance to the monastery. And, reaching a courtyard, picked our way to the guest quar-

ters along a balcony disclosing broad fissures of eternity between its creaking boards. The guest-master said that lunch would be ready in an hour. David lay down to read. Mark and I launched into the heat.

He walked up to the back to sketch. I, casting about for a vantage-point that might admit a level camera, noticed a platform of rock forty feet immediately above my head. Descending to a small chapel on the left of the path, which contained in its crypt the skulls of deceased fathers disinterred after three years and neatly docketed on shelves, I leapt down a bank of marrows; and, rounding a corner, came upon a gully that seemed to lead whither I had hoped. The ascent at first was easy: a mere creeping underneath the roots of bushes. But suddenly it took a right-angle – not to one side or the other, but in point of gradient. Perpendicular, it was not a gully, but a pipe. The sun was at its highest; the shaft in which I was imprisoned airless. All the view was the sea, awaiting the corpse that should come hurtling to its bosom. The stream, dry since May, trickled again, but red from lacerated flesh. Movement became fainter and fainter. Had not the sky reappeared, I should have remembered no more. Writhing like an Iroquois after a scalp upon the pinnacle of my desire, I poised the camera. Behold the result. And weep my life's blood.

Lunch, despite a protracted benediction, was welcome. Finished, we set out again, walking this time in the other direction, where the monastery is joined to the hill by a double-tiered aqueduct. From here its aspect changes. The pedestal of rock rises at the back of the monastery to within three stories of the roof, instead of, if the foundation walls of the front were windowed, approximately twenty. The domes of the church within the courtyard are visible. And the whole assumes an air of fantasy, like a Rhineland castle perched at the brink of an unscaleable crag, but made safe by the net of stone that hooks it to the hill behind. Below the scenic-railway entrance, the shadowy outline of ironbound double doors was visible, leading into the bowels of

FIG. 3 *Monastery of Simonos Petras: R. Curzon, London, 1849*

PL. 2 *Monastery of Agiou Pavlou (St Paul's)*

PL. 3 *Vrachaki l. (Kolitsou)*

the rock. Our curiosity was aroused. But their objective remained an enigma. It was presumably an older entrance, dating from before that ghastly fire, still recorded, when the entrapped monks could only hurl themselves down the precipices of the front to escape the flames. This was in 1625. A sketch of the building as it later appeared was appended by Robert Curzon to his Monasteries of the Levant, published in 1849. But, as the foreground of this is entirely imaginary, it is impossible to rely on the accuracy of his depiction. He makes it more whimsical in form than appears to-day, like a windmill on the scale of the Eiffel Tower. The present group dates from another fire of 1893, thus carrying the climax of Byzantine domestic architecture to the birthday of the twentieth century. For the monks built and designed unaided.

Those who have lived in Athens, and lunched, as Athens does, at Costi's, will recall the lovely Madame Kogevinas. Her husband, an artist, is the author of an etching which shows Simonos Petras from a peculiar angle, rising its most precipitous into the sky. This view I also had in mind to see. Searching the landscape for whence it might be possible, I espied a small brown patch among the trees on the farther side of the ravine. It was necessary to approach from the back. On a bridge over which the path was carried stood a number of mules, who double their near hind-legs in readiness for my ribs. But, alarmed at the unfamiliar imprecations which greeted this movement, they thought better and galloped off into the mountains. Their master, hearing the noise, emerged upon a balcony to vent his anger upon both them and me.

By means of a track scarcely a foot wide, coated with dry slippery leaves and tunnelling among the undergrowth at an angle that necessitated sitting, the brown patch was reached. And perseverance was rewarded. Far above, a huge tilted box, creamy gold, and striped with the shadowed silver of oaken struts and planks, was rocketed into the blazing turquoise sky. It lived; like the flowers of the mystic, it sang; insensate; irresistible; inexplicable.

Seated on a rock, I sketched. My pencil, prone to be romantic, fled over the page in ecstasy, exaggerating the tone of the sky to the ferocity of a thunderstorm. But the others were waiting. The progress of the ascent, owing to my sandals slipping two paces for every one they took, was dependent on the arms. The heat was insupportable; the handkerchief that might have solaced, plucked from its pocket by the barbed vegetation; and the last thorn added to my crown when I was confronted, after twenty minutes' climb, by an impregnable cliff. Returning to the bottom, I found another track. My mouth was so parched that, on entering the guest room, it would not utter, and the others feared for my reason.

Bidding the guest-master good-bye, we started the descent to the sea. It was my misfortune, when at school, to suffer from weakness of the ankles: a welcome safeguard against compulsory athletics; but one which jeopardised the hopes entertained by my house of my winning cups for its dining-room table – which I never did. Massage, therefore, was the remedy, applied by the Misses Dempster, ladies of frightening intelligence, who would invite me to consider the claim of a landscape 'permeated', as they said, 'with spires', to superiority over one which was not; or to analyse the composition of the uneasiest of Sargent's charcoal portraits, reproduced and presented them by Lord Spencer. Their house, indeed, was an illustrated Debrett, comparable only to the portraits of the Almanach de Gotha displayed on the walls of Madame Sacher's bar in Vienna. Massage finished, the ankles were tightly bound, and, thus reinforced, would gradually regain their strength. The morning of our visit to Simonos Petras, the muscles, long quiescent, had uttered a minatory twinge. Unwinding from a chintz bag some lengths of bandage provided by a parent

FIG. 4 *St Panteleimonos from the sea*

who had envisaged the dangers of glacier and crevasse, I performed the remembered operations. But in vain. And now, emerging from the monastery, I could scarcely walk. Nor were there mules.

The debility arising, as in the case of running-shoes, from my sandals having no heels, relief was only gained by remaining poised on the toes. Thus I set off, hopping from rock to rock like an inebriate ballerina. But the pace, in such heat, was not to be borne. And, the feet being comfortable in any position but their natural, I turned and went backward. Physically this was perfection; but the mental strain, owing to the precipitous twists of the path, was insupportable. Eventually I fell on David's arm and dragged behind him like a rag doll. We reached the shore; and, despite the presence of a small sword-fish, flung ourselves from the jetty. To tired, hot, and aching bodies never was bathe so delicious. Eyes shut; rocking on the ripples of a breeze, shaking the water to drink the fullness of its cold; eardrums vibrating to its tinny throbbing; we lay entranced, almost asleep; confronted, when the eyes opened, by the wide doors of the boat-house at the head of a causeway of logs; the monk's house, balconied and vine-shaded; the white arsenal tower; the hills around, full of large shadows; the black gulch; and at the top, alight with the sun, the great building, falling back into the sky, ready to kick its foundations down the trees and crush us in the water at the foot.

The fat monk opened his spare room to our toilet – a sunny apartment, and for that purpose chosen to contain a string of drying haddocks in the smell of which, festooned with blue-bottles, lay the secret of many of our meals. After an hour's journey in a boat, during which we slept, we arrived at Daphne.

There, while the boatman waited, we hurried ashore, excited at regaining this Sybaris of luxury. But our feelings were damped by the discovery that we could obtain neither a glass of beer nor a clean pocket handkerchief. A box of plates, and a kit-bag hitherto filled with food and unused films, were deposited with the shopkeeper. With a dozen fresh tins of sardines in our saddle-bags, we again set sail – this time literally, as a breeze had risen.

The sun was setting, striking hidden fire in the purple hills. While the water, as if in protest, turned a shivering glass-green. Schooners, vermilion and orange, lay at anchor. Another in full sail rode by, with a red gold on its bellying canvas. Then the wind dropped, and we took to the oars again. The sun was gone, and the twilight deepening, before the barracks of the Russian monastery of St Panteleimon loomed above us.

Monoxylites, 1941

SANDY THOMAS

Sandy was a New Zealand soldier who was wounded and captured in the Battle for Crete. He was shipped to a prison hospital in Thessaloniki, escaped, and walked across the top of Greece to the Holy Mountain, where he was sheltered and tended by the monks. He eventually found his way to the Turkish – Syrian border, where he was miraculously reunited with his brother.

This extract is from an unpublished letter to his parents written after the reunion. A few years ago Sandy asked me (PH) if the monks who made the wine he talked about, Monoxylites, would like to use his face to help advertise it. He always said that this wine went straight into his blood and that was what made his leg better!

... on the advice of the same mayor, fine patriotic fellow he was even in his fear, I moved along a small beach track towards the mysteries and wonders of Mount Athos, the Holy Mountain.

Mount Athos lies as one of the three fingers jutting from Macedonia, and is tied up with history throughout the ages. Xerxes had a canal cut at its base to enable him to manoeuvre his fleet, and used its heights as an observation point from where he could see all the Northern Aegean and even over to Constantinople. Nowadays the whole of this peninsula is peopled by some 8,000 monks of the Orthodox Church. For 1,200 years no female, nor even a feminine animal, has crossed the narrow isthmus of its borders. The kings of Greece have respected its identity – and have eased their conscience to the church by donating untold fortunes to the various monasteries, while even today the monks are tax-free. There are twenty monasteries, all in the most beautiful and rugged scenery imaginable, some perched way up on impossible heights where one feared the smallest puff of wind would dislodge them, with stone steps winding and zigzagging up to them giving the whole an appearance not far removed from our childhood conception of fairy castles. Built with ramparts, towers, great studded doors and sometimes draw-bridges these great forts have withstood many assaults by Greek and Turk alike.

The land is very steep everywhere, in fact it is difficult to find any flat area over one or two acres, but where they have built up their picturesque stone terraces the earth is rich and productive and the monks boast the best grapes, wine and olives in the whole of Greece. Dotted around the main monasteries are the monastery gardens and farmhouses, while everywhere are churches both large and small, their various bells ringing clearly up the steep valleys and ravines.

But let me get on with the story. I crossed onto the holy ground and after one or two adventures set off uphill to a large monastery I could see surrounded by great cypress trees. On the track a young monk stopped me and told me that it was a White Russian monastery and pro-German – that they had betrayed their sanctuary and given over two English quite recently. He himself was Russian and took me along the water's edge to a tiny cottage and church where I was welcomed by an old old monk.

All the monks wear long black robes, great flowing beards and long hair with a cap similar to a fez but black also. My host sat me down, took off my shoes and bathed my blistered feet in warm soapy water, gave me a meal of raw fish and olives and put me to bed in a tiny guest room. The next day I sat in the sun and watched the sparkling waves of the sea below, while the monk washed my socks and mended my shoes. With the walking my leg was discharging

PL. 4 *Monastery of Agiou Dionysiou*

freely and I bathed it in the sea. The monk was very worried and begged me to come to a doctor friend of his, so, agreeing, I followed him up the winding path to the monastery where I was turned away, and set off again just as dusk drew in. I spent that night on the beach lying in front of a fire I made from driftwood and eating the last of my precious bread.

Soon after dawn I set off toward the next monastery, taking a shortcut around the shore. As I was clambering over a rock I slipped and fell heavily on my bad leg, which immediately began to gush blood until I feared a major haemorrhage. I climbed slowly back onto the stony track and struggled my way so that at midday I was going only some ten or twenty yards between long rests and I think now that my morale must have been almost at its lowest there because I can remember almost praying for the appearance of a German to either finish me or take me to a doctor. I came over the saddle of a spur and saw below me a large stone house with the church attached. A most picturesque setting with a wonderful view of the sea. On the large open verandah partly covered by great grapevines sat two or three hooded figures. I stumbled down the track and approached them. This was the only time in my adventures that I begged. The leg of my trousers was soaked with blood while as I walked across the white boards of the verandah I left a trail of crimson. Approaching the oldest and most venerable looking monk, I bowed my respects and asked for sanctuary – I did not want a bed I said, but to be let to sleep under a roof, with a crust to eat. With no change of expression in his grave eyes, the monk clapped his hands, gave a rapid order, whereupon two younger monks took me, undressed me, washed and put me to bed with clean linen over my wound. They prepared a wonderful meal of shellfish fried in olive oil and some exceptionally good wine. I learnt later that the wine from this farm was famous, and supplied to His Hellenic Majesty's Court in Athens.

I stayed in bed there for five days and made many good friends. For a further five I went with them each day to the fields and while they would not let me join them in their work, they liked to see me lying in the sun watching them. And very quaint they looked too, their flowing gowns and beards, their wee caps and their weird pruning knives. I can recall amusement over one simple fellow whose hat kept falling off at every vine he bent to cut. It never occurred to him to leave it off for a while – time is nothing to these people, so he just patiently picked it up each time, readjusted the bun of his hair and put it on again. They had a great plan for my escape. I can't tell you about it, and

FIG.5 *Typical rough shoreline*

anyway it failed, so with Christmas just three days off I departed on another long shot to freedom.

And now I must mention security. Obviously it would be both dangerous and unfair to mention here the names of those friends, monasteries or villagers who were actively good to me and to many other English who passed that way. The Nazi hell is roughshod, and there are many less fortunate than I who might feel it, were we to talk idly of their goodness. Perhaps I might include here that it was not only their Christian convictions for sheltering us – the Macedonians have an overwhelming regard for the Englishman, most unusual in a foreign country. And now you will understand why I must be vague.

Christmas Day I spent on my own and very miserable. On Boxing Day snow started in earnest and I stayed in a monastery for ten days, in their hospital.

Inside a monastery it is like another world. The great gates are closed at night, and with the windows all heavily barred one might find that it akin to a prison, but there is life and freedom also. There are two types of monks – those who live communally and those who live really 'monos' or individually. This monastery lived communally and therefore were denied the pleasures of meat of any sort. They therefore made wonderful fish meals, especially, I remember, from octopus. At that time they were fasting as their Christmas was yet to come. You must understand they live in the old time – sunrise is 1 o'clock, sunset 12 o'clock and their calendar just thirteen days behind ours. Within the monastery the most important thing is the church, usually over 1,000 years old, the whole covered internally with mural decorations and polished brass work, and usually roughly circular, but with a partition for the priests on the walls of which are all the main saints. I intend to describe a church service in an Orthodox church later.

The head monk visited me each day. He was a fine, sincere fellow and highly respected. One day he told me he wanted a doctor to see my leg, and sent me by boat on a two days' trip to another monastery in the hospital of which I stayed. I remember we spent the halfway night in a delightful seaside farm where the famous painters from all the monasteries lived. Art from this farm is world famous.

Now this monastery was exceptionally good to me, kept me hidden even while fifteen German soldiers were staying there, and I wore the long robes of a monk for many days. While there I enjoyed their Christmas, on 6 January, and had lovely roast pork, honey, wine and plenty.

And from there, while the Aegean Sea thrashed and stormed in its winter fury, making a long sea voyage impossible, I made two major sorties both of which I am pledged not to put onto paper until after the war. They were long trips over snow and full of adventure, but after five weeks I returned to my monastery, was welcomed with open arms and, as my leg had reopened painfully, I was put to bed where I stayed for six long weeks, partly in the monastery and partly on various farms, mostly because of rather a severe attack of influenza. Looking through my shorthand notes of this period, I find a long list of promised boats which came to nothing, mention of strange meals such as snails, thistles and queer fish, and references to my very good friends, including the police of this area who knew of my identity. Also in this period I can recall many unusual ways I passed my time – pruning grapes, kneading dough for bread, cooking strange dishes, darning and patching my clothes, going to church for all-night services, going shooting with the police for the wild boar which were being driven down by the snow. Perhaps most outstanding was studies with textbooks especially obtained from distant Salonika. I was able to at last master the difficult Greek tongue, and arranged with the sergeant to let me know of the appearance of any other English in the area, and one day early in March he told me of the presence of one other, and I was able to get him a note with instructions to wait for the coming better weather. At that stage I was staying with a civilian in the employment of the monastery, one of my greatest friends, who had arranged for the purchase of a small boat. The monks were prepared to put up some of the money and I was to cover the balance with a cheque. During this period I was forced to assume the identity of a Turk, as a Rumanian monastery nearby were constant visitors, and indeed one who knew of my nationality became a very good friend. Poor fellow, given by his family to the church at the age of eight, he had never been away from the Monastery nor seen anyone but dull monks all his thirty-five years.

The weather continued to complete the worst winter Greece has known for many years, and while the sea still thrashed its fury on the rocky coast, things began to be very difficult, particularly in the way of bread, and we lived mostly on a horrible weed like a thistle cooked in olive oil, there luckily being plenty of this latter. Then however, the weather began to break, and the sea would flatten out into a silver mirror for often one or two days on end.

I made a journey to complete our bargain with the fishermen and came back very bitterly disappointed for, frightened by the regular patrolling of the coast by both enemy motor craft and seaplanes, he withdrew his offer of a boat, and curses and pleas alike were of no avail.

FIG.6 *Calm sea*

PL.5 *Shore near Monoxylites*

And so I decided it was time for action, for my own initiative. I am at heart a selfish rogue and I found it very easy to convince my conscience that the theft of a boat was in the scope of my duty as they really all belonged to the German master. I sent for the police sergeant, and asked for the other Englishman – he told me of his whereabouts. I immediately fell to completing minor arrangements for departure. At that stage there arrived a young Russian Air Force officer. I know that sounds rather vague, but to you he must just 'come out of the blue'. He was such a nice fellow, keen, good-looking and happy even in his adversities, and we got on famously. He knew of a boat we might buy, so the following day we did a round of farewells and set off by night. A long route it was and tiring, we stayed the following night with an old friend of mine at a wayside farm. I remember spring was really in the air as we moved further north and the track was just covered with primroses, tiny Virginian stocks and bulbs, so that I quoted over and over in my mind 't'was roses, roses all the way ...' and was very content with our chances.

But the Russian monastery would not sell their boat – they wanted food for it. This was out of the question so I dispatched Alex to collect the other Englishmen and I took cover in a monastery village. I must tell you about that. It was Good Friday and one of the many nights the monks spend in church. My host, sincere old soul, asked me to come too and I consented. Let me describe the service.

The church was a large one and had a central space with alcoves all round facing in. Great gaily painted stone pillars led up into a glittering ceiling of polished brass work. All along the main face were the saints, by each a tiny olive oil lamp suspended from the roof. Each monk on entering kissed first the Virgin and Child, then his special saint (each monk is renamed after some saint), bowed and knelt before the picture of Christ, and lit a lamp to one or other of the saints. Then one of the priests gave him a long candle and he took up his position according to his grading. I was led right up to the seats of honour by the high priests and while I was not asked to kiss the saints, they gravely requested that I should make the sign of the cross after each hymn to which I readily consented.

Gradually the hall filled up, along the far side one could see the boys with their sad girlish faces, on the other the monks and junior priests. In the centre was an altar. Then on a signal from my host, who was head monk, the lights of the great chandelier were extinguished and the church left with just the flickering candles of perhaps 150 of us throwing weird shadows on the walls and pillars. No one sits down, not for the whole night. There is a rest for your arms, and many monks managed to cultivate the art of snoozing while standing. I can remember one old priest next to me who kept dozing so that his head would fall forward and his cowling almost catching alight from his candle. I won't describe the actual service, I feel it was rather sacred, this Easter ceremony.

Well, the very next day we all met together. We were six now. The two English were Sgt John Coote, a tall fair lad from the commandos and Cpl Gavin Peacock from one of the yeomanry regiments and whom we dubbed 'Nicky' after St Nicholas whose picture he greatly resembled. We spent all morning exchanging news and experiences. Peacock had escaped from a working party in Salonika and had stayed with a wealthy family for one or two months so that he was dressed in a smart city suit which looked extremely odd amongst our rough clothes. Coote was a man after my own heart. His escape was one of the greatest determination I know. He led a party down the sewer pipes of the prison camp covering a distance of some 500 yards in four hours. When they had been underground over an hour they discovered it was quite impossible to work their way back and pushed on not knowing whether they would finish up in some underground tank or an opening. The three lads who made the break with them all died through privations during the winter and meeting him now I could see what a physical and mental wreck he was. He told me every ten days he had a bout of malaria and still did not think he could endure much more. The rest of the party was made up by the Russian, Alex, a Greek officer, and a discontented monk who wished to make a bid for freedom.

We made our plans.

Saturday night was the great day and all Greek Christians would be in church. The sea was reasonably calm and we, rogues that we were, intended to break into the boathouse and take our pick while this opportunity offered. Apart from some minor hitches all went according to plan, we smashed the door from its hinges, took a little food and water and launched a really snappy boat into a rising sea just before midnight. The Russian lad, Alex, claimed knowledge of the sea and we naturally gave him the role of master. As the waves were ever mounting we pulled around the point into a sheltered bay and at dawn had the boat well concealed in some rocks.

Here differences arose as to the state of the weather and the outcome was our departure before midday without the monk. We still had, however, a jolly and untidy little dog which the Greek officer had thrown into the boat to prevent it giving the alarm. It made great friends with me during that trip. We pulled out using four long oars with a will over a heavy swell. I remember we were very happy, singing from our hearts songs in every language imaginable. The great Mount Athos began to slip gradually into the sea, and now and then for brief periods we could use our sail to assist us.

Navigation was most important. It was necessary to pass a very dangerous point under cover of darkness. On a map of the Northern Aegean you will see two islands, Lemnos which is a German strong point and Samothrace which is a Bulgarian pressure point against Turkey. The channel between these two leads to Embos which is freedom.

By nightfall we were about forty miles from Lemnos, and a high wind was rising. We used it to advantage for a while until it became apparent from the dark clouds scudding over the skies that a storm was brewing, we sailed on to the twinkling lights of freedom until they vanished in the fury of the rising gale and left us forty long miles from anywhere, in an open boat with the sail we could not get down. Believe me it was serious. We sailed around in circles at some terrific speed, each gust throwing the waves up higher and higher until I think it was about midnight. Alex, child that he was, broke down at the tiller and crying that all was lost, that there was no hope, fell to screaming and praying with the Greek officer in the centre of the boat. I knew little about sailing and less about those queer boats Greek fishermen use, but John took over the sail and I the tiller and we held on for our lives. Peacock was prostrate with seasickness.

Well I prayed very earnestly. Not as you would imagine for a safe return – because the water was well over my knees and only some four inches from the top of the boat so that deliverance seemed just impossible. I can remember now how resigned I was – how simple it was all going to be, and how rotten for the people at home. I called out to John. He grinned back and called something I couldn't catch. Brave lad, he confessed later how hopeless he thought it all was. The dog whimpered and climbed up into my lap and we waited and waited.

With the water pulling the boat to a standstill, the sail could not stand the strain and with a crack it split into two, tore into countless flapped threads and blew away. I had thought this would happen and waited for the boat to settle, but now we seemed to lift over the waves better, so with fresh heart John set to bailing while I kept our pointed stern into the great rollers with the rudder and one oar.

What a terrible night it was. Dawn seemed to have forgotten us.

At last, light began to break over the waves, and what great mountains they were, each one rushing at us with such an incredible speed one thought it must be the last. For a long time no land was in sight, but about 10 o'clock the rain eased off and we saw high land to the north of us some twenty miles distant. What it was we had no idea and with new heart both Alex and the Greek officer slipped an oar in and even Nicky managed to exert sufficient energy to do some bailing.

Well we made it. We beached the boat in a more sheltered bay not more than ten miles from where we set out from. The storm had blown us some sixty miles back and off our course. Up on the beach was a locked house – with the last of our energy we broke down the door, lit a fire, prepared some food we found therein and fell asleep on the floor. Never had I been so exhausted. All the way in I had been seeing people before me on the waves – and strange scenes such as glimpses of home, and also of the battlefield on Crete.

About midnight I was woken by urgent shaking, and drowsily perceived my friend the police sergeant. Pressing his hand on my mouth for silence he warned me that he would be back in the morning to get the boat and arrest all the thieves. Then shaking my hand and kissing me on both cheeks he departed. Before dawn I awoke the sleeping band, we looked at the still furious sea and slowly and sadly took the steep track away inland again.

Having branded myself a thief I determined not to go back to my friends, broke the party into two, the English and the others, and we set off for pastures anew. Then commenced quiet an enjoyable period, the three of us visiting many fishing villages and making new friends, always however on the lookout for a boat. We had one good hideout from which we would sortie for reconnaissance. John and I spent much of our time filling our stomachs I'm afraid, for we bought fish, olives and snails wherever we could, and many places kindly offered us what meals they could spare. I received many urgent messages to return to my old friends but realised that my best chances lay with our repeating the theft with better luck.

Well we made two further unsuccessful attempts. One of them, a masterly theft off an open beach before the eyes of the unsuspecting village, was foiled by our failure to insert the bung before setting off. The other attempt was cut short by a patrolling police boat which did not however realise our identity but just warned us to get back inside the three-mile limit, which we did to be caught by the irate but luckily patriotic owner.

The final theft was a masterpiece and I am forbidden to enlarge on it. We six of us (one Greek, two Cypriots) were five days on the water because of unfavourable winds but finally landed some eighty miles north of Smyrna in Turkey, whereafter all was simple, was the greatest of fun (but security), and some two weeks later three smartly dressed young Englishman stepped over the border into Syria where, to my joy, I recognised not only New Zealand soldiers but my own regiment. I won't tell you of the wonderful reunion I had with the 23rd, and with my brother, Godfrey, then serving with them. It just overflowed my cup of happiness. I have been very lucky.

Captain W. B. Thomas
2nd NZEF
6.10.42

When Sandy wrote his best-seller Dare to be Free, *he omitted the last paragraph above. He felt that if this little miracle was included, people would treat the whole story as fiction! It is interesting to note that this book was part of the syllabus in the UK school system. I (PH) have met several people who tell me that their first interest in the Holy Mountain came from this reading.*

Citations, A Visit in 1944

PETER MCINTYRE

In November 1944, three New Zealand servicemen went to Mount Athos, to present citations
to various monasteries whose inhabitants, despite serious risks to their own lives and safety,
had been instrumental in caring for New Zealanders during the Second World War.
A talk, by one of the group, Peter McIntyre, the Official War Artist,
was recorded in Florence on 18 November 1945. The transcription follows.

I have been to a lot of queer places in my time; pocket republics like San Marino in Italy, Andorra in Spain, places like Monaco, but last month in northern Greece, I found one of the strangest of them all. A peninsula virtually cut off from the outside world, a state virtually self-governed, strange, mysterious and beautiful, a place of some 8,000 inhabitants, where there are no women, no roads and, incidentally, no advertising. When you come to think of it, rid yourself of those two things, women and motorcars, and most of life's complications and worries disappear immediately.

If you go beyond Salonica and over the mountain pass you come to the peninsula of Mount Athos. It juts out into the Aegean Sea. It is a lonely remote and utterly beautiful place. Since about AD 300 the peninsula has been inhabited entirely by monks. Dotted along its length, on high rocky crags and on the cliffs above the sea are huge old monasteries. They were built to withstand the pirate raids and they have great stone walls and battlements. There were three of us who went, all from Dunedin – Monty McClymont, Mac Miller and myself.

We went by jeep across country, through villages where they gave us roast pork and a fiery drink called ouzo. We went as far as even an army jeep could go, which is something. We saw the remains of the great canal that Xerxes tried to cut across the peninsula some 200 years before Christ. When the jeep gave up, we hired a fishing boat and we sailed along the coast. It was lovely.

The water was like glass, and you could see the starfish far below, with Mount Athos looming up away ahead out of the haze. Lying on deck in the sun we passed the last village on the coast, and there the fishermen pointed out the frontier guard. Women are forbidden by law from going past this frontier onto the peninsula. In fact, no woman has set foot on Mount Athos since the year 1026, although I believe many have tried. It gave you a sort of relaxed feeling. 'No women, eh?', said Monty, 'No women? Now this is a strange place for you to be in, McIntyre'. 'On the contrary, McClymont', I said, 'I am seriously considering becoming a monk. I doubt whether I shall ever leave this place' [FIG.7].

We put in that evening at a tiny harbour below the great monastery of St Paul and, as we climbed up the path, the monks came down to meet us. High black caps and robes, long hair and beards – strange looking fellows. My first shock was to find them not gloomy and solemn, but gay, even hearty and back-slapping. 'Welcome, welcome!' they kept repeating.

They are intensely royalist and pro-British. 'Greece must become a British colony!' was one of the first things they said to me. Eventually they realized from our shoulder flashes that

FIG.7 *Going to St Paul's*

PL. 6 *Monastery of Agiou Pavlou (St Paul's)*

we were New Zealanders and immediately chaos reigned! They all wanted to ask us at the same time how 'Thomas' was. 'Thomas' being Colonel Sandy Thomas of 2NZEF who, after escaping wounded from a German prison near Salonica, was sheltered and nursed by these monks. As they did with several New Zealanders and hundreds of British escaped prisoners, these monks eventually got Colonel Thomas away by boat to Turkey and freedom. They were frequently searched by the Germans but always managed to hide the soldiers in the forest around the monasteries. The young gardener monk who looked after Colonel Thomas was eventually imprisoned by the Germans.

Supper was an enormous meal, six courses with copious wine. A very joyful meal with much laughter and much urging to eat and drink more. At eleven o'clock we managed to escape to bed, spotless white beds with huge eiderdowns. At one in the morning all the bells in the monastery began to ring. I turned over with a deep luxurious sigh. These monks go to church to pray from one in the morning until dawn. At about three I was awakened again to hear a gong, a huge wooden gong, beaten in a sort of broken rhythm. Then a bell took up the rhythm, filling all the monastery with a pulsating sound. It was for all the world like being in Tibet.

FIG.8 *The Hermit Huts*

By boat again the next day, around the coast past the hermit huts. These hermits live all alone, each in a tiny cabin clinging incredibly to the cliff face high above the sea. Their food, dry bread and water only, is brought by boat and hauled up by rope.

It is interesting to note that these old boys thrive on this diet, and almost all live to be about ninety. To their last days they are able to clamber up and down the cliff like youngsters.

A storm forced us ashore at the cape and we climbed on foot to a Romanian monastery where they fed us on raw salt fish, wild honey and brown bread, in a room strangely enough hung with gaudy old lithographs of battle scenes. Among the most incongruous in this place was a scene of the relief of Ladysmith. From there we travelled by donkey through wild mountainous country, the paths were torturous, steep and rough, led round rocky cliffs and through deep forests. Two of us had nasty spills – donkey and all.

We would come to a monastery, sheer stone walls and a narrow gate, silent and forbidding. Sometimes Mac and Monty sitting on their donkeys under some battlemented wall gazing upwards would look to me for all the world like Don Quixote and Sancho Panza. At Great Lavra, the wealthiest and oldest monastery, we saw a whole library of ancient manuscripts. Priceless things, dating back to about the fourth century. Preserved there is the whole history of the Byzantine Empire. There were the robes and the jewelled crowns of the ancient patriarchs of Byzantium. There were quivers of arrows used 800 years ago to defend this very monastery against pirates. In the courtyard, a beautiful peaceful courtyard, was a huge tree that, by the monastery records, will be 1,000 years old in thirteen years. Though it had been rebuilt several times, this monastery was first built about 300 AD. The latest attempt to destroy the monastery was last year when the ELAS troops, knowing the royalist and pro-British leanings of the monks, set fire to the surrounding forests.

After another long journey by donkey, we reached the capital, Karyes. Surely one of the strangest in the world. Streets and shops and guest-houses, hostels and churches, but no women, no motorcars, no shop signs, no street signs. By law no shopkeeper may put up his name or any other sign. You may not even ride your donkey through the capital, you must dismount and walk.

These monks, too, have no sense of time! The day begins at dawn, so what you might think would be seven o'clock in the morning is, according to them two o'clock. Their calendar is thirteen days behind ours. In Athos you may

FIG.9 *In the forest*

think it is eight o'clock on 4 July but you are quite wrong; according to them it is three o'clock on 21 June. The whole thing leaves you are in a state of suspicious bewilderment.

The committee or parliament meets in the capital – one representative from each monastery. We were awakened at 6.30 in the morning by our own time to meet the representatives. Think of it – parliament in session at seven in the morning! We had had no breakfast, (the monks eat only two meals a day), and we were marched in with great ceremony. Promptly around came the trays of ouzo – at seven in the morning in parliamentary session! It was almost too much! After many flowery speeches we bade farewell, and led our donkeys off through the strangest of capitals. We rode down to the coast and to our fishing boat with a feeling of coming out into another world. So it was farewell to Mount Athos, land of no women.

We drove next day to Salonica, and there in front of a hotel was a woman, a little Australian Red Cross girl we had met on our way through. Her name was Penny. 'Penny', I said 'you have no idea how glad I am to see you!

Peter Howorth, editor, has an interesting addition to this story:

On the Holy Mountain, everything has a consequence. In the story above, the purpose of the expedition was to hand out what Sandy Thomas referred to as 'well done' letters. I know of several throughout the Holy Mountain, and certainly there is one in most of the monasteries and in Kavsokalyvia. The risk the monks took, and the assistance they gave to Allied soldiers was dangerous and often had tragic consequences.

During one visit to Greece in 2013, my passport, credit cards, and all other important stuff was stolen on the Metro from the airport into Athens. This necessitated a fairly rapid trip to the New Zealand Honorary Consul, a delightful fellow called Costas Cotsilinas. It turned out that he was Sandy's escort and guide while in Greece, and had just been with him for the 70th anniversary of the Crete landings.

The wonderful Greeks seem to be able to find justification for a party out of anything – away we went! In the course of the ensuing hilarity, Costas showed me packs of rolled certificates, all signed by the wartime New Zealand Prime Minister, and the Army Chief, General Freyberg.

'What are they for?'

'That is so we can give out new ones if the old ones are lost or damaged.'

We dealt with the details – the new passport was delivered in seven days, but I was able to uplift my diamonitirion by presenting my NZ driving license in Ouranoupoli! My wife, however, was still nervous about moving around Athens. She approached the ordered taxi with great trepidation, and started negotiations with the driver who responded ' Whereabouts in New Zealand are you from? I'm from Wellington and just over to give my brother a hand for a month or two'.

On this particular trip I visited Dionysiou for the first time. This monastery was one of Sandy Thomas's favourites. While there we were treated to an involved story about Sandy, his bleeding wound, and German soldiers. This was in Greek, from elderly Father Kallistos. At the end of this, he rushed off, and returned with the framed certificate from the New Zealand Government given during the trip described above. His face was crestfallen.

'It has been eaten by worms!'

'No problems – I'll sort out a new one straightaway!'

And we did – thanks to Costas the consul, and our good friend George Spanos. Everything happens for a reason, and everything has a consequence.

The Diary

JOHN WARRACK

1st April 1953. Donald Swann and I left Thessaloniki at nine o'clock, after a last-minute argument with an official about police permission. However, all was well, the Ministry's letter smoothing over the difficulty. The bus jolted across the country over dreadful roads and precipitous slopes, through streams where bridges had been blown up and over terrifyingly narrow bridges until after eight hours we arrived at Ierissos. On the bus we found several boys going to the Mountain to stay with relations, at least one of them intending to become a monk.

They told us of Donald's friends from his Palestine days with the Friends' Ambulance Unit during the war, Sydney and Joice Loch, now living further down and on the other side, in a Byzantine tower, Pyrgos, at Ouranoupolis.

The bus took us across the isthmus to Trypiti, the exit of Xerxes's canal, and from here we walked for two hours along the shore, with the sun setting behind us until suddenly ahead was our first sight of Athos in the distance – a white, Everest-like cone hanging in the sky, with a belt of mist cutting it cleanly away from the earth and supporting it on a white cushion.

Eventually we came to Pyrgos, where we found Loch and his wife Joice. He opened the door to us, and Donald greeted him, memorably, with, 'Sydney, I think we last met in the Garden of Gethsemane'.

Over supper with them, a plain meal with a little local, unresinated wine, they told us much of the Mountain, of the country, of the state of the monasteries and of the monks. They feel that the place is in serious decline. The monks are all old and poor, and there are hardly any novices coming in. Further, the Communists had actually 'captured' Karyes.

A force of men, including twenty-five women, had advanced up the peninsula and, according to Joice, seized the governor and chased him out of town. However, all the Greek army had to do was to close up the isthmus behind them, and they quickly disappeared. But the masculine sovereignty of Athos was broken, more than the landing by a 'Miss Europe' for an hour or so some years ago.

The Lochs have started a carpet industry among the villagers. Sydney collects ideas and designs from the monasteries, which he knows very well, and Joice copies them into a carpet design on squared paper and boils dyes down from local trees and herbs, and the girls of the village weave the thread on looms.

The results are wonderful – pale, translucent pinks and greens, deep blacks and blues and the whole with little symbolic or realistic animals, plants, trees, figures and images. The girls would stop if the Lochs didn't keep them going, and as it is they have had little worldly success. Sydney told us that the locals are not frightened of ghosts (that is more a Slav characteristic) but the loom-girls will not work in the tower after dark for fear of bogey men, what they call the Erapi: Arabs, an ancient fear of the Saracens and the swarthy Arab pirates.

Now we are on a little boat chugging along the coast with a boy of sixteen (looking much younger) who is going to stay with his brother in Great Lavra. He'll stay for a year, then he will be a kalogeraki, a 'little monk', go to Constantinople to study Byzantine theology, then return to Great Lavra and be a novice. He signs his name in this diary: Dimitrios Kotivas.

We arrived at St Panteleimon (Russiko) at about eleven, and having checked with the police, were admitted. The guest-master is a charming Russian who crossed from the Caucasus during the war and managed to get in here. He gave us tea (most welcome) and bread and olives, and then we walked up over the hill to Karyes (about two hours). We saw the police again, and got our diamonitirion from the Holy Epistasia.

Donald took some photographs of the Protos, the chief monk of the Mountain for the year (ending in May), and after buying some maps and postcards we went into the church of the Protaton. The Panselinos frescoes are won-

derful, notably that of the Baptist, a wild, tangled, inspired figure. The big icon of the Panaghia behind the Agia Trapeza was covered, not the others, most of them beautiful.

We took the wrong road out of Karyes but it turned out well, as it was better paved and more gradual in slope. It led us back to St Panteleimon by way of Xeropotamou. We had more tea with the delightful guest-master, who has given us a nice room. We are opposite the washrooms and lavatories (marked in Russian and Greek as 'Vaterklazet' and 'The Necessary'). Now we sit over candles writing all this up.

Panteleimonos Thursday 2 April. We spent a good night, and Father Gennady, the guest-master, gave us a fine breakfast of vegetable soup, caviar salad, fried potatoes, black bread and strong, bitter wine. Then we had more tea with him; he is a good and kind man. We saw the Abbot, an old man in a tiny, old office crammed with books with whom the half-Russian Donald happily chatted, then two of the churches, one large and Russian, thick with icons and chandeliers, the other smaller and Greek, but hardly less splendid. Then on we went in a little boat to Daphne, where we are now sitting waiting for another boat to take us on to Dionysiou. Donald's Greek is also usefully fluent from time with the Friends; mine rather less so from army days in Greece.

We arrived at Dionysiou to find the monks burying a brother who had died of flu yesterday. The service, of which we caught the last twenty minutes or so, was moving – a dark, close church with hooded figures silent in stalls round the edge, propping themselves up on their elbows and each clutching a thin yellow candle, joining from time to time in the service as the celebrating monk came by each one chanting out of an ancient book. As he intoned, so they followed him a few words behind. The effect was oddly moving. In the centre of the narthex was the old monk's coffin shrouded in black and standing on four legs with four handles by which to carry it. We stood in our stalls, holding our candles and listening though understanding little of this form of the liturgy. Then they picked up the coffin, having first all kissed the Bible on his chest, and carried him out of the church, through the monastery gates and along a path to the strip of land cut out of the cliff where they bury their dead. The wind tugged at the candles, and we followed trying to keep them alight and

FIG.10 *St Panteleimonos*

rekindling from a neighbour when necessary. After a final blessing they lowered their brother in his shroud into the grave, and sprinkling him with holy water, covered him up.

The service was led by Father Hilarion, an elderly monk who speaks English quite well but with a strong American accent. He took us into his cell, a small, airy room decked out like the cabin of a liner. He had once travelled to America on the Queen Mary, and now imitated the cabin in which he had been berthed, including a circular window painted like a porthole through which we could see the tossing waves of the Aegean. He showed us letters from English friends, and a book, *Dare to be Free*, by W. B. Thomas, a New Zealander he remembered who had spent some time on Athos after escaping from a prisoner of war camp and being on the run from the Germans.

Going down, we found the guest-master again. On our arrival he had kindly made some soup for us, having spotted us from his kitchen window as we landed on the quay. After welcoming us, he showed us round some frescoes of the Revelation by the church, explaining many of them in terms of present-day events (the beast with seven heads, a horrible looking creature, was the group of Communist nations, he declared). Thence to the wonderful refectory, through doors inlaid with squares of different coloured wood, and breathtaking images – saints, martyrs, holy men, devils, Lucifer and Christ himself throng the walls and legends and symbolic stories are illustrated with simple but highly charged paintings. One saint drew our attention, a Baptist-like figure with a beard reaching well below his knees.

There had been another such on the Mountain, said our guide, who had died fifty years ago. When he became a monk he had no beard, but he prayed to the Virgin one night, and woke in the morning with a beautiful long beard sprouting from his chin. For years he went about with his great beard, tucking it into a pocket for convenience, and when a Turkish commander came to the Mountain and asked to see this prodigy, the monk astonished him by waving in his face the living legend. There is a monk coming here for Easter who was present at his funeral and says that when they laid him in the earth his beard reached nearly a yard below his feet.

A long theological discussion with the guest-master and another over supper, confirming our feeling that the Orthodox and the Anglicans have much in common and much to learn from each other. We have decided between ourselves that we must have a little preparation before projecting ourselves fully into the Easter of the monks. We are not monks and we cannot be expected to attend all their services all through – indeed it would be in a sense presumptuous to do so. Tonight we shall sleep, tomorrow and thereafter we shall attend as much as we can. They do not mind us coming and going – they do so themselves when old or ill – and we cannot have the spiritual strength to attend and appreciate services that last from ten o'clock at night until three or four in the morning. We came here in a small and very unprepared way as pilgrims, and now that we are here we must do our best to spend a Christian Easter. Of course the word 'pilgrim' itself has romantic overtones that make us out to be more than we are; but if we are also Christians, well and good.

The monks spend most of the year working up to Easter, the last six weeks before it with rigorous intensity, yet when the first light of Easter strikes they greet the ancient miracle with ever fresh wonder. The stranger of another faith can catch a crumb of this, even if he spends only the last few days of Lent fasting instead of their six weeks. For the fast is no light matter. The services were very long and hard to follow; the monks, though kind and friendly throughout, were a bit abstracted, tired in body and distant and exalted in spirit, the beds were hard, the washing arrangements basic, and food consisted almost entirely of bean soup and black bread, with occasional slabs of dried mullet-roe and halva, washed down with water. No meat, of course, for the stricter monasteries never eat meat at all, no fish even, apart from sometimes the tough, acrid bakaliaros (dried salted cod), no cheese, no eggs, no wine, only coffee strong and welcome, tots of raki, even stronger and even more welcome, and a delicious tea made from dried flowers and herbs – only these to keep up our spirits which were flagging even if determination was, curiously, strengthening.

We are greatly supported and encouraged by the guest-master, Father Gabriel, a vastly entertaining character with a sweeping grey beard and a sparkling eye, and a strong tendency to behave to his charges like a benevolent but strict governess. He is a Byzantinist who has travelled and met church leaders and who despite the strictness of his vocation has a deep vein of ecumenical understanding. He wishes that the schism with Roman Catholicism might be healed, and he spoke well of German Lutheran respect for the Mountain during the occupation, even though the monastery had also risked destruction in order to help escaped British and other prisoners of war. He welcomes visitors to Athos so that its quality can be universally shared.

Father Gabriel had shown us the Revelation frescoes; we had also to respect, to venerate, relics of a fantastic if to us slightly gruesome nature. These included, in ornate containers, the right arm of John the Baptist (minus the forefinger, which is at Vatopedi), St Luke's right hand, and the complete skeleton, encased in a reliquary, of the Patriarch Nikon, second founder of the monastery. On the subsequent tour of the impressive library we were joined by Father Hilarion, with the Abbot. Even if we were unable to appreciate the books properly, the collection is vast and beautiful. On the second floor of the thousand-year-old tower (from which boiling water had once been poured on pirates) the door was opened by the Abbot with a gigantic key. The room is walled with books, codices, palimpsests and incunabula, all carefully catalogued. Even without expertness we could marvel at the exquisite calligraphy on vellum and the wonderful illuminations in the Bibles of the seventh and tenth centuries brought over from Constantinople.

By the Thursday of Holy Week we were getting distinctly tired and cross in spite of ourselves – the endless liturgies coupled with the rigours of the physical regime were telling on us – and by Good Friday we were more tired still though somehow not so cross with everything and were beginning to get the rhythm of the fast, even to draw from it. We had by now attended our first complete liturgia, lasting three hours. The fast has been strict, consisting of a daily meal of rice soup and bread, with an apple on Good Friday and a fig salad today. Monks and visitors are now entirely devoted to the rhythm of the Easter services. We are all hungry; the monks are also all weighed down by lack of sleep after two consecutive night services of five hours each. The elaboration of the service is striking, not to say exhausting. Although we have been much helped to an understanding of the service by having a prayer book each, we are still surprised by the ornamentation in the singing that can make half a dozen lines of print last twice as many minutes. We are, however, getting the feel of it, and can draw much more from it than even yesterday. All the elaborate lighting and extinguishing of candles and other minor rituals are beyond us, but then their comprehension is probably not important; the main thing is that the concentrated effort of worship is drawing us into its circle. We regret that

PL. 8 *Monastery of Agiou Dionysiou*

there are not better voices among the monks, but again, that is not the point and there are some unexpectedly moving moments in the chanting.

On Saturday evening, Father Gabriel bundled us off to our room with the comment, 'The first three hours are just sleepy old bores reading the Bible to each other. I'll wake you when things start properly'. We obediently disappeared, and slept fitfully for a few hours until we were wakened by the clacking from below of a semantron. Father Gabriel stuck his beard round the door over a spluttering yellow candle. 'Come now', he ordered quietly. We struggled into our clothes and crept down the creaking wooden stair after him. It was even colder in the dark courtyard. A wind was blowing off the Mountain, but a colder and danker one than the light breezes of early evening. The clock in the tower began to shudder before striking. Only an hour to Easter. We eased open the door of the church and slipped in. The chant welled up round us as we crept over to the two stalls to which we were motioned, and in the soft candlelight we could see Father Hilarion leading the chanting out of his parchment book. Round the circle he moved, stopping by each hooded figure in turn to read a little from his liturgy, always a word or two ahead of the strained, ornamented melody that followed. Sometimes the chanting would overlap as he passed to another pair of singers while the last one was still finishing, and the effect of the nasal voices whining the elaborate melisma against each other was almost unbearable in its intense fervour and grinding discords. Sometimes a peasant with a better voice would take up the line; then the ancient chant would fill and blossom, but always the whining voices would win the music back, and whatever the quality of the singing there was always the drone of the monk whose duty it was to hold grimly on to a bass note to keep the others firmly in the same key.

Gradually the long periods droned to a standstill, and as the candles were one by one snuffed by a novice, a great darkness settled. We remained in our stalls, half-stooping, half-hanging, choking over the acrid tang of the candle smoke, the only light in the church showing dimly from three tiny oil lamps in the great chandelier high above. With the ceasing of the chant the gloom seemed even more intense. Only a stray cough came from the back, with a few muffled sounds as the Abbot moved behind the choir screen. A chill settled on the church, and a kind of panic crept in, followed by a terrible sense of isolation. The impulse driving the long journey here had gone, and there seemed no reason for standing here shivering, cold and weak, for a sleepless night surrounded by these remote men, or why there should be any release. In the dark, the silent monks could just be discerned bowed over their dead candles, the older ones gaunt from the long fast and vigil, the silence total, yet, even as the bearded heads sank lower, filling with tension.

Without warning, the central doors were flung open, and the Abbot was standing there, holding a single strong, heavy candle burning with a steady flame. 'Christos anesti!', he called. 'Christ is risen!' With their robes rustling in a great sigh, the monks surged forward to greet the light, and one by one we all thrust our candles to the flame, taking and giving until in the swelling tide of light we could see now appearing for the first time that night the great fresco of the Christ Pantokrator in the dome above, His right hand raised in blessing.

Where there had been silence and darkness, all was now a blaze of rejoicing. The monks ran eagerly round to their special friends, and more shyly to us, whispering excitedly, 'Christos anesti! – Christ is risen, indeed he is risen! We too moved round, at first hesitantly, then with greater assurance as the delighted grins and bows of the monks encouraged our greeting. All except one young monk, who held back as if worried about something, then marshalling his few words of English, rushed across to me and blurted with a flash of white teeth, 'Merree Christmas!' Now the resumed chanting was quick and happy, and some of the younger monks were actually laughing out loud for sheer joy.

Overhead the huge chandelier was swinging recklessly to the answering glint in the eyes of the old men. But that discipline was maintained was brought sharply home to me: noticing me settle in my stall and cross my legs in an effort to get comfortable, he leant over and with a cheerful whisper, 'Temptation!', rapped me painfully over the knuckles with his candle. Then, gathering us all up, the Abbot, attended by deacons bearing a cross and the big scarlet and gold bible, led us out of the church. We followed with our candles into a side chapel, where he read the story of Mary Magdalene out of his bible. Then back into the church where the Easter canticles were sung, and so it proceeded, with readings from the Acts and chanting, all lasting some three hours until the service turned into confession, at which the guest-master came over and sent us off, saying that as we were not taking communion we need not attend this and we departed gratefully for bed.

It was now four o'clock. At half past six we were again awakened by the semantron, and went down once more to the church. Here the liturgy had begun, with all the monks joining in the canticles assisted by two laymen, a Macedonian peasant and a student of theology from Thessaloniki. All, except of course us, took communion, during which an immensely long communion hymn with elaborate ornamentation on every syllable was sung. By now the older monks were showing signs of fatigue from the all-night watch, but the younger ones seemed to thrive on it and once more were in the highest of spirits. We took the antidoron bread from the Abbot, and as the liturgy finished we passed into the refectory for the first meal of the feast. Here were abundantly soup, fish, bread, cheese, wine and eggs dyed a deep red in commemoration of the Blood of Christ. These we broke by tapping them against those of the monk opposite, and while Father Hilarion read from a holy book we made a good meal. A final ceremony was our individual greeting to the Abbot, when in his room we exchanged 'Christos anesti' again and he gave us each two more red eggs.

We thanked him for his hospitality and wished him 'Khronia polla' (many years). Quiet then fell upon the monastery, if quiet can be the word for the almost universal snores of the community recovering from the long night.

Athos Revisited

MICHAEL R BRUCE

Michael R Bruce, Emmanuel de Mendieta's translator, visited the Holy Mountain in 1957, 1959, 1962
and 1966. He wrote up his notes in 1971. After a space of sixty odd years it makes interesting reading
on the decline in the number of monks on the peninsula
and the apparent obsession with food.

The number of monks falls every year and the average age of those who are left increases.

In December 1957 there were 1,862 monks and this had fallen to 1,385 by 1966. In 1956 there were still 154 Russians, 34 Bulgarians and 129 Romanians – the figures for 1965 were 62 Russians 17 Bulgarians and 94 Romanians.

A few Russians and Romanians at last arrived in 1966, after negotiations which went on for many years. The diminution continues from year to year. How long can it last before there is a stand-still and something has to close?

Looking through the diaries there seems to be an obsession on the subject of food. Why should one record the menu at almost every meal?

Is this a desire to be able to tell one's friends of the hardships which one has endured during one's travels? Quite apart from monastic fasting and abstinence, the absence of milk and eggs, and the undoubted fact that monastic cooks do not hold the cordon bleu, we of the West are accustomed to regular meat, and while on Athos we are probably taking more exercise than we are accustomed to, appetite is a good sauce for a dull meal. A prudent philathonite will fill his pack in Thessaloniki with a supply of tinned meat and eat this when out of sight of his monastic hosts. There is a heinous monastic crime called lathrophagy – eating forbidden foods in secret! But there is no objection to bringing a supply of tea-bags, always an acceptable gift.

Even the least curious must gather some impressions to take home. But it is easy to see that, as the monks become fewer and older, this obligation of enter-tainment becomes an increasing burden on those monasteries, such as Great Lavra and Iviron, which are most visited. I cannot but recall my impression that one receives a more personal welcome at those houses which are off the beaten path. To the sensitive host, as to the sensitive guest, there is something repugnant in treating an institution as a peepshow, both to the observer and the observed.

Xenophontos 16 August 1957 … The guest-master received us with raki, coffee and water. The general impression was of old age and things running down. We then left and went round the headland to bathe, out of sight. The sea felt like a warm bath.

Karyes 17 August … At last we reached Karyes and collapsed in the auberge. '*Très mediocre*' (Guide Bleu) to drink a lot of retsina and have lunch, then we went to see the sights, but were sent back by the police to cover our knees with long trousers.

We had intended to walk to Great Lavra but waited with the promise of a boat, bathing and breakfasting on tomato and bean soup and olives at Iviron.

Panaghia 19 August … When we arrived we had a long wait for breakfast as plates and knives had to be washed from the previous sitting. Then we were served with tomato soup (good but not enough) and fish stew (horrid, all bones).

Dionysiou 20 August … A boatman took us to Dionysiou in return for a few cigarettes, we got off at the Quay but instead of going up we went round the

corner and took a siesta in a cave. We met a young monk cleaning the lamps and he told us that of fifty-three monks there were only six young ones.

Konstamonitou 21 August … Supper tomato soup, fried vegetables, melon and red retsina. In the morning we looked in our wallets to make the usual offering but when the guest-master saw our bank notes he asked us to wait as he ran back into his pantry and came out with large tumblers half full of the most powerful and delicious apricot brandy. We got down the stairs and through the gate with some difficulty. All this before sunrise!

Karyes 9 October 1959 … We went to visit Father Photios in his kellion '*Tou Prodromou*', just round the corner from the main square. We went through a high gate opening off the street and up a flight of steps. The cell consists of a well-furnished sitting room, a kitchen, four bedrooms, a chapel with early eighteenth-century frescos. On the ground floor is a cobbler's shop. I ate in the Inn … a horrid dinner, a plate of stone-cold haricot beans and nothing else. The Inn is indeed '*mediocre*' (Guide Bleu), downstairs are two dining rooms and a kitchen. The usual office is a hole in the floor of the balcony.

Panteleimon 18 October … This morning I had the same feeling of present evil during the Liturgy. Though I did not see any open irreverence the whole celebration was a travesty of worship and the whole atmosphere was so offen-sive that I felt forced to get out. I grabbed my pack and fled not turning to look back till I was well round the promontory. Then I had to stop, strip and bathe to feel clean.

Chilandar 20 October … Emmanuel was provided with a mule when we left and a small boy to bring it back. He chattered the whole journey and was about ten years old. He had been orphaned during the civil war and brought to Mount Athos when he was about a year old; he looks forward to seeing the world outside. If we understood him correctly he could never have knowingly seen a woman in his life.

St Paul 27 October … An excellent lunch pilaff of octopus. On going out of the dining room I noticed a heap of empty tins marked 'Best Californian Octopus American Aid to Greece'.

Dionysiou 28 October … Walked there on the kalderimi as there were no boats owing to the rough seas. After vespers we went to the trapeza for communal dinner (not too bad, cold fish and stewed apple).

I walked to Daphne and met Emmanuel there. Our housekeeping was so well organised that we ate our last tin of spam before getting the boat.

… Whither?

I recall sitting after lunch in Father Photios's kellion sometime during our 1959 visit and the inevitable question came up'. What will happen to Mount Athos if men do not come forward as monks?' Father P's reply was to this effect, 'We have had bad patches in the past, but we have always revived. It is not for us to worry about such things; if it be the good pleasure of God and the mother of God that Athos should continue, they will send young men once more'.

FIG. 11 *Monastery of Agiou Pavlou (St Paul's)*

* Emmanuel Amand de Mendieta (1907–1976) was a Belgian Benedictine scholar of aristocratic descent who specialised in the works of St Basil of Caesarea. He attained a brief prominence in the English-speaking world through his conversion to Anglicanism in 1962.

PL. 10 *Monastery of St Panteleimonos*

The Capital Town, Karyes

SYDNEY LOCH

In Karyes I ran into Charalambos, Dionysiou's representative on the Holy Assembly, as he rounded the post-office corner; he carried the black staff of his rank. His large face lighted up as we avoided collision, and blocked the traffic on the narrow thread of pavement. He had been my guest in the past and I must be his that night. He expected his own way and, liking him well, I accepted.

The ramshackle capital had grown up round the earliest of the Mountain's churches, the thousand-year-old Protaton, and looked bigger than it was because it rambled up and down over ravines. The main street was a lane of saddlers, monastic tailors and shoemakers, general stores and souvenir shops, spreading, with the Assembly headquarters, into suburbs of tumbledown country houses, the kellia and konaki of the twenty monasteries. The settlement made a better showing from the heights, where the pile of the Russian skete of St Andrew at one end, and the Greek monastery of Koutloumousiou at the other, the domes and crosses of churches and chapels gleaming in gardens and vineyards, improved on reality. The sea spoken of as the Holy Sea lay an hour or so away, and nearly two thousand feet below.

Originally the village had been known as Messi, or the 'Middle', from its central position; but by the end of the tenth century had acquired the name of Karyes, or the Hazels, from its nut-groves. Soon afterwards it was mentioned as the lavra of Karyes, and consisted of a number of cells under the Protos or ruling ecclesiastic. In the third typikon of 1394 it was written of as the skete of Karyes. To-day it had seventy cells inside Karyes, forty outside, and the Holy Community owned church, theological school, hotel, and cemetery.

Most shops and booths had passed into lay hands, and craftsmen from 'the world' were settled permanently as shoemakers and tailors, leaving the souvenir trade to the monks. Communities of monks, living by icon-painting and wood-carving round the end of the peninsula, sent work to this centre where tourists could see it; such humble stuff as tastelessly carved wooden spoons and salad forks, eucharistic bread-stamps, and rather intriguing wooden wine-jugs. The litter lay cheek by jowl on the counters with wooden and wire hairpins and combs for the long-haired monks, rosaries strung by wandering hermits of seeds picked up in the woods, walking-sticks straight off the trees, herbs, salves, scents and distillations, and picture postcards of the monasteries. Better and higher-priced work sometimes arrived in the form of carved and painted icons, holding rigidly to tradition, a type of handcraft mentioned in the sixteenth century.

Such a souvenir shop was close by, with a hermit like a forest bird inside, shyly offering his work to the habited shopkeeper. A monk who had obtained the appointment of police photographer was setting up the tripod of his passport camera outside the police station.

A lay shoemaker had a pigeon-hole of a shop just beyond, and shared a bench with an assistant who stitched by jerking two ends of waxed thread in opposite directions with a powerful elbow movement. A chair to sit on and somebody to watch at work was as much as the village ever offered at this hour, and two or three idlers already filled up the shop without more intention of ordering a pair of shoes than myself. Both cobblers were ready with local gossip in exchange for outside news. I took the free chair.

The master-cobbler, an up-and-down fellow, whistling if no ecclesiastic were by and sighing the moment after, pulled his last sheet of leather off a shelf. 'This finished, and up go the shutters', he announced, guffawing mirthlessly. 'Can I find a monk partner to get my leather in duty free for me? And how to pay duty on leather and charge the same as duty-free cobblers? Even holy men know the difference between good and bad bargains'. He was sighing again as a monk, bearing the furled umbrella carried on outings, went by with

a wiry step. One of the gossipers, in muleteer's homespun, shot to his feet, and went in pursuit.

'There's the sort of partner to be in with', the cobbler remarked, with a final hoot, watching master and man disappear to the waiting mule. 'That's Pavlos of ...' and he named a distant kelli, 'in on business. Before his wine goes away you see five barrels, four of wine and one of water. And if you're back in half an hour you'll see five barrels of wine in the same barrels, Pavlos having duplicated the first miracle of the Gospels, and then marked those barrels with red crosses to show they've been blessed.

'Who's having a day's change down here is Gabriel from up there', he went on, stabbing at a kelli on the heights with his awl. 'Went by five minutes ago, though not once a month you see him round this way'.

'Why should you?', the assistant asked.

'Why? why?', the cobbler exclaimed, opening his hand in the air. 'Have you called at that paradise up there?', he demanded, swinging round on me. 'There are four of them, and old Gabriel's their elder. What water! What air! What trees! And Gabriel full of money. One runs about for the rest, one gardens, one hunts. They leave Gabriel to sit all day on his veranda watching us here, where a mule can't sneeze without him knowing. What can't happen to a man full of money!'

He ran to the door to hail a handsome, foolish youth loitering by. He had won an hour's notoriety by claiming to have been called by nereids, tall, sweetly singing, golden-haired women with floating veils who are said to be encountered at the opposite hours of midday and midnight. In certain moods they look for a bridegroom, but are untrustworthy unless caught by the veil, whereupon they become obedient. But should she steal the veil again she vanishes, nor may she be sent to the well for water, for then surely will she find freedom. Marriages between villagers and nereids are known by hearsay, though generally the nereid turns out to be a golden-haired Swede or Norwegian.

'I hear you've been back to your village?', the cobbler called. 'Have you had more trouble?'

The youth signalled 'no' by slowly raising his cleft chin skywards. The cobbler helped him past the shop with a thump between the shoulders, then he leapt back to his last and brought his hammer on a boot heel, lamenting: 'Another lost five minutes!'

FIG.12 *Old Karyes*

He had not evened up the heel before another worthwhile spectacle had him at the door again. Two thieves had been taken on the Mountain, which led to the arrest of a couple of youths from Prosphori as receivers. The regulation was that thieves and receivers must be taken to the scene of their activities before serving sentence, and appear publicly with the stolen articles.

This warning spectacle now drifted past the shop door. The prisoners meandered between gendarmes down the middle of the road, handcuffed in pairs, decorated with watches, clocks, blankets, lengths of cloth, while a bored mule followed under piles of blankets and a carpet. One of the receivers grasped a cross, as if blessing the people who watched. His partner was full of bravado. But he with the cross hung his head. The out-of-step procession wandered away down the street, the mule yawning.

The cobbler bounded back to his last, exclaiming, 'How they're eating stick for their three meals a day!'

Finally he shot off the bench to welcome an elderly Russian monk who came to try on a pair of boots. These went on, and became fixtures; but the monk was an agreeable old man, and blamed his vanity for not having insisted on a roomier measure. The boots were still being stretched when we glanced at our watches and decided the morning must be gone. Mine, set by the 'world', stood at eleven-thirty; an Iviron monk, timing from sunrise, showed six-thirty; his companion from Xeropotamou, reckoning from sunset, had three-thirty. The cobbler's watch had stopped. The common interpretation was, it was time to break up the meeting. The cobbler's hoot followed me half-way down the street.

The street ran on for a hundred yards, to end at Assembly headquarters, and then turn into a lane leading towards St Andrew's Skete. I turned into an eating-house. Everyone sooner or later passed the window of its dining-room; but when I sat down shops were shutting for the siesta and would not open until after vespers, and the road, which had been full of striding and pacing monks, had hardly a human being left on it. Almost the last man abroad was the Mountain's senior monk, the Proepistates, handling his black staff, and trailing a full-bearded kilted guard at his heels.

The bare dining-room was full of munching labourers, and monks entertaining relations from the world. Talk drowned the clatter of cutlery. The Greek diner found enough in a little red wine, or a thumbnail glass of raki, to magnify a saucer of salted herrings and another of salted cucumbers into a repast, capable of being lengthened indefinitely by optimistic talk. A waiter moved between the tables calling, 'Command me!' but nothing of account was ordered, except a bottle of beer for me to garnish the beans.

Father Athanasios, whose dental chair had an unparalleled view of the Mountain, went gliding past the window. The amiable old man pinned his beard into his knot of hair before bending to fill a cavity. He had come to the Mountain at a time when they stood a comb in a man's whiskers to see if he was old enough. If the comb fell out the novice was not accepted until time had stiffened his hairs. There was an absence of terror-striking instruments in his surgery; he kept them in an old chocolate-box.

My hand-wave brought him to the window: 'That tooth didn't worry you?'

'Not a twinge, Father. Won't you join me in a coffee?' But he was in a hurry and dipped away down the street.

A gendarme made his way towards the landlord washing glasses.

'That's the new lad', observed my next-door neighbour to a companion. 'Seems the right kind'. But the old man he had jogged screwed both eyes at the gendarme's back and observed: 'There are white dogs in this world, and there are black dogs. Both are dogs'.

All the world would fall asleep for two hours, and so I could not call on the Holy Assembly until after vespers. I turned into the sun-stricken street, the last of the diners, as the waiter was slapping up the wine-stains from the tables. Crushed with heat I made my way to the first tree that offered its shade.

This extract is from ATHOS The Holy Mountain *by Sydney Loch (1957), Lutterworth: used with permission.*

Mount Athos, 1963

ROBIN PRICE

It was a good time to visit. The Holy Mountain was in hidden transition. Externally, it was dying. The monks were ageing, few were educated, the recital of offices and liturgy often perfunctory, the buildings decayed. The Holy Mountain was threatened with secularization. Few then knew of the hermits in the so-called desert and elsewhere on the Holy Mountain, whose banked spiritual energies would transfer to their disciples and later unlock the long stagnation and decline of the monasteries, whether cenobitic or idiorrhythmic. These energies began to become apparent and operative during the 1970s.

But my visit and pilgrimage with a friend and colleague, Michael, in late August 1963 was preceded by a much longer pilgrimage beginning in London on 3 August, originally set on foot by Richard whose lecture on his pilgrimages to the Holy Mountain I had heard the previous year. Accompanied by two friends of his, Dorotie, a stained-glass artist, fashion designer, and lecturer, and Meryl, a former ballerina, I stayed at places of spiritual significance in France, among them Chartres, Solesmes, Vézelay, St Benoît-sur-Loire, Taizé, taking in Paris (Notre Dame), even secular Rambouillet, and Versailles on the way, and the Jura and remote pastoral Switzerland as a final flourish. It was a tranquil and meditative time, still vividly and gratefully recalled.

Thereafter, with a life-long schoolfriend, Tim, we (that is, the two of us, plus the dashing coupé *Argo*, so styled as the vessel of our search for the Golden Fleece) traversed the High Alps via the Simplon Pass to Parma with its gorgeously operatic cathedral, and to Florence, where we stayed at the ever-welcoming Villa Pensione Bencistà just below Fiesole. The San Marco frescos touched, as ever, the heart of perception, as did the Donatello sculptures in the Bargello. But as this was a magic journey – indeed a pilgrimage – Tim and I encountered no fewer than three good friends staying separately and unexpectedly at Bencistà, an experience to be repeated many times in later years. As its sixteenth-century name indicates, it is ever good to be there.

On, now only myself and gallant *Argo*, to the inner shores of Venice, to Trieste, to Postojna in the Yugoslav People's Republic, to Belgrade on the rumbling stone setts of the narrow and almost empty main road down the spine of that sparsely populated landscape, mile after mile of huge sunflower heads on either side. Thence after a luxurious night in a once imperial hotel, magnificent yet in dingy red plush and faded gilding, we bypassed Skopje, not wishing to pry into the recent devastation of a massive earthquake. Here, outside the city was a ferro-concrete petrol station, crazily riven by the upheaval, but mercifully still functioning. As petrol stations throughout central Yugoslavia were no less than 200 miles apart, one station missed was a disaster indeed. The last stretch of sixty miles or so from Tito Veles to the Greek border was a nightmare of thick dust, stones, bumps, bashes, and potholes. A flat tyre, a dried-out battery, a blocked carburettor, were the heavy tolls exacted by the punishing conditions no tarmac-loving toy should be expected to endure. But *Argo* she was, and the Golden Fleece was yet, as always, to attain.

And it is, as ever, attained by uncomfortable, demanding, and daunting effort and circumstances, for Thessaloniki and the Via Egnatia were not the quietest and coolest places to encounter on nights in late August, especially when, as then, there were iron-shod trams shrieking, grumbling, rumbling, battering their way down the street only a few yards from one's open window. Nor indeed was the task on the next exceedingly hot day, 26 August, any less daunting: to visit before midday closure the very helpful and courteous British Consul, the Ministry of Macedonia and Thrace, together with the severely inquisitional ecclesiastical representatives of the Holy Mountain, before attaining the precious diamonitirion, without which nothing was possible. All this of course was long before the conveyor-belt Holy Mountain pilgrimage-tourism of the present day.

FIG.13 *Transport*

Michael's arrival that evening meant a diligent and well-practised repetition the next day of consular, ministerial, and ecclesiastical visits before setting off to Ierissos, and thence to sup and sleep at the little taverna perched above the wooden quay at Trypiti. From this point the exigencies of the journey meant that I failed to keep a diary. But the impressions remain. The vignettes of fifty years ago are strong, and I record some of them. At that stage of my life they were inevitably outer impressions of an exotic and medieval existence, absolutely untouched by the twentieth century. But within those impressions was the hidden indication, a floating touch, of the other Existence which the traditions represented. And how traditional it all was! For caique, with its few passengers under a canvas sun cover, was then the only transport to the Holy Mountain, and often too between the coastal monasteries, especially for those pilgrims weary, hot, sore of foot, and lacking a mule. Sailing and chugging, often late and generally uncertain of timetable, the caique compounded the problems of Western pilgrims, confused by coexisting standard time, Byzantine time, Chaldean time, and of course by caique uncertainties.

Walking, too, was for the pilgrim the only passage from coast to the capital at Karyes, in order to present the diamonitirion at the Holy Epistasia. There were then no roads, and there was therefore no traffic. It was wonderfully quiet. Where the footpaths, then well maintained, ran through woodland, it was shaded and green and cool. Once, beside a fountain pool we surprised a slightly embarrassed monk washing his long grey hair, and again encountered a senior monk or two rustling and pattering their way down to Daphne or to another monastery, the mules jolting and slithering on the worn paving. These were silent, unacknowledged, and slightly surreal encounters. We had entered a medieval dream world. It was also on the rocky hillsides mercilessly hot and exhausting, that Michael endured an unpleasant attack of sunstroke. Hydration was not then understood.

Karyes visited, diamonitirion approved, and duty done (I have, inexplicably, no recollection of Karyes on this visit), we stayed at the Great Lavra, oldest of the monasteries, and one of the very few houses where I recall a few (very youthful and cheerful) young monks, probably novices attending their idiorrhythmic masters, perhaps their relatives, awaiting the caique at the arsanas. Thence to Grigoriou, and St Panteleimon.

Of Grigoriou, recommended to us because it was newly guided by a dynamic abbot who had returned the house to the cenobitic and disciplined mode of life, I have powerful impressions. Returned to discipline it may have been, but apart from the friendly and jovial guest-master, it was still essentially medieval. The presiding monk of the kitchen was large, powerful, loud of voice, and dominant in a way which seemed to me, perhaps not aware of deeper significances, not much in the character of a monk. His wretched kitchen novice, when not being appallingly browbeaten, sat miserably within the huge fireplace, cauldrons steaming on trivets over great logs, plainly wishing he were elsewhere, anywhere but in a monastery. Before the great fire we few ate at a vast board, accompanying a toothless hermit soaking his stale bread in water and soup. Alas! Below the monastery, but out of eyeshot, I stole a forbidden bathe, perhaps mitigating the offence by recalling a significant phrase of the offices and liturgy just heard. I learnt subsequently with relief that others too have stolen a secular bathe in that same secret cove. And wholly secular was the famous loo in the Grigoriou guest house. Jettied perilously high above precipitous rocks and susurrating sea, it has inspired anxiety in the sturdiest pilgrim heart. Of plumbing below there was absolutely none, a discovery as surprising as it was unnerving – a delight to recall and recount, a challenge to the constitutionally timorous.

Of decay everywhere there was much. We visited the Romanian skete of Prodromou, probably on our way to or from the Great Lavra, which, like the Russian St Panteleimon, had not been refreshed by novices for many years. It was reduced to very few monks, and those scarcely able to work. The aged guest-master nevertheless welcomed us most warmly, and despite the poverty of his house offered us the usual generous hospitality of coffee, raki, water, and loukoumi, and explained in German (his and Michael's common language) the immense difficulty of maintaining monastic life, sustenance, and decaying buildings with so few left. One active monk of middle years, plainly vigorous, had been lent to them for essential work. All was clearly, and most sadly, dilapidated, impoverished, and decayed. How good to know that Prodromou is once again inhabited and renewed! But poverty can discover great generosity of spirit, as indeed in that house, and again on the morning when a hermit ran from his dwelling and insisted that we accept a few deliciously ripe figs from his one tree. So cheerful, grateful, and Christian a giver I have never before or again encountered.

There was yet more decay and sadness at St Panteleimon. Only a few aged greybeards remained, novices or young monks from before the Revolution.

Many of the huge later buildings were in freefall, windowless, and in visible inner decay. Of the once over 1,800 monks (plus a commensurate number of Russian pilgrims) only some twenty seemed still to remain. For us, almost their only pilgrims, with (I hope not cynical) generosity, they put on 'for the tourists', as I heard one propose, their star basso profundo performer; and profound, glorious, and moving his great Russian voice was. Here we had our last green beans, as indeed anything else, swimming in delectable Athonite olive oil. Fast period therefore it surely was not; and in that connection I can only record the objective open-handedness everywhere of impoverished monasteries to stranger pilgrims from a distant and apostate land. To be any kind of pilgrim then was to be most warmly welcomed.

As our caique sailed finally for Ouranoupolis, I stood beside a young White Russian whose tears lamented his parting from the last and decaying remnant of Holy Russia. And how sad and foreboding it all was.

But we were all wrong. The leaven was already working. The Holy Mountain would regain a new life. Holy Russia would be restored. Young and well-educated monks would take up the invisible golden thread. The Golden Fleece would again be sought. The monasteries would not be secularized. The Holy Mountain would again become a beacon to an estranged and aggressively secular world.

The End

JOICE LOCH

In 1959, Mt Athos was preparing to celebrate its thousandth anniversary as a monastic centre in 1963. And so seriously was that taken that the main road to Thessaloniki was being made much wider and was to be surfaced, not only to the Tripiti, where the boat for Athos is caught, but right into the village and to the very door of my tower. Along this new highway would pour the modern pilgrims, in cars, on bicycles, in buses, and there would come cigarette vendors; and men would bring little charcoal burners on which to grill lamb chops and souvlaki on sticks from lamb's meat rubbed in the dried wild marjoram from the mountains.

And there would be wine, and beer, and coffee, and even, perhaps, Coca-Cola! Then indeed would the old times be gone and the people no longer hammering on my door at midnight with the information that 'Fanoula can't make her baby! Please come to give strength!' Or the shepherd coming with a cracked head urgently requiring stitching; or the illicit fish-bomber with the splattered fragments of metal to be picked out of him; or the old man with the toothache; or the infant with the bellyful of chickpeas – shrieking until the family drowns its cries by pouring water first over the face of some holy icon, then into its mouth, as they cry aloud that it really has swallowed the devil this time!

All the immortal, simple people, who, full of faith, toil up to me at the top of the tower. It might be more peaceful, but a lot of colour would have gone from the world.

I trust that when Dion has been pumped clean of sand, the old ghosts will rise up out of the ruins. The shadow of the tower falls gigantic on the sunken walls both at noonday and in full moonlight, and its loveliness might fill the Dionites with nostalgia, so that they choose to come again to repeople their lost land, attracting the half-shy, birdlike attention of the villagers. Then our people will be caught for ever in the past, and never fully enter into the brave new world that is pushing away the old; for there will be little space left, and certainly no time to dream in the clear, deep shallows that flow so pleasantly over ancient Dion.

FIG. 14 *The Tower*

Now, in 1967, I remember a day at Prosforion, only a few years ago. The waves rubbed together as they slapped the beach, and a brisk wind blew from the Holy Mountain. This was the time of winnowing, and presently men and women stood with their huge sieves high over their heads shaking out the flying chaff. Chaff dust hung from their hair and eyebrows, and ringed their nostrils. And it ringed the noses of the donkeys, and mules, and bullocks, which trod the sheaves on the threshing floors. It trembled on their eyelashes like fringes. Every sort of animal was yoked together for the threshing, and each man slept on the ground by his own sheaves ready to start winnowing when the wind blew. Often it blew in the middle of the night. The feckless cicada sang her long, lazy song, shouting as she rocked on the tree tops: 'You dig, and you plow, and you plant, and you hoe, and you harvest and you thresh, and you winnow, and you grind, and you bake good pies, and you give to the ants, thieving, working ants, and I am left to die, in the cold hungry winter I am left to die; for, you dig and you sow ...'

There was no shame in the cicada as she rocked and sang her endless song, and the children and grandmothers sang it too; shouting it above the creak and swish of the threshing boards.

'This is the end', I said, staring at the road which toiled past me. None of us knew it then, although it was 1959 and the road slipped along to the tower.

It never occurred to them that possibly in a year or two they would have reached the NEW WORLD, and motors and threshing instruments would have taken the places of the ancient beasts.

The end, yes it really is the end!

This extract is from A Fringe of Blue *by Joice NanKivell Loch (1968), John Murray: used with permission*

Part Two

Encounters

Since 1972 slowly but steadily the number of monks started to grow. Now, more and more young well-educated monks are arriving, monasteries are receiving help, donations are coming from inside Greece and from abroad. The number of monks is over 2,500 and is continuing to grow.

This reversal of fortunes is due significantly to the influence of one man – Elder (now Saint) Joseph the Hesychast. He died over 60 years ago, yet the message of his life continues to touch Orthodox Christians around the world. He was born on Paros in 1897 or 1898. His father died when he was young, forcing him to quit school to support his mother and family. He found work in Athens, and at the age of 18 enlisted in the Greek Navy. He became somewhat successful, until one night he had a vivid dream.

He made his way to Mount Athos. He later wrote, 'On Mount Athos, we see monks who are doing well and those who are not … The monastic life does not consist of simply leaving the world and coming to Mount Athos and becoming a monk. That is easy to do. What is of essential importance is to find an elder who will teach us how the grace of God is obtained, how it is found, how it is dug up, and how this pearl of great price is revealed … I was looking to find where there is life, where I could benefit my soul'. During this time, he spent time in remote places to recite the Jesus Prayer.

Eventually he met Fr Arsenios, who was to become his co-struggler, and found that they shared a common desire for hesychasm, and decided to find an experienced elder. They found Elder Ephraim the Barrel-Maker, and they arranged their lives to provide the maximum silence for praying the Jesus Prayer. In addition to his work and his prayer rule, Fr Joseph went to a cave at sunset to recite the Jesus Prayer for six hours. After Elder Ephraim the Barrel-Maker's repose, Frs Joseph and Arsenios

FIG.15 *Elder Joseph (with walking-staff) and his disciples – Nea Skete*

spent summers moving from place to place around the peak of Mount Athos, so as to be unknown and to find and learn from spiritual monks. In winter, however, they returned to their hut in the wilderness at St Basil's. They possessed only their tattered monastic garments, and Fr Joseph ate three ounces of rusks (dried bread) a day, sometimes with an amount of boiled wild greens.

After approximately 13 years, the large amount of physical labour required to live there became too much, making most of the fathers ill. Elder Joseph moved the community further down the mountain, nearer the sea, to New Skete.

Elder Joseph reposed on August 15, 1959.

In October 2019, the Ecumenical Patriarchate of Constantinople officially recognized Elder Joseph and four other holy monks, Elder Hieronymus of Simonopetra, Elder Daniel and Ephraim of Katounakia, and Elder Sophrony of Essex, as saints of the Holy Orthodox Church. Saint Joseph the Hesychast was spiritual father to six monasteries and one cenobitic skete on the Holy Mountain, eighteen monasteries in Greece, six in Cyprus, two in Canada, and one in Italy. His disciples brought God, energy, and enthusiasm to the Holy Mountain.

Athos Forty Years ago

JOHN MCCORMACK

I am not so sure that asking me to write of memorable experiences on the Holy Mountain was a good idea, since, as is often said, 'The Devil has the best stories', and my encounters have not always been entirely edifying. But at least they demonstrate the rich diversity of monks who have, at one time or another, and for vastly differing reasons, come to call Athos home.

It was the reading of an 'O' level set book that introduced me to this extraordinary place. For a boy whose spare time was taken up by brass-rubbing, ecclesiology and the reading of Sir Walter Scott's novels, it was the romantic architecture of these monasteries that made an indelible impression on me. They seemed still, in the 1940s, to have had all the characteristics of medieval towns, as depicted in Sandy Thomas's wonderful escape story, *Dare to be Free*, where, after many privations, he is taken in by the monks of Great Lavra. 'It will all be gone', I thought, 'by the time I've grown up. And in any case, I shall never get there'.

But God moves in mysterious ways, as Cowper said, and in 1979 I found myself with a three-day diamonitirion, sampling the monasteries with a friend who had visited several times before and had primed me as to what to do and what not to do. So when we came upon an American air-steward whose casual curiosity had brought him to Simonos Petras and he proceeded to hang his washing for all to see on the external balconies, at least I thought myself well above such mistakes. I was soon to be discomfited, however, when, in a fishing boat (for some reason I've forgotten), the monk with whom we were travelling clapped me on the back and said, 'What about the Filioque then?' As an easy-going Anglican with no particular interest in the minutiae of theology, I had no idea what he meant. I soon learned!

On another visit soon afterwards, we stayed at Dochiariou, where a new abbot, Gregorios, was working his monks very hard indeed in order to restore this most beautiful of places. We celebrated a feast there, and the sight of him, splendidly robed and enthroned, lit by innumerable candles and oil lights, grasping his staff of office like an Egyptian pharaoh, was memorable enough. But when he moved around the katholikon, not at a stately Anglican pace, but sweeping all before him, robes billowing out behind, chanting as he went and roughly brushing aside pilgrims who always seemed to be in his way, medieval ceremony had come alive indeed. The following day, digesting this experience of the previous night, we were even more astonished when we turned a corner along our footpath to be confronted by the same Abbot, suddenly approaching out of the bushes, sitting erect on a mule like a figure from some Arthurian tale.

It was with these memories that I found myself back at Dochiariou last year, clearing some of those footpaths, staying once more in Gregorios's restored monastery, and celebrating Ascension Day on a perfect evening at one of the new chapels he had built, this one suitably sited on a summit, overlooking the coast far below. Now frail and supported by two monks, he was led to a seat after the service while we processed around the chapel with flaming torches, then feasted magnificently while Greeks were encouraged to sing folk-songs. All the while, one of two boys from the Athonite Academy who had come up for the occasion, stood behind the Abbot, rubbing his back. What a setting! What a lifetime of achievement was there! What memories for his monks, when they think back on him!

In fact, monastic life in Athos is extremely varied, and often, for all sorts of reasons, enthusiastic reformations gradually lose impetus until only a few apathetic old men are left, only to be helped along, either voluntarily or by edict of the Holy Epistasia, by a new brotherhood led by another dynamic or charismatic individual. On my first visit, with the American accompanying us and with time to spare at Filotheou, we decided to walk for half an hour down to the sleepy monastery of Karakallou for vespers, intending to return

PL. 14 *Outside trapeza, Dochiariou Monastery*

to Filotheou for the night. We had one of the most bizarre experiences that has ever come my way in Athos.

Karakallou, picturesquely set in woodland, and with a most attractive court-yard, surrounded by an amalgam of buildings from all eras, was at that time not just sleepy, but seemed to have entered upon an irrevocable torpor. It took us some time to discover the whereabouts of the guest-master, but in due course a somewhat slovenly monk, flopping around in carpet slippers, appeared, and we were ushered into a pleasant internal gallery. In the fullness of time, the usual tray of welcoming goodies was produced, except that the alcohol was so foul that as soon as the monk's back was turned, we all emptied it into a vase of flowers, expecting them instantly to wilt and die. We were left alone for a short while, but then the monk returned, and, beckoning to my friend, who was resplendent in as much of an Orthodox beard as he could grow, asked him to follow him. It was not long before we heard noises of crashing and banging in the distance, and when they reappeared, my friend growled into his beard that he had had to move several beds. But the monk immediately bade us all to follow him again, and we meekly traversed gallery after confusing gallery, as though in Gormenghast, until we found ourselves in front of some sheets of hardboard, which some idiot had placed against a wall at a low angle, so that they had bowed out of shape. These, we understood, we were to reverse so that they became straight again: in fact, most of them cracked, but the monk seemed not to notice. Instead, he beckoned us once more, and we began to look at each other, wondering what sort of interminable youth-hostel chores we had let ourselves in for.

Now we were ushered out into the courtyard and found ourselves in front of a gigantic boiler that looked like nothing so much as the Mouth of Hell. Nearby was a huge pile of tree-trunks, each approaching a foot in diameter and about six feet long. These, we gathered, we were to stack into two piles within easy reach of the yawning boiler. We split into two pairs, the monk and my friend forming one, the American and me the other, and, in the midst of swinging these timbers from one side to the other, I happened to look at my friend, who unaccountably was grinning. Since he always, for some unknown reason, sported one finger-nail over an inch long, and, as a lexicographer was not exactly cut out for hurling trees about, I asked him what was funny. 'The monk', he said, 'each time we pick up a timber, shouts out, "Take it easy; take it easy!" as we throw it'.

Well, having finished all this, the monk beckoned yet again, and our hearts sank, expecting that we would have to work on something else. But in fact, we were at last ushered into vespers. And what a service it was! The brotherhood had shrunk to just four monks, including the Abbot, who was stone-deaf. One monk, the cantor, was quite enormously fat, and belching loudly with every phrase he sang, was wedged into a stall with all his books arranged around him. A third monk seemed insignificant but aided and abetted the proceed-ings as best he could; and our strange guest-master busied himself continu-ally with doing everything he considered necessary. He went around with a little watering-can, lowering lamps and filling them with oil. 'Kyrie eleison' he shouted, as a lamp descended at speed. 'Kyrie eleison', he repeated, as an-other was hoisted back up. Then, hurriedly putting down his watering-can, he hastened to the iconostasis and hammered on it loudly, so that the abbot, immured behind, would respond as necessary. It was all quite extraordinary, and, close to hysterics at the afternoon's proceedings, none of us could keep a straight face.

From the church we were led straight into the refectory, and here everything was just as peculiar. Instead of a high table with others 'below', there was just one very long table, at one end of which sat the enormously fat monk, still belching. Everyone else sat at the extreme other end, including the Abbot, and placed at this end of the table was a huge stainless-steel tub of cold, congealed pasta in tomato sauce, into which our guest-master delved, serving some to each of us. That was the entire meal. Afterwards, fearing more beckoning, we lost no time, but quickly made for the gatehouse and returned to Filotheou. It was not many weeks after this experience that I discovered that these monks at Karakallou had barricaded themselves into their domain and defended themselves with guns when the authorities came to replace them with an al-ternative brotherhood. Later on, some of the most picturesque parts of the monastery burned down, but these days it is all running smoothly again, and this episode is just one of the nightmares of history.

One of my two favourite places in those days was the skete of the Prophet Elijah, inhabited by American monks descended from White Russians. Here was something the reverse of our experience at Karakallou. Just a few faithful people were endeavouring, with precious little funding, to maintain an enor-mous structure for posterity. They had inherited accommodation untouched since the Russian Revolution, indeed, from the time it was built. Latrines were literally 'long-drops' (holes in cubicles looking down a hundred feet). In one of them, the ascetic Father Ioannikios had ingeniously rigged up a shower, in the form of a watering-can balanced on a wall between two cubicles, tipped by pulling a string attached just behind the rose. Another monk with building experience specialised in attending to the lead on chapel domes by walking nonchalantly around the rims of them. And Father Hariton cut me a stick from a sweet chestnut tree that has since disappeared. The stick has a habit of disappearing too, though, 40 years on, I still use it annually. I have no difficulty bringing it out to Greece with Easyjet, but using the same company to transport it back from Thessaloniki is a different matter. I usually have a big struggle with officialdom. Last year, it vanished altogether for a month, when it miraculously turned up in Guernsey unannounced; if it goes on like this, it will soon qualify for commemoration by some icon. We tried our best to help the monks in those days. I remember painting much of the gatehouse, and down below in the two storeys of cellars, we banged the rust off Russian girders that supported a church which always seemed as big as St Paul's in London.

My other firm favourite was the kellion of St George at Kolitsu (or Colciu, as the Romanian monks there always called it). I was always welcome because a young monk, Father Pierre, was a French-Canadian and I could therefore make myself understood. With him, I remember taking a mule train down to the beach, 500 feet below, where we sieved sand for building by throwing it at a framework leaning on some sticks, then loaded it into the mule panniers and climbed back. The hegoumenos in those days was the saintly Father Dionysios, who had come as a monk in 1926 with five friends and started to do a lot of building, expecting more monks to join them. They never did, until Father Dionysios was in extreme old age, when he had the satisfaction of seeing many young men attracted to him and to Father John, almost as old. It was then that they needed more cells. The wooden framework was there, but not the material to build the panels. I suggested that the monks asked Father Dionysios where it was that he had dug clay to make daub in the old days, and to my great pleasure, this is what they did, and the walling was finished without further expenditure of anything other than hard work. Now, that has all been swept away by EU funding from Romania and all is concrete. It was while based at St George, in the 1980s, that I was able to measure up various other kellia in order to contribute a section on Athonite buildings for the Encyclopaedia of World Vernacular Architecture.

At St George they made their own soap from wood ash. They also distilled their own raki, using a totally traditional alembic, resembling the head and trunk of an elephant. The carefully tended terraces allowed them to be completely self-sufficient, and amongst many other things, there were apricot trees that I climbed to pick the fruit. I was instructed to drop any damaged apricots onto the ground, where I was astonished to see the monks driving the mules away from them. Instead, all were carefully collected up and put into sealed jars until the great day came for distilling, when everything, dirt and all, was tipped into a big copper boiler, the alembic on top, and heated until alcohol steamed out, dropping out of the 'trunk' as it cooled. It was tested by throwing a small quantity at the outside of the alembic and setting light to it. If it lit, the process continued; if not, it was just water, and everything was finished, except that the raki was boiled up again a day or two later, in order to add anise for flavouring.

There were footpaths all over the place in those days. I could cut down from the Skete to visit a Peruvian monk who had recently built himself new accommodation in great style while not disturbing the original buildings. Things were very civilised there. But coming back to the Prophet Elijah, my way led over the land of an old Greek monk. He invariably asked me in, and one threaded one's way across floors almost completely covered with onions drying. I was offered water in a cut-down baked-beans tin. Accepting with a smile, I somehow survived.

Other paths, some now vanished, led via Bogoroditsa very easily to St George. I used to reckon that I could go from one to the other in an hour and a half. One evening, when I had to return to the skete, I misjudged things and left St George too late. In Athos dusk falls quickly, but fortunately I knew my way well enough, and I had my stick with me. By the time I had descended to a bridge across the stream in the last valley, it was virtually dark. It had been a very dry summer, and this was one of the few streams still with running water. As I went along, I was aware of a great deal of noise from some large beast splashing and presumably drinking. I resolved to climb up the other side of the valley to stop for a moment to see if I could work out what animal it was. What happened was a very close encounter indeed, for I had stopped right alongside a wild boar, lying low while his mate drank. No doubt he heard the bumbling human coming and had decided to allow me to pass without reaction. But then I didn't pass: I stopped. Completely alarmed and with a huge grunt and

lots of other noise, he jumped up and missed me by an inch. I'm not sure who was the more astonished. But I can certainly vouch for the fact that pigs have amazing acceleration but probably no brakes. I can also muse on the fact that, once again, I survived completely unscathed.

A monk who had survived rather more serious upheavals in the Near East, as we used to call it before it became the Middle East to Americans, was Father Alexander, an Austrian. He had lived as a hermit for some years in Sinai, but eventually had to leave, and found refuge in Athos, where he had settled in a kellion, embowered in woodland quite close to Karyes. This he had adapted to look like an Alpine chalet, entered by a golden gate. Inside, there were prob-ably cuckoo clocks, though I can't remember, and, just as people with grand pianos in stately homes often stand photographs of family or friends for all to admire, Alexander had arranged photos of the Austrian royal family around his rooms, some members of which he had known. Everything was over-elab-orate, even his letters, which were multi-coloured and apt to burst into poetry. He kept body and soul together by making incense, rather dangerously. But his welcome was always warm, his hospitality overwhelming. How very bless-ed I have been, to come across such wonderful people, all individuals, all wor-shipping God by making the most of the richness of their own personalities, as well, of course, as using the liturgies they loved.

Short Trip to the Edge: A Pilgrimage to Prayer

SCOTT CAIRNS

In the spring of 2006, I first published *Short Trip to the Edge*, an account of my first three pilgrimages to Agion Oros, the Holy Mountain – a monastic peninsula in northern Greece that is more widely known as Mount Athos. It is, to be sure, a uniquely hallowed place, a hallowing place, one of those places our Celtic saints would have characterized as thin. I understand their sense of such thin places as physical spaces in which the veil between heaven and earth seems transparent or porous, sites whose immediate substance thins to yield apprehension of greater – or inexhaustible – substance; in my thinking, a more likely characterization of such scenes would be that they themselves have attained a palpable presence of the invisible enormity in which we live and move and have our being; that is, the places themselves register as thick, full, densely inhabited by holy presence.

Since those first three visits in 2004 and 2005, I have, at this writing, made an additional twenty-four pilgrimages. Much has happened in the interim. Therefore, I hope for this excerpt to bring the reader a sense of an ongoing synergy, the collaboration between Heaven and earth – which is what the Holy Mountain represents, and what the Holy Mountain performs.

Please accept this brief excerpt as one that offers a taste of the beauty, the efficacy, and the ongoing blessing that Agion Oros offers to those who would witness God's holy presence in the very midst of our slow-going way. Good journey, as the Greeks like to say – *Καλό ταξίδι*! Good road – *Καλό δρόμο*! Lord, I believe. Help my unbelief.

The boat is the Axion Estin, and I am finally on the boat.

The concrete pier at the bow marks the end of the world, where lies a modest village with an ambitious name; it is Ouranoupolis, Heaven's City. We remain bound to its bustling pier by two lengths of rope as thick as my thigh.

Any moment now, the boat will be loosed and let go, and we will be on our way to Agion Oros, the Holy Mountain.

The air is sun-drenched, salt-scented, cool, and pulsing with a riot of gulls and terns dipping to grab bits of bread laid upon the water for them. The Aegean reflects the promising blue of a robin's egg. A light breeze dapples the surface, reflecting to some degree the tremor I'm feeling just now in my throat.

I've been planning this trip for most of a year.

I've been on this journey for most of my life.

For a good while now, the ache of my own poor progress along that journey has been escalating. It has reached the condition of a dull throb, just beneath the heart.

By which I mean, more or less, that when I had travelled half of our life's way, I found myself stopped short, as within a dim forest.

Or, how's this: as I walked through that wilderness, I came upon a certain place, and laid me down to sleep: as I slept, I dreamed, and saw a man clothed with rags, standing with his face turned away from his own house, a book in his hand, and a great burden upon his back. He opened the book, and read therein; and, as he read, he wept and shook, and cried out, saying, What shall I do?

Here's the rub: by the mercy of God I am a Christian; by my deeds, a great sinner.

You might recognize some of that language. You might even recognize the sentiment. These lines roughly paraphrase the opening words of three fairly famous pilgrims, the speakers of Dante's *Divine Comedy*, Bunyan's *The Pilgrim's Progress*, and the Russian devotional favourite known as *The Way of a Pilgrim*.

In each of them I find a trace of what Saint Paul writes to the church in Rome in the first century: I do not understand what it is I do. For what I want to do, I do not do; but what I hate, I do.

I get it. I really do get it.

In each of these confessions I suspect a common inference as well: something is amiss. There is a yawning gap between where I am and where I mean to go.

Lately, the crux of my matter has come pretty much down to this: having said prayers since childhood, I startled one day – at the middling age of forty – to the realization that I had not yet learned to pray.

At any rate, despite half a lifetime of mostly good intentions, I had not established anything that could rightly be called a prayer life.

I have recently turned fifty. And though it is possible that some progress has been made in the intervening ten years, that progress has been very slow, negligible, and remarkably unsteady, with virtually every advance being followed, hard on the heels, by an eclipsing retreat – with hard words, harsh thoughts continuing to undermine any accomplishment in the realms of charity and compassion.

In his Christmas oratorio, *For the Time Being*, the beloved Mr Auden puts it in a way that never fails to resonate with me, to slap me awake when I recite his poem (which I do as a matter of course every Christmas Eve): 'To those who have seen / The Child, however dimly, however incredulously, / The Time Being is, in a sense, the most trying time of all'.

I get that, too.

Wise men and women of various traditions have troubled the terms *being* and *becoming* for centuries without arriving at anything like a conclusion. Every so often, though, I glimpse that some of the trouble may derive from our merely being, when – as I learned to say in Texas – we *might could be* becoming.

I wonder if we aren't fashioned to be always becoming, and I wonder if the dry taste in my mouth isn't a clue that staying put is, in some sense, an aberration, even if it may also be commonplace.

I have been a Christian virtually all of my life, have hoped, all of my life, to eventually find my way to some measure of … what? Spiritual maturity? Wisdom? I'd hoped, at least, to find my way to a sense of equanimity, or peace, or … something.

More generally, my life then reminds me of an often-repeated comment one monk made to a visitor to Mount Athos. I imagine it like this: The visitor asks what it is that the monks do there; and the monk, looking up from the black wool of the prayer rope he is tying, stares off into the distance for a moment, silent, as if wrestling with the answer. Then he meets the other man's eyes very directly and says: 'We fall down, and we get up again'.

A little glib, but I think I get the point.

Monks, it turns out, can be a little glib on occasion, and, I've noticed that they have a general penchant for the oblique.

Even if the monk's words do offer a glimpse of a truth that is available to us all, I keep thinking that – for the saints, for the monks, for the genuinely wise, presumably for anyone but me – the subsequent fall needn't seem so completely to erase all previous progress.

I keep thinking that, for the pilgrim hoping to make any progress at all, the falling down must eventually become less, that the rising up must become something more – more of a steady ascent, and more lasting.

I also have an increasing sense that the subsequent fall need not be inevitable.

I keep thinking that this is actually possible – the proposition of spiritual development that leads us into becoming, and – as the fathers and mothers of the Eastern Christian tradition would have it – into always becoming.

The question must be how to get from here to there.

And that question has pressed me to get serious, to slap myself awake, take up my bed and get to walking.

I hope to be, at long last, a pilgrim on the way.

The boat – whose name means It Is Worthy – is backing away from the chaos of crates and trucks and the crowd of very loud, very animated men burdening the concrete pier. With a shudder and a plume of diesel smoke, the ferry discovers a forward gear and angles out, pressing into the Aegean's dappled blue.

At that moment on the deck – with the breeze whipping up white caps on the Aegean, the ferry boat tooling along in what I swear was a confident, dactylic rhythm, and with the first monastic enclaves coming into view along the shore – I realized that I was really going to the Holy Mountain.

Mount Athos has always been a unique phenomenon, and, for most folks, it remains a downright puzzling one; its uniqueness and puzzlement are all the more pronounced in the twenty-first century, when ancient pursuits like monasticism, asceticism, and hesychasm strike the modern psyche as anachronistic, extreme, and maybe a little perverse.

The monks also follow the Julian, or 'old', calendar, and this involves a tweaking of dates to a point thirteen days behind where you thought you were.

Think of it as a cosmic pressure to slow down – or, maybe better, as a metaphor for our failure to know, even, where we stand, or when. Then don't think about it again. The monks are, for the most part, gracious enough to suppose where and when you think you are, and will play along.

PL. 17 *Katholikon, Stavronikita*

Oh, and one other thing: the clock. The hours of the day begin at sundown rather than at midnight. Not to worry; you'll catch on.

The easternmost of three peninsulas – easily the steepest and rockiest of three long fingers of steep and rocky land – reaching south into the Aegean from that region of northeastern Greece known as Chalkidiki, the peninsula of Mount Athos is about thirty-four miles in length and varies between five and eight miles across, covering less than 250 square miles total; the sharply rising terrain moves precipitously from sea level to 6,700 feet, which is the summit of the Mount Athos peak itself, very near the southern tip of the peninsula.

In physical terms, then, the area of the Holy Mountain isn't much. In spiritual terms, it is immense, impossible to chart.

Archaeological evidence suggests that since as early as the second century ascetics have lived here in pursuit of prayer – in pursuit of, rather, lives of prayer.

Since the third century – and perhaps even earlier – ascetics desiring lives of prayer have lived in community here. Over the next seventeen hundred years, the precise number of these communities has varied, witnessing intermittent increase and decline; some documents indicate that as many as 180 such communities flourished at one point. The establishment of these communities appears to have occurred in two distinct waves, an early wave during the third through fifth centuries, and a second, more pronounced wave commencing in the tenth century and continuing into the fourteenth century. (Megisti Lavra, founded in 963, is agreed to have been the earliest in the second wave.)

Today there are twenty such communities recognized as 'ruling monasteries'; because Mount Athos operates as a virtually autonomous political state, representatives from these twenty constitute the Holy Mountain's governing body. While seventeen are identified as Greek, one as Bulgarian, one as Serbian, and one as Russian, the Holy Mountain includes a full array of Orthodox nationalities, including significant numbers of Romanian, Moldavian, Ukrainian, English, American, and Australian monks. There are also a dozen or more sketes and countless, smaller brotherhoods; some of the sketes appear very like monasteries, but ostensibly – with a few notable exceptions – smaller. Each skete is a dependency of one of the twenty ruling monasteries, on whose lands it rests. Some, like the Romanian Skíti Timiou Prodromou (named after 'the Forerunner', St John the Baptist), the Russian Skíti Agios Andreas (Saint Andrew's Skete), and Skíti Profiti Ilíou (Prophet Elijah Skete), look very like full-fledged monasteries, with a central katholikón (or kyriakon) protect-

ed within a high-walled structure; others, including Skíti Agias Annis (Saint Anne's Skete) and Nea Skíti (New Skete), appear more like thriving residential communities spread across the steep Athonite slope, dotted with churches, chapels, and monastic kéllia, or cells. There are, as well, throughout the Athonite wilderness, many scattered, communal farm dwellings, kalýves (communal huts), kathísmata (smaller huts for single monks) and hesychastéria (squat huts or simple caves etched in a cliff face for the most ascetic of hermits, an increasingly rare breed).

The twenty ruling monasteries are now all cenobitic, in which the monks all follow a common rule. Until recently, some were idiorrhythmic, in which the monks pursued more individualized ascetic practice, often allowing for a more demanding rule. The idiorrhythmic approach – still observed in many of the sketes and smaller dependencies – is thought by some to be an aberration of the ideal monastic community, albeit an historic necessity brought about during foreign occupation by Franks, Turks, etc. Others understand the idiorrhythmic rule of the skete to be more aptly suited to those monks who are permitted a more strenuous ascesis.

In either case, the monastic rule has always revolved around prayer. And fasting, too – but fasting as a tool assisting prayer. It is safe to say that nothing about life on Mount Athos is understood as an end in itself, and that everything deliberate about life on Mount Athos is undertaken to accommodate prayer. Prayer is undertaken to accommodate union with God – what those in the business like to call théosis.

We should probably stick to prayer for now, but théosis is the crux of our matter, and that is where – I pray – we will eventually arrive.

Odd as Mount Athos may appear by contemporary standards, the Holy Mountain is visited by hundreds of pilgrims every month. The generally balmy weather and calm seas of spring, summer, and fall bring boat-load after boat-load scrambling to visit the steep and rocky slopes, the deep forests of chestnut, pine, and juniper, and the ancient enclaves; though wintertime draws relatively fewer, they arrive daily and by the dozens, even so – whenever the weather-driven surf allows the ferry boats to dock.

That is to say, year-round, pilgrims arrive at Mount Athos virtually every day, looking for something. One friend (now a novice monk at Simonópetra) told me that a good many visitors come in search of healing from serious illness – their own or that of a loved one. Some arrive because their marriages are failing or have failed, some come to kick an addiction or two, and some few arrive because they are drawn to a fuller sense of prayer.

Most of them are Orthodox Christians, and most are from Greece; a good number arrive from other parts of eastern Europe, notably Romania and Russia. Concurrent with the rise of Eastern Orthodoxy in English-speaking countries, many also come from England, Australia, and North America. Many non-Orthodox arrive as well; from what I could gather, many of these are from Germany and other parts of western Europe.

On the Axion Estin, leaning into the headwind at the bow, I was waking to the fact that I, after many months of planning and anticipation, would soon arrive, setting foot on a land blessed by centuries of prayer – genuine prayer, prayer of a sort I could only suspect, and desire.

Soon, I'd be walking through what the Orthodox call 'the garden of the Theotokos'.

I hoped, moreover, to come upon a holy man, an adept, a spiritual father, who could help me to pray.

It was more than a little daunting.

This extract is from Short Trip to the Edge *by Scott Cairns (2007), HarperCollins: used with permission*

God's Reason for a Pilgrimage to Mount Athos

FR RICHARD EDWARDS

I'm not sure what I expected or hoped for when a friend asked me if I would like to make a four-day pilgrimage to Mount Athos in 2008. For as long as I can remember I have carried two very strong drives, which have sometimes seemed to be in tension with each other. On one hand, a deep desire for family life and community and on the other, an equally strong desire for space to be alone; a deep desire to love and be loved unconditionally and the deep desire for silence and solitude, to make sense of my questions of being and purpose.

That first pilgrimage was a tantalizing taster of the way that those two drives are unified as part of the monastic vocation. I had always sensed that this may be the case and my regular 'retreats' in male or female religious communities, had pointed to it. My first pilgrimage to the Holy Mountain plunged me into a form of monasticism that reflected what I had thought only existed in history, not in the present. It was tantalizing because we were staying briefly with men who had answered the call to monasticism and yet we had little time or opportunity to talk with them and ask questions.

The following year, 2009, I joined a group of men drawn together by John Arnell, to clear the ancient footpaths of Mount Athos. By the beginning of the twenty-first century taxis and buses were increasingly being used by pilgrims to visit monasteries rather than using the ancient and often overgrown footpaths. Some years earlier HRH Prince Charles had shared his vision with members of FoMA to restore these ancient paths so that pilgrims could travel from monastery to monastery by foot. John had accepted the challenge of organizing this huge exercise and the base for our group was the Monastery of Vatopedi.

It was a wonderful fortnight of hard work, worship, adequate and sometimes beautiful food, 'well-water', friendship and hospitality, allowing time for conversation. Emerging from the sea of black monastic robes, long hair and beards I began to identify the different characters and personalities of the monks and the different reasons for them coming to the Holy Mountain. Also emerging was my awareness that their new life was not always in line with their expectations for making the initial commitment to join an Athonite religious community. I relished the blessing of time, to talk, listen and to be silent.

On our last evening at Vatopedi we were invited to take refreshments and meet with Abbot Ephraim, the leader of the community. During the course of that meeting Abbot Ephraim told us, through Father M who was acting as interpreter, 'No one comes to the Holy Mountain by accident, whatever reason they think they are coming for is not God's reason'. Ever since then I have reflected on those words and shared them with friends who plan to visit the Holy Mountain.

Jesuit Priest, Gerard Hughes describes God as a 'God of Surprise' in his book of the same name. The hospitality, work, worship and fellowship of the Athonite Monasteries has helped me in my ongoing desire to be part of creating community where love flourishes and space for silence and reflection is enabled. In this space we can be alert to the surprise, of God's reason for our being and God's purpose for us. Perhaps God's reason for my time on the Holy Mountain was to help me see that I face the same challenge as each monk; to become the person God created me to be. As I live my life in the world I recognise that footpath-clearing was my reason for being on the Holy Mountain and continue daily to seek 'God's reason'. I also continue to be grateful for The Communities of Mount Athos, and I'm constantly surprised by God.

Journey's End

NICHOLAS SHAKESPEARE

A strange osmosis takes place when you write the life of another person. After Bruce Chatwin died, his widow Elizabeth gave me the maté gourd that he had taken with him on his travels, together with its silver bombilla – the metal straw through which he sucked his addictive tea, like any Argentine farm hand. At times over the next seven years I had the sudden deep conviction that I was absorbing the world through his perforated silver straw.

In the course of following Chatwin's songline, I met his family and friends – some of whom became my friends. In Birmingham, I had tea with the charlady responsible for dusting the contents of his grandmother's cabinet, including the scrap of giant sloth that had formed the genesis for *In Patagonia*. 'It used to put the creeps up on me, an old bit of blacky, browny bristly stuff as didn't look very nice at all [...] I thought it was only monkey fur.' In 1991, I drove with Elizabeth from Buenos Aires to Tierra del Fuego, to the cave on Last Hope Sound from where Chatwin's cousin had salvaged the original hide – believed by the infant Chatwin to be a piece of brontosaurus. In Sydney, I poked my nose into Ken's Karate Club, a 'sex on premises venue' designed in imitation of a fantasy Roman baths, with horned satyrs and concrete putti (from a garden supply shop). Near Alice Springs, I camped under the stars with the man on whom Chatwin had modelled Arkady, the protagonist of *The Songlines*. And so on, through twenty-seven countries.

My biography was published in 1999, ten years after Chatwin died of Aids. But in all the travels I had undertaken, there was one significant journey I overlooked. In 1985, following his second visit to Australia, where he had picked up a mysterious illness, Chatwin was in Greece, grinding out another draft of *The Songlines*, when he interrupted his work to make a pilgrimage to Mount Athos. Before leaving, he wrote breezily to Murray Bail: 'Athos is obviously another atavistic wonder'. Up until that moment Chatwin had not impressed friends as religious. 'There was never, not a word

talked about God', says Patrick Leigh Fermor, his host in Greece, reflecting on their conversations over five months. Elizabeth was, and remains, a practising Catholic. In preparation for their wedding, Chatwin had taken religious instruction from a Jesuit in London. 'Nearly became a Catholic', he wrote in his notebook. Then, just before they were married, Elizabeth's parish priest in New York State gave her a leaflet explaining why she should not marry a non-Catholic. 'That put Bruce off forever', says Elizabeth. Thereafter, his religious faith became subsumed in his nomadic theory: he believed that movement made religion redundant and only when people settled did they need it.

Since his illness, there were signs of a sea-change. One entry in his notebooks reads: 'The search for nomads is a search for God'. Another, 'religion is a technique for arriving at the moment of death at the right time'. While recuperating with Elizabeth in Nepal, his thoughts had turned to a man's ethos, 'in the Greek sense of abode or dwelling place – the root of all his behaviour for good or bad, his character, everything that pertained to him'.

Of Chatwin's friends, the diarist James Lees-Milne and the artist Derek Hill were regular visitors to the sacred, all-male enclave. He importuned both to take him. Lees-Milne recorded in August 1980: ' "No, Bruce", I said, "you can't." I was, I fear rather bossy'. Next, Chatwin asked Hill, who had visited Mount Athos fifteen times. Hill was a friend of the Abbot of Chilandar monastery, who could facilitate their permits. Finally, in May 1985, Hill agreed to accompany Chatwin. He told me, 'I was slightly apprehensive because he was a great complainer. I thought he'd find the monks smelly or the beds hard or that the loos stank. But it was a revelation to him'. One afternoon after his usual maté (mistaken by the cook for hashish), Chatwin walked to the monastery of Stavronikita, once painted by Edward Lear. He puffed towards it with his heavy rucksack. 'The most beautiful sight of all was an iron cross on a rock by the sea'. From where he stood – just below the monastery – the black cross appeared to

be striving up against the white foam. Then these words: 'There must be a god'. Beyond this entry in his notebook, Chatwin was uncharacteristically silent. 'He didn't talk about it, but I knew by his whole bearing that it had affected him', said Hill. The artist had known Chatwin for twenty years and had no doubt that as Bruce gazed down on that iron cross he was ambushed by a spiritual experience that unfroze something in him. 'I think it hit him like a bomb'.

Elizabeth says, 'When he came back, he said to me: "I had no idea it could be like that". It wasn't like his other voyages of discovery. It was completely internal'. The memory of that moment returned to Chatwin a year later when he collapsed, hallucinating, in Zurich. One of his hallucinations was of a fresco of Christ on Mount Athos. Back in England during a brief period of remission, he went several times to see Kallistos Ware, a bishop of the Greek Orthodox faith living in Oxford, to discuss the possibility of becoming Orthodox. 'What he wanted was to be received by baptism on the Holy Mountain since the Holy Mountain had played such a decisive part in his conversion'. Unknown virtually to anyone, Chatwin planned a second trip to Athos in which, as part of the baptism ceremony, he would renounce the devil, breathe and spit on him and return to Christ. 'I offered to receive him myself', says Ware, 'but we were overtaken by events'. On 19 January 1989 Chatwin died in Nice. At his memorial service in the Greek Orthodox Church in Bayswater, Ware relayed his wishes to a frankly astonished congregation: 'Bruce was always a traveller and he died before all his journeys could be completed and his journey into Orthodoxy was one of his unfinished voyages'.

Last September, after finishing with Elizabeth the editing of Chatwin's letters, I decided to visit Mount Athos. My aim was simple: to find that simple metal cross. But an English priest warned me on the eve of my departure, 'Nobody goes to Athos by accident. Whatever you think you are going for is not the reason'.

Mount Athos is actually a finger of steep wooded land that extends fifty-six kilometres into the Aegean, culminating in a 2,000 metre peak of crystalline limestone. The peninsula is dedicated to the Virgin Mary, who stopped off here on her way to Cyprus and jealously forbade any subsequent woman to set foot. This rule, enshrined in AD 970 in the charter of the Great Lavra, the first of Athos's twenty monasteries, stated that monks 'may not defile their eyes with the sight of anything female', a stricture not relaxed even in favour of chickens. Under Greek law, a woman caught on Athos today faces an automatic prison sentence of up to twelve months.

'With no one to nag them, the monks often live to a hundred'. The speaker is a stout pilgrim whose whiskers sprout at a brigandish angle from his chin. We are on board the ferry from Ouranoupolis, the only way to reach Athos.

It's a bright hot day. I elect to walk to the monastery of Vatopedi where I am staying the night. The journey takes all afternoon, the white cobbled path twisting through woods of Spanish chestnut, past ruined stone fountains, over bridges spanning dried-up rivers. My shirt is soon splotchy with sweat. Thirsty and perspiring, I long for a fresh-water stream to plunge in – although from a former British diplomat I have gathered that Athonite monks deplore nakedness. John Ure told me how, as a young pilgrim here, he once stripped off to splash himself in a stream, when an old hermit emerged from a cave above him, screamed and ran off covering his eyes. Later, Ure arrived at the Great Lavra to find the monks in a state of terrific excitement. They had received a visit from one of the holiest hermits on the peninsula, who had broken his vow of silence to report a vision he had seen: John the Baptist baptizing in his local stream – his tell-tale body radiating with 'a shining whiteness unlike any normal mortal'. Already they were discussing the erection of a stained-glass window.

The gatekeeper at Vatopedi is Father T from Brisbane. Does he miss Australia? 'The grace of God sustains you. You forget the past and keep an eye on the future'. He is dead to the world he has left behind, which is why he wears black. But Father T is far from gloomy. He brims with news of a minor miracle that occurred at Vatopedi last July. An old monk, Father Joseph, had died in huge pain with a terrible expression on his face. 'We couldn't close his mouth. We asked the Abbot if we should bind it shut, but he said, "No, let it hang open"– and when we came out of the liturgy his mouth was closed in a tremendous smile. Look, I have a photo'. From his black robe Father T produces a portrait of a bearded corpse with cheeks like polished doorknobs, beaming. 'That is what sanctification is. It comes from within you'.

Vatopedi, founded in 972, is the peninsula's second oldest monastery, and largest. Its luxuriant church accommodates 107 monks from twelve countries. I watch them at vespers flit across the water-veined marble floor. Their destination: half a dozen holy icons which they proceed to kiss in a way that reminds me of a scatter of swallows sipping the surface of a glassy pond; then, adjusting their hats, they sit down in squeaking stalls, faces in mid-distance reverie, beneath frescoes which Robert Byron, revered by Chatwin beyond all writers, considered the finest in the world.

Chatwin was so enthralled by the repetitive chanting of the Kyrie eleison, the words unchanged for over a millennium, that he made a scene with some noisy Greek pilgrims, 'demanding hushes at once and interrupting the service'. My solecism is to sit cross-legged. From nowhere, a black stick appears and wallops me – the wielder, a small wax-faced monk whose long white beard accounts for a quarter of him.

Chastened, I uncross my legs and go on listening. To the singers, the plain-song serves to enthrone their veneration for the Mother of God. Whatever one's belief – and as Patrick Leigh Fermor reminds us, 'no living man, after all, is in a position to declare their premises true or false' – the mysterious scallops of sound are absolutely transporting to hear live. 'To anyone who has sojourned beneath the Holy Mountain', Robert Byron wrote of Athos, 'there cannot but have come an intensification of his impulse to indefinable, un-analysable emotion'.

In roughly such a state, Chatwin must have shouldered his rucksack and wandered down to Stavronikita.

Father T watches me leave. He arrived on Athos twenty years ago, but has never done the walk to Stavronikita. 'I liked walking when I was young, but all things in moderation'.

It's late in the morning when the castle-like building comes into sight, perched on a cliff above the Aegean. There is no swell and the sea is smoother than shell. Suddenly I spot it. A small black metal cross on a ledge of white rock, facing the empty bay. It's too dangerous to clamber down, so I stand and contemplate it. I shall not attempt to describe the sensation of trying to shed the load of a nineteen-year involvement, but my anticipation is shot through by an extraordinary blankness. I realise that I had been willing for some sign or emotion, however slight, to tell me that my journey was really over.

After a long interval I turn and walk up the hill to the monastery, where a surprise awaits me. Fumblingly at the gate, I explain my mission to the monk who brings out a silver tray containing the traditional offering of Turkish delight, ouzo and water. He invites me inside to look at the church. I follow him through a door, into a chapel at once more intimate than at Vatopedi, small, dark, marvellous. In pride of place beneath the gold corona, staring out from the top of a base shaped like a squat grandfather clock, is a glassed-in icon of a bearded man. The face is composed of mosaic fragments and there is a deep gash from the left brow down to the lip.

FIG.16 *Daphne*

The monk explains that the icon arrived over the sea of its own volition from Byzantium. 'And the gash?' Caused either by pirates who tossed it into the sea, or else by an oyster that a local fisherman found clamped to its forehead when he dragged it up in his net. 'Who is he?' The monk gives me an impatient glance. 'St Nicholas!' – to whom Stavronikita is dedicated.

A name can mean nothing. But in that moment, in that space, it humbled me to learn, as I gazed around at frescoes that depicted scenes from the life of my patron saint, a name can mean more than a lot.

Holy Mount Athos: Station of a Faith

NICHOLAS TALBOT RICE

In 1926 my father David Talbot Rice and a companion joined Robert Byron on his famous pilgrimage to the Holy Mountain. David's role was to photograph the relics, frescoes and mosaics to which they were given access. His photographs illustrating Byron's seminal book, *The Station*, bring to life how Athos looked between the wars. These notes record my journey in my father's footsteps ninety years later.

April 2015: It is dawn and a chill wind blows across the empty courtyard, while inside the Koutloumousiou katholikon elderly monks huddle together for warmth in dark and muffled corners. Still half asleep, my eyes stinging from the early start, I stand discreetly at the rear watching the theatre that is the morning Liturgy unfold.

At 6.30 a.m. we all cross to the trapeza where a simple meal awaits, accompanied by flagons of robust red wine which will help sustain us on our long trek to Vatopedi. We stop briefly in Karyes for supplies and I dig out Robert Byron's *The Station* from my rucksack and standing outside the little restaurant I turn to my father's photograph of the village and hold it up to compare it with today's vista.

The photograph of Holy Ghost Street I am looking at was taken by my father in 1926 and although it shows only one shop, the view in front of me has changed very little in the intervening ninety years since he stood on this same spot. As Robert Byron says in the closing words of *The Station*: 'This is the Holy Mountain Athos, station of a faith where all the years have stopped'. This spine-tingling moment is the first of many spiritual encounters I am to experience and seems somehow to embody much of the mysticism of the Holy Mountain.

Fifteen years earlier I had received out of the blue an email from a Father Ioustinos at the Monastery of Simonopetra. He was in charge of the Holy Mountain Photo Archive. In his email, Father Ioustinos referred to my father's photography as 'pioneering work' which has 'always inspired admiration and respect' and asked for my help in allowing access to the original notes, negatives and prints which added so much to *The Station*. Although I was determined to visit Simonopetra, on this occasion we were unable to get permission to stay, and I would have to wait a further five years before I was able to close the circle and visit their library.

September 2019: As the ferry Mikra Agia Anna rounds the headland, the famous outline of Simonopetra comes into view, hanging from the edge of a single rock 330 metres above us. Now, five years on from my first pilgrimage, we have been offered an overnight stay. We disembark at the arsanas and make our way up, up and up towards the monastery along a broad kalderimi which zigzags its way through olive groves and gardens, offering spectacular views of the coastline below. Eventually, after many stops in the hot afternoon, a long vineyard tunnel leads on to a small square and we arrive at the monastery's heavily fortified main gate.

At the archontariki I mention Father Ioustinos's email of 2000 and it is early evening before I am able to track down a Father Niphon who has been assigned to us to give a private tour of the monastery library. A simple door gives no indication of the fascinating world which lies beyond. Like Alice going down the rabbit hole, we stepped into a descending labyrinth of stairs and doors and vast areas of exposed rock. When, five floors down, we finally reached the library we met an intriguing mix of state of the art sophistication and unchanged thousand-year-old tradition.

Father Niphon tells us of the two catastrophic fires which have ravaged the monastery, the many rare and precious books and manuscripts which had been lost forever and why the library is now located so far underground, to protect it from further damage. He proudly shows us a selection of books and has placed my donated copy of *The Station* in a most prominent position. I ask Father Niphon if he can look out the 1925-26 guest registers which my father would have signed on his visits. At the same time, I experience strong emotions as I too sign the guest register, as my father had done all those years before. This moment, and that of five years earlier on Holy Ghost Street, will remain with me forever.

The following morning, we leave Simonopetra, climb into a 4-wheel drive and roar down the road to Daphne. Our friendly monk-driver is in a hurry and anxious to knock five minutes off the usual journey time. But we feel safe – he crossed himself before setting off. Athos, station of a faith.

The Single Gospel

NEIL AVERITT

Neil wrote the book The Single Gospel.

Like many Americans today, I grew up with religion playing very little part in my childhood life. This was a change from family tradition, because my ancestors had always had a strong Christian bent. Some members of the family were Huguenots – French Protestants who endured prosecution for the sake of their faith and eventually fled to England. Others were English Puritans, who suffered a different kind of persecution for their own faith and eventually fled to Jamestown in the new colony of Virginia.

Once here, people in one branch of the family embraced the Church of Jesus Christ of Latter-day Saints – the Mormons – and braved the wilderness with Brigham Young to make new homes in the western desert. All were willing to endure great sacrifices for the sake of their beliefs. This same religious commitment continued into more recent times. The family has produced many ministers and preachers.

Some of them helped to found Averett College, a Baptist-affiliated school in southern Virginia. Another, the Revd James Battle Avirett, was the Episcopal chaplain of Turner Ashby's cavalry regiment during the Civil War. Working for the success of the other side in the same conflict, my own great-grandfather served as a doctor in the Union Army and then went on to spend the rest of his life in the ministry in Kentucky. We were an educated family, however, and the Age of Reason had a strong influence on our thinking. By the time I was born, religion had gone out of style in America.

My parents were scientists – geologists who were more inclined to study what they could see and measure: the stones and rock formations that make up the physical universe. They were fair-minded people and respectful of religion, but not religious themselves. And so I grew up virtually without a re-

ligious education. We seldom went to church. From time to time my parents took us to services in the little Mormon farming towns of southern Utah, where my father spent summers doing geological work. Back home in Washington they took me to a local church one Palm Sunday when I was in grade school. There I saw children my own age waving palm fronds; I recognized some of them as my classmates, but had little idea what their actions meant.

Once when I was very young I was asked by an elderly relative if I understood the meaning of Easter, and responded that I certainly did. It was the day, I explained gravely, when they nailed George Washington to the cross.

On other subjects, however, I was able to give better answers, and so I went to Harvard, the London School of Economics, and Harvard Law School. Religion remained absent in all these places. I spent my time amid throngs of intelligent people who were trying and often failing to find meaning in their lives. I enjoyed the sight of Memorial Church, a building that dominates the centre of Harvard Yard and faces the main library; but I went inside only to see the lists of the Harvard men who had gone before me, and who had died in the First World War. I also travelled during those student years, riding a motorcycle through Europe.

One day I visited Mont Saint-Michel in France and was struck by its beauty. A thin spire rose high above the cloister of the monastery, and its proportions reminded me of Memorial Church. But here too my response was just an aesthetic one – I thought it was a beautiful building with glorious architecture. Then later that day I had a serious accident. I hit a break in the pavement of the road, flipped the motorcycle, and broke my collarbone. A kindly motorist picked me up and took me to a nearby hospital affiliated with the Roman Catholic Church. At the end of the day the nuns paced down the hall-

way chanting something beautiful and otherworldly. I couldn't understand the words, but for the first time I had an inkling that the world might contain other sets of values.

Visiting the cathedral of Notre Dame while recuperating, I looked with interest at the frieze of sculptures around the choir showing biblical scenes. It wasn't until many years later that someone explained that these depicted episodes in Jesus's life, designed to tell the Christian story to people of the Middle Ages who were illiterate. Here I was, a highly educated man, but I was less able to read that story than a person who could not read at all. I sometime paused to think that this cathedral – and the churches of my own country – represented a huge investment of the time and wealth of earlier generations. Clearly they were expressing some message that those people had thought was vitally important to hand down to us. But the message wasn't reaching me. As I moved into adult life, however, it became increasingly clear that our contemporary world was missing something that had been central to successful cultures and to successful individual lives in the past. I thought back to the European towns I had seen on my travels, and the classic American towns with churches at their centre, and realized they had helped to build a sense of community that was no longer with us.

The rational secular laws I had studied in law school didn't seem to be providing a similar structure for people's lives or making them particularly happy. There were a lot of alienated strivers in our world. But what was the alternative? One alternative began to appear when I first encountered a true community of faith, and saw what lives lived in Christian understanding might look like. This experience could happen to a person anywhere, but in my case it happened on a visit to a place in Greece called Mount Athos.

Mount Athos is in Greece but not really of it. It is a self-governing, largely autonomous monastic republic in the northern part of the country, literally a piece of the old Byzantine Empire, a part of the doubly unfamiliar world of the Eastern Orthodox churches. It occupies a remote, mountainous peninsula that reaches thirty-five miles out into the Aegean, terminating in the steep-sided peak of Mount Athos itself, which rises seven thousand feet directly out of the ocean. No road connects the peninsula with the mainland, so it is for all practical purposes an island. Scattered across this isolated landscape are twenty large monasteries, a few small towns, innumerable farmhouses and hermitages, and about 2,000 monks.

Even the buildings themselves are dramatic, built of stone and fortified, with Byzantine and medieval influences predominating, the monasteries sometimes standing near the sea and sometimes clinging to crags a thousand feet above it. The entire community functions as a religious republic – a sort of 'Christian Tibet' – under a charter granted by the Byzantine Emperor in the year 972. For the first-time visitor like me, the experience was as strange as being suddenly dropped down on Mars.

Although Mount Athos was undeniably exotic, it did not seem likely to be the place of my spiritual awakening. After all, I had gone there as a cultural tourist, to see the architecture and the unique institutions surviving from the classical world. I was a visitor. Once there, however, I found faith in forms that I had not seen before. For one thing, the monks did not have, as one might have expected, a dour and burdened attitude toward their austere lives. Instead, the life they had chosen for themselves seemed to have made them calm and cheerful, and at peace with the world. The country lanes around some of the monasteries were so quiet that you could hear the sound of birds' wings and of bees in the trees, and a sense of age-old peace lay over the land. One of the monks recommended to me a line from the Psalms, 'Be still and know that I am God'.

The monks' faith was not just a response to a tranquil environment. It was grounded, not in a freedom from aggravation, but in a sense of continuing communion with something larger. Every act, it seemed, was imbued with religious significance and done for the greater glory of God. The monks rose for services at 3.30 in the morning and prayed steadily for about four hours as the night gave way to dawn. At one monastery even the gardener's wheelbarrow was decorated with a cross painted on the side.

Where all these elements came together, it seemed to me, was in the lamps that lit the night-time services. These burned olive oil and were dimmer than our paraffin candles of today, and the light was further muted by shining through bowls of coloured glass, often red. They were calm and intimate, close at hand. And they symbolized, at least to me, a different way of looking at God – not distant, transcendent, remote, but rather as something personal and close by. They conveyed a sense that the infinite was accessible by looking within yourself. But if this was the experience at the monasteries, what were my own beliefs? What elements of faith did I take away from the experiences? In some senses the answer to this question is easy.

The Nicene Creed and similar pledges have long defined the essential elements of Christianity – belief in the Trinity, in Jesus's incarnation as both God and man, in the resurrection, and in a number of other basic tenets. Yet while these are all key elements of the Christian faith, they do not all present themselves in exactly the same way to every person. Some elements have come to me more forcibly than others and have presented themselves with special vividness. One particularly clear connection has been with Jesus in his earthly incarnation as the Son of Man. I find it easy to picture Jesus the human teacher walking the paths of his native Galilee, gathering disciples and teaching, and eventually making his way to the final confrontation in Jerusalem. His lessons speak fundamentally to the human heart, and they carry wisdom to our own day.

When he tells us to 'Love your enemies' and to seek out 'treasures in heaven' he is giving a profoundly corrective message in a strife-ridden and materialistic world. Another close connection has been with the third element in the Trinity – the Holy Spirit. Jesus described the Spirit as the Counsellor, who will 'bring to your remembrance all that I have said to you'. The Spirit is more abstract than the other persons of the Trinity. But this abstract quality also makes it all-pervasive, helping us feel our connection with all the parts of the material world, and also helping us shape our own judgments in accordance with the teachings of Jesus, making us better able to sense and to intuit the proper path in life. I had come to realize that I wanted to know more about Jesus and his life. And as I came to learn more, I found that my own truths had changed.

For one thing, the Christian teachings have made me more patient with the other people around me. I have become more willing to accept each of them for who they are, rather than looking for whom I wish they would be – to see them, insofar as I am able, as God sees them. The words from the Sermon on the Mount have not encouraged me to set aside my judgments, but rather not to judge in the first place: for your heavenly Father 'is kind even to the ungrateful and the selfish'. For another thing, faith has opened the door to a different way of looking at all the business and practical dealings of daily life. It made it suddenly clear that it is possible to live in the world by different values, and to perceive both troubles and opportunities in ways very different from our society's customary practices. A follower of Jesus might 'live in this world but be a citizen of heaven'. And so, because of these values, I have become more at peace with myself and with the wider world. All things are related, and all things are sacred. The red lamps, which symbolized for me the presence of the Holy Spirit, also symbolize this universal, unifying presence of God. The calm, low, inward-turning focus of the lamps ultimately leads, somewhat counter-intuitively, to a connection with the whole world.

The seventh-century church father, St Isaac the Syrian, expressed this connection well: be at peace with your own soul; then heaven and earth will be at peace with you. Enter eagerly into the treasure house that is within you, and so you will see the things that are in heaven; for there is but one single entry to them both. The ladder that leads to the kingdom is hidden within your own soul. Flee from sin, dive into yourself, and in your soul you will discover the stairs by which to ascend.

And so, at long last, I had relearned what had once been so well known in my family that it seemed to be in our DNA. And I had come to feel that the gospel story was something that I needed to work through, absorb, put into more understandable form, and make available to a general readership. I therefore began a seven-year study of the history and theology involved in the various English versions of the gospels. I also acquired a working knowledge of Greek through various studies, including a course taught by the Dominicans. Then I considered whether it would be possible to build on the work of the earlier editions of the gospels by bringing some new skills that have not been a prominent part of religious publishing in the past. By profession I am an antitrust lawyer and a former editor of my school's law review. I could bring to the task an editor's ear for language, and a lawyer's ability to combine a variety of authorities into a coherent whole. Those seemed to be the relevant skills for the new kind of volume that was most needed; and thus the book.

PL. 23 *Arsanas, Esphigmenou Monastery*

Wandering

JOHN CAMPBELL

It is over fifty years since I visited the Holy Mountain but the memories are still fresh. At the time I was driving east to India via Tehran to visit historic sites and buildings that I had studied or learned of. Mount Athos was on the way and sounded interesting.

It was like a time machine into the past. No roads, no electricity, no women, no sheep, no chickens, nothing but holy men and ancient monasteries perched on defensible hilltops. And also some clearly not holy men too. Genial encounters on the trails. Hollow half-logs to carry irrigation water to gardens.

Terrible maps except for two German priests with splendid military topographic mapping produced sometime during the war.

No English spoken at the monasteries but my Greek grammar managed to bridge the gap. Sanitary facilities on the walls. Especially vivid was catching a lift around the far end with a company of visiting eastern European bishops from Iviron to Simonopetra. No holy men there either, I thought.

But I wander.

FIG.17 *Pantokrator courtyard*

FIG.18 *Simonos Petras*

Athos in 1985

TREVOR CURNOW

My first visit to the Holy Mountain was in October 1985 (or September 1985, as my diamonitirion insists, because it was dated according to the Athonite calendar). At the time I knew little of Athos or Orthodoxy. My constant travelling companion in those days was a copy of David Talbot Rice's *Art of the Byzantine Era*, and I was there primarily to see the icons and frescoes.

Having completed the paperwork in Thessaloniki, I set off for Ouranoupolis, about which I remember little. The bus was met by people offering rooms in their houses, and I stayed with a woman called Maria and her mother. Also staying there was a Dutchman. He left for Athos the next day. Of him more later.

I set out the day after. The boat took us to Daphne, from where possibly the most clapped-out bus in the world, let alone in Greece, took everyone to Karyes. The system then was that an entry permit had to be exchanged for a diamonitirion at the Holy Epistasia in Karyes. The process was less than swift, but at least it afforded the opportunity to visit the Protaton and get my first taste of the Byzantine art I had come to see. The system then also meant that there was only a limited distance that could realistically be travelled on the first day, so most visitors headed for one of the monasteries nearest to Karyes. I, along with a handful of others, chose Stavronikita.

It did not disappoint, and the frescoes in its katholikon are always a pleasure to behold. When we got there the monastery was still abuzz with the events of the day before. (My Greek in those days was non-existent, but one of our ad hoc group was a Greek-Australian called Steve who proved a valuable interpreter.) Some time after dark on the previous day there had been a loud and sustained knocking at the bolted monastery outside door. When it was opened, there stood the Dutchman. He had walked from Karyes to Pantokrator, but something about the place had so disturbed him that instead of spending the night there he had walked in the fading (and then non-existent)

light to Stavronikita. I never saw him again or discovered the reason for his flight.

The next day Steve (who had visited Athos before) said he was heading for Filotheou. That was pretty much my plan too, so we agreed to walk together. It was a damp morning and one of the monks was concerned about my lack of wet weather gear, so he fashioned an improvised waterproof tabard for me by cutting some holes in a discarded plastic cement sack. Thus elegantly attired, I set forth.

We headed towards Iviron. Steve wanted to see Father A, who was living in a cell just outside Iviron then. He was busy making incense when we arrived, but he broke off from his work to provide refreshments and engaging conversation. Then we went into Iviron itself, which was idiorrhythmic in those days. I think Sir Steven Runciman once said that an idiorrhythmic monastery reminded him of an Oxford college. Certainly it didn't have much of a monastic feel to it. But we saw the person Steve wanted to see and then walked on to Filotheou, where Steve planned to stay for a while. I think he had ambitions to become a monk there, but I have no idea whether those ambitions were ever fulfilled. Although I have some pictures of Filotheou, I really remember very little of it.

The next morning I was offered a lift to Karyes. There were few vehicles on Athos then, but Filotheou had a truck that it used in its logging activities. It seemed too good an opportunity to miss, so I took it. Deposited in Karyes I walked down to Daphne, and then set off south past Simonos Petras and Grigoriou to Dionysiou (I was fitter then). The view from the balcony of the guest-quarters there might best be described as dizzying. By this time I had come to realize that not being Orthodox, I would not necessarily be permitted to enter every katholikon, and that was the case at Dionysiou. As I sat outside it a passing monk took pity on me and gave me an apple.

The next day I was told that a small boat would be calling at the monastery and heading for Daphne, and that this was the best way for me to get back there. It did and it was. However, after waiting at Daphne for some time it became apparent that the boat to Ouranoupolis was not coming that day. This was scarcely a problem as it meant an unexpected extra night on Athos. A few of us decided to head to St Panteleimon. There we were given something to eat and shown to the guest-house, which lay outside the walls of the main monastery enclosure. Much of the massive complex was in a ruinous state. In the evening I sat outside the katholikon and heard the most beautiful music ema-nating from within. At the end of it all, a handful of elderly monks shuffled out. It was difficult to reconcile the sound with the vision.

The next day I headed back to Daphne again, this time with a brief visit to Xeropotamou on the way. This time the boat to Ouranoupolis arrived, and that was the end of my first visit to Athos. I had become interested enough in the place to want to return, and sure enough I did, but not until 2003 when I joined the ranks of the FoMA footpaths team. The first place I was sent? Pantokrator!

Pantokrator and Me

TREVOR CURNOW

I have tried to write a coherent and continuous account of my relationship with the Holy Monastery of Pantokrator, but I find I cannot. What appears below is episodic in nature, but I hope it conveys something of what I would like to say. I have decided to leave the identities of all but Abbot Gabriel obscure.

I well remember the first time I ever saw the monastery of Pantokrator. I had volunteered for the FoMA 2003 footpaths group. After being told I was on the reserve list, I was subsequently informed (not long before departure day) that someone had dropped out and a place in the group was mine if I wanted it. A bit of hasty reshuffling of my work schedule and I was off. I was assigned to Pantokrator (which would not have been my first choice) for the first week. For some reason the expected transport did not materialise at Daphne, so improvised arrangements had to be stitched together on the spot. After a lengthy wait in Daphne, and another at Karyes, two of us decided to do the last stretch of the journey on foot. There is a point along the route, just after the road takes a turn to the left, when the monastery suddenly becomes visible for the first time. It stands far below, looking like a medieval castle sitting on its cliff top. Many times since that day I have paused to take in and admire the view.

One of the great benefits and privileges of visiting the Holy Mountain with the footpaths group is the ability to spend a week in a single monastery, which affords a very different kind of experience from the arrive-one-afternoon-leave-next-morning experience of most visitors. Of course, 'different' does not necessarily mean 'better', and in some places a single night might be more than enough for many people. For me, the week at Pantokrator flew by and I was sorry to move on. Who knows why we make connections with some places rather than others? All I can say is that I strongly felt that some kind of connection had been made during my first visit there.

The next year I was back with the footpaths group again, and again despatched to Pantokrator (now very much my first choice) for the first week.

Before the end of the week one of the Fathers mentioned to me that if I wished to return to the monastery on my own, I was welcome to do so. The invitation was far too good to turn down, so in October 2004 I returned for my first solo visit to Athos since 1985. As I had to take time off work, and did not wish to abuse the monastery's hospitality, I planned to stay at the monastery for less than a week. Since then I have revisited the monastery on twelve further occasions, for anything from three days to three weeks. It has become, if not quite a second home, then at least one of my homes.

During my stays I have been privileged to be present at three tonsures and one ordination, and to spend two Easters there, as well as one Christmas and a Feast of the Transfiguration, to which the monastery is dedicated. While the feasts are busy times in terms of visitors, the busier times for the monastery are the days of preparations preceding them. As a temporary resident, I have found myself on many occasions spending time cleaning the church, whether dusting, mopping or refreshing the shine of the silver.

As I am a coffee drinker, the monastery's guest-house has tended to be a magnet for me, and if there is any washing-up in the kitchen there that needs to be done, I am always happy to do it. On one occasion I was busy at this task when three Russian monks walked in. The conversation (in basic Greek on both sides) went like this: 'Is there coffee?' 'Yes'. 'Three medium sugar!' 'OK'. 'Is there ouzo?' 'Unfortunately, we do not have any ouzo'. When I relayed this to Abbot Gabriel later he told me that they used to keep a bottle of spirits openly available in the guest-house, but on a couple of occasions one or two visitors drank the lot, and it was decided to keep it under lock and key thereafter.

Different seasons bring different types of visitor. Because the Feast of the Transfiguration takes place in summer, the weather is more attractive for many. At one time, I believe, the Greek government sought to actively promote a positive image of Mount Athos and monasticism because many Greeks view monks as too other-worldly and lazy. In my experience, a number of Greeks who visited Pantokrator for the first time were surprised by the lack of luxury they encountered, and by how hard the monks worked. And many of those had no intention ever to return.

It was during the same stay that a group of people turned up at the monastery one Sunday afternoon. They were Serbians travelling by tractor and trailer, making a tour of a few monasteries within easy reach of Karyes. I was invited to come and see them at the Serbian house in Karyes. The next day, I walked up there and found that the Serbian house occupies perhaps the most spectacular view of anywhere in Karyes. And I was made most welcome. I find hospitality to be the norm across the Holy Mountain, wherever I go.

Because no one is born on the Holy Mountain, all those who live there have had previous lives elsewhere. Some have had very colourful lives. While some become monks very young (at least two monks at Pantokrator became monks in their teens), others become monks after having had careers and families. The late Father Damaskinos of Pantokrator was perhaps one of the most extreme examples of this, having been a celebrated puppeteer with thirteen children. Becoming a monk after his wife died, he lived to be 100.

While I have been at the monastery when it has been at its busiest, I have also been there when it was at its quietest. On one particular December's day in 2005, there were only two pilgrims staying at the monastery, and the other one was unwell so he spent the day in his bed in the guest-house. I had (for me) the unique experience of being the only person in the church for the liturgy that day who was not a monk.

My reason for visiting the monastery in winter was in order to try and write a book about Athos and Orthodoxy, and being there during a quiet time of the year gave me the best opportunity to spend time with the monks. I was generously given the use of a computer in an office I shared with one of the monks, and spent hours conversing with others. I have always felt slightly embarrassed at how the Fathers find time for people who must really be a distraction for them. On the other hand, after all this time, I count several of the Fathers of Pantokrator among my personal friends. When my students used to ask me why I went there, however, my stock answer always was: 'They give me wine for breakfast!'

When I visited the Holy Mountain in 2018, I was surprised by how many people were on the boat, on the bus, in Karyes, etc. Russians, in particular, seemed to make up a lot of the numbers. As is my habit, I stopped in Karyes for refreshment before heading down to Pantokrator, and my reward was hearing a beautiful Russian hymn sung by the people at the next table.

For reasons I cannot explain, Pantokrator has become an important part of my life. But Mount Athos is a place where many things happen that defy explanation.

My Recollections of Mount Athos, and an Encounter on London Bridge

BEN MARTIN

I first went to Mount Athos more than fifty years ago when I was about twenty years old. I remember the phut-phutting of the single cylinder diesel of the little caique which took us, a handful of passengers, from Ouranoupolis to Daphne.

In the early 1960s Mount Athos was at a low point with perhaps no more than 2,000 monks across the whole peninsula. The only road was the one that went from Daphne to Karyes but I can't recall whether we walked or found some form of transport. In Karyes I had my first sight of the frescoes in the Protaton by Manuel Panselinos. Later I was to acquire in Athens a slim volume with colour plates of his paintings there.

The following day in company with two others we set out on foot for Vatopedi and as the sun went down we became anxious that the monastery gates would close before our arrival and we hurried along. There was no electricity in Vatopedi nor I believe in any of the other monasteries at that time. We crossed the great Vatopedi courtyard in near darkness and were led up to the guest-quarters by oil lamp. After a frugal meal we sat with the guest-master on the balcony overlooking the sea and watched the flashes of a distant storm on the horizon. Of all my memories of Mount Athos the visit to Vatopedi is one of the most deeply engraved – vast and beautiful, a scattering of silent monks and an overwhelming medieval atmosphere.

On my second visit about ten years later I went with my father, who was recovering from a heart ailment. In Ouranoupolis we called upon Joice Loch and sat with her in her old stone fortified house. Her husband, Sydney, had died in 1955 but Joice had carried on living in Prosphori Tower until her death in 1982. Not until much later did I realise what a champion she was for refugees. When

Bones washed in Water and Wine was published in 2012, I learned too what a great deal she had done to help the poor villagers of Ouranoupolis.

I have no record of this visit but I know we went to Dionysiou and St Paul's and also stayed in a skete on the steep slope of the short south eastern edge of the peninsula under the mountain. The few monks in the skete kept at prayer in the chapel most of the night. We gratefully accepted a single spring onion and a slice of bread each to eat. Before dawn I set out on my own to try to ascend the Holy Mountain. Stumbling around in the dark I disturbed and frightened a group of mules or ponies, hearing them but not seeing them. I never found the path which leads from the main pathway along the edge of the Mountain to the summit.

Like me I think my father was uneasy about the gender exclusivity of Mount Athos. It troubles me to think that for the many years she lived in Ouranoupolis, Joice Loch was unable to step a single foot into the peninsula whilst Sydney was able to wander at will there. It is also disquieting that there are esteemed academics of Byzantine and other studies who are unable to visit. I believe that one day there will be modifications to this sacrosanct rule but that it will not be for several generations more and after much theological debate.

By the time of my third visit the boat from Ouranoupolis to Daphne had become a good-sized ferryboat carrying cars and many pilgrims. There was one exciting moment when there was a cry of '*delphini*' and a rush to the guardrails to scan for dolphins.

There were four of us on this pilgrimage and it took us along the coast from Stavronikita to Great Lavra and round to St Paul's. It was particularly

pleasing to visit Great Lavra and to see, amongst other things, the huge porphyry basin or phiale. Setting out from Great Lavra in the morning we found the little path which leads up to the Panaghia chapel, lying 1,000 feet below the cross on the top of the Holy Mountain. We stopped at the chapel, unhitched our backpacks, scouted the weather and then we set off late in the day for the summit. Returning to the chapel in the evening it was cold at a height of 5,000 feet above sea level so we lit a fire of pine cones beneath an arched chimney at one end of the building; then in the darkness we lay down to sleep on the stone floor. Robert Byron in *The Station* describes a similar scene and I imagine that many of those who overnight in the chapel make use of the plentiful pine cones surrounding the chapel.

Here I must mention that one of our party decided not to join us on the ascent of the mountain but to continue on the path from Great Lavra to the skete of St Anne's. This was uncharacteristic of Stephen, a strong and determined walker, and we had some concern for him. In the stunning location of St Anne's on the steep slope of the mountain we caught up with him the next day, he seeming to be in good health. In the quiet of the small monastic community of St Anne's, Stephen, I think the only guest, had found rest and peace and was much uplifted by it. Indeed I think his solitude in this isolated and beautiful skete had given him a spiritual experience such as many seek on the Mountain. He may even have had a foretelling of his mortality, as within a few months he was to die suddenly and unexpectedly at the age of fifty-seven.

I won't be going again to Mount Athos. Like Philip Sherrard, who after many visits decided he could no longer accept the roads, the vehicles, and the large number of visitors and stopped going, I will live with my memories. On my last visit, which is now more than twenty years past, I saw how the number of visitors was rising strongly. Now in the autumn of 2019 the shipping line which runs the ferry service from Ouranoupolis to Daphne is to increase capacity with a vessel which carries 500 passengers and seventy-five cars. It will require much skill from the monastic authorities and from the monasteries themselves to accommodate this growing number in such a way that the pilgrims can come to the Holy Mountain to visit the monasteries and experience a little of the monastic life whilst at the same time allowing the monks themselves to have the tranquillity and undisturbed time for devotion which they seek.

I conclude these recollections with mention of an encounter on London Bridge. It was after my third visit to the Holy Mountain that one day as I was walking across London Bridge I saw an Orthodox monk coming towards me. Divining he might be from Mount Athos I stopped to talk to him and he asked me the way to the National Bank of Greece. As I guided him to the bank he told me that he was indeed from the Holy Mountain and that he lived in a skete near Karyes. He was Peruvian and on his way to take a vacation with his family in Peru after ten years on the Mountain. He invited me to visit him at his skete. This short and extraordinary encounter reminded me again of the worldwide appeal of monasticism and of Mount Athos, and of the hospitality and humanity of the monks.

FIG.19 *Kiosk at Hilandar*

Two Rather Different Pilgrimages

SHAUN LEAVEY

My first pilgrimage to Mount Athos was in May 2012 with three friends. Of those three only Charles, formerly of the British Foreign Office, was a fluent Greek speaker. Max had visited the Holy Mountain when a Cambridge undergraduate (and had got very lost one night when looking for the monastery where he was due to stay). Christopher was a former Royal Navy submariner and more recently a lawyer. I had been a soldier long ago, and forty years previously had worked in Greece for two years as a farm manager – but had forgotten most of what little Greek I ever knew.

Our arrival at Dochiariou coincided with a bad accident on the road above the monastery when the vehicle returning monks from a festive occasion had overturned. From the adjacent room to the guest room there came the sounds of groans, and monks could be seen hurrying about with bandages. We explained that we had made every effort to secure a reservation, but that it had not been possible to get any acknowledgement. After a mild rebuke for not obtaining confirmation of accommodation, and some reservations about the Anglican church's position on homosexuality (perceived as not sufficiently strict) we were admitted to a very large dormitory. The beds were very close to one another and there was an extremely low ratio of washing facilities to the number of dormitory occupants.

We attended vespers. However I was not aware that crossing one's legs when seated was likely to provoke frowns and the wagging of fingers. We were subject to quite a bit of this until we took to rebuking one another for any such infringements of monastic protocol. I don't think any of us slept particularly soundly. However we were dutiful in our attendance at the following morning's service. During breakfast, I (as the person who had planned the route) was somewhat daunted by the serious doubts of other pilgrims about our capacity to walk later that day up to Chilandar where we were due to spend the night.

We agreed we would ignore this advice. It was a fairly long, but very memorable walk. Initially we went along a coastal path to the landing place for Zografou monastery, and then struck up a valley towards that monastery. It was quite a demanding walk, but the final approach to the monastery was reached by a beautiful cobbled path.

One had the feeling that one was taking exactly the same route as earlier pilgrims had done over many hundreds of years. When we got inside we were able to get some cold water to drink and – most importantly – guidance on the next leg of our journey to Chilandar. When we eventually reached the Serbian monastery of Chilandar we received a warm welcome from a young English-speaking monk and – unusually – four mugs of tea. We were again allocated to a large dormitory also with rather inadequate ablutions for the numbers accommodated. Despite my having visited Serbia twice, and many of its monasteries, some of the other pilgrims seemed less friendly than in Dochiariou. I was treated to a complaint about the situation of the Orthodox monasteries in Kosovo ... for which the UK was (inexplicably to me) deemed to be entirely responsible. However we were shown a part of the treasury which contained some wonderful icons. Again the vespers service was very impressive. But the night in the dormitory could most politely be described as 'disturbed'.

We were up for the morning service, and another rather challenging breakfast. Our plan was to walk to the nearby monastery of Esphigmenou, and from there to Vatopedi. We were within a mile of Esphigmenou when a kindly monk passing in a Land Rover stopped to give us a lift. This did not seem to be a common practice on Athos where too often a rather commercial approach was taken to all forms of vehicular transport. The view of this monastery with the sea on one side and wooded hills around it was especially striking. Despite Esphigmenou's banner stating 'Orthodoxy or Death', they could not have been

PL. 28 *Courtyard of Iviron Monastery*

FIG.20 *Pantokrator courtyard*

more friendly to us. One monk who was formerly a sailor insisted on accompanying us for the first part of our walk on to Vatopedi.

Vatopedi is so well known to almost all those who have visited Athos that little need be said about our stay there. Father M was not only a conscientious guide, but also offered his skills as a cobbler to repair one of our party's boots which had started to fall apart on the previous day.

Among the breath-taking items on display in the Treasury there was a ground level shelf given over entirely to items related to the Prince of Wales including one of his water colours (of Vatopedi) and two enamelled tins. These had contained the slices of his wedding cake (at the time of his marriage to Camilla) which had been sent to the Abbot and Father M. They had been permitted to eat the cake, but apparently cenobitic rules had required that they did not retain the tins!

On Sunday morning we were taken by bus to Karyes, and had the expectation that – after exploring the town – we could travel on from there to Grigoriou. However – perhaps because it was a Sunday – there was a dearth of any transport. Our Greek speaker was deployed to bargain with an extraordinarily cantankerous minibus driver (who turned out to be Romanian). Eventually he agreed to drive us down to Daphne for a grotesquely large cash payment, and with some relief we just caught the ferry.

Grigoriou was idyllic, and we were billeted together in a clean room overlooking the sea with only two other occupants. One was a very young American who had been there for six weeks and was studying the Greek Orthodox faith – seemingly with a view to becoming a priest or monk. With this in mind he had been re-christened Seraphim. His relief at sharing his room with other English speakers was very evident, and we were keen to off-load some of our surplus food on him.

There was one other occupant of the room whom we chose to call Cherubim although from his appearance this seemed rather inappropriate. Before we turned in for the night we had collectively expressed the hope that the adage 'Cherubim and Seraphim continually do cry' would not be the case whilst we shared a room with them.

Not having done any walking that day three of us decided to walk over to Dionysiou monastery before vespers. By the time we left it had got significantly hotter. The map indicated that Dionysiou was not far away. Initially we were rewarded for our climb up the hill behind the monastery by a magnificent view down on to the roofs of Grigoriou. We then started a very steep descent down into a ravine and up the other side. That ridge revealed another ravine and we set off down into it.

At the bottom we crossed a stream and looked up to see a spectacular waterfall many hundreds of feet above us. We then climbed up the next slope. When we crested the apex of this there was still no sight of Dionysiou, but instead another similarly deep ravine. Reluctantly we agreed to return without accomplishing our mission. The paths were difficult, the heat oppressive, and the slopes very steep. It was some consolation on getting back to the monastery to be told by a monk that this was one of the more difficult routes between monasteries on Athos. I was less pleased when he added that we would have had a much easier walk if we had headed west and gone to Simonos Petras monastery.

The following morning we attended the early service and ate our meal, but then enjoyed a couple of hours sitting on the balcony reading and watching both monks and other pilgrims on the quayside. At about eleven o'clock the ship to take us to Daphne arrived. At Daphne we fought our way through the unmanned customs control on to the second boat which took us back to Ouranoupolis, lunch, and our transport back to Thessaloniki.

Three years later Christopher, the former submariner-turned-lawyer, and I agreed that we should return, and persuaded Michael, a friend of mine to join us. I had talked to a Greek acquaintance in London who had visited Athos on many previous occasions. He listened sympathetically to my tales of mild discomfort in some of the monasteries, and proposed that our next visit should be mainly based at the Skete Prophet Elijah. He spoke of the extremely high standards set there by the Prior (reported to be a former Chaplain General in the Greek army), and insisted I would find conditions there very similar to an 'officers' mess'. Suffice it to say that whilst there were certain differences from the officers' messes I inhabited during the 1960s as a young cavalry officer we could not have found a warmer welcome or a more hospitable host than the kind and charming Father F. We did not formally meet the Prior, but ate with him on several occasions.

On Thursday morning after the service and a de minimis, but quite adequate, breakfast Father F showed us the Skete's church. Christopher (whose name day it was) had the honour of being given the key so as to open up the vast doors. The iconostasis was breath-taking. It had originally come by ship

FIG.21 *Iviron Monastery*

from Odessa. While we were there a small group of Ukrainians (understood to be from the pro-Russian part of the country) came in with a priest and conducted an extempore service. The history of the Skete was difficult to unravel, but gradually we realised why Russian speaking pilgrims were so keen to visit. During the time prior to the revolution, when the majority of the monks had been Russian, the cellars were used as both workshops and storerooms. When the revolution occurred many monks are thought to have returned to the Tsarist army leaving behind enormous quantities of stores (medical, cookware, bottles, sewing machines, and some weapons including swords, revolvers and rifles). It is amazing (but perhaps less so on Athos) that none of this material appears to have been looted or acquired by the Greek authorities over the many years that elapsed after the departure of the Russian military from the Skete. Recently it has been collated, restored, and incorporated into a museum.

There was rumoured to be a tunnel going all the way down to Pantokratoros monastery on the coast, but this was doubted by our guide. However we were two floors below ground level when I noticed a manhole cover. We opened it and were amazed to see a flight of stone steps go down to an even lower level – which none of us felt inclined to explore.

From the Skete with its moving and very splendid services we were due to move on to Iviron via Stavronikita monastery. The path was often steep and the weather got warmer. However, the tree cover protected us on much of the route from the worst of the sun.

By the time we got to the monastery we had enjoyed wonderful scenery – the sea below us on one side and a steep mountain above us. Nevertheless, we were glad to have the chance to take on more water at a spring on the outskirts of the Stavronikita monastery, and even more glad when a kindly monk emerged with a tray of ouzo, more water, and some loukoumi.

At Iviron Father L, the Archontaris guided us to what was – by all monastic standards – a small suite (including shower and WC) with a balcony looking out over the monastery gardens, a stream, and beyond that the vast wooded mountainside. The word idyllic is much over-used, but for me that was the only way that one could describe the situation.

Father L spoke fluent English having studied in the USA after his mother re-married a US serviceman. He had decided that the USA was not for him, and had then committed himself to a monastic life in Greece. We had an interesting talk about the reaction of his parents to his becoming a monk ('par-

ents are happy when their children are happy'), and found him a most insightful and impressive person. We attended a service before supper (pilgrims ate separately from the monks who were fasting), but were confined to the outer porch so saw little of it. The following morning we were all at the early service, and then had breakfast – amused by the strident protest of one uncharitable Greek pilgrim about its perceived inadequacy.

Our departure was stressful for me, as the organizer of the visit, as there were doubts as to whether or not the fast ferry to Ierissos would operate that day. I was enormously relieved to see a boat with a vast bow wave rounding the far point. After we had boarded we realised why it would not sail in any swell. We had – by chance – sat far enough back on the top deck not to get completely soaked (as most other passengers did) when the wind caught the spray generated by the ferry. In typical Greek fashion the journey was enlivened by an explosive row between the collector of tickets and one of the passengers who seemed not to have imbibed much spiritual value from his time on Athos and had declined to pay.

For us three pilgrims it had been a fascinating and enlightening experience. Christopher and I reflected on the significant differences between our two pilgrimages – the first something in the nature of a 'hard landing' and the recent one a far more restful one with greater scope for contemplation. But both had given us extraordinary experiences that were unique to the Holy Mountain.

The Holy Mountain – Personal Fragments

ROUMEN AVRAMOV

Before my first steps on the Mountain, for me Athos was a synonym of a mystical, remote, and inaccessible site. Twenty years, twelve journeys and three climbs to the top later, the existential question of what draws people there, again and again, is still haunting me. It is common sense that there is no standard answer to it and that one can only share his personal truth.

Religious faith is the genuine motive for pilgrimage. What then does a secular, atheist, and rationalistic academic look for in the Holy Mountain? I think, it is a conscious or implicit quest for spirituality in the broadest sense, a thirst for history, art, nature and friendship. There are not so many places on Earth where those elements blend in such a harmonious, holistic, almost institutionalized way. *Spirituality* is everywhere and even if one is not able to grasp all the intricacies of the monastic mindset, the undisputed reign of high matters and values commands respect. Imprints of *history* and *art* are embedded in all the tangible and intangible heritage of the Mountain. Crossing the peninsula the old way, by walking up and down the footpaths, opens your eyes to sublime, dramatic or delicate *natural landscapes*. Moreover, FoMA offers the opportunity for a special communion with nature if you dare to join, as I did in 2014, the Friends' path-clearing teams. Finally, all those gifts to the senses, the soul, and the mind are savoured in a unique ambiance of *friendship* and conviviality. Talking quietly with your fellows during the long journey, with the hospitable monks, or with pilgrims you meet fortuitously is an experience you never forget.

Mount Athos is supposedly a stronghold of traditionalism. Continuity is the quintessence of the monastic republic and we are not always ready to face transformations there. And yet, this is a realm where – as it is the rule in history – continuity and change intermingle both on the macro scale and within the micro cosmos. An ostensibly small, albeit telling example of such change that I witnessed and which impressed me during my twenty years of wandering is the metamorphosis of Zografou monastery's library. Thanks to the inspiration and tireless efforts of the current librarian, Father A, this remarkable, once opaque, collection has evolved into a modern repository, responsibly opening its treasures to researchers.

The Mountain does not loosen its grip when you are away. The conventional bond remains through the books. Piles of them are being read in insatiable efforts to understand the different facets of Athonite life. Although with time the searching tools employed to satisfy our curiosity became digital and seemingly limitless, they never substituted for the charm of paper. It was thus a privilege to have had as friend and as fellow traveller in seven instances Dincho Krastev, the late and much lamented erudite, bibliophile and director of the library of the Bulgarian Academy of Sciences. From the very beginning, I was also interested in the great variety of maps – both historical and those guiding us into the Mountain's dense network of routes. After meeting Peter Howorth in 2013 for the first time, I was happy to be able to occasionally help him with some details of his impressive cartographic achievement.

For a scholar in the fields of social sciences and the humanities, the Holy Mountain is a rather peculiar society, a rare instance of contemporary theocracy. I could not resist the temptation to immerse myself professionally in this extraordinary universe. Driven by the impetus to learn how such a community and economy functions, I organized an international research network dedicated to the history of monastic economy. It gathered over thirty academics in a series of workshops and individual projects where the study of the Athonite legacy occupied a prominent place.

The cliché that every contact with the Mountain is an enriching event is actually supported by indubitable evidence. One is certain that his next journey will lead to discovering new itineraries, meeting wonderful people, gaining deeper knowledge, and ultimately better understanding oneself.

PL. 30 *Restored building, Zografou Monastery*

The Bumblebee

ROBERT W. ALLISON

In 1977 I began a project, funded by a grant from the National Endowment for the Humanities and sponsored by the Patriarchal Institute for Patristic Studies in Thessaloniki, to produce a descriptive catalogue of the Greek manuscripts of Filotheou Monastery. That was before the days of electrification and central heating on the Holy Mountain, when even telephone communications were very rudimentary and unreliable. At Filotheou they had installed a turbine powered by water flow from their irrigation pool to generate electricity for basic needs like refrigeration and the operation of tools in the workshops, but there was no electricity in the library, which was then located in the tower over the monastery's arched entryway. I was an object of curiosity to the fathers as I set out my portable solar panels each day to recharge my battery-operated imaging equipment and my lights for working in my cell in the evenings. During those first weeks working at Filotheou, most of the monks kept their distance as I lived and worked and moved among them.

I think that I was also, to some degree, an object of suspicion. As a Protestant I was not permitted to attend services in the katholikon or eat together with the fathers, most of whom only saw me as I moved about between the library, the trapeza, my solar panels and my cell. In the evenings, when pilgrims and foreigners were mingling with the monks, I had to be recording the results of my day's work with the manuscripts and preparing for my next day's work. Every weekend I left the monastery to return to my wife and two young sons, who were living in rented quarters above a pantopoleio (general store) in Ouranoupolis. In a peculiar way, I was importing into the monastery my own, very American kind of weekday/weekend schedule, which had the effect of alienating me from the monastery's pattern of life.

In addition, I found, to my surprise, that being a research fellow at the Patriarchal Institute did not help. Relations between the Institute and the monastery were, at best, tenuous. The fathers had legitimate concerns about losing control of their own heritage as embodied in their manuscripts, compounded by lingering suspicions that the Institute was profiting from sale of the microfilms and photographs that it was producing. They sometimes felt disrespected by the authoritative approach taken by professors and theologians of the Institute, as well as by government-funded researchers from the archaeological services whom they had to accommodate. The presence of this young foreign scholar, a Protestant research fellow of the Patriarchal Institute, must have seemed highly anomalous to the monastery's fathers in the 1980s. Thus, I found myself living a peculiarly isolated kind of existence at Filotheou.

At the same time, I remember being deeply appreciative of the warmth and consideration shown me by the Gerontas Ephraim and by his protégée, the younger Ephraim, who later died in a tragic auto accident in Thessaloniki. Father Chrysostomos, who ran the kitchen in those days, always went out of his way to bring me special treats, and Father Georgios often invited me to have coffee with him. For Father L, who worked with me each day as the librarian at Filotheou, I know my presence was a heavy burden. As an elder in the monastery, he already had many responsibilities before I came upon the scene, and often seemed aloof when they were weighing upon him. Some people who had dealings with him feared him because of the appearance of severity that he projected. As time passed, however, he became, for me, a source of continuing enlightenment, as my education in monastic life and spirituality began at Filotheou, not to mention a valuable contributor to my manuscript descriptions. But above all, he helped me to understand the presence of the Panaghia on the Holy Mountain.

My regular routine at Filotheou began each day when I ascended the stairs to the upper floor of the tower, where I would wait for Father L in front of the massive, iron-clad door to the library. About 10 a.m. he would arrive, bearing a correspondingly massive iron key. When that door swung open, our working

FIG.22 *Near Hilandar*

day began. His day began with cleaning off the work area on the large wooden table in the centre of the room, after which he devoted himself to his daily greetings (haritismoi) to the Virgin. For me, that moment held a special meaning that came to define my relationship to Father L. It wrapped our time at work with the manuscripts, and the unusual relationship we shared, in the aura of the presence of the Panaghia. My work began with laying out my notes and taking from the shelves the codex with which I would begin my day's work. There we remained, except for an hour-long break for a midday snack, until the first semantron for vespers sounded. One day as I worked I found a marginal note written in one of the codices by a monk of a bygone age, 'When you hear the semantron, run'. I showed the note to Father L, who always welcomed the sound of that semantron and indicated it was time to end our work for the day. 'When you hear the semantron, run!' became our mantra when we heard the first call to vespers late each afternoon.

The midday snack was a simple affair, typically fresh-baked monastery bread with water or wine, depending on the day of the week, and some halvah and fruit. I ate quickly, usually sitting alone in the trapeza. Afterward I often walked down the vehicular road a short distance to sit down and read. The road was still quite new, with steep, raw embankments cut into the earth on the uphill side of the road that had been bulldozed not long before. I would find a comfortable-looking spot along the road and sit there in front of the embankment, sometimes leaning forward, elbows on knees, as I read, sometimes leaning back against the embankment. One day early in my work at Filotheou, I began reading a version of the Philokalia in Greek. It required great concentration, but it was helping me in my continuing effort to understand better the nature of the monastic spirituality I was encountering at Filotheou. As I read, I gradually realized I was hearing an insistent buzzing sound behind my head. I knew what it was. I had by this time seen many of the enormous bumble bees that pilgrims to the Holy Mountain will know are so characteristic of Mount Athos. The fathers at Filotheou had cultivated beautiful gardens and placed containers around the courtyard of the monastery with roses and all kinds of flowering plants, which attracted these bees. So I was quite familiar with them.

I turned my head to observe this one that was so persistently hovering behind my head. As I watched it, my focus gradually expanded and I realized, with a shock, that directly behind the bee, entwined around some roots protruding from the embankment, was a small, greyish coloured adder. I had heard about the adders on Mount Athos, which were reputed to be very deadly. From my Boy Scout training I recognized immediately the significance of the pronounced, triangular head on this one, only inches away behind my neck. If I had leaned back one more time against the embankment...

Moving very slowly, so as not to startle the snake and induce an attack, I retreated from the bank. When safely out of reach of the snake, I slowly stood up and backed into the road, my eyes fixed on the snake. Only then did I notice two monks coming down the road from the monastery with their walking sticks and bags. They were eyeing me quizzically, wondering what this peculiar foreigner was doing. As they drew near, I pointed out the snake, still shaken from my close encounter. The monks immediately sprang into action. One attacked the snake with his walking stick and killed it, while the other turned to me to ask if I had been bitten. When they were sure I was OK, I told them how I had been reading, occasionally leaning against the bank, and that if it hadn't been for the bumble bee, I would undoubtedly have leaned back again as I read, my neck coming down directly upon the adder. As we walked back up to the monastery, the fathers told me that it was the Panaghia who had saved me, that Mount Athos was the garden of the Panaghia, and she often appeared in her garden in the form of the bee. The Panaghia, they explained, was the protectress of all who came to Mount Athos.

When we reached the monastery, the two fathers led me back to the trapeza, where Father Chrysostomos was still working with some other monks in the kitchen and some novices were cleaning the tables. The two monks told them how the Panaghia had saved me from the snake that would otherwise surely have killed me. Father Chrysostomos confirmed to me that the Panaghia was present everywhere on the Holy Mountain, and that it was indeed She who had protected me. I thought of how Father L began his day, every day, by greeting the Panaghia in the library.

From that moment on, the remoteness, the sense of suspicion, that I had been feeling since first arriving at Filotheou disappeared. Some of the fathers began greeting me by name. One invited me to work with him in my spare time making incense, and so I did. Another, an iconographer, invited me to come to his kellion to see how he painted icons. Father G, a photographer whom I came to know well, shared with me his interest in documenting monastic life in photographs, and his woodcarving. I was now, he told me, a Philotheïtis.

Impostor Syndrome

CHRIS THOMAS

Don't know much about history. Don't know much theology. Am a bit rusty on architecture. I am slightly under-read on Byzantine iconography. My knowledge of the flora and fauna of the Athonite archipelago has failed to flourish. Am no legendary footpath clearer. An inability to construct long and/or coherent sentences has prevented me from becoming a distinguished author. My painting skills are non-existent. I am not a world-class mapmaker. The only stunning photographs I have taken were accidental. I am shy and a bit awkward with people. My Greek is poor.

Mount Athos possesses a magical, magnetic and divine filter – its holiness, spirituality and relative remoteness attracts 'givers' in the first place. In the rare event that a 'taker' sneaks through, the misdeed is only temporary. The Holy Mountain only rewards those who want to keep on giving so the 'takers' quickly lose interest and move on to less-demanding shores.

Until someone spots the anomaly and has a quiet word in my ear about this place being strictly for grown-ups, I intend to take full advantage of the benefits of this unique club I have somehow been allowed to join. I return to the mountain time after time not necessarily having anything to give other than my willingness to learn.

Try and stop me discussing Gregory of Nyssa with my great friends Bart and Peter. And why would one not wish to explore post-classical Greek literature with Graham or the latest map-making techniques with Peter? When that's done, it's time to move onto spiritual renewal with Andrew and then a quick twenty minutes with John about an inspirational royal visit a few years back followed by a catch-up with the other John about some blessed wine at Zografou. And, given the tumultuous local history, it is rather appropriate to finish off with an hour on the geopolitics of the Eastern Mediterranean with Dimitri.

If only all humanity could be this clever, this selfless, this generous – what a wonderful world this would be.

FIG.23 *Friends at Cape Akrathos*

The King's Wine

JOHN MOLE

Visitors are asked not take photographs of monks without their permission or the blessing of their abbot and I think the same goes for writing about them. These conversations with monks are as verbatim as I can recall. But I have changed their identities out of respect for their privacy.

The Catalan strongroom of Vatopedi monastery has manuscripts, icons, crucifixes and many other priceless treasures of the last thousand years. Among them is a pink and green tin that contained a slice of the wedding cake of Prince Charles and Camilla Parker Bowles. It is empty as the Abbot ate the cake. Prince Charles has been coming on private visits to Athos for many years. He is a celebrity among the monks and not just those of Vatopedi, as we discovered when four of us were billeted at a smaller monastery as part of FoMA's annual path-clearing project.

Father G was a useful man to know as he was the cellar master. One evening in the cool of his cellar we sat around a table among massive barrels with a tin of smoked fish and a jug of decent red from a demi-john, the gift of a Transylvanian well-wisher in thanks for a successful intercession to the Virgin, whose icon is a treasure of the monastery. We did not suspect that he harboured a special mission for us.

'You must know that our abbot was called to be a monk by St George. He was a young man on the ships. His name was Dimitris then. One night he was on watch in the middle of the ocean and a sailor who he did not know stood next to him. He shone in moonlight but there was no moon. He asked Dimitris where they were heading. Dimitris said he didn't know. "That is where you are going," said the stranger and pointed ahead and Dimitris saw they were heading straight for the rocks under a high mountain. Dimitris sounded the alarm bells and the captain and all the sailors ran out of their cabins. But the mountain and the stranger had disappeared. They were in the middle of the ocean. The captain said Dimitris was dreaming or drunk and gave him many punishments. Dimitris left the ship in Piraeus.

He went past a shop that sold religious things and saw a picture of the high mountain he had seen in the middle of the ocean. It was the Holy Mountain. He came straight here and told the Abbot. The Abbot said he had a dream in which St George came to him and told him to take in a young man he had rescued from the sea'.

'How marvellous'.

'Well I never'.

'Good Lord'.

'Of course it was a miracle!' said Father G.

'Obviously'.

'St George comes to the Abbot once or twice a year to see how he is getting on and give advice'.

'Very considerate of him'.

'Of course. Two years ago, St George visited the Abbot and said he must make wine for King Charles of England. You know St George loves England too', said Father G.

'Oh yes. His flag is everywhere'.

'On churches'.

'On football shirts'.

'But he is *Prince* Charles. Not King'.

'A great country must have a king', said Father G.

'We have a queen'.

'Of course, but that is a woman. The ruler should be a man. Byzantium had two emperors. England can have a king and a queen'.

'Fair enough'.

PL. 33 *Entrance to katholikon, Vatopedi*

'The Abbot gave me the blessing to help him make the wine for King Charles as I was in charge of the cellar. We had a novice to help us. The three of us picked the best grapes with our hands. We pressed it down here. See, there is the press. And there is the barrel. It is ready now. It is organic for the health of the King'.

'Do you use sulfites? Or do you rack it?' I asked.

'Nothing', said Father G.

'How do you stop the fermentation?'

'Of course, when wine gets to fourteen degrees it kills all the bacteria and the fermentation stops. You must taste'.

Father G picked up a glass jug, rinsed it under the tap and took it over to a hundred litre wooden cask lying on its side with a crown chalked on the front. It had been tapped and Father G turned the spigot. This was not going to be pleasant.

I have experience of wine-making. With my friend Panayis we made 5-600 litres a year in my cellar in South London with grapes from Covent Garden Market. I suspected this would be strong as sherry and tasting of dead mouse with hints of camel urine and fartleberry. Father G filled our glasses and invited us with a flourish to sup the royal brew. After sniffing, holding up to the light, a loyal toast to Charles, England and St George, anything to put off the moment of truth, we steeled ourselves not to pucker and sipped the littlest of sips. Then swigged. Swigged again. Held out our glasses for more. It was excellent.

'You must take it to the King', said Father G.

'How, Father? How do we get that barrel to London? Through the customs of several countries? We can't take it on a plane. You need a shipping company'.

'We have tried. They will not take it. It is not certified. You must help us. The Abbot is most anxious. What will he say to St George? Take some bottles'.

'We can't turn up at King Charles's palace with bottles of home-made wine. Monastery-made, I mean. They have security. They'll want to know what's in it'.

'Of course. Wicked people wish to poison the King. That is normal. We will send a letter with the seal of the Abbot. When the butler opens the door of the palace you will give the wine to him and he will taste it before he gives it to the King'.

He looked so expectant, so imploring. He was under pressure from his boss and his boss's boss, St George.

'We can take two bottles each. That's all we are allowed'.

Relief and happiness flooded over Father G's face. He chose eight dark-green bottles from a bin of empties and gave them a good rinse. He opened a new packet of corks and dragged out a floor-standing corker. We gathered round the spigot and filled the bottles, with hearty tastes to make sure the quality was consistent. Each of us had a turn corking two bottles and took photos to prove it. Father G found a roll of yellow masking tape and a felt-tip to make labels that he wrote out in elegant ecclesiastical script. Finally we tore up cardboard boxes for packaging that we sealed with the tape.

Two months later three of us turned up at Clarence House, Prince Charles's official residence, to deliver the wine to his private office. We were kindly received by some very senior staff and a letter of thanks signed by His Royal Highness was sent to the Abbot. I hope somebody got to drink the wine. It was rather good.

The Mountain

D J CASO

Chances are that in a previous life (not that I am particularly superstitious in that way, mind you) I was a struggling stand-up comedian, which is why I ended up on Agion Oros in the first place.

No, it wasn't for open mic night, though I will be the first to admit that by the time I stepped off the Holy Mountain and onto the ferry back to Ouranoupolis, I was awestruck by the show I had witnessed – both the sheer natural beauty of that rugged sliver of land jutting out into the turquoise vastness AND the enthralling life stories of the monks I had met, some of whom turned out to be funnier (funny ha-ha, not funny-looking, even if sometimes there was a bit of both) than Louis C.K. at the Gotham. But I digress, so let me go back to the beginning.

I had just moved back to Bulgaria (yes, it's a country, and yes, it's in Europe – just north of Greece, and as a matter of fact only a few hours' drive from Thessaloniki) from the United States, where I had spent most of my formative years and beyond, when, in an attempt to get to better know my parents now that we were all reasonable adults, I 'boomeranged' back to their Sofia apartment for a while. The first or second weekend of me squatting in my old bedroom, in itself a somewhat surreal experience, my Dad happened to organize one of his trademark motley gatherings of friends, collaborators, colleagues, and sundry acquaintances (a ragtag and, frankly, somewhat funny looking bunch of older and mostly married men ranging from brainiac Brahmins and accomplished architects to Ivy league professors and geeky bookworms and plenty of others way, way, way more learned than me), dudes with a fitting jumble of the alphabet soup tagged onto their last names. The conversation that night bounced back and forth between the finer points of the historiography of the late European Renaissance and a particularly thorny dilemma concerning sums of Poincaré duals of the homology classes of subvarieties – something I later learned was actually the crux of the yet unsolved Hodge

conjecture in algebraic geometry, whatever in the heck that was. It made no difference, for it was all Greek to me. As a matter of fact – no, it was more like medieval Mandarin Chinese, for I am actually one-sixth Greek, to be precise. The point is that I felt out of place, like a junior varsity backbencher in a championship bowl game, as if I wasn't up-to-snuff. Because truth be told, I simply wasn't and the deer in headlights look on my face probably belied my 'seemingly interested in the exchange' demeanour.

And so, in an admittedly pathetic attempt to avoid the Mark Twain conundrum ('Better to remain silent and be thought a fool than to speak and to remove all doubt'), I turned to doing one of the only things I do fairly well – cracking jokes. Somehow at the time it seemed like a good idea. And no, alcohol wasn't a factor. Some of the jokes were pretty funny, some less so, and some were downright awful ... Derp! And yet, I had no shame, which in retrospect was perhaps my saving grace on the night. You gotta swing for the fences – go big or go home, I egged myself on! And then it dawned on me – I already was home! Do or die time.

And so, there I was, punch-drunk in my knee-slapping and wise-cracking haze, when, at some point during the tomfoolery I felt compelled to trot out this humdinger out of my bag of laughs (advance apologies to the ladies, gentlemen, and any other sensitive souls) – Hey fellas, do you know why husbands die before their wives? Well, because they want to! (insert drum roll here, followed on the double by a staccato Zildjian crash cymbal). Yeah, that's how low I can go sometimes. In my defence, it was a rough crowd. Balkan intellectuals, what can I say?

Luckily though, this one got a few laughs. Just then, one of my father's friends – Boyan, a jovial and portly economist who could have been former Fed Chairman Ben Bernanke's out of shape double – pulled me aside and got an oversize photo-book from one of the upper shelves in the study. On the

cover was a beautifully shot image of what looked like the Mediterranean twin of Eiger in the Bernese Alps. The title of the book was simply *Mount Athos*. For a moment I thought that unbeknownst to me my favourite musketeer had purchased a picturesque private island off the coast of Southern France, and that someone had given my father a coffee table album about it.

'Listen, if you think heaven is where we married guys go to have fun without the wives, you ought to come with us to this amazing place', said Boyan, shoving the album in my hands. 'You're gonna like it!' Little did I know that my Dad and his cabal of friends had already made thirteen consecutive annual pilgrimages there. Nobody had ever mentioned a word about it. I looked at the sheer granite cliffs on the book cover. The mountaineer in me didn't need a second invitation.

Fast-forward five months, to the spring of 2013. Dockside in Ouranoupolis, waiting to board the Agia Anna at the crack of dawn, I was quietly observing the mass of ferry-borne humanity destined for Daphne. It was a veritable ecumenical melting pot – a bunch of Serbs with matching 'Greater Serbia' T-shirts, a group of ruddy and over-equipped English gentlemen in matching khaki beanies who looked like they were getting ready to race up to the top of K2 and be back to base camp just in time for five o'clock tea service (I later found out they were actually footpath-clearing volunteers with The Friends of Mount Athos, a very fine non-profit group which I joined that very same year), a few married Ukrainian priests in black kamilavkas who were taking selfies and waving goodbye to what ostensibly were their wives on the pier, a gaggle of bishop-chaperoned Romanians who could have easily been extras on the set of Gadjo Dilo but who were likely just normal God-fearing parishioners, three chiselled and stone-faced Russian KGB-types who were surreptitiously giving the Ukrainians the hairy eyeball, a half-dozen loud and oblivious to their surroundings Bulgarians, a couple of Columbia-clad frappé-sipping Americans, a tightly-knit bloc of Germans who were busy double and triple-checking the Karyes shuttle timetable, and of course tons of Greeks as could reasonably be expected, including a sunburnt and chatty trinkets-hawking monk who was selling assorted Mount Athos themed bracelets and necklaces, most of which were clearly made in China. Globalization!

'It takes all kinds', I said to myself, 'so the more the merrier!' – just as we pushed off and got under way. The backlit silhouette of the undulating and craggy coastline made for a beautiful sight as the ferry plied the crystal-clear

FIGS. 24–25 *The Holy Mountain*

blue water. The sun was slowly creeping up on the other side of the peninsula, and the Aegean Sea stretched out as far as the eye could see, rising up to kiss the azure sky somewhere out there on the sparkling horizon. A few arsanases later the summit finally came into view, and my jaw dropped to the floor. To say that I was amazed wouldn't do it justice. I was in awe of that jagged granite spire knifing straight up into the clear blue sky as if it was trying to touch the sun. Maybe it was the sea and mountain contrast. Maybe it was the over-two-thousand-metre vertical rise. Maybe it was the invisible aura of the divine which enveloped the entire mountain. I had never seen anything like it – I mean, I had seen it once from the beach in Sikia across the bay, but that was at least thirty or thirty-five kilometres away. This time, I was up close and personal, and I was enthralled. I knew I had to head up to the top as soon as we hit land. I had to climb it. Now.

I told my Dad and the rest of the group that I was going to heed the mountain call for the time being, and that I was pretty much abandoning them for a few days. Promising to rejoin them later at whatever monastery or skete they happened to be, I then hurriedly got directions (I had no map and no idea in what direction to hike, other than up) on how to get up to Stavros the fastest and where to fill up on water before making the push up to Panaghia and onto the summit.

After the obligatory shot of tsipouro at the archontariki of Saint Anne skete, I hit the trail for Stavros while feasting my eyes on the 300 metre vistas straight down to the water's edge. The stony path zigzagged through a heavily wooded area, crossed several sprawling rock rivers, and then climbed sharply for an altitude gain of another 400 metres, finally plateauing out at the saddleback between the conical Profitis Ilias and the main massif. I left my backpack at the water spring and hiked up to the top of the Profitis Ilias to admire the 360-degree view of a number of sketes and the deep blue sea on one side and the steep couloirs undergirding the summit another 1,200 metres up. As soon as I emerged from the thick scrub which had almost completely covered the footpath leading to the top of the butte, I immediately regretted having left my sunscreen at the bottom. The midday sun was beating down like a hammer, and the difference in feel-like temperature was striking – down by the spring at Stavros, in the thick shade afforded by the old growth forest, the hot air was still bearable. Standing out in the open on the Profitis Ilias summit felt like being in a sauna and the thirty-three degrees my thermometer was indicating

felt more like forty-three. I glanced at the trail which snaked up the side of the big mountain and realized that I was going to have to spend the rest of the day baking in the desert-like conditions, for practically all of the rest of the way was above the tree line. I wondered if I had brought enough water bottles to fill, unsure of what I would find at Panaghia and the peak itself. Everyone I had talked to told me there was no water anywhere past Stavros. There was only one way to find out. I trotted back to the spring, wolfed down a banana and two cereal bars, guzzled as much water as possible without bursting at the seams, filled up every single watertight container I had, strapped my backpack on, and headed up.

No sooner had the trail come out of the shady woods and onto the exposed long ridge covered by low-lying brush than I was already drenched in sweat. I knew that donning loose-fitting long sleeve shirts and hiking pants, as well as avoiding the blistering midday heat, were two of the best coping strategies when venturing out in such conditions. I had done neither. And to make matters worse, I only had three litres of water. Who knows, I thought, maybe I'll get lucky and run into someone with some water to spare. The thing was this though, there was not a soul to be seen or heard anywhere. It was just the mountain and me. And the blazing sun. A thermonuclear blast furnace only eight light-minutes away. Yet there was no turning around now. Huffing and puffing like an underpowered freight train engine, I trundled on up.

A couple of hours later, still sweating like a Kentucky Derby racehorse in the thirty-five-plus-degree heat, feet ablaze in my hiking boots and eyes foggy from the melting sunscreen and my dripping wet bandana, Panaghia as elusive as ever somewhere up there at over 1,500 metres, I heard heavy grunting coming up behind me. Since I hadn't seen, met, or heard anybody aside from a couple of mountain goats ever since leaving Agia Anna, I was puzzled, and my heat-addled brain somehow glommed on to the image of a hungry Kodiak grizzly hot on my trail. I turned around to take a gander, and what I saw wasn't that far off the mark. Gaining fast on me in the precipitous section of scree covered footpath I had just covered (about twenty or thirty feet from where I was standing) was a gargantuan red-headed monk clad in several layers of black from head to toe. When I say gargantuan, I mean it quite literally. The man looked like a cross between Rasputin and Paul Bunyan. His eyes were pinwheels, his toothy grin full of daggers, and his bright orange hair a lion's mane. He looked to be close to seven feet tall, and the black Converse sneakers he was climbing in reminded me of dolphin flukes. The only non-black accessory he was wearing – his polished silver belt buckle – was the size of a pie tin. I sure hope Babe the Blue Ox isn't following behind him, I said to myself, or else I am in real trouble – seeing that there were no trees to rub on anywhere around.

As soon as he noticed that I was looking at him, he slung his single-strap black knapsack around to the front, reached in, took out something round swaddled in a raggedy black cloth, folded back the four corners, and unceremoniously whipped out a human skull. A human skull!

Picture this, if you will – here was this mountain of a savage looking colossus, a physical specimen to make Andre the Giant tremble in his boots, taking Goliath-sized strides towards me with a human cranium in his outstretched hand, and a Cheshire-cat grin plastered across his face. Understandably, far outside the mainstream of human civilization as we were at the moment, in the back of my mind I started hearing the crazy plinking banjos from 'Deliverance'. Probably because of the prolonged direct sun exposure that day, however, neither fight nor flight kicked in. I just stood there stupefied. With just three steps the leviathan was next to me, beaming knowingly down at me the way anteaters perhaps chortle upon discovering a hidden anthill. I stood stock still. In hindsight, it must have been quite the Kodak moment.

While I was busy ransacking my memory like a thief going through another man's billfold for any inkling on what all this could possibly mean, the giant in black said something in Romanian. After he saw the blank look on my face, he repeated it in English, which I still couldn't comprehend right away because of his heavy accent. Finally it dawned on me that he wanted me to kiss the skull. OK, then. As if to make doubly sure I had understood correctly, he demonstrated by giving the skull a smackaroo right between the empty eye sockets. Not daring say no to the Samson of Athos, I quickly pressed my lips to the skull's forehead, wondering whose body it had once adorned, and hoping the man in black would be satisfied since I didn't really have a plan of action in case he decided to be cross with me.

Fortunately for me, he turned out to be a gentle giant – just a regular monk from one of the sketes in the foothills, and to lighten things even further, we were finally able to communicate in an amalgamated mixture of Greek, Russian, and English which would have made the Rosetta Stone software proud. He even told me about the well of drinkable water in the Panaghia chapel,

FIG.26 *The Peak*

where he was headed to perform a service to honour the respected Russian hieromonk whose relics he was carrying.

When I heard about the water, well, I must have looked like a bright-eyed and bushy-tailed Irish Setter – if I had a tail, it would have been wagging. I followed the gentle giant up the slope like pilot fish, and in under fifteen minutes I was scooping up fresh water from the well in the cool shade of Panaghia.

After another two hours spent slugging under the scorching sun and scrambling over the nearly vertical terrain on the final ascent, I finally made it to the top, where the temperature promptly dropped down to the low teens, and where the air had that fresh-scrubbed quality that only comes with altitude. Talk about a thermal shock! As sunset approached, I was thanking my lucky stars for having actually taken my winter-grade sleeping bag, and for having found the tiny mountain cabin with bunk beds practically carved into the side of the mountain just twenty metres below the summit (but on the opposite side, so not so easy to find). Out of all the nights I have spent on the peak since, I have never again had the good fortune to find its door unlocked. And the interior of the (now remodelled) church is frequently off limits too, for one reason or another. All this is to say that if you ever decide to spend the night on the summit, plan ahead and be ready to rough it out in the open, with everything that entails and requires. A high mountain, especially one surrounded on almost all sides by deep water, has a mind and weather of its own, as any experienced hiker will tell you. So please be heedful of that. But I digress.

As to witnessing and experiencing sunset and sunrise on top of Mount Athos, let me just say that my underdeveloped sense of aesthetics leaves me unable to adequately describe and express the glory of these moments. As a matter of fact, it is not something that can or should be put to words. It has to be lived, and I wholeheartedly urge you to do so for yourselves. It's truly a once-in-a-lifetime, feeling-closer-to-God moment, whether you consider yourself a mountaineer or not, and your efforts in getting to the top will be vastly and undoubtedly rewarded not only by the sweeping views but by seeing and feeling airstreams and lights billow out from the sea and the monasteries below, swirl only inches from your heads, and then dive and bounce back down the ravines and ridges on the other side. The sheer exhilaration of just being in the present moment will make you experience how awe-inspiring Mount Athos can be, in particular if you happen to have good weather (and the conditions around sunrise and sunset have a tendency to always clear up for a while, even on otherwise overcast days).

Being one with nature on the top of Mount Athos is to my mind sufficient proof that God often reveals himself in the orderly harmony and otherworldly natural beauty of places like the Holy Mountain. But don't take my word for it. If you've never been, go see for yourselves! For me personally, every time I set foot on the summit I am able to enjoy that sense we all seek, that knowledge we get a few rare times in life, that the themes of our life are all connected and that the seeds of our ending were there in the very beginning. And vice versa, of course.

From Space

VERONICA DELLA DORA

As a radio ham, I had my first contact with sv2asp/a on 20 September 1996, on the twenty metre band. I was then a student in Venice, my hometown. I did not know who was hiding behind that callsign, nor did I know exactly what Mount Athos was. I had simply heard somewhere that it was a place in Greece with some monasteries where women were not allowed. And of course, as a radio ham, I knew it was a rare place to connect to. This is all I knew.

On that early afternoon, his signal was quite strong, but there were many, many people calling him. I was actually quite surprised when, after several attempts, he caught my call-sign despite my modest power and simple vertical antenna. I was overjoyed by the unexpected 'new one'. Such was my first contact with the Holy Mountain – a quick exchange of signal reports and a new tick on my list of 'radio countries'.

In 1998, I happened to enrol in a summer school for foreigners near Thessaloniki. I wanted to pick up a new language, just for fun. Having studied ancient Greek in high school, I thought learning modern Greek was a logical choice. Besides the language classes, every weekend the school organized visits to major archaeological and tourist sites in Macedonia and other regions of Greece (for example, Pella, Vergina, Meteora, and Kavala).

On the last weekend, they took the boys to Mount Athos, whereas we girls were offered a little cruise along the western coast of the same peninsula. The evening before, the school had invited a professor from the Aristotle University of Thessaloniki to give us a short lecture on Mount Athos. We were presented with many beautiful slides. I was captivated by those magnificent buildings and by those black-robed monks 'living like centuries ago'.

Our boat left Sithonia (the second 'finger' of the Chalkidiki peninsula) early in the morning. The sea was flat and crystalline. At some point, the dark pyramid of Athos's summit began to loom on the horizon, veiled by the thin summer haze. I was totally charmed by the silent presence of that mysterious mountain emerging from the water. As the boat drew closer, the first coastal monasteries started to appear. Those ancient structures then began to parade before us in all their splendour, one after the other. At some point, towards the end of our journey, the loudspeaker announced that the beautiful monastery we were passing by was called Dochiariou. When I heard that name, I suddenly remembered that I had once talked to someone from there through ham radio. 'Hold on! How could a monk be a ham radio operator?!' In my mind, I started to picture austere clerics studying ancient manuscripts in their dark cells illumined by dusty oil lamps … and right next to them the technological radio-shack cell of the ham radio monk! This image amused me, and yet at the same time it deeply intrigued me.

Thus it was just out of pure curiosity that I decided to put the Greek that I had learnt to use, and wrote a letter to that strange ham radio monk. In broken (or rather, disastrously broken!) Greek, I wrote him that I was an Italian student, that we had once talked through ham radio, that I was in Thessaloniki because I wanted to learn Greek, and that earlier on that same day I had seen his monastery from the boat. Best wishes. And that was it. On the following day, I returned to Venice.

Weeks, maybe even months, passed by. 'Who knows, perhaps monks are misogynists and don't write to women…', I thought. I then totally forgot about the whole thing. One day, however, an envelope arrived stamped with the Byzantine double-headed eagle in my mailbox. 'Dear Veronica, I am sorry it took me so long to reply, but over the summer I was working in the mainland, and I have just found your letter'. It turned out that he and a small group of fellow monks were building a nunnery near Sochos, a small village in the Lagkada area, in northern Greece. The guy must have felt for my broken Greek and offered help. 'I am glad you are trying to learn Greek, not only because it is my mother tongue, but because it is the language of the Gospel. As a monk,

PL. 35 *Dochiariou Monastery*

however, it is not appropriate for me to keep a correspondence with a woman, unless you have spiritual interests. Do you have any?' How to answer him? Ham radio interests I had plenty at that time. Cultural interests I might have had too. It was, however, ages since I had last set foot in a church (like the rest of my family). I resolved to simply tell him the truth: 'I am agnostic and know nothing about Orthodoxy, but I would like to learn'.

We started to correspond – initially through letters, later over the phone (those were the years before the Internet). His Epirus accent was too fast for me and I struggled to understand him. At the beginning, the poor guy made an incredible effort to slow down. I asked him about his daily routine and his faith. With infinite patience and fatherly care, he listened to me, corrected my mistakes, taught me new words, and introduced me to his world. Sometimes, together with his letters I received photographs from the monastery with some comment hastily scribbled on the back. Other times, I received a book – from simple books to St John Climacus's Ladder of Divine Ascent (when my Greek had progressed enough). Other times, I found a little icon. Others, blessed bread from the last feast, flowers from the Easter epitaph, olives from the last harvest, a little wooden cross hand-carved by some Athonite hermit, or some other object from that distant world that had already become a part of my life.

I met Father Apollo in person for the first time in summer 1999, at the nunnery in Sochos. That encounter surpassed any picture my mind could have possibly crafted. He was excavating the foundations of a new building with some other Fathers under the burning midday sun. A bunch of sweating, dust-covered bearded men dressed in rags; their faces sunburnt; their hands hardened by the continuous heavy work. Most of the monks were excavating with their shovels inside a trench. Father Apollo was opening the way on a noisy bulldozer. This was certainly not the image of monk I had in mind! At some point, he got off the bulldozer to welcome me. I remember his wide smile, his bright face, his warm voice.

That night I attended a long vigil at St Anna, a little white chapel in the nunnery's cemetery (the nunnery was then still in its early stages of construction, and the main church had not yet been completed). The dusty workers had suddenly transformed. I remember their dark silhouettes standing around the lectern. Behind them was a small window through which I could see the Macedonian countryside bathed in the golden light of the sunset, as it slowly faded into the night. Mystical melodies cut the silence of the hill and travelled to-

wards heaven. The fragrance of the incense mixed with the scent of the night. Polychrome lamps illumined the peaceful faces of the saints on the icons, and the trembling light of the candles lit the sunburnt faces of the monks. I tried to discern Father Apollo amidst them. And yet, in the darkness, the Fathers all looked the same to me, with their black hoods and their long beards. I could nevertheless discern his chant, his low tones. His voice was warm and comforting. Above the little church was a sky so full of stars as I had never seen before. It was as if we were standing on the top of the world – and a bit closer to heaven. It was my first time in an Orthodox church.

Of course, I could not pick up a single word of that service, which felt endless. I actually became quite tired by the end of it. However, that melody kept echoing in my mind for a long time after I returned home. During my stay in the nunnery, I had a chance to talk with Father Apollo at length. I revealed to him personal problems and anxieties. He provided me with sound advice, which I treasured over the years and which totally changed my life. I found a safe shelter in him. I regained my faith.

I was baptized in the nunnery on July 15, 2001, about two months before I moved to Los Angeles, where I continued my studies. I arrived in the U.S. just a few days before 9/11. For a 23-year-old who had never lived by herself, let alone abroad, being catapulted to the other end of the globe under such

FIG.27 *Father Apollo*

dramatic circumstances was not easy. In the midst of daily uncertainties, Father Apollo stood by me like a sleepless guard. He lived all my anxieties, especially in the aftermath of 9/11. I knew that every day he lit a candle to the Mother of God for me, and this gave me strength. I found solace in the thought that every night, as Europe was still asleep, the monks would get up to go to church and pray for the entire world. Every day, I saw a little miracle happen and felt closer and closer to the Holy Mountain, even though I was so distant. Through Father Apollo, Mount Athos became the most stable landmark in a life of continuous changes and moves, away from my homeland.

For twenty entire years, Father Apollo and I used to communicate on a daily basis. Every summer, I used to visit him at the nunnery, which in the meanwhile became a most beautiful shrine similar to a Byzantine castle. Someone seeing it today would hardly believe that it was built from scratch by a small group of monks! Throughout the years, I met dozens and dozens of people who turned to the monastery. They were people of all ages, social backgrounds, and occupations. They were usually broken, suffering people: poor families and mothers of drug-addicted teenagers; couples who had lost their only child, and childless couples; victims of domestic violence, orphans, terminally ill. The monks provided each one of them with comfort, prayer, sometimes even with financial help.

What always deeply touched me, however (probably because I experienced it personally), is that those monks did not 'preach', but lived people's daily sufferings from within. Father Apollo was not a priest-monk, so he did not confess people. He nonetheless had a special sensitivity towards the suffering. It was as if others' sufferings and their problems were always his own. Since he was the person responsible for the construction of the nunnery, at the beginning, he was the only one of the Fathers who had a mobile phone. His old Nokia would ring non-stop all the time, regardless of whether he was working with his bulldozer, building the electric system of some new building, fixing a pipe, or driving his truck. His mobile was on even at night, during his few hours of sleep (normally no more than four). 'Someone might be in need', he used to say. Everyone dumped their sufferings and problems on him. He patiently listened to them, he comforted them, and took their suffering to the Mother of God through his ceaseless prayer (I never saw him without a prayer rope in his hand).

Whatever gifts people gave Father Apollo he would never keep them for himself, nor for the monastery. He would always give them to those in need, be it money, clothing, food, or any other thing that might have helped them, or at least, cheered them up a little bit. I was often saddened, as I wanted to send him something, but he would immediately give it away – to poor families, to orphans, to widows who had just seen their pension cut. When he started undergoing treatment for his terrible illness, I saw him suffer the cold of the winter for the first time. I therefore sent him some warmer clothes. He immediately told me off and gave those away as well. 'That's not appropriate. I am a monk'.

Father Apollo was a simple and direct man. Whatever he thought, he would always say without false kindnesses, political correctness, diplomacies, or hypocrisies, as we from 'the civilized world' often do. He had his own special way of approaching and helping everyone who was in need. With his jokes and his genuine love, he managed to open up people's hearts. Thanks to him, many regained their smiles and hopes. Even if he did not speak foreign languages (other than his basic ham radio English), he also helped a number of amateur radio colleagues from abroad with his prayer. He believed that, regardless of their nationality, gender, or social class, humans are the same, and suffering is present everywhere. He used to say: 'God speaks to the heart of every single person. And yet, how many listen to Him?'

The 'ham' spirit, I believe, naturally fitted his open-mindedness and his unconditional love for his neighbour. He nourished the highest esteem towards colleagues involved in emergency networks. He told me many a story of emergency situations in which he found immediate relief through ham radio, especially when mobile phones had yet to come. In its own way, ham radio somehow extended the boundaries of his world, even though he was a serious operator and he never discussed religious matters on the air (nor any other thing unrelated to the hobby). He believed that technology is neither good, nor bad. 'It can do a lot of harm. It can, however, also do good. It depends on the way in which it is employed', he used to repeat.

Father Apollo had a special gift for operating anything mechanical or electronic – from heavy machinery to computers. He never refused to try out a new programme, device, or mode when we offered it to him (though more so as to make us happy, than out of personal interest or curiosity). When we first met, I had a mania for satellites. I remember, at some point I explained to him how to work the Russian low earth orbit satellite communications with his simple equipment. I passed him the uplink and downlink frequencies, and told him to mind the Doppler effect. I then sent him a list of orbits for Greece for the following days. As soon as he found a moment in his extremely busy monastic pro-

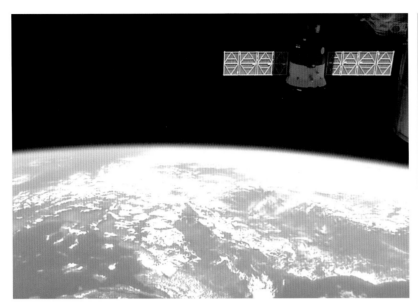

FIG.28 *Mount Athos and Greece from orbit*

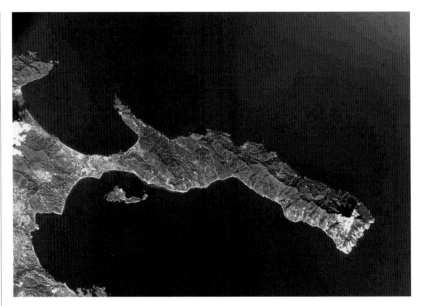

FIG.29 *The Holy Mountain from the ISS*

gramme, we managed to organize a schedule. After our short talk, he started to create congestion even via satellite!

When I told him that I used to talk with the astronauts on the MIR space station, however, he appeared a bit sceptical, and even more so when I told him that he could do it too. In north Italy, where I used to live, one needed power and good antennas, in order to break through the European radio congestion. Out of curiosity, he started to leave his VHF open on the downlink frequency whenever he happened to be in his cell, or nearby. One day, as he was setting the table in the Fathers' refectory in Sochos, the communication suddenly opened up. It was Jean-Pierre Haigneré, the French astronaut who spent six months on the last mission on the MIR. Father Apollo rushed to his cell and called him. Jean-Pierre immediately got back to him. I think this first contact with space enthused Father Apollo. And the French astronaut probably got even more enthused (and intrigued) when I told him who that Greek operator was!

Since I moved to the U.S., I stopped my ham radio activities, except for some occasional help to my university radio club during Morse-code contests. In summer 2002, however, while I was spending my holidays in Venice, I was told by some colleague that Valery Korzun, with whom I used to have daily contacts during his stay on the MIR in 1996, was back in space and was asking

about me. He was now leading the first mission on the newly-launched ISS. It is hard to describe the joy of that first contact after six years!

Valery and I started to talk to each other again on VHF on a daily basis. We also exchanged messages via packet, and sometimes photographs. After sending me wonderful pictures of Venice and L.A., he asked what other place I wanted him to photograph for me. I asked him to take a picture of Mount Athos, since in the meanwhile he had made some contacts with Father Apollo. At the beginning, he did not quite understand (we originally got a picture of the Peloponnese!) However, when I sent him the coordinates via packet, he suddenly got very excited. 'Aphoi! Aphoi!', he started to shout. 'You know, Veronica, this is the holiest place for us Orthodox!' I told him that SV2ASP/A, with whom he had talked, was actually a monk from Mount Athos. That was just the beginning of a very special and lasting friendship between the two of them.

Every day, when the ISS passed over Greece, Valery used to call Father Apollo and receive his blessing. They exchanged letters and messages, which I translated for them, as well as plenty of photographs. Valery sent Father Apollo images of the Holy Land, of the summit of Ararat, of a hurricane over the States, and of many other places, as he saw them from space. In exchange, Father Apollo sent him photographs from the monastery and the latest liturgical feasts. Every night, Father Apollo used to light a candle to the Mother of God for Valery and his crew. Valery always asked for Father Apollo's prayers before going out on a space-walk, or in difficult situations, like when they experienced the start of a fire onboard. They remained in orbit for six months.

When Valery returned from his mission, we somehow lost touch with each other. A few years later, I received a phone call from Father Apollo while I was in Venice on vacation (I remember I was on the waterbus at that moment). Full of joy, he told me that Valery was there with him and he wanted to say hi to me. My thoughts immediately went to our common friend Valery KB2FIV from New York, who every year used to go on a pilgrimage to Mount Athos. 'No, it's not that Valery!', he said. 'It's the other one, the astronaut!' Valery Korzun, the Russian cosmonaut, had come to Mount Athos with his spiritual father, because he wished to meet and thank in person that ham radio monk who had supported him with his voice and with his prayers during his space mission for so many months.

FIG.31 *'To Holy Mountain Dweller "святогорец" Father Apollo, with gratitude for love and spiritual support during our space flight. Valery Korzun'*

I think this says a lot about the outreach of the voice of Mount Athos through Father Apollo – and about the power of that voice too. As some radio magazine wrote, his recent departure leaves a devastating void in the international amateur radio community. Those of you who are reading these lines and knew him personally are probably mourning a beloved colleague; perhaps some of you are mourning a special friend, or even a brother. As to myself, not only have I lost my spiritual father, but a true father, and the most precious thing I had in this world. However, I believe that from where he is now, beyond the earth and beyond space, he is continuing to pray for all of us who loved him, as he always did. And as a colleague said, 'one day we will catch up again' – it's just a matter of the Doppler effect …

This piece originally appeared in Greek in the radio magazine SV NEA, September–October 2019. Many thanks to Fr Maximos Constas for his help with copyediting the English translation and to Peter Howorth for his help eliminating the technical jargon and making it more accessible to a broader audience.

FIG.30 *Fr Apollo and cosmonaut Valery*

'The Highest Place on Earth': Climbing the Mountain

GRAHAM SPEAKE

It is a fine, sunny morning within the season of Easter at the start of June 2013. We are a party of four – three Serbs and myself, all Orthodox and all but one Athonite veterans. The neophyte is experiencing a baptism of fire. We convene at St Anne's skete in the heat of the mid-afternoon. The guest-master's tray of raki, coffee, loukoumi, and water is gratefully received after the gruelling climb up the concrete stairway from the port 400 metres below. Having made reservations, we are among the fortunate few to be given beds in an otherwise unfurnished room. Other pilgrims are not turned away, but some have to sleep in the corridor outside the church. Most of them are Russians, but there are also Spaniards and Swiss. We put our feet up while we have the chance. At 6.30 p.m. the pilgrims are summoned to the kyriakon where the relics are brought out to be venerated, chief among them the left foot of St Anne. At 7 p.m. a fasting meal is served in the guest-house: spaghetti, tomato, olives, apple, water. We take a short stroll in the soft light of evening to admire the fine views from this skete that clings precariously to the already precipitous slopes of the mountain itself, and turn in around 9 p.m.

Next morning we rise at 5.15 to attend the liturgy being served in a small nearby church and taken at a brisk pace. Apart from the celebrant and two or three chanters no other monks are present. It being Friday, there is no meal, but coffee and rusks are produced from the guest-house: a rather insubstantial foundation for the rigours ahead of us. I perch on a low wall to anoint my knees with ibuprofen gel, the first of several applications over the next few days, and encase them in the knee braces that I have brought for this exercise. I have had problems with my knees for many years, particularly on steep descents over slippery stones, and I am taking no chances. For the past month I have been swallowing daily doses of glucosamine sulfate, omega-3, and fish oils; I have kept up a daily routine of knee-strengthening exercises; and I have equipped myself with two lightweight, adjustable hiking poles. 'Time for your massage', Radoman grinningly reminds me every four hours, and I take five

minutes out to apply more of the gel. The performance is mildly amusing to my companions, but it would be too frustrating to find that physical discomfort prevented me from reaching the summit, and I know that once that particular agony sets in, every step is a form of torture. Happily, the regime has paid off and my knees remain entirely free from pain throughout both ascent and descent.

We are on the road by 8 a.m., climbing steeply up a stone or sometimes concrete track through dense woods. After a couple of hours the path levels out and offers occasional spectacular views down to the port of St Anne's, now 700 metres below us, and along the entire west coast of Athos. It is easy to pick out the bay of St Paul's with its seaside ruin and the beetling heights of Simonos Petras, and to the west the neighbouring peninsulas of Sithonia and Cassandra, and snow-capped Olympus rising above the distant horizon. The sun has now caught up with us, but it is not hot and there is a cool breeze creating ideal conditions for walking. This is a well-travelled route, being the principal track to the west coast, not only from the summit, but from the Great Lavra as well as the sketes of Prodromos and Kafsokalyvia. Mule droppings define it and a succession of mule trains pass by in the opposite direction, some laden with building materials (roofing stone, timber, etc.), others with overweight pilgrims and/or their baggage. The mules hesitate and stumble on the often slippery surface but their heartless drivers spur them on relentlessly with sticks. Our progress is slow but we are taking our time, unlike some striplings who overtake us at speed, intent on ascending and descending the peak within the day.

Around 10.30 a.m. we reach the place marked by a wooden cross (Stavros) where five roads meet, from Great Lavra, St Basil's, Karoulia, St Anne's, and the peak. Here there is a wayside spring with deliciously cold running water, the ideal place for some refreshment and a short rest. Here pilgrims, monks, and mule trains pass through, bound for any of these destinations and more.

PL. 36 *The Holy Mountain from near Kaliagra*

A young Romanian pilgrim is relaxing beneath a shady tree. It feels like the heart of the Athonite desert, far from any motor road or monastery, deep in the silent woods where only nature's sounds are heard. We choose the path to the peak, signed 'Panaghia 1500m', the refuge some 500 metres below the summit where we plan to spend the night. We still have to climb another 750 metres to reach it: this is only the half-way point to the Panaghia.

We continue to climb through woods. The sun is rising in the sky, but as we gain altitude, so the air becomes cooler. 'Christos anesti!' is our greeting in Greek to every passing pilgrim. 'Voistinu voskrese!' is the Slavonic reply nine times out of ten, though the respondents are not always Russians but may be Serbs, Ukrainians, Bulgarians, Moldovans, or Romanians. The relatively few Greeks give us 'Alithos anesti!', and a couple of Americans 'He is risen indeed!' Everyone has a story to tell and a question to ask: how far is it? How steep is it? How many hours? There is a camaraderie among the pilgrims; and whether they are Orthodox or not, they are surely all pilgrims. No one is here just for the sport.

Eventually the trees begin to thin out, the terrain turns to bare rock, and colourful carpets of wildflowers are rolled out in every direction. Finally, just as we emerge from the trees, the Panaghia refuge comes into view, our goal for the night. Facilities are rudimentary here: a chapel, dedicated of course to the Mother of God, with some lamps burning, numerous icons on a brand-new iconostasis, and a lingering aroma of incense; a large dormitory containing half a dozen double-bunk beds, some of them provided with foam mattresses, blankets, and sleeping bags; a rather bleak and spacious kitchen; a sort of saloon with a large open fireplace and a covered well, fed by rainwater from the roof. Any washrooms there may have been once are locked. Outside, hanging over the entrance, there is a bell with an inscription in Russian for summoning the faithful or guiding the benighted; a radio mast, providing a very intermittent signal for mobile telephones; a tub of fresh water brought up by the mules; and one of the best views in the world. A party of five or six Russians, who have arrived before us, soon depart with their mules laden, clearly intent on sleeping at the summit, leaving us in sole possession of the refuge. We lay claim to what appear to be the least worst beds and feast on our meagre rations of biscuits, nuts, and dried fruits. It is of course a fast day, so no wine. Not that we had any anyway.

The sun sets early behind the Mountain, a wind gets up, and it starts to feel chilly. We take to our beds as there is not much else to do, only to be roused by the arrival of a noisy party of four Greeks. Scorning the beds, which creak hideously at every turn, they drag mattresses out to the saloon where they settle down for the night, leaving us in possession of the dormitory. The windows are sound and exclude the wind, and the sleeping bags and blankets provide adequate warmth, but the constant creaking of the beds and the ceaseless chatter of the Greeks conspire to deprive us of sleep. We rise next morning at 6.30, unslept, unfed, and slightly grumpy. Slowly we make our preparations for de-

FIG. 32 *Monastery of Osiou Grigoriou and the Holy Mountain*

parture and tidy up our belongings which we are to leave here, so that we make the final climb unencumbered. At 7.30 a.m. we begin the ascent, deliberately not hurrying, but stopping regularly to admire the view or photograph the many varieties of flowering plants, some of them endemic to the mountain, looking down to watch the Panaghia gradually receding, looking up to glimpse the summit still tantalizingly distant. A number of pilgrims pass us on their way down, presumably having slept at the top, if passing the night in these places can be called sleeping. Eventually, exhausted after two hours' climbing, quite unexpectedly and suddenly, we round a corner of solid rock and there it is: the top! 'Beyond, a void', exclaimed the travel writer Robert Byron at this point in a strikingly terse, three-word paragraph.

All the agony of the climb, the lack of sleep, the lack of food, the grumpy start to the day, all these things are immediately dissipated. We scarcely notice the party of Greeks who were with us in the refuge, who have preceded us to the summit, and who depart very soon after our arrival. Apart from one single and silent Greek, who also leaves in due course, we have the summit entirely to ourselves. The weather is utterly perfect: not a cloud in the sky, one hundred per cent visibility in every direction, not cold, not windy, just pleasantly sunny and warm. How blessed we are!

The highest point is surmounted by a three-metre-high iron cross dated 1897. The rock on which it stands retains traces of numerous, partly legible inscriptions in a variety of languages and bearing dates mostly from the nineteenth century. A few metres away there is a chapel dedicated to the Transfiguration, similar to the one at the Panaghia but filled with natural light and with monastic stalls round the walls. It is right and fitting to linger here, to light a candle and give thanks for our deliverance and for all the wonders that have been revealed to us. The Jesus Prayer comes to mind, but otherwise we are strangely silent and even the Serbs refrain from their usual banter. Somehow the awesomeness of the location transcends any need to converse.

Here spread out at our feet like a large-scale map lies the whole of Mount Athos: a complete 360-degree panorama in perfect focus and unimpaired clarity. From the rocks that destroyed the Persian fleet immediately below us, turning clockwise, clearly identifiable on the west coast we see the port buildings of St Paul's, the monasteries of Grigoriou and Simonos Petras, the harbour and domes of St Panteleimon, the arsanas of Zografou, and the tower at Ouranoupolis; coming down the east coast, the monasteries of Pantokrator

and Stavronikita, Karyes and the Serai, Mylopotamos, Karakalou and its port buildings, the bay of Morphonou overlooked by the tower of the Amalfitan monastery, the sketes of Provata and Lakkou, and still just visible below us the Panaghia refuge. To the north the hideous scars made by the roads stand out starkly like contours drawn across the hills, hills that are otherwise apparently clad in a soft, velvet-like down. To the south there are no signs of human intervention, just bare rock, a few scattered trees, some denser woods on the lower slopes, and the deep, deep blue of the sea almost immediately below. The view beyond Athos is as Byron described it; nor is it fanciful to imagine that one is looking on the plains of Troy. It is a spectacular and breath-taking moment.

But it is also much more than this, much more than just an amazing view. Here, far away from any of the monasteries, any of the roads, any of the cars and cranes and computers, is a simple chapel, dedicated most appropriately to the Transfiguration of Our Lord on Mount Tabor. To this single point, this tiny pinnacle of rock, come pilgrims – Russians, Greeks, Serbs, Romanians, even Americans and Englishmen – pilgrims from every corner of the Orthodox world and beyond. They converge here in order to experience this one sublime, spectacular, and breath-taking moment, the nearest thing that most of us will come to an earthly transfiguration, a truly transforming point in time and space. And for me, this is a symbolic revelation of the true pan-Orthodoxy of Athos. This is the eternal, immutable summit of the entire Athonite pilgrimage experience. 'Come, let us rejoice, mounting up from the earth to the highest contemplation of the virtues: let us be transformed this day into a better state and direct our minds to heavenly things, being shaped anew in piety according to the form of Christ. For in His mercy the Saviour of our souls has transfigured disfigured man and made him shine with light upon Mount Tabor.'*

This account of my ascent of the mountain was first published in the second edition of my book, Mount Athos: Renewal in Paradise *(Limni, Evia, 2014), pp. 259–64.*

---

* The opening sentences of the small vespers
for the feast of the Transfiguration of Our Lord.

Travelling Light: Mount Athos

ALASTAIR SAWDAY

The village was abandoned, the roofs gone, and only a few swinging shutters and doors hinted at a more animated past. Em and I trod paving-stones worn by the feet of villagers over many centuries. Each street led neatly to another, to a square or a church. It was clearly once prosperous and well-ordered, and had been left in a tragic rush. The inhabitants of Livissi, after years of persecution during which many thousands of Greeks were deported, tortured or sent on forced marches, were given just twenty-four hours to leave by the newly triumphant Turkish government of Atatürk.

Thus ended, in 1922, over two thousand years of Greek settlement in Asia Minor. The upheaval was vast, with more than a million Greeks from Asia Minor forced to resettle in Greece, and three hundred thousand Turks having to come home from Greece. Livissi remains empty, some say, as a mark of respect by the local Turks who refuse to repopulate a place abandoned by their friends and neighbours. It is a moving reminder of the trauma that reshaped Greece, and of the sensitivities that shape Greek responses to the world. If they feel unreasonably burdened by the current financial and refugee crises, it is no wonder.

The story of Greece doesn't get better until long after the Second World War, so it is natural to sense the layers of history behind every encounter one has there. In Crete, in 1975, Em and I met village elders who would gleefully mime the slitting of throats and the shooting of parachutists as they drifted to the ground during the German invasion. Being British, we were, much to our relief when contemplating the alternatives, made to feel welcome. The British were still treated as wartime saviours, though some historians berate us for our military incompetence.

Luckily, Patrick Leigh Fermor's translation of the book *The Cretan Runner* by George Psychoundakis, has rescued our reputation and allowed us all to bask in his glory. Fermor kidnapped a German general and was chased with his Cretan partisans through the mountains. It is a great story and we landed on the island wearing our admiration for the brave and ill-treated Cretans on our sleeves.

We knew that the Greeks are hospitable, but inviting ourselves to an evening meal in a private house was a genuine error, if not my first. In those days Loutro, to which we came by boat after a magnificent day's walk down the Samaria Gorge, was scattered among the rocks, many of the houses standing alone against the setting sun. It was hard to see any shape to it all, and we wandered awhile, hungry from the walk, looking for a café or signs of food. One house was bigger than the others, at the top of a rock-strewn mound. Such was the general air of conviviality emerging from the three tables of old men outside it, that we experienced that familiar traveller's relief at finding a restaurant, sat down and ordered. Em, whose minimal Greek outshone mine, asked for a menu, but the woman who had welcomed us reacted with puzzlement. There was no menu, but in Greece you often eat whatever is on offer so we pointed at the food the old men were eating and she disappeared to the kitchen. We waited but it was only moments before she returned with a dish of goat's liver bubbling hot in a rich brown sauce, succulent and delicious. The woman, who now so sweetly served us, had cottoned on to our gaffe and went along with it. The evening turned gay with laughter and misunderstandings, and for both Em and me it was, and remains, one of the best meals we have ever eaten – which shows how atmosphere and context are vital to the enjoyment of a meal.

I have also, since then, learned again and again how poverty and generosity often go hand in hand. So we are resolved to be kind to unknown foreigners intruding upon our meals. (We are, as yet, untested.) That day of walking

down the Samaria Gorge turned out to be significant in our lives. It showed us that we should leave London, and Bristol beckoned. After the walk and our goat's-liver dinner, we returned to Chania, on the north-west coast, for a night in the Imperial Hotel on the harbourside, a ramshackle old place with a battered but heavily made-up face.

In the morning we were awoken by the sounds of vigorous slapping. Peering groggily through the windows we watched two fishermen rotating their arms like windmills, each rotation bringing a small octopus crashing down onto the harbour wall. Were they killing them, stretching them or softening them? I'm not sure, but I felt for the octopuses.

We returned to Crete in 2014 for a yoga holiday and stayed again in Chania, now overwhelmed with tourists. The exquisite Venetian lighthouse was still there at the end of the harbour wall. We ate on the harbourside, served by an unusually sophisticated waiter who earned a trifling salary as an air-traffic controller and needed to boost his earnings. The crisis had laid waste to people's finances and many were returning to the land: Greeks hold tightly to their rural roots and return to them when the going gets tough. Yakis was philosophical about it, for he had a family smallholding just outside town where he grew vegetables and kept bees. That gave him a sense of self-sufficiency in a topsy-turvy world.

The part of Greece least affected by the economic crisis is probably the part that has for centuries detached itself wholeheartedly anyway, Mount Athos. Monasteries all over Europe have been abandoned in the past centuries, but Mount Athos and Meteora remain as refuges for those seeking an ordered spiritual life. They are remote, a challenge to reach. I have never been to Meteora, but photographs of monastic buildings clinging to the highest pinnacles are captivating. Mount Athos is different: constitutionally independent, isolated from the rest of Greece by a border, and with the wisdom to stay so. It is three times the size of the island of Jersey, with twenty monasteries, about three thousand monks and a number of sketes, or daughter houses. There are also hundreds of remote hermitages. Most of the monasteries are also cultural and artistic centres, preserving and encouraging the arts. The monastery of Iviron, for example, has a famous icon, the Panaghia Portaitissa, and some sumptuous architectural features and frescoes. There is a silver lampstand with thirty silver lemons, plus a library of more than fifteen thousand books and two thousand parchment manuscripts. It is no wonder that Athos has had an immense influence on orthodox art.

The whole area is called the Holy Mountain, and it really does feel sacred. There is no space for the braggadocio and delusion of the outside world. This is deeply reassuring, a living reminder that humans are capable of creating communities of holiness in a cynical secular world.

There is more to it, of course, than this. Farming is a major part of monastic life and the monks are famous for their organic produce and for their maintenance of rare plant species. Athos is a laboratory of conservation, nurturing ideas, plants and traditions that may serve us in the future.

I spent a week there in 2012 with friends from Bristol. We walked from monastery to monastery, staying the nights as guests, motivated by a mixture of curiosity and admiration. My curiosity had been aroused further by the story of the sudden flight of a friend's Greek hairdresser from London, leaving a note on his shop window declaring, 'Gone to Mt Athos'.

Mount Athos is a provocative place to be, for it challenges many of our modern assumptions about how the world should be ordered. The buildings are semi-fortified structures, some of them of great beauty, all different. One, Simonos Petras, is perched upon a rock over the sea; another, Vatopedi, is like a village, with a population of monks from all over the Christian world. Our guide there was Father C, large, boisterous, chuckly and French, only recently joined after a life as a restaurant owner in London. He still seemed to enjoy a good chat with 'the clients' – unusually, for most monks kept their heads down and greeted us only if they had to. They have, after all, fled the world of casual chat. I kept an eye out, meanwhile, for a monk who looked like a London hairdresser – tricky, for they become more visually alike as their beards and their hair grow. We discreetly attended vespers. The chanting was hypnotic, part of a thousand years of unbroken tradition. The monks sat in deep pews to the side, coming up to the altar or lectern one after another to recite, read, pray. It was hard for us to understand the services, but just witnessing them was very moving. Dinner afterwards would be silent, our group seated self-consciously together, with readings by a monk. Each monastery had its own traditions, but always served good food, often with a glass of its own red wine.

The Mount Athos diet is famous for ensuring a long and healthy life, largely free of many problems such as cancer, diabetes, heart disease, strokes and dementia. The monks eat no meat, a little fish, lots of pulses and spices such as dill, onion, garlic and cumin. Some days each week are reserved for a more austere diet. The absence of stress may also contribute to longevity and well-being. Simplicity, structure, companionship, hard manual work and the constant presence of Mother Nature must play a part too. And faith, perhaps?

We slept in dormitories, or simple shared rooms, in the guest-quarters under the care of the guest-master. Sometimes we shared the bathrooms with monks, which I was unaware of until I emerged from the shower to startle some monks into alarmed retreat. We would get up early for the morning service and then breakfast on eggs, bread and coffee. Then we would file out of the monastery for the day-long walk to the next one. The countryside is thickly wooded, well-tended in places by the different monastic communities and often within sight of the sparkling sea. We succumbed to temptation one day and plunged naked into the water, only to be admonished by two passing monks. We were embarrassed to have broken their rules. To have insisted, even among ourselves, on our right to do as we wished in a free world would have been inappropriate. This was their world.

Some of the paths between the monasteries have been neglected during thin times, and a British charity, the Friends of Mount Athos, has volunteer path-clearers who annually work on path maintenance, encouraged by their patron, Prince Charles, who loves the Holy Mountain.

At a particularly handsome monastery, with wooden balconies cantilevered out from high defensive-looking walls and not unlike monasteries I had seen in Ladakh, I was taken by the excellent English of the small, twinkly-eyed, grey-bearded monk who looked after us. He didn't respond easily to questions about himself but I did tease out of him that he had run a small business in London, was without family, and had arrived recently. That was my hairdresser, surely – but I hadn't the heart to say so, for he had left London to start afresh and anonymous in another world.

What is the Mount Athos community there for? Or, as people ask me cynically, what is the point? It is a question that will enrich debate for centuries to come, even if it doesn't preoccupy the monks themselves. They are there to worship their God. However, there is a secular response: it is an example to us all, while the rest of us are destroying our life-support systems with reckless consumption and leading lives shorn of meaning and purpose. The communities of Mount Athos are sustainable; they produce nearly all their own food and energy, living lives so materially simple that they demand little of the ecosystem. The rest of us depend on others to sustain us, whether through accepting our pollution or producing and buying goods. But this is to state the obvious. Among the many roles of a monastic community is the keeping open of a door to the possibility of God, to explore other ways of being, of knowing ourselves. Not one of us was a practising Christian, yet the devotion of so many fellow men touched us deeply.

The fact that no living female creatures are allowed there, other than those one cannot control, such as mice (and cats to chase them), is mystifying to outsiders. It can hardly be sustainable, surely? But the population is replenished by a fairly reliable supply of monks.

Those of us who secretly hoped to spot a crack in the monkish carapace of perfection were satisfied to hear that there had been near-conflicts between monasteries in the not-so-distant past. One community, Esphigmenou, had even hung banners to protest against the visit of the Ecumenical Patriarch of Constantinople, whose remit they would not accept. Not every monastery is beautiful. The Russian foundation, St Panteleimon, was, we were glad to see, even a touch vulgar. Too much new money.

Greece, or those of its citizens who care about its environment and its autonomy, is battling on many other fronts, one of which is in Chalkidiki, the northern region from which springs the peninsula of Athos. The Canadian mining company Eldorado intends to mine for gold there and the locals want to stop them. It is an epic struggle, one that has gone on for decades. It is even possible that the local community will win. They know that profits would be expatriated and run through a subsidiary in another low-tax country, as happens with many international companies. Yet again, for the Greeks, it is them against the rest.

At the beginning of this chapter I wrote of the heartbreak of the Greek exodus from Asia Minor. A second heartbreak was the suffering of the Greeks during the Second World War, and then for many years afterwards during a vicious civil war. The role of the British was not one of which we can be proud. Churchill, a committed monarchist, poured resources into supporting the monarchy and the establishment against the progressive left and the communists. All this in a country broken and impoverished by a war of which it had wanted no part, but into which it had been dragged by Mussolini's invasion. So it is painful to see Greece yet again overwhelmed by outside forces and tens of thousands of migrants for whom life has become impossible in their own countries. Greece, I believe, bears no responsibility for this last great migrant crisis, but bears much of the brunt. It is hard for those who have lived a long time to see their country torn yet again.

But Greece has been with us for a while and will keep its head; and it still has much to teach us.

Visits to Mount Athos

DANIEL ERIKSEN

Raised a Congregational Protestant in New England, I had been received into the Orthodox Church in Boston in 1981 and I loved our small parish (OCA), with all the young new converts from local colleges and around the area; we became a family of enthusiastic seekers of truth, and good friends.

Looking back, a number of us from the years 1979 to 1984 have pursued vocations: two became monks, two nuns, three choir directors, three professional iconographers, one deacon, an abbess of a monastery, three priests, one bishop, two professors of theology and two of us, including myself, earning degrees in theology at SVS but not priesthood. So I guess we were all quite focused in various ways!

The very next year, in 1982, I felt a need to know if 'God is really real' and my priest who was a priest-monk himself said, 'Go to Mount Athos, and also Father Sophrony's monastery in Essex, England.' So I did. I stayed on the Holy Mountain a total of fourteen months over a ten-year period, mostly at Filotheou. I would like to offer some recollections of those things we call 'miracles' that God uses to increase our faith and instruct us.

Like most visitors, I took the boat to Daphne and then went to Karyes. On the way, huge monasteries came into view from the boat, like majestic ancient castles. That evening, my first formal encounter with an Athonite monk was with Elder Aimilianos, Abbot of Simonopetra. I was invited into his cell and my first naive question as a spiritual 'tourist' was, 'Which is the best monastery for me to visit?' Gerontas said to me, 'Visit them all and stay at the one where a flame is felt in your heart.' That first night, spent at Simonopetra, an unusual thing happened, something that would become more common over the next many months. I had bought a small cassette recorder to tape the beautiful chanting but when I was shown into my room and about to go to vespers, I was chagrined to find I had forgotten batteries! Just as I had that thought, looking at the recorder in my hand, my foot kicked something under the bed.

There was a brand-new pack of AA batteries that someone had dropped. God was listening?

My journey was starting. The next months carried me by boat, monastery truck, mule or by foot to various monasteries and sketes; but first I arrived at Filotheou and I knew I had found my monastery for future visits. The Elder Ephraim seemed to me to be the incarnation of the first century apostles, his kindness and visage.

During my first days at Filotheou, Father L, an older monk, agreed to hear my 'theological' questions. I was told that he was 'enclosed' (*enclistos*), not leaving his cell often, his work being deeper prayer. We sat in a nice 'study' near the trapeza and I had my long list of questions, expecting profound answers as to who God really was. After eight or nine very serious questions, Father L leaned back and said, 'You are a typical Westerner, you have questions before you have had any experience'. That was lesson number one.

I had been at Filotheou a while by now. On this evening there was to be a festal vigil for the next day, so at the small compline (short prayers after the meal), there were lots of visitors. I was in the far back corner outside of the front nave. I looked over at the Elder Ephraim about twenty-five feet to the right front. Suddenly I had a very strange and unsettling thought. I knew it was not my thought because it startled me. At that moment, Father E who was in the far-right corner, with dozens of pilgrims between us, turned and stared right at me. He then got up and walked into the front of the church and I lost sight of him. That night about an hour later I was in my cell getting ready to sleep for a bit and heard a knock on my door. Father E, one of two in charge of the monastery under the Abbot, appeared and his first words were, 'You know that thought you had?' and he described exactly what it was and how it related to certain of my passions that I had to fight against. This sort of discernment became part of my experience on Mount Athos during my time there.

PL. 39 *Pilgrim accommodation, Hilandar Monastery*

A curious thing happened while working one afternoon. I had noticed that two Greek-Canadian novices were sharing the same room, which was not usual. One of the monks explained that since they were so young (in their teens), the demons wanted to scare them back to Canada, make them quit the hard monastic life. While in their separate rooms, at night, they would be 'attacked' by loud laughter and their beds would shake and jump off the floor violently. They were so frightened that the Elder allowed them to keep each other company for a while. I understood quite clearly that the calling to be a monastic was not an easy thing.

Another night, at 1 a.m., I went for the usual blessing to start church which lasted until about 5 a.m. Gerontas Ephraim held his hand up to bless me so I could go to my 'stall'. But this time he didn't look at me with a kind smile and pat me on the head as usual. He was staring into the air above my head while blessing me, transfixed as if I were not there. As he exhaled a powerful fragrance wafted over my face. I was startled and pulled back and audibly made a sound, 'Oh!' I did not understand what was happening. I had heard about fragrant relics and myrrh-streaming icons but wondered why these realities were not more present in Christian communities back home. What was different about these monasteries? A good question.

At this point I asked Gerontas Ephraim if I could leave my large backpack and complete what Gerontas Aimilianos advised, to 'visit them all', even though, amazingly, I had already found 'the one where a flame is felt in your heart'. He also gave me a 300-knot prayer rope. I stayed for a month before going on a trip around the entire peninsula to see other monasteries and sketes. The prayer rope had the sweet scent of 'myrrh' from the moment I took it from his hand. The scent vanished when I left. The fragrance did not return even when I got back the next month to Filotheou. I stayed another few months before returning to 'the world' and America.

But back to that trip, by foot around the Mountain. I met a wizened little monk on a boat going from Iviron to the far end of the peninsula. He suddenly had the urge to tell me a story: 'I was going to a feast day at a large monastery and had to return late at night. It had been raining heavily. The river that I had crossed earlier in the day was swollen and raging with broken tree branches carried along. The path was flooded and I did not know what to do. I prayed, took off my shoes to carry as I waded across, but suddenly I fell asleep. Just as suddenly, I awoke to find myself on the other side of the river with

my shoes next to me.' He made me understand that an angel had carried him across. Another lesson, we need to hear these stories of Orthodox life to carry us through future storms.

On the other side of the peninsula, I spent the night at Grigoriou monastery, where the Abbot Gregorios was one of the rare ones to speak English. I had a wonderful conversation with the Abbot. 'As far as work as a lay person in the Orthodox Church in the USA, which is weak, Protestantized and lukewarm; the most important work now is to help develop monasteries there. Without a strong monastic life, Christian life will remain shallow. You must pray for help from Mount Athos for America and ask that we send holy monks and confessors regularly for two to four months as Father D did from Simonopetra. Invite us. In ten to twenty years we will be sending good monks and confessors to stay in the US and build monasteries. The strength of Orthodoxy today lies in the Holy Mountain'.

The next evening at Dionysiou monastery, I talked with Father John, an elderly Greek-American monk, retired American Navy. A wonderfully cheerful and grand-fatherly person, he had been there many years. As we were sitting in the trapeza having a snack, suddenly we heard a great commotion out in the courtyard. Loud talking and a scuffle. Father John calmly said, 'Maybe someone is demon possessed, let's go see'. What an odd comment to make! Instead, it turned out to be an all-night drama involving a large yacht in the dock below. A wealthy family had sent detectives to go to Dionysiou under the guise of 'pious pilgrims' and kidnap their wayward son who wanted to be a novice monk. The Abbot even asked me, as a visitor, if I had a camera so they could photograph the 'detective pilgrims' to show to authorities in Karyes. The visitors left the next morning without the young novice.

From there I went to St Paul's monastery marvelling at the relics: the gifts of the Magi, gold, frankincense and myrrh; I never knew they looked like that! The hand of Mary Magdalene still covered with soft brown skin, warm to the touch (although the latter could have been at Simonos Petra, in retrospect). As a former Protestant I did not imagine that the Church had kept such things. I met Father D while there and he offered to take me up to the skete of St Anne, a collection of monks in a 'village' of monastics living separately but sharing a church together. He wanted to visit his friend, a solitary monk, Father G, who had just moved into an old abandoned cottage he was renovating. We met him high up the mountain and they wanted to take a walk along the steep trail; the terrain went up on the left and down on the right quite precipitously. A beautiful view of the sea far below, no trees in sight. I looked down and saw a broken-down fence and some hand-forged nails sticking out loose on the ground. As they were walking about fifteen feet ahead of me, conversing with each other, not looking back at me, I had the thought, 'I wish I could take one of those nails home as a souvenir.' At that moment Father G turned around and looked at me saying, 'Take it, you can have it.' I have it here in my study. If God wanted to get my attention, He was doing a good job of it.

Another time I was visiting Konstamonitou, inland from the sea. It had no roads for vehicles. The Abbot was a spiritual child of Elder Ephraim of Filotheou. There were not many monks at that time. It was the end of that visit to Mount Athos and I was leaving back to Thessaloniki. But there was a bus strike and we had to wait. No one could leave the Holy Mountain including the Abbot. We all were gathered together at the boat dock waiting for the boat to Ouranoupolis, the first town back in 'the world' as they called it. I was walking around outside with about twenty-five or so other visitors and monks. I smelled a wonderful strong fragrance in the air. I asked someone, 'Is there a flowering tree nearby, what is that fragrance?' He replied, 'It's the myrrh-streaming icon inside'. I ran up the steps into the room above the dock and found the Abbot sitting by an icon. It was on a small table and hundreds of large drops of a thick, oily substance were accumulating on the face. They were running down onto a thick wad of cotton wrapped around the base of this icon of Christ and the Theotokos. I asked the Elder how this was happening and he told me God gives us this gift on special days to encourage our faith. As I expressed amazement at it, he cautioned me not to talk too much about miracles to people because it would not be understood easily. He said the goal of the Christian life is to repent and pray, not see miracles.

A couple of months later I was walking to St Panteleimon monastery with an American monk, from Simonopetra. We went to greet the Patriarch of Russia coming by Greek battleship escort, a state visit. There were hardly any visitors, just the monks and his patriarchal choir and attendants. This was just before 1985-86 when the monastery was allowed more monks from Russia and began to grow. The antiphonal choir was quite a contrast with the few resident monks on one side and the patriarchal choir on the other. The monastery was just holding on due to the communist regime in the USSR. I remember picking up a few Tsarist Russian military coat buttons, an eagle on them, from the ashes of the burnt-out guest building, long since abandoned.

I also met monk Daniel in the upper 'desert' of Mount Athos, a Romanian hermit living in a cave. The only reason I went to Kerasia, so far above the sea on the side of the mountain, was that I met a retired Greek Air Force officer who invited me along as he knew the monk. I was impressed with his joyful expression and animated voice. Simple clothing, sleeves made from cotton bath towels on his ragged cassock. He ate wild greens and the few tin cans of 'pachsimadi' (dried bread) brought occasionally to him by the monastery that he was attached to far below. His cave was walled up with a door. About five feet deep by ten feet long, it had a couple of boards with the head angled up at one end as a bed. No mattress. Only his icon corner and books were in the 'room'. How did he live here for fifty years after his fellow monk died? Yet nothing but a joyful and peaceful presence was felt by listening to him.

Back at Filotheou, Father T had returned from the mainland with Father Stavros of Rethimno (in Crete) carrying in procession a large piece of the True Cross that had been in his family. (His is an amazing story, well known.) I have a photo of the procession. I found out that Father T, second in charge at Filotheou under Gerontas Ephraim, had been healed of a serious illness by this piece of the True Cross. He had been sent out of the monastery to correct a serious bowel problem, and the doctors in the hospital on the day of the surgery had told him he had a fifty per cent chance of survival. He had been sick for years. He met Father Stavros (well known for his healing ministry in Greece) that day in the hospital and was asked if he wanted to see if God would fix it. And God did. The doctors didn't know what to do except send him home and cancel the surgery. So here he was in procession into the church in Filotheou with many monks and visitors lining up the next day to be healed of various ailments. My turn came because I had had a sharp pain in my lower left side for the past year and my doctor had no idea as to what it was. I went into the side chapel and stood in front of Father Stavros. I started to show him where the problem was and he said, in the simple Greek I could understand, 'Don't tell me, the Cross will diagnose, it will stick (tha collai)', and he started, after prayers, to touch the Cross to my head, ears, eyes, methodically working his way down my body. Sure enough, it got to the painful spot, and it stuck! He said, 'It is here.' The pain never came back.

There were many wonderful visits and experiences over these ten years.

(As I understand the Greek word for 'miracle', it means simply a 'wonderful thing' which we should see in everything God gives to us. No need to overturn the laws of nature all the time!) We learn to pay attention in a heightened way when visiting these monastics.

A few more stories. A visit with Father (St) Paisios was arranged by two monks at Filotheou. We started walking, a long way by dirt road but just outside of Filotheou, this was far from his cottage, yet we found him already on the road almost as if we were expected. I had talked with him four years earlier, at his cottage outside of Karyes about the importance of Baptism, where he told me, in his common sense way, 'It is like plugging an electric cord into the sun and the energy of the Holy Spirit can flow down to us.' This time, on the road, his white hair actually seemed to be glowing in the sun around his face. I remember having an impression of seeing St John the Baptist at that moment. We talked for about half an hour with great advice on what to do if I wanted to marry although first he asked me if I wanted to be a monk. 'No? OK, no obstacle, but marry soon and don't marry anyone under twenty years old. A young woman needs experience apart from her parents to be ready.' And he gave me much more advice. Curiously my wife, whom I met years later, was at the time exactly twenty.

Forward to 1992 and a feast day at Iviron monastery. The feast of the Portaitissa icon, a miraculous icon with a long history. I had heard the stories of how this huge icon in the main part of the large church would foretell events by the swinging of the large oil lampada hanging before it. I heard that the Second World War was foretold by the oil lamp swinging in an erratic pattern for two weeks before the outbreak. The lamp was similarly supposed to warn of earthquakes. But I did not expect to see such a thing myself (they were just stories, right?). There were many of us visitors and monks from around the monastery present. I remember that we took the huge icon off of the iconostasis and two men at a time carried it up into the hills above to be venerated by monks in sketes. We returned to the monastery and replaced it. We had a wonderful festal meal in the large trapeza. I still remember the power of all the men's voices singing after we finished. We then filed out into the courtyard in front of the church. Suddenly a young novice came running out of the church and exclaimed, 'It is swinging, it is swinging!' We all went in and sure enough, it was. A big arc of several feet. It kept going as we watched. The laws of physics didn't seem to slow it down. The Abbot stood behind us as we all watched and

simply but profoundly said, 'It is the finger of an angel pushing the lampada; it is God celebrating with us'. So it was true. But this was not enough for a young monk I knew from Filotheou, he had to test it. After everyone had left, just three of us remained entranced by the sight of it. We were basically waiting for it to slow down when he reached up and stopped the lampada. It was still. We waited. And it started swinging again all by itself.

I met Father M again, a Great Schema monk formerly at Filotheou now living at a small skete called Marouda, above Karyes. He said, 'We shouldn't pay much attention to the "last days" talk or even writings. It distracts us from our real work as Christians – prayer, obeying the Commandments, going to Communion in Church, and such. A number of young novices went to a big monastery here at Athos because these are the "last days". Their foundation as monks is shallow because their motivation is such. In twenty or thirty years they will grow weak and perhaps leave monasticism'.

Father PA talked about these 'last days' as well. 'Our work now is especially to repent and pray, go to Church, take Communion. There will be few physical martyrdoms to come, a great persecution like that will not occur. The battle will be inward, mentally and spiritually, a "noetic martyrdom". Strive to keep your thoughts pure, your mind clear of passionate influences to be able to discern what is occurring'.

This last story I am hesitant to relate, not because it is not valuable, but because it has to do with the 'hearing of a word from an angel or a saint' and what that could mean to us ordinary people. As a Protestant on the college campus, I had been very upset and sceptical when the Evangelical students would talk about their personal relationship to Jesus, and say things like, 'The Lord told me …', or 'God spoke to me and said to do …'. I was always turned off by the seeming delusional thinking of Christians. I had rejected Christianity for years since my confirmation at age thirteen as a Congregational Protestant. It was an unfortunate experience when my minister, who had been educated at Yale Divinity School, told me after my catechism, and my confession that, 'I didn't believe in God', that, 'It's ok, you can join anyway'. Right then I thought all religion was false and that Christians didn't know what they were talking about. No real experience. Didn't someone say, 'I am the truth'? But I hadn't found that in any Christian. Probably my own blind judgmental attitude; Orthodox Christians do not have a monopoly on 'goodness', but can only claim the fullness of truth.

As a new Orthodox Christian, I had read of how the saints, elders in our monasteries, and spiritual fathers, if free of the passions, could truly 'hear God's voice' and give someone if God wills it (it's not automatic or magic) a true 'word' as it is called. A true understanding of God's will for each of us, at that moment, can be given. For sure. This seemed a real leap of faith for me. They said that these people would take the first word to come to their mind and consider it the word of God for that person or themselves. Hard for me to trust.

But this is what happened to me when I visited St Panteleimon monastery in 1992. I went with a friend as we were both staying at Filotheou. We both wanted to venerate the relics of St Silouan, probably my favourite saint. I came into Orthodoxy primarily reading Father (now St) Sophrony's books on St Silouan. I knew his story thoroughly and had spent many months at St John the Baptist Monastery in Essex, England over the years. It was like home to me spiritually. Of course, Father Sophrony had been a monk on Mount Athos for many years before starting his monastery in England.

We entered the monastery and were taken by the Abbot, a hieromonk, into the room with the many relics. The skull of St Silouan was a prized relic in the reliquary venerated by many visitors. He was revered around the world because of Father Sophrony's popular books. I stood in front of the box holding the skull on a tall wooden pedestal and noticed the colour, deep yellow and the large letters engraved somehow on his forehead in Russian, 'Silouan'. I leaned over and kissed his forehead and a strange thing happened that I would never think of doing because it would be inappropriate or even rude. Without any premeditation at all, no thought whatsoever, I turned very matter-of-factly and said to the Abbot, 'May I have a piece of the relic?' I think in Yiddish they call it 'chutzpah'. I felt very calm and totally normal as the priest without hesitation replied, 'Of course'. My friend was visibly unnerved. How could I be so rude? The priest returned with pliers and as if this was an everyday and reasonable request, lifted the entire skull out of the box and broke off a piece of bone the size of half of my little finger. I took it and put it away thinking nothing unusual had happened.

The confirmation for me that God does act in such mysterious ways came when I was on the way home to America, stopping at Father Sophrony's monastery for the last time (1992 was my last trip to Europe) and showed the relic to Father Raphael who was quite surprised. They supposedly had the only piece of relic, as I was led to believe at the time, all but the skull lost in the charnel house? So Father Raphael asked me if I would give a piece of it to their monastery and he went to get permission from Father Sophrony to do so. He came back and relayed the message: 'No, St Silouan wants to go to America'. So I guess my 'rude' request was from God. I somehow now knew God 'Is' and my youthful agnosticism dissolved away more completely. We sawed the relic into three pieces and I gave one portion to a friend and one to a bishop in America, along with the chips I had saved to various monks and monasteries in the US.

I do wonder sometimes why God gives us such amazing confirmation of our faith but then I remember St Sophrony's words in his book on St Silouan: 'At the outset man is drawn to God by the gift of grace; and once attracted, a prolonged period of testing sets in. His freedom as a man and his trust in God are put to the test – sometimes "harshly". At the initial stage of his conversion his prayers, urgent or not so urgent, are miraculously granted almost before they are uttered'. That's where I am now, the easy gifts of grace lessened. It is time to grow up spiritually and if the Saints had to struggle and Christ's way is that of the Cross, then we have to follow. We cannot have consolation like in the beginning all the time. He doesn't leave us with blind faith, but can give us *empiria*, experience. The 'deposit' or 'earnest' (*arravon*) of things unseen as Scripture promises. As Corinthians 1:21-22 says, 'Now it is God who makes both us and you stand firm in Christ. He anointed us, set his seal of ownership on us, and put his Spirit in our hearts as a deposit, guaranteeing what is to come.' (See also Cor 2: 5:5; Eph1:13-14.) Not only our minds, our rational faculty, but our hearts are touched. This is where He speaks to us in that special way, beyond the merely 'scholastic'. Wasn't it Thomas Aquinas who said at the end of his brilliant life's work that it was all merely 'straw' (*stromata*)?

To end, I believe through the experiences on Mount Athos which many of us have had, that God 'talks' to us in many ways, through his Saints, both in the past and living now.

PL. 41 *Cell of St Paisios, Panagouda*

Fifty-Four Years as an Athonite Pilgrim

KALLISTOS WARE

'A high mountain apart'

Among all the sacred places on this earth, the Holy Mountain of Athos is the one that I personally find most immediately attractive. Since my first visit in 1961, I have been drawn back to the 'mountain of monks' more frequently than I can now remember: perhaps some fifteen times, possibly more often. With good reason Athos has been styled 'the monastic magnet', and certainly its magnetic force is something I have felt continually since my initial pilgrimage fifty-four years ago, and indeed for a number of years before that.

During those fifty-four years, what have I come to understand about the inner meaning and the spiritual message of the Holy Mountain? What changes have I seen? What have I come to regard as its contribution to the wider community of the outside world, throughout the Church as a whole and, indeed, beyond its boundaries? 'We know that when any one of us falls, he falls alone', states Aleksei Khomiakov, 'but no one is saved alone'. How, then, do the monks of Athos contribute to the salvation of others?

Let me begin with what has been for me the single most memorable experience on the Holy Mountain, when I ascended alone during the night to the summit of Athos in summer 1971. My intention was to reach the peak at sunrise. I was about to set out from St Anne's around 10 p.m., when there was a sudden and violent fall of rain; and I wondered if it might be prudent to postpone my journey. 'Go', said Father Elias, the monk with whom I was staying, 'you may not ever again have another such opportunity. And if you go, you will never forget your experience'. I am glad that I took his advice. In fact there was no more rain that night.

It was a lengthy climb. My starting point at St Anne's was about 300 metres above sea level, but to reach the summit I had to mount upwards for another 1,700 metres or more. I had chosen a night when there was a full moon, but in practice the moon was less helpful than I had expected; for I had forgotten that much of the walk was through thick woods where the moonlight could not penetrate. My immediate objective was the little chapel of the Panaghia, about 500 metres below the summit, where I intended to rest before embarking on the final stages of the ascent. I came out from the woods into a rocky wilderness where the chapel ought to have been, but I could not see it anywhere. To make matters worse, I lost the path. Moonlight has the effect of flattening the landscape and making everything appear different. Blundering about in confusion for many minutes, eventually I sat down defeated. Then I looked up and saw to my surprise the chapel no more than 200 metres away. How strange that I had not noticed it before!

After a short sleep on the chapel floor and a drink of cool water from the nearby cistern, I set out in the pale morning light for the peak of the Holy Mountain. The path is good, and there is no danger at all as long as one does not wander from it. But I kept in mind that, not long before, three Germans had left the proper route and fallen to their deaths. I arrived at the summit just as I had hoped, at the exact moment when the sun emerged in the east from the low clouds across the sea.

I was confronted by an astonishing spectacle. After gazing for some time at the rising sun in the east, I turned and looked northward, and saw the whole Athonite peninsula, thousands of metres below me, stretching away towards the mainland. It was like a relief map, with rocks and paths standing out with an amazing clarity. I could distinguish all the paths that I had been following for the past ten days, and even the exact points where I had missed the right turning (for in those days there were few effective signposts). Then, with my back to the rising sun, I looked westward, once more over the sea. The sight that met me was something I had never expected, and it will always remain etched in my memory. I saw the shadow of the Holy Mountain as a great pyra-

mid of darkness, extending many miles over the sea and shrinking perceptibly as the sun behind my back rose higher. Surely there are few places in the world where such a phenomenon can be seen.

As I stood in this way, alone at sunrise in the piercing cold on the top of Mount Athos, beside the (then) ruined chapel of the Transfiguration, I was given a dim inkling of the significance of the Mountain as a holy sanctuary, as a point in sacred space, a 'thin place' where the wall of partition between earth and heaven, between the present age and the Age to come, becomes so attenuated as to be virtually transparent.

Wolves, snakes, and frogs

I have begun these recollections of my visits to Athos over fifty-four years by speaking of the Mountain itself, and this I have done for an important reason. Athos is indeed a mountain full of holy persons, of dedicated monks; and of this I shall speak in a moment. It is also a Mountain full of holy objects, of churches and chapels, icons, relics, chalices, crosses, and illuminated Gospel books. But, beside all this, it is more fundamentally in itself a holy mountain. While admiring the saints and ascetics who have dwelt and still dwell there, and while rejoicing in the spiritual beauty of the many works of art that it contains, we need also to appreciate the physical reality of the Mountain as such, the intrinsic sacredness of the material environment in which these persons and objects are to be found. In the words of Father Nikon (1875-1963), the hermit of Karoulia who inspired the English translation of the Philokalia, 'Here every stone breathes prayers'. In common with other holy places – such as Jerusalem and Patmos, Iona and Walsingham – the Holy Mountain of Athos acts as a sacrament of God's presence, as a burning glass concentrating the rays of the spiritual Sun with an especial intensity, manifesting the immediacy of the Eternal.

To appreciate this physical reality, this intrinsic sacredness, the best way for the pilgrim is to travel on foot – not to be driven in a minibus or Land Rover but to walk, if possible alone. This will frequently prove exhausting. The ancient mule paths are often steep, sometimes neglected, full of loose, sharp stones and overgrown with brambles. In summer the pilgrim will inevitably suffer from heat and thirst. But only so will he come face to face with the basic reality of Athos as a centre of stillness, a shrine of the Divine Presence.

Along with the holiness of the Mountain, the pilgrim who travels on foot will also be struck by its outstanding natural beauty. Because of the presence of streams on every side and the absence of marauding goats, Athos – especially in springtime – is a veritable paradise. There are meadows bright with wild flowers, and trees covered with blossom; and everywhere there is the surrounding sea, with waves breaking over the rocks. Prince Mishkin's words come to mind, in Dostoevsky's novel *The Idiot*: 'Beauty will save the world'.

This Athonite beauty is not vacant and static, but it is full of sounds and movement; for the Mountain is a refuge for many living creatures, non-human as well as human. On my earlier visits, as I set off to walk alone through the more remote uplands, the monks warned me to beware of the wolves. I never saw any, but doubtless they saw me as they looked watchfully from the thick undergrowth beside the paths. I am told that there are now no more wolves on Athos, because they have all been shot. This is in some respects a pity, for wolves in their own way are hesychasts, seeking solitude and avoiding contact with humans; and so their continuing presence was an assurance that the Mountain has not ceased to be a place of seclusion.

While I have never seen any wolves on my Athonite wanderings, I have twice met wild boar. The first occasion was just outside the skete of the Prophet Elijah. The second was in the deserted region above the Serbian monastery of Chilandar, on the path leading to Chromitsa, close to the border with Ouranoupolis. Here I encountered a whole family, father, mother, and two youngsters. Not more than fifty metres away, all four of them stopped in their tracks and stared at me, with curiosity but without apparent hostility. After I greeted them, they continued peacefully on their way, disappearing among the bushes.

The solitary walker will also come across snakes, both great and small, which abound on the Holy Mountain. When I was staying for several weeks at Chilandar, working on the English translation of the Philokalia with my friends Gerald Palmer and Philip Sherrard – both frequent visitors to Athos – I used to go alone for a walk each afternoon in the surrounding woods. Every day, in exactly the same place on the path, I met a snake some three metres long, basking in the sunshine. On the first day I banged on the ground with my staff, but he showed no inclination to move, until I had addressed him politely, asking him to let me through. Then he slid into a gap in the adjoining wall; but as soon as I had passed I heard a swishing sound immediately behind me, as he slid out once more to resume his place in the sun. On the second day I had no

PL.43 *On the coastal path to Agiou Pavlou (St Paul's)*

need to bang on the ground, for as soon as I asked him he moved out of the way. On the third day I did not even have to ask, much less to bang on the ground, for of his own accord he moved aside as soon as he saw me approaching. Such is the rapport with the realm of nature that even a town-dweller such as myself can quickly establish during visits to the Mountain. The monks who live there permanently, especially the hermits, frequently build up a relationship that is far closer. The many stories in monastic sources about beasts and saints are not mere legends.

Not all my encounters with Athonite snakes have been as benign as my acquaintance with the snake of Chilandar. Once, in one of the more solitary regions of the Mountain, I heard nearby a strange sound, and I turned aside from the path to discover the cause. A rabbit had come down to a pool to drink and a large water snake had seized hold of its head and was gradually swallowing it whole, as the rabbit screamed aloud. I took note that it would be sensible not to bathe in isolated pools on the Mountain. The monks may not eat meat, but there are other residents on Athos who do so.

I wondered at the time whether I should intervene to try and save the rabbit, but I decided that it was not my business to meddle in the affairs of Athonite wildlife. I bore in mind the experience of a friend of mine who was making his way through the woods on the Mountain in the company of a monk. My friend has the ability to imitate bird song; and since the Athonite woods are full of birds he practised this gift as the two of them walked together. He called out to the birds and the birds duly replied. In tones of disapproval, the monk said to him: 'Would you mind not doing that?' 'Why, what's wrong?' asked my friend. And the monk replied severely, 'You are disturbing the natural order'.

Along with the snakes and birds, Athos is home to innumerable frogs. I know few sounds in nature as attractive as the singing of frogs, and Athos is one of the best places in which to enjoy batrachian harmony. Once I was staying, around the season of Pentecost, at the skete (or monastic village) of St Anne's. Here each of the scattered dwellings has a garden, with its own cistern and its own contingent of melodious frogs. As I sat on a balcony around sunset, first I could hear the frogs many metres below me on the steep hillside, and then came an answering group many metres above. Others joined in from various cisterns on either side, and before long the whole evening was alive with frog-sourced music. I wished that it would never end.

There is an Athonite anecdote, typical of the monastic sense of humour, about a group of monks who were celebrating the morning service. The frogs in the cistern outside were making an astonishing noise. So the superior went out of the chapel and said: 'Frogs! We've just ended the Midnight Office and are about to begin matins. Would you mind keeping quiet until we've finished?' Whereupon the frogs replied: 'We've just ended matins and we are about to begin the First Hour. Would you mind keeping quiet until we've finished!'

Decline and renewal: threats and hopes

Having reflected on the natural environment, both inanimate and animate, of the Holy Mountain of Athos, let us turn our attention to the monks themselves. I am grateful that, on my first visit in 1961, I was in time to see Athos in what may be termed its 'pre-industrial era'. There were at that time virtually no roads suitable for vehicles, and indeed no actual vehicles to use such roads. The pilgrim, arriving at the port of Daphne, did not find a bus to take him up to the monastic capital of Karyes; he had to walk. But coming events cast their shadow before: on my second visit, in 1962, I found that a vehicle road from port to capital was under construction, in preparation for the celebrations of the Athonite millennium in 1963. In 1961 the only vehicle road was from the Russian monastery of St Panteleimon, leading up far above to the woods that belonged to the monastery. The community had a lorry to bring down timber to the harbour. Through the modest sale of this timber the Russian monks hoped to raise a little money, for their economic position at that time was altogether dire. This road, however, did not connect St Panteleimon with any of the other monasteries. With this one exception, I do not think that in 1961 any monastery possessed a lorry, Jeep, or Land Rover. I was told that the Serbian monastery had a tractor donated by Tito, but I never saw it.

Alas! Today the situation has changed beyond recognition. A network of vehicular roads – many of them ugly gashes across the hillside – now joins all the twenty 'ruling' monasteries to one another, with the sole exceptions (as far as I know) of Grigoriou and Dionysiou, which nevertheless have outlets immediately on to the sea. Vehicles are to be found everywhere. The monks are surprised that I deliberately choose, whenever possible, to walk from one monastery to another, not out of voluntary asceticism, but because of the delight which such walks afford. They consider that this behaviour is unsuitable for a bishop.

Other aspects of the 'pre-industrial era' on Athos remain clearly in my memory. There was no electricity, and lighting was provided by oil lamps or candles. An electric system had been installed in Vatopedi in the 1920s or 1930s, but when I visited in 1961 it no longer worked. There was no running hot water in the monasteries; it had to be heated on a cauldron balanced on a primus stove. The monasteries were not connected directly to the outside world by telephone, although there was a primitive and inefficient telephone system joining the monasteries to each other. I believe that this was set up during the German occupation in the Second World War. It is easy to look back with nostalgia to the days of Athonite oil lamps, but more modern devices certainly have advantages from a practical point of view. There is, after all, nothing intrinsically numinous about primus stoves and oil lamps.

Coming to Athos in 1961, all around me I saw evidence of decline. The monks constituted a shrinking and ageing population. Everywhere I was surrounded by grey beards, while the few beards that were black stood out as a marked exception. The fall in numbers was by no means new, but had started before the First World War. In 1903 there were 7,432 monks, more than half of them non-Greeks. By 1913 the number had dropped to 6,345: this was due mainly to the expulsion of some 800 Russian monks in the course of the dispute concerning 'Glorifiers of the Name' (Imyaslavtsy). Following the 1917 revolution, no more recruits came from Russia, and few Greeks chose to join the Athonite monasteries; in consequence, by 1943 there were only 2,878 monks, and by 1959 the number had fallen to 1,641. A low point was reached in 1971, by which time there were only 1,145. Most of these were over sixty years of age, and so there was every prospect that the decrease would continue.

Surprisingly this did not happen. In 1972, for the first time since 1914, the number of monks actually increased, rising by a figure of one from 1,145 to 1,146. This upward movement has steadily continued since then, and today there are perhaps 2,000 monks on the Mountain. More importantly, these are not predominantly elderly, but are distributed more or less evenly among the different age groups. Indeed, there are monasteries where it is difficult to discover a grey beard among the serried ranks of black whiskers. Recently the overall numbers have ceased to grow noticeably; there has, however, been no significant diminution.

This growth in numbers has been accompanied by a major alteration of spiritual atmosphere in the different communities. In almost all the monas- teries that I visited during my visits in the 1960s, on a practical level there was a lack of hope among the monks, an absence of any expectation that the demographic situation would improve. Those with whom I spoke did not doubt that the Mountain enjoyed the special blessing of Christ and His Mother; but they viewed the future with quiet resignation rather than with any sense of confidence. I remember, for example, a conversation I had in 1968 with Father Evdokimos, the senior epitropos in the monastery of Filotheou (it was at that time idiorrhythmic). 'We are seventeen monks here', he said, 'but we are mostly old men, and so all the work has to be done by about three or four. I am afraid that Athos will soon become like the monasteries of Egypt – just ruins'. (In fact since then there has been a notable revival of monasticism in the Coptic Church of Egypt; but that is another story.)

I do not hear any of the Athonite monks speaking today in the way that Father Evdokimos did fifty years ago. Today, combined with the quest for inner stillness, there is among the monks a sense of practical purpose, of dynamic energy. Sometimes one hears the phrase 'springtime in the garden of the Panaghia', and this aptly describes the prevailing mood. Everywhere buildings are being restored – sometimes, I fear, unwisely: there was a disastrous example some time ago at Dionysiou when a substantial part of the attractive external balconies was destroyed. But at any rate there are no longer the signs of structural decay that were all too apparent in the 1960s. There is better sanitation in the quarters both of the monks and of the visitors; there are proper washing facilities, with hot water, and there is electric light. In most monasteries there is a welcome improvement in the cooking: no longer do lukewarm beans form the main staple of the diet, but eggs, green salads, and fresh fruit are usually provided.

As for the monks themselves, there has been an evident change in educational level. In 1961, throughout the whole of Athos, I doubt whether more than a dozen monks had received a university education. Today in virtually every community there are members with university degrees – not exclusively in theology but often in subjects such as medicine, law, or politics – and there are a number who have studied outside Greece in western centres of learning. Several are authors of substantial doctrinal texts. Some of us, recalling the humble simplicity and the purity of the vision found so notably among the monks of an earlier era, may feel that there has been a certain loss. Needless to say, university education does not necessarily produce good monks. Yet so long as Athos contained virtually no monks who had pursued higher studies,

it was difficult for the Mountain to provide the articulate inspiration and leadership that are so greatly needed by the Church at large.

One of the most encouraging changes has been in the liturgical worship on Athos. In the 1960s, despite the lack of younger monks, the daily round of services was conscientiously performed in full; but often this was done in a hurried and perfunctory manner. A non-Orthodox visitor said to me in 1961, 'They perform their worship as a duty, but without joy'. I thought this unduly harsh, but I saw his point. Now, however, in almost every monastic house the outward prayer life is markedly different. The standard of singing is greatly improved; the reading of the Psalms is more intelligible; the ceremonial actions are carried out with greater reverence; there is less talking in church.

Most important of all, there has been a decisive revival of frequent communion. When I first visited the Mountain in 1961, it was the practice almost everywhere for the monks to receive the sacrament no more than once every forty days, that is to say, ten times a year, even though the Liturgy was celebrated daily, except in Lent. It was also the custom for them to observe before communion a strict fast of two or three days, without any use of oil in cooking. Since oil is allowed on all Saturdays throughout the year, with the sole exception of Holy Saturday (the Saturday immediately before Easter), this meant that, apart from Easter day, the monks never received communion on Sunday, but as a rule on Saturday. This was surely a strange anomaly.

On my first visit to Athos, I attended the feast of the Nativity of the Mother of God (8/21 September) at the Great Lavra. If I recall rightly, the feast fell on a Sunday. There was an all-night vigil, with the participation of some eight priests and four deacons. But, when we came to the Liturgy, this was served by a single priest, without a deacon. At the moment of Holy Communion, out of a congregation of about 150, monks and lay pilgrims, to my astonishment not a single person came forward to receive the sacrament. I had a sad feeling of anticlimax. Today it is unthinkable that this should happen at a great feast in any of the main Athonite houses. At Simonos Petras, for example, it is the norm for lay monks to receive Holy Communion two or three times a week. Throughout the Mountain there has been a true Eucharistic renaissance.

What has been the main reason for this increase in the number of monks on the Holy Mountain, and for the renewal of the spiritual and liturgical life? Among the various possible answers, the most significant reason in my view has been the presence on Athos, over the past fifty years, of charismatic elders

(*gerontes*), endowed with the gifts of discernment and pastoral guidance. The ministry of the abba (or 'father in God') has been a constant feature of Eastern monasticism from the time of the first monks such as St Antony and St Makarios of Egypt in the fourth century up to the present day; but there have been periods of decline followed by periods of revival. On Athos the second half of the twentieth century has definitely been a period of revival. Prominent examples of such charismatic elders, from the 1960s onwards, are Father Vasileios at Stavronikita and Iviron, Father Aimilianos at Simonos Petras, Father George at Grigoriou, and Father Ephrem at Filotheou (he has more recently established some sixteen monasteries in North America). It is a striking fact that, when Athonite monasteries have revived, this has been particularly in houses where the abbot is endowed with the gift of eldership. Today young people drawn to the monastic life are attracted not so much by the abbey as by the abba. They are looking, not primarily for a famous house with a distinguished history, but for a personal guide.

Spiritual fathers on the Holy Mountain are of course to be found not only in the main monasteries but in the sketes such as Great and Little St Anne's and Kafsokalyvia. One such geronta, in the middle of the twentieth century, was Father (now Saint) Joseph of New Skete (1898–1959). He gathered round himself a group of disciples who practised the Jesus Prayer with special devotion. Setting out from New Skete, his followers have played an important role throughout the Mountain and elsewhere. More recently, a greatly revered elder was the hermit Paisios (1924–94), who was glorified as a saint in 2015. I shall never forget the two hours that I spent with him in 1971, when we spoke at length about St Isaac the Syrian. I was greatly struck by his lightness of heart and his spirit of joy.

Guarding the walls

What, finally, has been the contribution of the Holy Mountain to the outside world? Although, as already noted, there are now well-educated monks on Athos who are authors of serious spiritual works, the Holy Mountain is by no means a centre of scholarship, in any way comparable to the Benedictine Maurist congregation in eighteenth-century France. What is said by Father Theoklitos of Dionysiou, a leading Athonite spokesman in the mid-twentieth century, is basically true, although somewhat overstated:

In the Eastern Church, the existence of the 'scholar' monk is quite unknown … The monk finds no justification, under the ascetic and mystical theology that has been developed by the Fathers, except as a worker of virtue, as a contemplative soul called by God, giving to his brethren in Christ, because of his love for them, out of the abundance of his experience of the divine … Hence, the cell of the monk is not a room for scholarly research and writing, but a place for prayer, work, meditation and the tempering of the soul for special spiritual struggles, in an unworldly, solitary, quiet region.

Much more important than scholarship and literary work is the provision of hospitality by the Athonite monasteries. From the earliest beginnings of monasticism this has been seen, in both East and West, as an integral part of the monastic vocation. As St Benedict of Nursia insists in his Rule, 'Let all guests be received as Christ Himself, for He says 'I was a stranger, and you welcomed me' (Matt. 25:35)'. Such also is the tradition of the Mountain. Abbot Gabriel of Dionysiou once said to me, 'We divide all the money received by the monastery into three equal parts: one third for upkeep of the buildings, one third for the monks, one third for hospitality to visitors and pilgrims'.

Yet here there is today a major difficulty. In the past the majority of the visitors were genuine pilgrims and, because travel was difficult, their number was relatively restricted. When I stayed for a week at Great Lavra during October 1962, for the whole of that time I was the only visitor. Today, especially throughout the summer, the main monasteries are all but overwhelmed by a constant influx of visitors. Despite a strict quota system, the numbers are disturbingly large: perhaps nearly a hundred each night at the more accessible houses. What is more, most of these visitors are tourists rather than pilgrims; they come to Athos out of curiosity rather than religious devotion. The monks do their best to cope with this incursion, but the inevitable result is that one no longer finds on Athos the stillness and silence that was such an impressive feature on my visits to the Mountain fifty years ago.

It is only to be expected that those who come to the Holy Mountain as genuine pilgrims are in many cases not content simply to attend the church services and to venerate the icons and relics, but they also hope to find monks to whom they can open their hearts, and from whose words they can receive healing. This brings us to a second way, alongside hospitality, in which Athonite monasticism serves the Christian community at large. From the very beginning of its history the Mountain has nurtured elders, charismatic guides who can offer spiritual direction. We have already spoken of the crucial role played by these elders in the revival of monastic life on Athos during the past half-century. Not only do these elders provide assistance to the monks permanently resident on the Mountain, but they also minister to the many pilgrims who seek them out. But the visitor should not expect that he will easily and casually discover such elders. Often they are hidden.

It is of course true that the ministry of eldership is not limited to monks. Spiritual guides are to be found among the married clergy and in monasteries for women as well as men, and likewise among the laity, both men and women. There are many ammas as well as abbas. But it can justly be claimed that the Mountain, while enjoying no monopoly, is yet to a pre-eminent degree a centre where such Spirit-filled counsellors are to be found.

What is it that enables someone to act as a spiritual father or mother? It is above all their entry into the deep mystery of inner prayer. The true geronta is not merely someone who says prayers from time to time, but someone who is at prayer all the time, a living flame of prayer, without interruption day and night, whether in solitude or in the company of others. And so we come to a third way in which Athos serves the world. Today, as in the past, the Holy Mountain continues to be an oasis of living prayer. I am not thinking only of intercessory prayer, although this does indeed play a prominent role in the prayer life of the Athonite monk. Yet beyond this all prayer – not only prayer of intercession and petition but prayer that is exclusively contemplative – supports and strengthens the Christian community as a whole. Every place where genuine prayer is offered, and par excellence each of the monasteries and hermitages of the Mountain, acts as a focal point, a powerhouse of noetic electricity, that renders the desert of the secular world less arid and forlorn.

This, in the last resort, is the only way in which a monastic centre such as Athos can find its justification and raison d'être. For those who do not believe in the value of prayer, monastic life on the Holy Mountain will appear futile and pointless, a perverse waste of human talent. But for those who believe that the world is upheld by the prayers of the saints, the Mountain is indeed providing a service to the world that is creative and indispensable.

The value of the Holy Mountain, and equally of every monastic house of prayer, is well illustrated in a story from fourth-century Egypt. When the young Palladios was suffering from discouragement, he went to see his spiritual father Makarios of Alexandria and said to him, 'Father, what shall I do? For my thoughts afflict me, saying: You are making no progress, go away from here'. Makarios replied, 'Tell your thoughts…For Christ's sake I am guarding the walls…'.

I am guarding the walls: the Church is like a city; the monks are sentinels on the walls, keeping watch so that the other inhabitants of the city can pursue their occupations in safety and security. Against whom are the monks guarding the walls? The monks of Athos have a clear and specific answer: against the demons, who are the common enemies of humankind. The warfare waged by monks against the forces of evil is thus a battle fought on behalf of every one of us alike. With what weapons do the monks fight? With the weapon of prayer, and beyond that with the totality of their ascetic dedication and their personal sanctification. Such in essence is the way in which the Athonite monk assists the world: not so much by what he does as by what he is; not actively but existentially; not primarily by preaching, teaching, writing, or by external works of mercy, but by his very existence, by his continual prayer of the heart.

Because there are persons of living prayer on the slopes of Mount Athos, our lives wherever we may be – in North Oxford, in Chelsea, or Camden Town – are rendered more stable, more fruitful, more joyful. We are never alone. Let us bless God for our Athonite companions, for the mystical support of our monastic partners and fellow workers.

Mount Athos: The Artist

DOUG PATTERSON

Although it is very difficult to put one's experiences of Mount Athos into words, I first visited in 2002, taking the boat from Ouranoupolis to Daphne, where I disembarked, changed boats and then sailed along the coast to Karoulia.

Nothing in my life had prepared me for this unique journey, its monumentality and grandeur and the intimacy of the vistas. I was overcome with emotion by the architecture of the monasteries perched like eagles or nestled into the cliff faces, I sketched furiously to try to express the subtle tonal graduations and capture the fleeting effects of light and the atmosphere.

I realized this was without doubt a unique and sacred place in the world, and I decided immediately to illustrate a complete Mount Athos portfolio. This was the beginning of numerous visits. I was given the rare privilege to be allowed to draw and paint all the monasteries and sketes with the blessing of Father I, who supported my work throughout my many visits, and introduced me to my second major discovery, the work of the travelling artist Vasili Grigorovich Barsky (1701-1747) who made incredible architectural drawings of all the monasteries and landscapes in 1745.

I made many friends during my work on Mount Athos who have shown me different paths. These experiences have tugged at my soul and raised my spirits, and encouraged me to undertake a similar journey to illustrate the twenty Buddhist dzongs (monasteries) of Bhutan.

Over the years I have travelled extensively with paint brushes and sketchbooks in the long tradition of the travelling artist, and this has given me an intimate insight into a place and the people who live there, but Mount Athos opened that door, and reminds me that God is just a whisper away, wherever you are.

FIG.33 *St Panteleimonos*

FIG.34 *Simonos Petras*

A Visit

ANDREAS CHRYSANTHOU

Nothing could have quite prepared my family and me for the beauty that awaited us.

The transition from our frantic efforts to find parking by the port of Ouranoupolis to the tranquil scenes of the Athos mountains is indescribable. From the first peninsula we came across in the distance, we knew that we had embarked on something special.

The beautifully coloured and crafted monasteries high up in the clouds towered somewhat regally over the calm sea and golden shores in a way I've never seen before.

On the outbound journey I had expected to be amongst old Greek ladies dressed in black but the demographic was a packet of all sorts; from young ladies in Orthodox head coverings to old men strategically manoeuvring their worry beads, men in military uniform to curious holiday makers in short trousers and sneakers.

Everyone had their very own personal reason for visiting this Holy Mountain and whichever it was, the curiosity and excitement on their face resonated with me as it matched mine. As the boat neared the anchor point where we were to be met by monks, there was an air of excitement on the boat.

Everyone hurried downstairs towards the back amidst pointing and cheers. In the distance, you could make out a speedboat heading our way and had I not known better, it was as if Elvis himself was on it. As the speedboat neared and docked to us, three smiling and welcoming monks joined our deck where they were greeted like rock stars.

Nonetheless, even without anyone corralling the crowds, no one pushed or shoved; the calm showed was overwhelmingly respectful. One by one the crowds formed an orderly queue to either receive a blessing from one of the monks or buy locally sourced and produced goods from the other two, (I later found out they were assistants, not monks themselves). Their offerings included olives, olive oil, tsipouro (distilled grape pomace), wine or a plethora of icons and charms.

As the queue slowly drew down and my turn came for a blessing, my children were greeted first where the monk asked their names and one by one proceeded to give them an individual blessing followed by them kissing his hand and the cross he was bearing. Next came the turn of my wife and me, where he pulled us close together, blessed us and to our surprise, thanked us for coming. How humble, I thought!

Whilst the crowds waited patiently, he took his time and asked us where we were from. 'North London', we said to which he replied (translated),

'I was in London last month, I was on the Piccadilly line in Cockfosters'.

Within a matter of minutes of talking to this monk we had just met, he became an almost intimate figure to us and someone we both felt a personal bond with. Over time, I came to realise that all monks I met from the Holy Mountain have this unique gift in common. It's their ability to make you feel comfortable, welcome and, more importantly in my view, familiar.

That feeling runs through the entire place as well. The first time I made that journey, without even stepping foot on the mountain, I experienced an overwhelming feeling of solace and warmth which has been the driving force behind the desire to keep going back. Definitely a humbling place to visit!

PL. 45 *The morning pilgrim ferry*

Ad Limina: On the Boundary

DOUGLAS DALES

Whenever I arrive in Ouranoupolis on my way to visit Vatopedi and Simonopetra for my annual Lenten retreat as an Anglican priest, I always walk out to the land boundary of the Holy Mountain. It is a fine experience in the spring, after an early start and flight from Gatwick, and then an epic drive across the mountains above Chalkidiki. The path winds past rural villas full of early flowers and up through a lovely set of olive groves, where the ground is usually covered in anemones, set off by the bright yellow of the broom. Then down a small ravine until the restored curtain wall of the Frankish castle comes into view. This was built during the time of the Crusades, around the year 1206, and is in the process of restoration. In the middle of it is a fascinating archaeological site, which is of great importance for understanding the early history of monasticism on Athos – the monastery of Zygos.

The first life of St Athanasius, who founded the Great Lavra in 961 at the other end of the peninsula, describes how escaping from court life in Constantinople to explore Athos, he came first to Zygos. There 'he met an elder who was very simple and free from worldly cares, and was living a life of spiritual tranquillity outside its walls'. It seems that Zygos was in fact the first centre of monastic organisation on Athos, mentioned in a document from 942, before it moved to the safer inland location of Karyes. Archaeology has confirmed that Zygos had been an inhabited site, close to the sea but sheltered from view, since prehistoric times. The little hill between Zygos and the sea is still called Viglia, which means look-out place.

It was therefore at Zygos that St Athanasios received his formation as an Athonite monk and the recent archaeological excavations have exposed a primary monastic site, complete with its church, of the kind that may still be seen on a larger scale at Great Lavra and Vatopedi. Because the other monasteries are still functioning communities, the archaeological evidence underlying them remains largely obscure. But Zygos gives an opportunity to see the shape and proportions of an early Athonite monastery, which still retains some of its marble decoration and frescoes, as well as evidence of the more practical buildings of a monastery such as the olive press. The church itself dates from the early eleventh century. It was later extended to become a small katholikon of the type seen at Great Lavra and Vatopedi and elsewhere. The site was vulnerable to attack from the sea, however, and the monastery seems to have succumbed to the turbulence of the twelfth century. In 1199, the Emperor Alexis III gave the abandoned monastery to the newly created Serbian monastery of Chilandar as a convenient port where they could keep a ship. Today it hosts a small police outpost.

To visit Zygos and its environment is to stand on a boundary in more than one way. There is the modern land boundary with its notice prohibiting access on foot. There is the quiet place where it runs down to the sea where you can sit and look across at the holy territory just within reach and listen to the sea and the wind. It is also a geological boundary, full of very interesting stones where the little stream debouches into the sea. It is normally approaching the boundary of the day, with sunset appearing over the elegant profile of the Ammouliani islands just across the water, backed by the shadowy shape of the next Chalkidiki peninsula. It is also a boundary in time between normal life in England and this special time of seclusion and prayer in so holy and beautiful a place, and among such welcoming monastic friends. It is a historic boundary inasmuch as it was the place where St Athanasios took the decisive step of becoming a monk. It is a spiritual boundary, which the physical boundary represents and respects, because to cross it is to enter the wilderness of the saints, the earthly paradise of the Mother of God.

PL. 46 *The border and ruins of Zygou Monastery*

My First Visit to the Holy Mountain

ARTUR SCHOLTES

In 1975 I spent a holiday in Greece, taking advantage of the fact that our semester break was to last more than six weeks. At that time Chalkidiki, and especially Sithonia, was not yet on the tourist map. Therefore we could easily find a lonely cove in which to pitch our tents, living for the moment, and taking things as they came. I confess that our interest in swimming, snorkelling and fishing far exceeded our interest in cultural events and the historical sites of Greece. But after a few weeks of lazing around a friend of mine accidentally came across a short article about the Holy Mountain in a travel book.

The story about the secluded monk's republic with its medieval monasteries quickly captivated us. It sounded like a real adventure, especially as we could not simply go there, but had first to get permission through a seemingly difficult procedure. So the reason for my first visit to the Holy Mountain was not at all spiritual or religious interest, it was pure love of adventure.

A week later we left Ouranoupolis on the boat to Daphne. Before that we had to go to the German Embassy in Thessaloniki to get a written recommendation, which we had to present to the Police Department of Northern Greece. They checked it and issued the permission to board the boat that took the pilgrims to the harbour of Daphne.

At that time there were not many pilgrims on the boat. But when we arrived in Daphne, it turned out that the old and rickety bus, which took the pilgrims on the old dusty road to Karyes, was too small to pick up all the pilgrims who had arrived with the boat. When my friend Wolfgang tried to get into the already overcrowded bus, a member of the monastic police drew him back and threatened him with an impressive wooden truncheon. So he quickly handed his backpack over to us through the window and the bus started without him.

Wolfgang was the sportiest of us and started the hike to Karyes, cutting across every hairpin turn of the potholed crushed rock road. So he played the hare and the tortoise with the bus. But the mountain is rather steep in this area and after a few hundred metres we saw him vanishing in the dust cloud the bus had left behind.

When we arrived in Karyes we had more than an hour to stroll around in this strange looking little village till Wolfgang arrived. Together we went to the Protaton to receive our diamonitiria. As it was already 3 p.m. by the time we held them in our hands, we decided to hike to the next monastery, which we thought would be Simonopetra. At that time there were no reliable maps of the peninsula available so we used the small sketch in a book for our orientation.

A narrow path led into the forest in the direction we had determined as the right one to reach Simonopetra. No signpost gave us any hint where to go. After two hours of walking, the small path broadened. It was lined with large blackberry bushes generously draped with ripe berries. After an extensive break– we hadn't eaten anything since our breakfast in Ouranoupolis – we quickened our pace as we were afraid we wouldn't reach the monastery before sunset. The path through the forest was very beautiful, but because of the lush vegetation and the dense wood, we had no view to the coast for our orientation.

What was meant to happen, happened. After having taken decisions at a few crossroads of the path, we had lost every bearing. Our last chance was to follow the light of the sinking sun, which we hoped would lead us to the western coast of the peninsula. Dusk was already falling when we saw light through the trees. But, to our frustration, the path suddenly ended at a steep cliff. As it was too far to get back to Karyes and we were sure that we would not reach Simonopetra before nightfall, we decided to look for a place where we could spend the night.

To make matters worse, it then started raining. Fortunately, we found a clearing with a very big tree in the middle before it was completely dark.

PL. 47 *Small ferry approaching Nea Skete*

Under the large leaf canopy of the tree we found shelter from the rain. We unfurled our sleeping bags and despite the adverse conditions we soon fell asleep. The next morning had a surprise for us. The big tree seemed to serve normally as a kind of open-air barn for mules. Our bed had been a big layer of mule droppings, dried by the sun when we arrived, but soaked by the rain during the night. The tang of mule dung was quick to welcome us as soon as we woke up.

We left the place as quickly as possible. The sun was shining again and we washed our sleeping bags in the next creek we crossed and dried them in the morning sun. The sun helped us to orientate ourselves again and three hours later we saw Simonopetra below us. I will never forget my first view of this extraordinary building residing on the rock above the blue sea.

After the long walk through the forest, the rain and the night below the mule tree, we did not look particularly trustworthy. When we approached the gate of the monastery a monk was sitting on the small stone bench at the entrance. He stood up and looked at us with a blank stare. Later, when looking at the photos we had taken – there were no digital photos at that time, so that we viewed the photos in the weeks following our return home – we understood his surprise. The monk could only speak a few words of English and so he greeted us with the words: 'You look like playboys'.

Nevertheless we were generously accepted as guests and given a room on the uppermost floor below the roof. The view from the wooden balcony down to the sea was awesome, the wooden construction of the balcony in a different meaning was awesome, too. We quickly stepped back and decided to enjoy the view from the inside of our room.

Soon after we were invited to celebrate the mass with the monks and then we had our meal in the trapeza with the monks. It was at that time that our mood changed. We felt that this was more than a little adventure. We were impressed by the deep religiousness of the monks. When the monks invited us for the morning mass, I was quite sure that most of my friends would stay in their bed at four o'clock in the morning. But to my surprise everybody was present.

When we left Simonopetra the next morning and hiked towards Grigoriou and further to Dionysiou, new topics were added to our conversation: the meaning of life, our personal future, religiosity …

Retrospectively our visit of Dionysiou was the most impressive part of my first visit to the Holy Mountain. The monks involved us more in their monastic life than we had expected. The holy service, the common meal in the trapeza, the night service and the 'breakfast' in the morning, everything was an intensive religious experience, comparable perhaps to the feelings I had as a child when attending midnight mass at Christmas with my parents.

When we left the Holy Mountain four days later, I was sure I would one day come back. It had been more than an adventure of six friends; the door had opened to new experiences. Since then I have visited the Holy Mountain more than a dozen times. Each time, I have hiked with friends from monastery to monastery through the beautiful Garden of the Panaghia which is an integral

FIGS. 35–36 *Playboys*

PL. 48 *Kellia at Vigla*

part of my spiritual experience of this wonderful place. We have had numerous enriching encounters with monks and pilgrims from all over the world.

Five years ago, when I walked from Kavsokalyvia to Great Lavra in the pouring rain with my brother, we thought of asking our twenty-five- and twenty-two-year-old sons, Jan Felix and Frederic respectively, whether they wanted to accompany us the next year. We were not sure if they would share our enthusiasm for the Holy Mountain, but to our surprise and delight they have both become new Friends of Mount Athos. This year, my son Frederic has visited the Holy Mountain for the fourth time.

Evlogite – O Kyrios!

How I got lost and met a Saint

DEREK SIMONS

The first visit to Mount Athos is always going to be the most impressionable experience and in August 1992 waiting in Ouranoupolis for the boat I had little concept of what to expect.

My wife and I had become Orthodox in 1989, and in 1992 we had a young monk, Brother Aidan Hart, staying with us. He was an icon painter, and as I am an artist, we had much in common. We had helped him find a derelict cottage on the Stiperstones Hills in Shropshire to convert to a monastery, but first he was sent to Mount Athos to experience the life of a monk. We decided to take him ourselves, driving through Europe and Northern Greece to Thessaloniki and on to Ouranoupolis.

Brother Aidan and I landed at Daphne and caught the bus to Karyes. It was already full and I had to stand. A small black-bearded Serbian monk decided to practice his English on me. He asked me about the royal family and then proceeded to tell me the Mark Twain story of Henry VIII's son Edward substituted for a commoner. He thought Henry was a good and clever man for defying the Pope and proceeded to do mock genuflections much to the amusement of the whole bus.

At Karyes we collected our visitor permits and caught the bus to Iviron monastery.

Iviron is like a small fortified village. A massive tower guards the bay and another badly damaged one is in the walls. Inside the gateway is a small church built to house the miraculous Portaitissa icon. The monks were cleaning the brasses from the main church and pieces of huge chandeliers were laid out in the courtyard. We were welcomed by Father J and the gatekeeper Father Ja. who spoke excellent English, French and Greek. After a meal in the guesthouse and compline we explored the grounds. This was going to be Brother Aidan's monastery, but they weren't expecting him for a few days, so he had a blessing to show me some of the nearby monasteries.

After the liturgy the next morning we set off for Stavronikita. The path went along the beach and then followed the coast up and down the cliffs through shady tunnels of trees, marked occasionally with red painted arrows. The monastery is approached through a long pergola covered in purple and green grapes. We were welcomed with a glass of water and loukoumi, shown the church and invited to stay for a meal. We then walked to Pantokrator, a short distance along the coast, where we planned to get a boat to Vatopedi. I did a quick sketch until we saw the boat coming. There was a slight swell on the sea and the boat had difficulty getting near the jetty. At last it came alongside, Brother Aidan threw his bag on board and leapt at the prow just as a wave carried the boat away. He heaved himself over the edge and fell into the boat with much shouting from the crew. Off they went with Brother Aidan waving a bottle of water and shouting, 'You'll have to walk!'

FIG.37 *Iviron by Derek Simons*

PL. 49 *Funeral at cell of St George, Kolitsou*

I set off and found a small red painted arrow with 'Vatopedi' on it and followed a well-made stone track which, after a short distance, disappeared under a mound of rubble. I found what I thought was my path but after a time the stones became cobbles and then boulders and finally a sheer rock face. I was following a dry stream bed. I turned and went all the way downhill picking up, every now and then, little tubes of water colours which had fallen out of my rucksack. I looked at the map and decided to go to the Prophet Elijah skete which I reached after a long, hot, uphill climb. The gate was blocked with pieces of wood but I climbed over hoping to find an outside tap or a well. I found the main entrance, rang the bell and sat disconsolately on a wall looking at my map.

Suddenly a young Greek monk appeared at the door. He spoke English and asked me in to have a drink. He produced loukoumi, a glass of water with something like icing sugar in it, and a glass of plain water. He showed me the vast Russian church and relics in their golden caskets. We chatted. I was the first English man to come to the monastery since seven Greek monks had taken it over. He had been to Essex when he was aged seven with the Boy Scouts.

He asked me to have a look at a letter the monastery had received. It was a photocopy of the probate of an American, Alex Limar, who had left $2,000 to the monastery. This they understood but were not clear what to do. I explained what the legal language meant and wrote out a brief, formal reply for them to return. After a glass of orange juice he gave me a bottle of water and a small carved wooden cross and I set off again. I was to follow the path to the skete of Bogoriditsa and from there to Vatopedi.

The path seemed fine at first and continued upwards but soon became so overgrown with tree heathers that it almost disappeared. It followed a rocky ridge with steep wooded slopes either side. I reached the skete, climbed over another gate and found a man painting the roof who waved me uphill to Vatopedi. The path eventually joined a broad sandy road and I could see the monastery a long way below me. I arrived about 7.30 p.m., found Brother Aidan, and the guest-master gave me some supper.

We stayed a day at Vatopedi and the next day returned to Iviron so that we could get the bus to Karyes at 2.00 p.m. I met Father Ja. again and we discussed my walk and what a pity that the old paths were beginning to be lost and were not repaired or cleared any more. Brother Aidan went off to the sewing room to see if a lightweight rason could be made for him.

At Karyes we set off with two Greek boys to see Father Paisios, a hermit, much respected and looked on as a living saint. He lived about a twenty-minute walk from Karyes down a winding path through ferns, oaks and sweet chestnuts, scented with herbs and wild flowers. At various junctions there were notices saying 'This way to Father Paisios. Do not bother us'. The other hermits got fed up with visitors knocking at their doors asking for directions. Father Paisios did not receive visitors to order and we passed some men who had not seen him. However, Brother Aidan took us to a back gate which was locked. There was a tap and drinking mugs and a large tin of loukoumi in the fork of an oak tree. We sat on two small benches and Brother Aidan said we should wait and pray, not to ring his bell and see what happens. After about twenty minutes, I stood up and took a photograph of his tiny house through the wire fence. Seconds later Father Paisios appeared at his door, came down the steps and smiled at us. 'Have some loukoumi', he said and disappeared inside. A minute later he reappeared and came to the gate.

Brother Aidan told him who we were and he unlocked the gate. We sat on a low bench near the house and the two boys sat quietly at the end of the garden. Father Paisios was a lovely old man, quite sprightly, a face full of smiles and chuckles. His front teeth were missing and his side teeth glinted with gold fillings. While he was talking he was busy weaving a prayer rope and when he was asked a question would complete another knot while he considered his reply.

Derek: 'Father I live in the world, am married, and have two children. How can I please God?'

Father Paisios: 'By living simply. A person can't follow God easily if he is weighed down by the cares of this life'.

Derek: 'How can parents bring their children up in the ways of God? Many children nowadays are attracted to the life of the Church but at the same time find the attractions of the world greater'.

Father Paisios: 'Parents must lead, primarily, by example more than by words. There are people who try to teach with many words but if their words aren't followed by the example of their good lives then the words will prick and prod people rather than bless them. What is your work?'

Derek: 'I am an art teacher and a painter'.

Father Paisios: 'Ah! If you read The Philokalia and try to do what it says then you will make yourself into a work of art. The Philokalia is a collection of sayings and writings of saints and means 'the love of the beautiful'. Everything that we do – whether it be iconography, writing, translating or whatever – is a reflection of the state of our hearts. If we have good hearts our words and actions will be full of God's grace. People in the West tend to live too much in the brain; it is ultimately through the heart that we come to know God'.

Derek: 'Should monks be cut off from the world?'

Father Paisios: 'A monk's job is to seek God, to know Him. How God sees the world is another matter. A monk will love the world in the way God guides him, but his primary aim is to follow Christ. As Christ said, 'Follow me and I will make you fishers of men'. A monk isn't a hater of men but a lover of men. He will love them best when he follows Christ fully'.

Brother Aidan: 'I desire to be a monk and also am concerned that people in the West come to know Christ and the Orthodox Church. How can both these be done?'

Father Paisios: 'By example. The monastic life makes people stop in their tracks. They see that a monk does all sorts of things that seem to him to be unpleasant, to be a denial of life, and yet also they see that he is full of joy. He doesn't have all the things that the world says are important, even necessary for happiness, yet he is happy. He fasts, has all-night vigils, does prostrations, gives free hospitality to many and so on. This makes the unbeliever or the lukewarm person reconsider their life and so, by being as good a monk as possible, you will be the best possible missionary. How many monasteries are there in England?'

Brother Aidan: 'Two or three with more than three monks, Essex being the largest with twenty-five and then a number of individual monastics live in hermitages. Tell me Father, I have been a monk for four years and God is leading me, by circumstances, towards a semi-eremitical life. Is it possible for me as young as myself in the monastic life to live well in this way? Bishop Kallistos is my spiritual father'.

Father Paisios: 'It is possible. Have a daily programme of prayer, work etc. Know what you are aiming for and centre your programme on that. Spiritual life is like schools and universities with its different grades. Aim for what is appropriate for your level. Bishop Kallistos is a good spiritual guide. When you read, don't read to fill merely your head with knowledge, but read to struggle better against your sins. Some people read and then fall asleep; read and struggle. It is a blessed thing to return to England and start this skete. England needs monasteries, without them it is difficult for the Church and the world to draw near to God'.

After this long conversation he scurried inside (he was like a small blackbird), reappeared and gave each of us a prayer rope that he had just been making. We made our way back to Karyes. Brother Aidan was elated to have had so much time with Father Paisios, and I was happy that we were doing the right thing in helping found a new monastery in England after some opposition to the idea.

A year later Father Paisios became seriously ill and died in July 1994. He was declared a saint in 2015. Brother Aidan returned to England in 1994 and began to restore the cottage on the Stiperstones.

Twenty-six years later our little bit of Mount Athos, the Monastery of St Antony and St Cuthbert is still there with Father Philip Hall and novices and full monastic services.

I have visited Mount Athos a number of times since but never returned to the skete of Prophet Elijah to see if they ever received their legacy.

My first visit to Mount Athos had been short and a whirlwind of impressions. I had made friends with some young monks and I needed to return to talk to them in a more leisurely fashion instead of constantly moving on to somewhere else however equally fascinating. A year after my first visit my fellow trustees of the monastery that we hoped to set up decided we needed to go to Mount Athos to see how Brother Aidan was getting on and to discuss with the Abbot of Iviron when he would be allowed to return.

My wife Margaret, and Michael and Soula Kakoulis, our co-trustees, set off in October 1993 for Thessaloniki and went straight to the Bureau of Northern Greece to collect our papers. Then on to the Mount Athos office only to be told, 'No you can't go. You must phone Iviron'. Luckily we had a letter of invitation from Iviron and Michael explained I was Orthodox which did the trick. We then caught the bus to Ouranoupolis and found our hotel. The wives would stay there while we went. The next morning three men sat near the harbour issuing passports which had been prepared the night before and the boat left at 9.30.

The boat was much larger than the previous year and a number of lorries and tractors were being delivered.

The weather was sunny and warm, the sea blue and clear. This time I had binoculars with me to look more closely at the buildings we passed. A large building, without roof or floors, I was told, was being built by the Russians for tuberculosis patients in 1917 and never finished. Likewise, at St Panteleimon Monastery, big six-storey blocks were now derelict.

FIG. 38 *Church of Fr Maximos*

The bus from Daphne to Karyes took about thirty-five minutes up a steep zigzag track, over the top of a hill and down to the capital. Father Aidan was waiting for us and gave us a big hug. We had to get used to calling him Father as Brother is not a title on Mount Athos. He had to get back to Iviron to light the lamps for vespers so there was not time to show Michael the marvellous church of the Protaton.

The old track from Karyes to Iviron, much of it through Iviron land, was laid with stone flags with raised stone ridges on the steep slopes. It winds down through mature sweet chestnuts, plane trees, olives, and evergreen oaks past Elder Paisios's house. We saw autumn crocus, cyclamen, mallows and other late flowering plants. We talked all the way with news from back home and the various parishes and people he knew.

We called in to pay our respects to Father Maximos, a monk in his nineties, who had built a wonderful little church complete with a dome alongside the road. It commemorated the appearance of the Mother of God to a travelling monk who, tired and hungry, had collapsed under a tree. She gave him a gold florin to return to Iviron to pay for food. In amazement, the monks went to the holy icon of the Portaitissa and there was a gap where the gold coin was usually fastened. Father Maximos was bed-ridden but cheerful and looked after by a young monk. He gave us a few nuts wrapped in a twist of paper. A few years later I found his hermitage and church locked up and was told the ninety-six-year-old had been instructed in a dream to return to the monastery where he had been a novice so, despite his age, he had departed taking his carer monk with him.

We hurried on as Father Aidan needed to start lighting the lamps at 2 p.m. He took us to the guest-house saying he had reserved the best room for us. Since my last visit they had renovated more rooms with fine chestnut doors and new windows. Each room had a narrow entrance area and an inner bedroom with a log burner for colder days. Vespers was in the main church and afterwards Father Aidan showed us around. We saw the big timber workshops where he was making a carved wooden stand to support the icon of the Portaitissa when it is brought into the church and then his studio in a large room at the corner of the monastery with views in three directions. He had collected old tools and knives from around the monastery and displayed them on the walls. It was dark at 6 p.m. and although there were oil lamps at strategic points the monks all retire early. So it was bed at 7 p.m. – a very hard bed and pillow in fact, and I slept badly.

Early the next morning we were woken by Father Aidan knocking the talanton 'tune' on the door. The Divine Hours were held in the narthex and then moved into the church for the liturgy. You progress, in the dark, from an outer porch into the eco-narthex, then into the narthex, the doors are opened and you enter the church lit only by candles and lamps. There were huge brass candle sticks and an intricately carved icon screen with large icons. Above each icon were numerous silver oil lamps and overhead three large chandeliers.

Later in the day, when it was light enough to see more clearly, I saw that the centre chandelier had a brass fat cherub at the top complete with bow and arrow. Surrounding this chandelier was an enormous 'corona' decorated with icons, candles and more lamps. Flanking this were two more chandeliers. Behind the icon screen we were shown rare and beautiful icons and these and the exquisite wall paintings made me reflect that history of art books in the West rarely mention Byzantine frescoes, icons or mosaics, the quality of which certainly equalled that of Italy at the same period. Also behind the screen you could see that the marble columns that supported the roof were fluted on the inside and smooth and polished on the side facing the church, betraying their pagan temple origins.

We walked round the back of the monastery passing the gardener's house with its vine-covered pergola and oil pressing mill. A river bed, dry at that time of year, ran at the back, beyond the garden walls. At some time in the past the rights to extract gravel had been sold which had created a considerable mess. As the river bed widened near the sea there was a pool, more of a puddle really, where a family of terrapins lived and heads appeared and disappeared as we walked past. We met Father G who looked after the gardens and he invited us to see the walled gardens. Huge blue cabbages, onions, pointed peppers, celery, kale, spinach, dahlias, marigolds and much more grew in long lines below the monastery walls. In another walled area were oranges, persimmons, pomegranates and figs. Father G split the skins of some pomegranates and gave them to us to eat.

We walked back and found Father Aidan busy with another of his duties. This time in the bakery with its wood-fired oven and wooden troughs for the dough. It was the first time I had tasted sourdough bread. He showed us some of the other rooms on the courtyard, the candle-making workshop and the huge wooden wine vats – or the top quarter of them, as the lower part was in the cellars below. Down in the cellars we met a monk who gave us a sample of (sour) wine to try and a glass of raki.

I spent the next few days drawing and painting at the monastery and along the coast. One morning we visited Father S the Peruvian, a poet and writer, in his exquisite new hermitage in the hills above Stavronikita. On the last evening I wanted to talk to my two monk friends so I arranged to meet them after vespers. One of them was still living in his 'studio apartment'. The monks of previous generations had lived independent lives with facilities for cooking, working and sleeping but these would soon be banned when all the renovations were complete. I had taken teabags and Scottish shortbread. They produced a teapot, teacups, a kettle and (surprisingly) milk, and more biscuits. We chatted about the world outside, the world inside, and much more until 9.30 p.m. On Mount Athos, Byzantine time takes over so 9.30 p.m feels as if it is late. They listened at the door after putting out the lights, and we returned to our rooms.

Archimandrite Vasileios was away so we could not ask him about Father Aidan's return to the U.K. so we made our way back to Ouranoupolis. Our wives had had a restful time and had been on a cruise along the coast to view Mount Athos from the sea. Monks had told us how intrusive the noise of loudspeakers from the tourist boats was. In future years, my wife would visit the great female monasteries of Ormylia and Souroti whilst I went to Mount Athos.

Athos Diary

JONATHAN DUNNE

Koutloumousiou

Today has been an extraordinary day. After the early-morning service in the church of Filotheou monastery, I prepared to leave on the only minibus out of there, which was due to depart at 7.15 a.m. Two Danes introduced themselves, they were also going to Karyes, and did I know anything about the bus? We went to stand in the little square down from the monastery, then at the first fork in the road – no bus. It was raining and blustery, the clouds that had descended yesterday were firmly in place, concealing the central ridge of the peninsula and only allowing us glimpses of a choppy sea. We talked about life in the West and the East as the minutes ticked past, and they eventually decided to walk to Iviron to venerate the Portaitissa icon and pick up the bus to Great Lavra – their reason for going to Karyes from there. I was left with the option of walking for three hours in the cloud, and this is what I did, descending into a little valley with an impressive waterfall and then climbing the ridge. Several watercourses you wouldn't even have noticed in summer had become raging torrents – OK, gushing streams – and I had to take off my socks and shoes and hitch up my trousers to get through the largest of them. I think for a moment I became all water, my bare feet in the ice-cold flow of the stream, my head in the clouds, my body wrapped in moisture. I stopped at a fountain to take a little refreshment, and three horses appeared out of the mist. Three then became six. They were a little anxious when they saw me, and I climbed the side of the path to let them pass. The rear three had lost all fear by this stage and made a point of lapping the puddles at my feet. They then disappeared back into the mist as if they'd never been there. Thoughts are like mist, insubstantial. The track climbed and turned corners, vistas were severely rationed, most of the time it was white nothingness and the occasional red signpost, much like life, until I crossed a bridge and came into Karyes. I had a warm to-mato and onion pasty from the bakery, the guard at the Office of the Holy Executive asked me what day it was and I had no idea, and I ended up coming to stay the night at Koutloumousiou.

Koutloumousiou – Xeropotamou

The cold continues. The rain makes pitter-patter on the roof. Larger drops make thud-thud somewhere else (in my imagination). It has been raining probably for forty hours, and the first thing I'm going to do when I get home is sit with my back against the radiator and drink a hot cup of tea. The cold seeps into my bones. It is difficult to know what to do when circumstances, events, overwhelm your own defences. We like to keep everything in order, which means everything in limits that we can control, and find anything that surpasses this to be extraneous and threatening and must be stopped, cut out at the root. We are reluctant to go beyond familiar frontiers, as when you are swimming, one, two, three strokes, up for air, but one, two, three, four strokes is already a little uncomfortable, one, two, three, four, five is pushing it, building up our reserves, making us stronger, more faithful. What must the martyrs have thought when they were subjected to inhuman tortures? What must the forty Roman soldiers from the Legio XII Fulminata have thought when they were forced to stand overnight in a freezing lake to espouse their faith in Christ before the cruel governor or whatever he was? One soldier fell away and a guard took his place, as so often happens, impressed by their faith, as St Alban's executioner refused to lift the sword and bring it down on the protomartyr's neck whose passing feet had just caused the river to dry up and flowers to spring from the ground. Unusual things, things outside our control; the executioner himself was executed, one mother whose son was still alive pushed him back on to the cart of forty martyrs in Sebaste, ran with him so he wouldn't

miss the opportunity of a martyr's crown. The river begins to flow, the lake feels empty, the flowers go through their cycle of bud, blossom and wilt, petals falling to the ground or being eaten, hanging upside down by the radiator, we are small things in need of small comforts, a chair, a helping hand, a warm bowl of food, the bowl is warm, I gather it to me, seek its heat, it resists, sticks to the plastic that protects the cloth. I look up and a thousand faces, a thousand stars, are watching me. The saints, the company of the saints. They are still living.

Xeropotamou

Xeropotamou is a beautiful monastery whose church is dedicated to the Forty Martyrs of Sebaste, surely one of the most impressive icons in Orthodoxy, the forty martyrs standing, freezing in the lake, the water like a blue veil that mixes with the breath of their mouths, one would-be martyr unable to withstand the pain, the cold, emerging from the water, his face in his hands. We are called on to endure a certain amount of pain in this life, the pain that acts as a poultice and humbles our spirit, turns us to repentance, literally a changing of the mind, a reorienting of our lives. There cannot be repentance if there is not a realization first of our own sinful state, we thought we could go it alone and then we realized that our own resources were limited. We thought that the world could give us everything we need, especially if we play by its rules, and then the pleasures it offers become hollow, we suddenly become aware that what the world is offering us is not for our sake, is not to our benefit, it doesn't make us better people, it has stolen our innocence, but a glimmer remains, a spark that urges us forward, urges us to repent. Having recognized our sin, we must confess it to a priest. And the thoughts flicker and fade, insubstantial as ghosts, it is the cold that is keeping us awake, it is the cold that is preventing us from falling into a deep sleep, but we cannot do this on our own, we must turn to Christ, who will help us to bear our burden. We become part of his body and, through Communion, he forms part of ours, not connected, not joined like the slabs of marble in Filotheou church, not running side by side like a pair of railway tracks with sleepers between them, the onward movement buoying us, the gravel cushioning our fall, from one destination to the next, unfamiliar faces gazing at us through the misted-up window, the journey a repetition, a rehearsal, a going over of the lines, prompted by the still, small voice in our head, not the anxious, fretful prattler, the one who would make us worried. Just because you have a thought doesn't mean you have to follow it, it can be ignored. What Christ wants, St John Chrysostom tells us, is to be interwoven with us so that there are no boundaries. We accept that he is telling us the truth, because only the Truth opens our eyes, makes them whole, round as patens.

Xeropotamou – Thessaloniki

Time is a metal gate, solid, ribbed such that when you walk over it you might trip, a car will jostle from side to side, rocking you in your seat, barely interrupting the conversation, a slight recognition out of the corner of your eye (out of the corner of your mind), a flicker, a flit, like a seagull cutting through the air, or the plush seat on the bus, the diesel engine, holding on momentarily to the handle or the seat in front of you. Time is a metal gate moving over the rough, granitic surface, the contact with the land, a hand held out containing a cross and an icon, containing years of studying, of application, cupped hands ready to splash the face with water, ready to caress a child's face in greeting, ready to put an arm around a person's shoulder, ready for prayer, warped from the air and the moisture. The surface is almost arthritic, it is rough to the touch, if your skin came into contact with it, it might graze, there might be a speck of blood, this is the underside of time, the one we walk over so carelessly, our gaze fixed on a point in the future, our destination, the silhouette of land and cloud that is still visible, thoughts wandering as they do to things that are non-existent. Time plays tricks on the mind, one moment you are here, you try to concentrate on the moment, to extract the prayer, to devote yourself, not to become dizzy as the lamp sways slowly from side to side, rocking you in your seat, as you stand. Time is a crumpled surface like a crisp, like a sheet, with ridges that can be climbed (we would say surfed if they were water, but it comes to the same thing), time is the meeting of hands that shake and part, the meeting of hearts that share a common purpose, time contains understanding, it rattles over the surface. At this point you realize it is chained, there are figures standing on it, it is not stable, it moves in a circle, it seems to have a purpose other than your own, and you stand on the side gangway, aware that you have been tricked, and remember the gorse flower that shone bright in the rain yesterday, in the mist, the background of bush, greenery, blurred, out of focus, shone bright, shone yellow, came into focus. Eternity is the time between the parting surfaces.

PL. 51 *Monastery of Xeropotamou*

A Catechumen

BART JANSSENS

Μη ζητάς φίλους, να ζητάς συντρόφους. Don't ask for friends, ask for companions
—Nikos Kazantzakis, *Askitiki*

My friends in Belgium jokingly ask me not when I will return to Mount Athos, but rather when I will decide not to come home from such a visit. Less jokingly, a monk in one of the monasteries once challenged my two Orthodox companions by asking them why they had not yet convinced me, a Roman Catholic, to convert to Orthodoxy despite sharing several days of company on the Holy Mountain. Neither is currently my ambition, but it cannot be denied that both the Mountain and Orthodoxy have put a permanent spell on me.

I first visited Mount Athos and walked the historic footpaths in March 1997, when I spent a year abroad at the Aristotle University in Thessaloniki. It was not until years later that I came across the Mount Athos path-clearing project via the FoMA annual report and newsletters (I had recently joined as a member following a chance meeting with Graham Speake and Simon Jennings during the Patristics Conference at Oxford in 2011). I immediately knew that I would want to sign up for the footpath pilgrimage one day since the project's mission statement combined so many of my passions: Greece, Athos, hiking, nature, serving – once a Boy Scout …

However, I continued playing hard to get for a couple of years, actively reaching out in an email to Andrew Buchanan as late as April 2013. Although Andrew replied immediately and warmly, I still let pass the 2014 and 2015 expeditions. The main reason were time constraints (sixteen days off in mid-spring is not obvious for a young father with work commitments), but then came the news that, as an experiment, a small number of one-week places would be made available on the 2016 team.

Eventually I made it into the 2018 team as a 'one-weeker', joining the main team in Daphne on changeover day. Although a newcomer without previous experience in path-clearing nor a first aid certificate, my training as a Classicist and Byzantinist and my command of spoken Greek as well as my portable stove and a tin of Nescafe (to this day, I am in the dark as to what exactly made the difference in the recruitment procedure in my favour) qualified me as a footpath warrior stationed at the Great Lavra. My expectations were greatly met and my vocation confirmed. It was indeed the first of many such missions and I am happy to say that I am already signed up for the 2020 pilgrimage.

At the risk of getting lost in the inextricable crypts of semantics: is it a selfish thing to keep setting time apart to return to Mount Athos? I do not think so, since we are so fond of sharing the experience, especially with those loved ones who are not allowed to go and see for themselves. Is it a form of egocentrism, then? I do not believe so, because we value our companions so much. It is rather a sense of duty shared among many, like warriors going into battle or troops of ascetics being drawn to the desert and transforming it into a city, or at least into a moderately accessible place. Man does not need friends, he needs brothers in arms – very fitting for a meticulously run operation like the FoMA path-clearing team, even if our arms be only clippers and a pair of gloves.

A monk is not merely running away from the world: by his voluntary seclusion he is rather transforming it into something new and better. Prayer, too, is more than a personal dialogue between Man and his Maker: it is at least partially intended to benefit the world at large. Equally, our relationship with Mount Athos is partly personal, because of the hours spent in silence and darkness, but also largely social, for the sake of the men we meet, nature, life itself, and – at the risk of being lured into the rather less well-signposted intricacies of rhetoric – for the planet and all mankind. And at the end of the week, upon returning home, the days spent on Mount Athos always feel like days well spent, and that alone is no small thing in a human life!

PL. 52 *Iconostasis, Skete of Profitis Elijah*

Nineteen Ninety-Eight

COLIN WHORLOW

*Back in 1998 my friend Michael Groves and I spent four days on Mount Athos, staying at
Grigoriou, Dionysiou, Simonopetra and St Panteleimon. Whilst there I wrote a daily account of our
experiences in the form of a handwritten letter to my then girlfriend Linda, now my wife.
Linda has managed to unearth it and I have typed it up.*

Grigoriou Monastery, Mount Athos, 1/8/98

Dear Linda,

It is now around 9 p.m. and I am sitting on my bed in the monastery guest-house wearing my head-torch. Apparently the light switches start working at 10 p.m. An unusual day so far, beginning at 5 a.m. in our room in Thessaloniki, and then getting a taxi, a bus and a boat before reaching Daphne, the port of Mount Athos, at 11.50 a.m. We had had to rush around at Ouranoupolis before getting on the boat, partly to buy the boat tickets, but also to get our diamonitirions, which are our official travel passes, and are very Greek and official looking.

The boat was quite full – about 300 people including a scattering of monks. (PAUSE – I'm now upstairs, where it's light). However very few of them looked like walkers. When we arrived at Daphne via stops at various monasteries' landing stages there were heaps of people, a bus, jeeps, minibuses etc, and everyone seemed to get into those. Michael and I donned our packs and headed south up a dirt road, rather surprised to be the only ones on foot. It turned out subsequently that there is a boat south, but walking seems the appropriate way to travel so we'll probably stick to that.

The road was easy to follow and went steadily up for about an hour, and then levelled out and began to descend. We came across a tap, and a shaded

bench, which were both very welcome. After about another hour we arrived at Simonopetra monastery and were directed to the guest-house. I was rather surprised to see someone I recognised from the Friends of Mount Athos AGM, but that was very useful as he spoke English and Greek so could explain what was happening. Monks were rushing around everywhere spring-cleaning the monastery for the big feast day on Tuesday. It would therefore be inconvenient for us to stay overnight, but we should come back on Monday afternoon. Though busy, the guest-master presented us with water, Turkish delight, and raki. We therefore continued to Grigoriou Monastery, another hour down, up and down a steep track.

We arrived just after 3.30 p.m., entered the guest-house and phoned the guest-master who invited us to stay. After a rest, a chat with some other guests, and a shower, it was time to go to the church in the monastery for the end of vespers. Being non-Orthodox all we can do is sit in the outer chamber, whilst all the activity happens in the inner two chambers. After half an hour of this, with people wandering in and out, lighting and extinguishing candles, and kissing icons, we were summoned to dinner. This was an aubergine pie, tomato and watermelon, and very nice and filling it was too. This is eaten in silence – and at great speed! After dinner we went for a stroll and came across Father D, an English monk, born in London, of Greek extraction. He offered us a 'cool water' between us, and we had a long conversation, sitting out on a sort of verandah, with the green and rocky mountain behind us, and the

FIG. 39 *Monastery of Agiou Dionysiou*

bright blue Aegean in front. We talked about how he came to be there, other monks, bar codes, Schengen, how one achieves an inner life, saints, miracles, computers and a lot more.

At 8 p.m. a seven-hour service started for St Elias day (or something). 8 p.m. is midnight to the monks. We went to part of it – lots of intoning, then came back to the guest-house – where I wrote the first few lines of this letter – and then went back to the service to see if it had changed – which it had, to chanting. We came back here, hence I am writing this again! Bed soon – it's 10 p.m. Michael has already gone to bed as he is thinking of getting up at 5 a.m. for the next mass! (I should have mentioned earlier that dinner was in the refectory – which has lots of tables and benches and is painted throughout with icons on a blue background.)

Dionysiou Monastery, Mount Athos, 2/8/98

I was woken at 7 a.m. by a monk banging on the door to say that the service was beginning. I got up, slowly, and joined Michael in the church at about 7.40 a.m. Breakfast followed this a bit before 9 a.m. This was fish (sadly) and tomato, cucumber. A monk was reading and when he finished it was a case of everybody out, whether you had finished or not! Father D met us after breakfast and showed us around the church, which was very interesting, particularly the stories associated with the various icons. (Before breakfast, whilst we were sitting outside the church, he had introduced us to Father P, who was the 'whizz kid' monk, and ran the monastery computers, and built their radio aerials!)

After the church tour, Father D showed us another tiny chapel where the monks can go for services so as not to be 'on show' for the pilgrims (i.e. visitors). He then gave us some postcard-like icons for us to take away.

We left Grigoriou on foot and got to Dionysiou at about 1 p.m. after ninety minutes' walking. As we came down the hill just before the monastery, we saw the boat unload about thirty people – so we joined them. We were met in the guest-house by water, raki and Turkish delight, as before, and then shown to our dormitory, which we are sharing with four Germans.

They accompanied us on a walk to St Paul's monastery, the next one down the coast. The walk up to the monastery itself was knackering, and we couldn't go in the church when we got there – so we sat about and drank water and then walked back. We had a quick walk round the church at Dionysiou – much older than Grigoriou. I located the shower in Dionysiou, which I was very grateful for, and after one I joined the service in church for half an hour prior to dinner. As with breakfast, there was a monk reading, so I knew I had to eat as quickly as possible, with the result that I finished most of the meal in the allotted time!

Then I sat overlooking the sea, and then lay down for a bit, and then wandered, and then wrote this. The four Germans are in bed upstairs and they intend to get up for 3 a.m. to attend the 3-7 service. I don't! Time for bed – it is 9.30 p.m. after all!

Simonopetra Monastery, Mount Athos, 3/8/98

I am writing this mid-afternoon, sitting out in a courtyard of Simonopetra monastery. I'm in the shade, but it is boiling hot in the sun – as ever! I woke up this morning still knackered from yesterday's exertions combined with less food than usual, and the heat. (The Germans were still in bed – I might add!) 7 a.m. was breakfast time, and that was served to us guests in the guest-house, and consisted of mint tea, olives and bread. Not a lot!

We had decided last night to get the 9.15 a.m. boat back to the Simonopetra landing stage – which is about 1,000 feet below the monastery itself. This went against our original plan to walk everywhere, but it meant we would get to the monastery sooner and guarantee a place. I had a Snickers bar whilst waiting for the boat as a breakfast supplement. Having got the boat, and then climbed the 1,000 feet – along with some monks and chaps carrying suitcases, amongst others – the first person we ran into was Dr Dimitri Conomos – the chap from the Friends of Mount Athos we ran into here two days ago. To our surprise – and delight – given it was only 10.20 a.m., he told us that lunch was about to be served! So we went in, ate stuffed tomatoes and a wedge of watermelon at double-quick speed. I accidentally poured Michael a cup of white wine, under the impression it was water – but he didn't seem to mind!

(Interlude – sitting here on a stone bench I was resting this on a book on my crossed legs – and I have just been ticked off by a monk with a stick. Crossing your legs, like putting your arms behind your back, is frowned upon as negative body language. This next bit may therefore be even more illegible.)

After 'lunch' we were shown to our room – it's a mattress on the floor tonight! I spent most of the next few hours lying there, apart from getting up to see the Bishop arrive for the feast which is tonight. Much hand kissing and hugging. I have just been for a wander around the monastery – vertiginous galleries surround the stone tower, and have taken some photos. I signed the visitors' book – and noted that the last UK visitors came on the 4th of June – one from Fairford and the other another member of the Friends executive committee!

It's now 4.25 p.m., and I believe there is a service at 6 p.m., followed by dinner, and then a fourteen-hour service to celebrate the feast day of St Mary Magdalene.

St Panteleimon Monastery, Mount Athos, 4/8/98

It is now about twenty-four hours since I wrote the last section, and I am sitting on my bed in a cell in St Panteleimon monastery. It's been an odd twenty-four hours! As I thought, there was a short (about forty minutes) service at 6 p.m. followed by dinner, which yet again was very nice but had to be eaten at speed. The refectory at Simonopetra is mostly white-walled, with a few icons hanging, rather than being entirely covered with wall paintings like the previous ones. They were also different in that at Grigoriou the paintings were only a couple of years old (and Father D had helped paint them) whereas at Dionysiou they were seventeenth century. Incidentally everything, the utensils, is metal in the refectory including the plates and the drinking vessels.

After dinner we sat around for a bit and then got chatting to a Canadian hermit. He had been at a hermitage on Mount Athos for some time, but was currently only on a visit back, as he had recently set himself up as a hermit in Ontario. A very friendly fellow, who told us that the Bishop we had seen earlier had apparently been lined up for the bishopric of Albania, but then hadn't been selected, so he was currently without a seat – and so he would have to stand!

The fourteen-hour service began at 8.30 p.m., and we watched the first half-hour – lots of chanting, and then wandered around. We came back to the church area after it got dark. The church itself is relatively small, and there were a lot of people sitting outside, including many monks. I found it a little sinister to see all these black-clothed, bearded people sitting round, with just the candlelight from the church windows. It was quite ok, incidentally, to stand by these windows and peer in.

This morning we got up around 7.30 and popped up briefly to see how the service was going, eleven hours in. It seemed much the same, but I saw a mass being conducted. There were still heaps of people sitting round outside.

As we had been dropped by the boat yesterday at 9.30 a.m., we walked the 1,000 ft down to the landing stage to be there in plenty of time. However, the boat didn't appear until 10.20 a.m! In the meantime a monk appeared who was also waiting for the boat, and when he established that we were not Orthodox he accused us of being heretics – much to Michael's irritation. We were particularly glad when the boat finally arrived!

The boat took us to Daphne, where we had a Sprite and a piece of cake (golden syrup tart, I think), in a café, before catching the boat to St Panteleimon. As we got off the boat, a fellow traveller, a monk, spoke to us in English and said he was the guest-master, so we followed him to the guest-house, which is in a six-storey building site surrounded by scaffolding. A monk called Boris brought out water and Turkish delight, and then the first monk summoned us into a room full of icons and crosses etc. He asked us our names, and then gave us wooden icons of St Nicholas (for me) and St Michael. It then transpired that we were in a shop so we had to pay for them!

Boris, whose English is very good, then explained that they shouldn't really have guests at the monastery as they were preparing for the feast of St Panteleimon next week. However, we could stay if we were prepared to do some work. We said we were, so after showing us to our cell he asked us to clean the windows on one floor of the building. This was tricky as we had only one cloth, one piece of wire wool and a quarter of a bottle of Ajax between us, also the windows had been splashed by cement during the building work. Furthermore some were broken and others were covered in netting. Still we made a start, and after an hour we paused for a break just as Boris appeared. He offered us a coffee (very strong) and said we had done enough, and some other guests would carry on. He suggested we look round the monastery (which we did, and it is very beautiful – with green towers above marble walls) and said when we returned he would like to show us the ossuary. Before we returned to take him up on his offer we were approached by one of the workmen, who turned out to be a Russian who taught English at the Academy of Sciences in Moscow. We talked to him briefly and then

accompanied Boris to the ossuary, where the skulls of former monks are laid out (two to three thousand of them, I estimate). He said there was a similar ossuary at St Catherine's monastery in Sinai – and as it happens we were there last year so I was able to agree and describe the differences! Boris, it turns out, is a novice monk, who studied international relations in Moscow for five years and then did a thesis at Cambridge. He is quite young – younger than me, that is! After showing us the ossuary he asked if we could help him carry some blankets up some stairs and lay them out on bed frames. We did that and then were invited to rest before vespers (which is at 5.30 Greek time and about 8.50 Athos time!) and dinner.

Augustou Hotel, Thessaloniki, 5/8/98

It is now the early evening here and we are resting after having eaten and before popping out for a beer. To start with the bad news: shortly after finishing the last section I found that someone had stolen most of the contents of my wallet whilst I was cleaning windows etc. I had stupidly – and about for the first time ever – left it in my room in my day sack. Losing the money is annoying (principle as much as anything) but more upsetting was that he took the little red card that you gave me in my Valentine's card. It looked like a credit card I suppose. I hoped he might have thrown it away immediately but I couldn't see it anywhere round, or in any of the bins so I am afraid it has gone for ever. Please will you give me another one. It is particularly galling to have something stolen that is of great value to me and no value to anyone else.

Still, after discovering the theft we headed up to the pre-dinner service, which was in the 'big church' on the top two floors of one of the monastery buildings. Very large and gold everywhere. I sat on a bench outside for most of it and admired the view of the monastery roofs. I was joined by the Russian I mentioned earlier – Mikhail – and we had a good chat. Dinner was very good, in a refectory designed for 800 but only having about eighty (if that) people in it. Very good frescoes in the refectory – more realistic than the other ones we've seen.

After dinner we went for a stroll by the water and spent some time skimming stones and throwing them at a rock. Very therapeutic! We returned to our room after I reported the theft to Boris and the guest-master. They were very sympathetic, but there wasn't really anything they could do. Our room had no lighting apart from an old oil lamp. We lit this, but in the process almost set fire to the room! It didn't give much light anyway so we turned it off. I'm not surprised that monasteries keep burning down though!

This morning I got up just in time for the very end of the pre-breakfast service at around 8. Good timing! Before breakfast a monk called Paul took us aside and showed Michael how to make the sign of the cross properly! I had seen people doing it so I knew – but Michael wasn't doing it quite right! Breakfast was ok although the only drink seemed to be potato juice. After breakfast we sat around. An old man asked if we had an English coin for his foreign coin collection but neither of us did. Later we had a coffee in the guest-house and I read a book which quoted Winnie the Pooh hunting the woozle as a metaphor for certain biblical scholarship! Then we said goodbye to Mikhail – we couldn't find Boris – and waited for the boat back to Ouranoupolis. That came at about 12.15 p.m. and so we had a brief Mediterranean cruise in the sun, before a long bus ride to return to the heat and noise of Thessaloniki.

So there it is, a summary of a very bizarre four days. You probably can't read most of it so I have probably helped you decipher it by now! Sorry it's a bit dull – I was trying to include as much detail as I could remember. Thinking of you. Very much love.

Colin xxxxx

Twenty Years of Gratitude: Life since Athos

CHRISTOPHER DELISO

I have seen many remarkable things on Athos. One image that recurs is that of an elderly monk beginning the evening prayers in an empty chapel, lighting candles briskly as the dark grew from without. It wouldn't have mattered, I thought, if no one but the monk was present; so long as human participation in the great ritual of Athonite spirituality continued, the very future possibility of that spirituality itself was confirmed.

This was not just a philosophical observation; at that time (January 2000) only about three monks inhabited Agios Andreas Skiti. This vast Karyes-area dependency of Moni Vatopediou had become a forlorn, rambling wreck by the time I visited. A loss of Russian patronage under Soviet communism meant that it fell neglected until Greek monks began reviving it in the 1990s. This was a significant task, considering that the monastery in its nineteenth-century heyday had hosted 500 or more monks. But during my January 2000 visit, it was all but empty, which made it ideal for spiritual reflection.

How I got there is a story in itself. In the spring of 1999, as an Oxford MPhil researcher in Byzantine Studies, I enjoyed a travel grant to visit the bygone imperial capital (along with a friend who has since become a University of Athens professor). Rather by accident, we happened to be inspecting the Ecumenical Patriarchate precisely when the patriarch himself passed through with his entire entourage. Somehow, we were invited to join them for lunch; at trapeza, a monk disclosed that renovations were then underway at an unknown monastery on Mt Athos, and invited me to see the works should I ever go.

Up to that point, my closest experience of Athonite tradition had come in the form of Orthodox theology lectures given at Oxford by Bishop Kallistos Ware. His great booming delivery and jovial presence thoroughly filled the room and enlivened a subject which also informed several aspects of my studies in the hagiographical and philosophical realms. By the time I had finished

my studies (and taken in another summer of Greek language studies at the university in Thessaloniki) I was more than ready to make good on the monk's invitation to experience Athos for myself.

In all, I spent three weeks on the Holy Mountain during that first visit in 2000, much of the time at Agios Andreas Skiti, with its long creaky corridors absent of pilgrims, its grandiose central church, and ramshackle courtyard. It was, like me, a work-in-progress, something under repair, with high hopes for the future but no guarantees, either. It was also a good base from which to explore the rest of Athos. I greatly enjoyed the long walk in the winter woods to Vatopediou, with its staggering opulence and serene waterfront. Also walks to the more distant places like Iviron far down the east coast, and, rising high from a cliff-top on the west, Dionysiou, where my historical imagination raced at the sight of the miraculous icon of the Theotokos, according to tradition wielded by the patriarch on the walls of Constantinople during the Avar-Persian siege of 626. Somehow, just the simple experience of seeing such a relic made my previous two years of studies much more real; as a repository of the cultural and spiritual heritage of Byzantium, the Holy Mountain continued to play a vital role in the living history of that civilization. What my Greek classmates had taken for granted or at least always known from their upbringing was to me, a simple foreigner, entirely new.

While interesting and relevant in the bigger picture, my visualizations of the role of tradition, ritual and history on Athos were not relevant to my being. When it came to the state of my soul, what was actually important was something inherent and utterly intangible in the Holy Mountain's nature. Coming from a writer who is not particularly religious, this is probably going to sound strange. But in the last two decades since my first pilgrimage, there have been visits when I have prayed very hard and others when I have prayed but a little: whatever the case, Athos is always working on you, restoring you

PL. 54 *Entrance, Xeropotamou Monastery*

to strength, giving you the answer to a dilemma and preparing you for the return to the outside world.

Most fundamentally, the Holy Mountain returns you to that world a better man than when you arrived. What more can one ask for than that from any sort of spiritual experience? It seems pretty good to me.

A full twenty years have passed since my initial pilgrimage to Mt. Athos; what luck that the present volume materialized right in time for an overlapping anniversary. I joined FoMA not too long after that first visit and my involvement with both it and, more recently, its sister organization (Mount Athos Foundation of America) has reconfirmed for me how lucky I have been to visit Athos – and indeed, to write about my experiences for a worldwide audience – when so many others will never get to visit the Holy Mountain, due to distance or circumstance or imperial edict.

As a writer, the responsibility I feel towards both the monastic community and the 'outsiders' (both pilgrims and the general public) derives from my sense of gratitude. Athos has taught me some of my life's most important lessons. Over time, the Athos experience has instilled in me a sense of respect for its traditions, and a desire for service, so that in some small way I might give something back.

Fittingly enough it was at Agios Andreas Skiti – the place where my Athos encounter began so long before – that I would first stumble across a tangible sign of success. An American friend who had always wanted to visit Athos asked me to join him, and so we went, in September 2018. While showing him the skete and recounting my own stories, I noted whole rows of ornate bells, and recalled that we (at the Mount Athos Foundation of America) were awarding a scholarly grant for documenting the monastery's bells. From what I had heard, the project had gone successfully, forwarding our mission of highlighting the Holy Mountain's material and spiritual culture.

Even better than seeing the bells was noting how lively the monastery was in general, and how significantly it had been transformed since my initial visit. The beleaguered monk dealing with hospitality seemed nearly run off his feet by the volume of pilgrims coming in; he lamented that the smaller monasteries would send on the overflow crowds to find lodging at the skete, since after the long renovations and expansion of the brotherhood the place was perceived as capable of handling anything. I had to smile. After all, in my mind I could still see that image from almost nineteen years earlier, of a solitary monk, lighting candles and reciting evening prayers in a dark winter chapel. At its essence, the continued existence of Athonite spirituality – whether attested by a lone monk in an obscure place or a well-attended Easter service – is itself a sort of miracle, and one that never fails to resonate whether the days between be centuries or a mere handful of seasons.

An image from spring sparks my final reminiscence. Flowers blossomed on the thick bushes that lined the kalderimi path, its occasional stones interspersed with grass, where I came down from the woods into the pure blue sky of mid-morning, cheery birdsong scattered on the warm breeze all around. For no particular reason, I thought that this was the sort of landscape the Philokalia would look like, were it not a book.

It was 2011 and I was writing a kind of book very different to the classic compendium of Orthodox spirituality. As just a travel guide to Greece, it would not contain anything more about Athos than necessary– and certainly would not divulge the name of the monk I had just visited, an ascetic who had achieved significant fame on the Holy Mountain. Some pilgrims, I had been told, sought out his counsel, at his kelli way out in the forest. As always with Athos and me, the encounter had ultimately come about by complete accident; a friend-of-a-friend in Thessaloniki happened to be a relative of the monk, and a few days earlier had penciled in for me the exact location of where his kelli was not listed on an otherwise quite detailed hiking map of Mt Athos.

I was grateful to get to share a good fifteen minutes of conversation with the ascetic, who lived, I had been forewarned, in a simple house without phone or electricity in the forest. That sounded remarkably like the hut I had once inhabited, in a placid olive grove in the south of Crete. I had written the island's name in a notebook while on my first pilgrimage to Athos, in January of 2000; I know not from where this inspired idea came, but it did answer the burning question of the time, namely, where to live. That ensuing year in Crete was terrific. The idea to go there, of course, I owe entirely to the Holy Mountain.

As it turned out, my 2011 encounter with the forest ascetic was to recur too. This soft-spoken monk with the deep, distant gaze would re-emerge in my Athos experience seven years later – again, by coincidence, when another one of my other Greek contacts in Thessaloniki named him as a close friend. This did seem auspicious.

There was only one problem. Perhaps the American pilgrim accompanying me would regard a forced march on poorly-signposted kalderimi in the early morning, followed by an unspecified wait to see a monk with whom he could not communicate, as detrimental to the larger goal of touring monasteries. Luckily for me, he was affable and considered the excursion part of the general adventure.

While still in Thessaloniki, I had been forewarned about the monk's increased fame: "get there early," the mutual friend had instructed me. I judged that we would be safe if we set out from our lodgings (at Moni Iviron) by 6.30 a.m. Carrying our backpacks into the fresh sunrise over the sea, we passed through the gates and then walked and walked, before eventually catching a monastic vehicle that left us at the right spot to start tackling the forest kalderimi. We would be there plenty early. Wrong assessment.

When we finally ascended to the kelli, a sprawling mass of other pilgrims was already gathered outside. I was confounded. One Greek pilgrim handed me a list, to preserve a record of our place by order of arrival. My name was scrawled down in big Greek letters on a paper after the vacant entry number twenty-seven. The first pilgrims had arrived there at 4.30 a.m., we were told. Two other monks passed by occasionally, though the man everyone had come to see was still asleep. There was no guarantee that he would see everyone, no matter how long we waited, we soon learned.

As the hours slowly crept by, I began to feel guilty, like I was ruining my friend's Athos experience. I said I would understand if he wanted us to abandon the mission after a certain time. He just laughed and munched another of the powdered pieces of Turkish Delight the monks had left for us all, next to a tankard of water. 'No, man, I'm cool,' he said. 'If you gotta see your monk, you gotta see your monk. We'll wait as long as we need.'

As morning turned to afternoon and approached evening, I enjoyed numerous conversations with other pilgrims who had also come to share a few moments with the charismatic ascetic. I was struck by how important and how varied participation in the Athos experience really is; yes, Athos is the monks, and it is about the monks first and foremost, but it is also about those who come to seek their blessings and to engage in their own spiritual betterment. Athos is thus, at a certain level, the sum of the interactions enjoyed and bonds forged among the pilgrims. It has been that way since the beginning and always will be so.

The long day of waiting in the woods allowed me to speak with several other pilgrims, all of whom had unique and profound stories behind their visit. Of all these, my favourite perhaps was Charalambos, a good-natured theology student from Athens, who was just a spot ahead of me on the list. We passed the time talking about various topics from religious history and contemporary life. I told him of my previous studies of the Church Fathers back at Oxford. He told me that he was concerned with the practical challenges facing the family in modern Greece, considering the poor economy, secularist ideologies and so on. We talked until it was his turn to speak with the monk. The sun was receding and most of the crowd had dissipated.

Finally, after waiting for almost thirteen hours, it was my turn to go down to sit across from the monk, at a wooden table under a sort of pagoda that I did not recall from seven years earlier. Charalambos, coming up the pagoda steps, looked very happy.

"So, what did he say to you?" I asked, setting foot on the stair.

"He confirmed what is my dream," replied Charalambos. "I will become a priest in Athens and help the regular people. The father believes I am strong enough for that challenge. I am very happy."

I congratulated my fellow pilgrim and shook his hand before descending to where I too could hopefully gain some vital insight. I have no doubts that, should I visit Athens again someday, I can ring up the number Charalambos entrusted to me and continue our conversation exactly where we left off.

For truly, Athos has an enduring role and eternal function; it is the great joy of anyone who has ever visited to know that the Holy Mountain will exist inside of you, wherever you may happen to be in the world. Inevitably, this means that this joy of the Athos experience is shared with those who have not been, or who cannot go. This is one response that can be offered to those critics who argue that monks do not 'do anything.' In fact, Athos means the world.

A Family Affair

TERRY SWEHLA

After a two-year Christian spiritual odyssey, on Holy Saturday, April 1995, I was chrismated into the Holy Orthodox Church. Joining me that day was my wife and our three teenage sons. During our journey we had immersed ourselves in the richness of the Orthodox tradition and history, including the lives of unfamiliar saints and distant holy sites. Interestingly, none of this had been revealed to me during my prior Lutheran seminary studies.

As I grew into my new Orthodox world I found that references to Mount Athos, the Holy Mountain, kept appearing in my readings. Eventually I discovered the Friends of Mount Athos (FoMA) and found that their commentary kindled a deeper interest in learning about this unique place. In 2005, I joined FoMA so that I could immerse myself further into the life of the Holy Mountain's unique, other-worldly communities.

The annual FoMA reports spoke of teams clearing footpaths between monasteries while having the opportunity to live and worship with various monastic communities. The thought of joining such a work party began to percolate within me and in the fall of 2011 I decided to apply. By then my family had greatly expanded. My sons had completed their college educations, married faithful wives and had provided my wife and me with nine grandchildren.

I reached out to my sons and invited them to join me knowing that their lives were quite full supporting and raising their respective families. To my surprise, one of them, Ryan, accepted my invitation. Our application was accepted by team leader Andrew Buchanan and in April 2012 we departed on the nearly 7,000 mile (11,000 km) travel from California's West Coast to the Holy Mountain, with stopovers in London and Thessaloniki.

Our time on Mount Athos was like discovering a new world: some things were familiar, much was anticipated through our reading, but unforeseen wonders awaited us. Our stay was divided between the monasteries of Vatopedi and Zografou. While at Vatopedi we rose early and spent most of our days working alongside other team members trimming vegetation along the paths. We worked primarily along the ridge line above the monastery and on the paths leading to Zografou. Even after an exhausting day of working and hiking, joining the monastic community for vespers and the evening meal in their historic refectory was a rejuvenating and deeply rewarding experience. Occasionally we were blessed to have evening discussions in our dormitory room with Father M, an American convert to Orthodoxy who had lived many years as a member of the Vatopedi community.

We used the same trails we had cleared to hike to Zografou monastery where we would spend most of our second week. Our only companion was a wonderful Greek teammate, Dimitris Bakalis. His assignment was to map and evaluate surrounding paths. Ryan and I were asked to clear the trail leading to the monastery of Konstamonitou. This path had been quite neglected and we spent quality father-son time identifying the trail and hacking away the obstructing brush.

During our stay another team member, Roland Baetens, who had visited the Holy Mountain on numerous occasions, joined us and guided us to the cave of St Kosmas. Near the end of our stay, Roland suggested that we join him in travelling down the coast to New (Nea) Skete. He wanted to introduce us to a monk that he had visited on prior trips. Little did Ryan and I realize that this journey would lead to a life-long relationship with this holy place.

Upon arriving in New Skete we were greeted and led to their guest-quarters. That evening we walked up the eight hundred steps to the cell of St Charalambos where Elder H and his small brotherhood resided. We found life in a skete community to be a different experience from the cenobitic life within the walls of a monastery.

That first afternoon and evening we sat on Elder H's veranda and enjoyed his hospitality while nature provided a spectacular view of storm clouds and

PL. 55 *Nea Skete from path to Agia Anna*

lightening over the Aegean Sea. We talked into the night with Elder H gently guiding our conversation. The next day was again spent at Elder H's kellion. We learned that he had been given the blessing to move to New Skete by his spiritual father, Elder Charalambos, who had been a disciple of recently canonized Elder Joseph the Hesychast. We were spending time with the spiritual 'grandchild' of a saint. As the day passed, he invited us to return and encouraged Ryan to consider bringing his two sons on that future visit.

On our journey home Ryan expressed that he felt a deep, immediate connection with Elder H. This was affirmed as they began communicating via VoIP applications. Now on the feasts of Pascha and the Nativity of Our Lord we enjoy participating in conversations with Elder H.

In September 2014, my wife and I and our son, Ryan, and his wife and their three children travelled to Thessaloniki. During the intervening years Ryan and Elder H had remained in contact. For this trip Elder H met all of us in Thessaloniki and was our family's personal guide through Thessaloniki's rich Orthodox history.

The following morning Ryan and I and his two sons (nine-year-old Matthew and seven-year-old Andrew) travelled with Elder H to New Skete. During our four day stay we had the opportunity to visit the Holy Monasteries of Dionysiou and St Paul's, St Anne's skete and the cave and tomb of Elder Joseph the Hesychast. Matthew and Andrew were able to experience a lifestyle very different from their California lifestyle. Together we worshipped in Elder H's chapel, enjoyed hiking the footpaths along the base of Mount Athos and added to our Orthodox knowledge and piety. We experienced our first all-night vigil for the Feast of the Elevation of the Holy Cross at New Skete's kyriakon. For my two young grandsons to be in the presence of so many monks, amid the sounds of Byzantine chanting and in the shadows created by the candlelit setting, was truly an other-worldly experience. We noticed that their presence seemed to bring a joyful expression to the monks who understood the biblical guidance to enter into the Kingdom with a child's heart.

Four years later, in August 2018, my other two sons, Joel and Matthew, were able to join Ryan and his sons for another trip to the Holy Mountain and Elder H's residence. For one of my sons (now Father Matthew serving within the Greek Orthodox Archdiocese of America) who had been unable to participate in his seminary's class trip to the Holy Mountain, it was the chance to complete an important part of his spiritual formation as a priest.

FIG. 40 *Zografou Monastery*

Together, the brothers hiked to Kavsokalyvia to visit the cell of St Porphyrios. Through Elder H's gracious efforts all five of them visited the cell of St Paisios and spent a night at Vatopedi monastery, where Ryan and I had first stayed six years earlier.

Our family's connection to the Holy Mountain continued this past June with Ryan and his sons once again visiting Elder H. This time Ryan left his sons in Elder H's care an additional week so they could enjoy their own special time in that sacred place. They are looking forward, God willing, to many future visits. As Ryan commented, 'The boys have developed a fond relationship and wonderful memories of Elder H and the brotherhood. They have spent time on their own there: playing and exploring, gardening and helping the brothers, learning to write icons and visiting the dwelling places of saints'.

God's Spirit has graciously worked wonders throughout our family by way of these journeys. Together, we have had opportunities to venerate some of the most sacred relics of our Orthodox Church and to pray before numerous miracle-working icons. Our faith has been enriched with tangible experiences of the Panaghia's precious work on Her Holy Mountain. Mount Athos has become a focal point of our family's experience even though our homes are thousands of miles away. The time we have spent on the Holy Mountain bridges the time and distance that physically separates us. And our encounters with those who live there and maintain prayers for us have enriched all of us, even those family members who could not step on its shores.

As Ryan reflected on deciding to join me seven years ago on FoMA's Footpath Project: 'Getting away from work and family commitments for two weeks was very difficult, but it turned out to be one of the best decisions I ever made'. At the time neither he nor I realized the real impact our participation would have on us, our family and future generations. Today, our family is blessed to enjoy a living connection to the saints of the Holy Mountain.

Waves of Eternal Praise

THOMAS STOOR

I was twenty-three-years old when I visited the Holy Mountain for the first time in 1978. I was working at the Scandinavian Seamen's Church in Piraeus, Greece, visiting Scandinavian vessels in the harbour of Piraeus. I had already heard about the Holy Mountain of Athos from a Greek student I had met, and through the book The Way of a Pilgrim, the Jesus Prayer was already a part of my prayer life.

While working in Greece I saw the opportunity to visit Mount Athos for the first time, not only through literature and art, but as a pilgrim myself. I told the Swedish seamen's pastor my plans and we decided to go together that spring. With all the documents in place we took the train from Athens to Thessaloniki, and then the bus to Ouranoupolis and found our hotel for the night. The next morning, when we were to enter the ferry to the port of Daphne, the Swedish seamen's pastor, was refused entry. As he was an ordained minister of the Evangelical Lutheran Church of Sweden he needed an additional document from his bishop, which he did not have. So for him it was 'no entry' to the Holy Mountain. What could we do? We decided to stay one extra night in Ouranoupolis and try again the next morning. But, unfortunately, the same officer was at the ferry, the same refusal, so my friend had to go back to Athens.

Alone, I went on the ferry that morning and finally entered the holy ground of the Mountain. With me I had my prayer book, a copy of Metropolitan Kallistos's book *The Orthodox Church*, and a letter of introduction that I had received from Professor Constantine Scouteris of Athens University. He had recommended that, after receiving the diamonitirion at the building of the Holy Epistasia in Karyes, I go to the skete of St Andrew in Karyes and the Athonite Academy. There I would present my letter of introduction to the Fathers in order to get advice how to travel and spend my four days as a pilgrim on the Holy Mountain. The Fathers and teachers kindly received me, but I noticed a certain suspicion and curiosity as to why this young, Protes-tant student of theology wanted to visit the chief centre of Orthodox monasticism. I remember that I said that I had come to experience the source of Christian faith and tradition, which Orthodoxy had preserved unchanged since the time of the apostles. The Fathers seemed very pleased with my answer and gave me an excellent plan concerning which monasteries I should visit and how. During my stay I visited the monasteries of Stavronikita, Iviron, Esphigmenou, Chilandar, St Panteleimon, Grigoriou and Simonos Petras.

With my diamonitirion in hand I started to walk towards my first goal, the holy monastery of Stavronikita, where I was going to spend my first night. During my walk I was amazed by the peace and the beauty of nature that surrounded me. The sight of the sea in front of me and the mountain in the distance filled me with a deep inner joy. I felt the whole of nature was filled with praise and thanksgiving towards God. With every step I took I prayed the Jesus Prayer and I felt that in my heart I took part in cosmic praise to God for the beauty of Creation.

At Stavronikita, I was greeted by a monk who showed me to the guest room. I was the only pilgrim and my bed was right next to the window. As the sun went down and I went to bed, I heard the sound of the waves outside. The sight of Mount Athos in the evening light from my window gave me a feeling of great calm and deep gratitude towards God. Something of the stillness and inner peace that the writers of The Philokalia describe as hesychia filled my heart.

The next day, and thanks to the possibility of using the boat, I went to the monasteries of Esphigmenou and Chilandar. At Chilandar, a young Serbian monk offered me lunch and time to rest in the guest room in a part of the monastery that was tragically destroyed by the terrible fire in 2004. I still remember the old furniture and the pictures on the wall of Serbian saints and royalty, all destroyed in the fire and now gone for ever.

At the Russian monastery of St Panteleimon I was the only pilgrim to stay overnight. I was alone in the huge pilgrims' accommodation near the sea. At the refectory, built for 500 monks, I sat together with fewer than thirty monks at the table, under damaged frescos of serious ascetics and saints from the deep forests of the Russian Thebaid. During the divine service in the church, with the golden iconostasis, I noticed an old schema-monk who stood in silence behind a pillar. Perhaps he came from Valaam monastery in Lake Ladoga, the 'Athos of the North', that I have visited several times. His silent presence reminded me how close Orthodox monasticism had once been to my own country of Sweden, only on the other side of the Baltic Sea.

My most unforgettable memory from my first visit is my stay at the monastery of Simonos Petras. It was the evening before the Feast of the Ascension of our Lord. One of the monks invited me to follow him to the balcony, high up, towards the sea, for a coffee and a talk on spiritual matters and my life in the world. There, near heaven, far from the busy world in Athens, my admiration and love for the Orthodox faith and tradition was planted in my heart. As the evening came, I experienced the same scenery that Robert Byron described in his book *The Station*; 'The sun was setting, striking hidden fire in the purple hills. While the water, as if in protest, turned a shivering glass-green … The sun was gone, and the twilight deepening …' (see p. 21 in this book).

Later that evening, the sound of the talanton called me to church and the night-prayer began. The prayers, the hymns, the smell of incense and the swinging of the great chandelier enveloped me and all my senses. After a couple of hours I went back to my room. I was alone. Deep under my window I could hear the eternal sound of the sea and the waves that for thousands of years had broken on the coast. At the same time, I heard the singing and the hymns from the church. The monks' praise of God for the glorious Ascension of Christ, our Lord, met the praise of nature in an everlasting song of praise from man and creation towards the Creator and Giver of life. Surrounded by this hymn of praise from man and nature, I fell asleep.

Finally, what about my friend, the Swedish seamen's pastor? Did he ever visit the Holy Mountain? When we parted, some forty years ago, we promised one another that one day in the future we would go together, with the right documents, as pilgrims to the Holy Mountain.

So in 2007 we went together and encountered quite a different Athos, with more roads, more vehicles, and monks talking on mobile phones.

But my memories from a more peaceful and quieter Athos remain with me, as a constant source of spiritual inspiration and gratitude to the Lord, who gave me the opportunity to be a pilgrim on the Holy Mountain.

PL.57 *Entrance to Stavronikita Monastery*

An Athonite Childhood

ANNA CONOMOS-WEDLOCK

My monastery story began before I was born.

My parents, Dimitri and Danae Conomos were married in Oxford in 1979 and they decided to spend their honeymoon in Greece, in a monastery, but not the same one. My father went to Simonos Petras on Mount Athos and my mother to the sister monastery of Ormylia in Chalkidiki. When the time came for Dad to pick Mum up she complained, 'Why didn't you bring me here before we got married?'

The nuns of Ormylia love to retell this story. I'm glad Dad didn't take Mum there before the wedding because if he had I am sure that my sister, brother and I would not be here today to tell the tale. But they did do the next best thing. They revolved all school holidays, long weekends, all possible time off with visits to Athonite monasteries. They even bought a flat in Thessaloniki so we could have a base close to Athos and Chalkidiki. And this was our childhood.

Athonite monasteries were our life. Our real life. Everything else was what we did in between, until we were able to go back. And this defined all our formative years. I can safely say that the monasteries gave us a unique and precious schooling. My first (sung) words aged eleven months were: 'Κύριε Ἐκέκραξα' (Lord I have cried), which I had already heard countless times at the long monastic vigils that I would scream my way through as a newborn baby. While the other children at school were singing 'Baa baa black sheep', I was singing Byzantine chants in the first tone. While others were bringing their favourite toys to our 'Show and Tell', we would bring the prayer rope that we had been taught to knit using nine knots to represent the nine ranks of angels. And while other children were spending summer holidays by the sea we were baptising dogs and chickens on the monastery farm and building our own mini monastery in a barn by the farm house.

The farm was the designated children's space; in fact we were so proud of it that I spent my lunch-breaks at school in Birmingham collecting rubbish from the playground in order to raise money for our 'mini monastery church' in Ormylia, which we had dedicated to St Modestos, the protector of animals. We had already chosen the roles for our 'mini monastery community': I was the chanter, my brother the priest, my sister a nun, our best friend the abbess (she is now a nun at Ormylia, she became a novice at sixteen), her brother the abbot and so on.

And so this was my precious other life, the one that was so close to my heart. I would relish the long walks through the camomile and poppy fields, listening to nuns telling us stories about St Mary of Egypt or St Seraphim of Sarov or the Mother of God. And my favourite stories were about the nuns themselves, how they used to escape from home secretly at night to go to midnight services, how their mothers had vehemently disapproved of their calling and then ended up becoming nuns as well!

I also loved the all-night vigils! Lining up in the semi-dark church to receive the blessing from the Abbess, feeling her squeeze my hand in that special personal way, being given a chair up the front if I could prove that I could stand v-e-r-y still. And then our favourite moment! At the half-way point in the service, all the children (and only the children!) are hurried out of church! We are taken through the starlit night, across the sweet-smelling courtyard, all the way to the children's centre, our hearts are bursting with excitement! We are treated to the most delicious sweets and to the most spine-tingling stories about the legendary Vlahouli, the monastery dog, who saved the lives of so many sheep, goats, rabbits and chickens from greedy predators! Then we return to the vigil just in time to watch the gold 'polyeleos' (chandelier) spinning round and round in the centre of the church to the rhythm of the chanting, we join the nuns at the choir stand and we bellow out 'Kyrie Eleison' and for those few hours, we are convinced, that the whole world revolves around us.

We would always prepare a special play or concert to entertain the nuns on Easter Sunday and in the process, we would each discover and develop our talents. We never knew the fear of performing in public since we were given so many opportunities to do this at the monastery and the nuns are the most encouraging and enthusiastic audience imaginable! Once a year, on Easter Sunday, we were taken up to the bell tower and taught to ring the bells and the semantron in the unique Athonite rhythm, we were allowed to make as much noise as we pleased!

We loved being included in the 'diakonimata', the monastic obediences which included fruit-picking, the painting of stones to sell in the shop, cleaning, and serving Greek coffee and loukoumi to visitors. The visitors were always very curious when they saw us working at the monastery.

'Why are you in the monastery?'

'We are having a holiday here'.

'REALLY, why?'

'Because there's nowhere else we would rather be, the people here are the happiest people in the world and my experiences here are the most joyful part of my year'. We knew that we had a constant source of prayer and love to draw from, the monastics were always there, watching us grow and change while they remained unchanging and full of love. I remember we would even use them as a measuring tape to see how tall we were getting while they seemed to get shorter! As an adult I can see how these experiences gave us everything: faith, freedom, discipline, routine, creativity …

For my sister Thalia, it was the drawing. She went on to study iconography and mosaics at the Prince's School in London, and is now an artist and teacher. For my brother, it was the practical side of life: woodwork, metalwork, carving and building. For me, it was the music and the stories. I developed a low voice like the nuns of Ormylia who were instructed by Abbot Aimilianos to sing with 'andreia' (manly strength and depth). And so my voice evolved accordingly. It was unusual and now, in my profession as a storyteller, I use all these skills that the monastery freely gave to me.

When I got married, I could not wait to take my husband to Ormylia and give him a taste of the life that I had the privilege to know. It was an experience that perhaps I and all of us Athonite children took for granted. After our visit my husband said, 'You must be so grateful to your parents for sowing these seeds for you, so that it was all ready-made for you when you were born and you were given an Athonite childhood which I now have the privilege of sharing and knowing as well'.

FIGS. 41–42 *An Athonite childhood*

Part Three

FoMA Footpaths Project

*Visitors to Mount Athos today may not realize that
many of the paths they walk along were impassable, or
even completely forgotten about, only twenty years ago.
The fact that they are walkable today is largely down to
the Friends of Mount Athos footpaths project, which was
the creation of John Arnell. Given food for thought by an
idea aired by HRH Prince Charles, John set about making
the idea a reality. Accounts of the project's progress have
become a regular feature of the FoMA Annual Report,
and it continues to go from strength to strength.*

Early Days

JOHN ARNELL & TREVOR CURNOW

Reprinted below are John's first two reports on the project,
which began with one small team based
in one large monastery in 2001.

Clearing the Footpaths – First Years: 30 April – 10 May 2001

Many pilgrims to the Holy Mountain in recent years have been concerned about the deterioration in the condition of the footpaths and, in many cases, their virtual extinction as the roads and forest trails have been developed. Notwithstanding the wonderful maps and the working parties led by Herr Reinhold Zwerger, the condition of the footpaths has continued to deteriorate. At the reception for the Friends of Mount Athos held on 2 August 2000 at Highgrove, His Royal Highness the Prince of Wales expressed similar concern and suggested that the Friends should put their minds to this problem to see what could be done.

Having had some responsibility for our local footpaths, I contacted the British Trust for Conservation Volunteers (BTCV), from whom I have received excellent training in footpath clearance in the past. They were enthusiastic to help with the project and introduced me to one of their senior international project leaders, Andy Rockall. Together we worked out an outline plan of action, a system to document the state of the paths and the work completed, and a shopping list for tools and equipment.

Volunteers included members of the Friends, BTCV members to act as team leaders, representatives of the Prince's Foundation, and my local Footpaths Officer from Essex County Council. They proved to be a long-suffering and very good-humoured group, despite disparate backgrounds, experience, and ages.

The team of twelve met for the first time at Heathrow airport to travel to Thessaloniki via Vienna. Most of the party were visiting the Holy Mountain for the first time, so I had taken great care to ensure they were well briefed on what to expect in terms of accommodation, food, and facilities. I was really pleased to see that everyone arrived at Heathrow with minimal luggage, especially as we had two substantial packages of cutters, loppers, saws, choppers, etc. to take with us.

We arrived in Thessaloniki in the late afternoon and had made arrangements to stay overnight. This provided the opportunity for some 'team-building' in the evening, but we were all on parade at the crack of dawn for our coach to Ouranoupolis. The coach didn't arrive! We did eventually wake the driver and get the trip underway, but we had to have some rapid processing of our documents at the office in Ouranoupolis to get to the ship in time. Then the magic of the Holy Mountain started to take charge. I suspect that all pilgrims find that boat journey something rather special, an opportunity for reflection and to shed some of the thoughts that trouble our daily lives.

It was with considerable relief that I found two monks from the monastery of Vatopedi waiting to greet us at Daphne and transport us across the mountains to the monastery that was to be our base for the next two weeks. We were accommodated in two dormitories adjacent to one another; and, having settled in, we were introduced to Father M, who was to be our main point of contact with the monastery during our stay. We were greeted by Father A, the deputy abbot, and Father I. We spent some time that evening discussing the footpaths that we should work on. We also took a look at the condition of some of the nearer paths and then got the team together for a talk on the safe use of the equipment we had brought.

The next morning we were breakfasted and on the road by 7 and put our first efforts at clearing on the path leading from the monastery to the monument on the ridgeway known as Chera, 'The Hand'. We split into teams of three or four, depending on the conditions, and each team would take a twenty-five-metre stretch of path. We found that much of the pathway had been reduced down to no more than half a metre, which we cut back to generally about two metres. The constrictions varied from bracken to substantial trees up to ten centimetres thick which had to be sawn down and then cut into pieces for disposal.

The work was slow and demanding, and drinking water quickly became a vital commodity. We had a brief stop at around 10 a.m. to review progress, refuel with water and perhaps an apple if that was on the menu for the day. We then worked until about 1 p.m. when we took a more substantial break for food and to rest. We were supplied with lunch provisions by the monastery. These included olives, bread, apples, cheese on a non-fasting day, and occasionally halva and raisins. We settled in quickly to the relatively frugal diet that had been a cause of concern to many people before the trip, and as time progressed, secret stashes of Mars bars and other chocolate delights started to appear.

We finished between 3 p.m. and 4 p.m., depending on conditions and the distance we had to walk back to the monastery. Then started an orderly queue for the shower, washing and airing of clothes, writing up of notes, and perhaps a short rest before joining the monastic community in the church for the evening service. Supper was taken as part of the service, and after supper we met with the Holy Fathers to discuss progress, outline a plan for the following day, and, as the days progressed, to discuss various other issues, many well removed from footpaths. We came to learn much about the organization and planning that are necessary to keep the monastery functioning. Their plans for the future are ambitious and include the complete renovation of the olive groves as well as considerable building and renovation work around the monastery and at the derelict school building. Major work is already in hand to underpin the structure of the church and to continue the renovation of the monks' quarters. We were privileged to stay in completely renovated accommodation, this work having been done to the highest standards throughout.

After the first few days the quality and speed of our work on the footpaths had improved and the monks were taking an increasing interest in our work. Attendance in church was increasing as the members of our team began to understand more of the significance of aspects of the services. It was also noticeable that the levels of chatter both inside the dormitory and around the monastery significantly diminished.

We had one really testing day of heavy rain. A decision was taken first thing in the morning that we should press on with the work planned for the day. This decision was far from unanimous. We set off in heavy rain; but after just a couple of hours of cold wet conditions things brightened up; and by the time we had completed our day, clothes had dried out and spirits improved.

One evening we were very honoured to be offered a tour of the new museum and the old library. The library contains some amazing treasures, including very ancient illuminated manuscripts, and we were able to view the thirteenth-century copy of Ptolemy's Geography with its wonderfully coloured maps. The continuing work on the library will enable these priceless manuscripts to be preserved in good condition for future generations.

His Royal Highness had indicated his intention to visit the monastery during the period of our stay. As the time of his visit approached, one could sense increased urgency around the monastery. For our part, we had earmarked a particularly interesting stretch of path that we thought included a wall and a fountain but was all very heavily overgrown. This was in case His Royal Highness should wish to join us in our task. On the evening of his arrival Andy and I spent an hour or so with the Prince of Wales to brief him on the work we had done and what we felt needed to be done in the future. He seemed pleased with what we had achieved, and concerned at the amount that remained to be done across the territory of the Holy Mountain, but also concerned that our team appeared to be short on luxuries. We had tactfully referred to the impact of the smell of bacon early in the morning emanating from the royal accommodation which was situated below our dormitories. Immediately after this discussion two bottles of a suitable luxury were delivered to our dormitories. The smell of bacon was quickly forgotten.

The Prince of Wales and two of his party joined us to help clear the fountain area. This turned out to be a very substantial task, but was interrupted by the appearance of a lone pilgrim who we found was from Khabarovsk, in the very far east of Russia. He was a little taken aback to be introduced to the

Prince of Wales who greeted him with enthusiasm; lost he decided to join in our efforts and stayed on to share our lunch. It was a wonderful day and we were all impressed with the energy and enthusiasm shown by the Prince of Wales. We had cleared an area bounded by a stone wall in quite good condition with steps to the olive grove above, and the remains of an old fountain: a real reward for our efforts.

On several days we sent out survey parties, usually consisting of two people, to evaluate the condition and the work necessary to recover various paths, should it be possible to organize further visits in the future. Several we found to be all but impassable. Most of our work was in the area around the monastery and we estimated we cleared some five kilometres of path to a good standard. A further twenty-six kilometres were surveyed. This certainly represents no more than five per cent of the total task, but it is an important beginning. The monastery has also started renewing the waymarking of their paths. We took care to sharpen, oil, and grease all of the tools we took with us and these have been locked away together with some notes for the guidance of others who might have time available to continue our work.

The end of our last day's work was a very thoughtful time and the walk

PL.58 *On path*

back offered a period of inward reflection. For those visiting the Holy Mountain for the first time it had been a profound experience. Losing a little weight was just one of the good things that happened to most of us; but the return journey to our everyday lives was nevertheless a profound shock.

We decided, perhaps unwisely, to take the boat from Vatopedi to Nea Roda to where we had redirected our bus. The boat then stopped for several hours at Esphigmenou, putting our timetable at some risk. In the event we made our flight in good time but had to change planes in Vienna. For some reason I cannot fathom, half of our party avoided the 'Transit' signs and took themselves out through Austrian customs. By the time they made their way back, the rest of the party had found a small restaurant area where we could slowly wean ourselves back to our normal diet. We all noticed the noise, the colour, and the speed of things around us as we sat in the airport, especially when invaded by a party of football fans, celebrating some victory, no doubt.

Since returning, we have produced a short factual report both for the Friends and for St James's Palace to distribute to our various sponsors. We have laid plans for future visits, and I anticipate we shall be able to mount a similar effort in 2002.

PL.59 *Below cave of St Kosmas*

This project came about at the instigation of the Prince of Wales and we are especially grateful to His Royal Highness for his help and generosity in making it a possibility. A number of organizations have contributed in various ways including the funding of travel and equipment: the Latsis Organization, the Alliance of Religions and Conservation, and of course the Friends of Mount Athos. The help of the British Trust for Conservation Volunteers was invaluable in providing the experience and guidance that ensured good and safe progress was achieved. We are most grateful for all of this help and most especially for the assistance and hospitality of the monastery of Vatopedi.

Back Again! – Paths for Pilgrims: 2002

In last year's Annual Report I recounted how this project had been started at the suggestion of the Prince of Wales and how we had brought together a team of twelve people, equipped with the necessary tools and equipment, and spent two weeks in May 2001 surveying and clearing footpaths. That year we based the project at the monastery of Vatopedi and cleared paths towards Esphigmenou and the monument known as Chera ('The Hand').

The volunteers: The article in last year's Annual Report aroused considerable interest amongst the Friends and encouraged a number of people to volunteer for future work. In addition, publicity in British Trust for Conservation Volunteers (BTCV) and other publications including the Friends of Mount Athos website led a number of non-members to volunteer their services. Hence, when the opportunity arose to pay a further visit in 2002, we decided to increase the size of the team to eighteen and to work from two additional monasteries, Pantokrator and Koutloumousiou. Our team included both an artist, James Horton, and a photographer, Richard Storey, whose resulting work has been seen by many members of the Friends both at the seminar at Highgrove last summer and at the reception at Bridgewater House, shortly before Christmas.

The team members are selected as far as possible on a first-come basis together with experienced footpath conservationists from BTCV and some members from previous years to ensure we have a good body of seasoned workers in each of the teams. We also look for specific skills, people with first-aid training, knowledge of Greek, or experience in work of this type, for example. Everyone is sent a briefing well in advance, giving some indication of what they might expect, and advising them specifically to bring earplugs and Mars bars or whatever, to provide a supplement to the diet and comfort food. Whilst the suggestion of earplugs caused some amusement, one of our number this year was able to arrange sponsorship from Mars resulting in a donation of several hundred Mars bars, weighing well over thirty kilos – a substantial weight to haul to Mount Athos but much appreciated both by the team and occasionally by the monks.

The team came from a wide geographic spread – Sweden, USA, the Orkney Islands – and a variety of backgrounds – bookseller, composer, an oil broker, a professor of genetics. This mixture added to the richness of conversations whilst working through the day or during more relaxed moments in the evening.

From my perspective, I correspond with all of these volunteers, but we do not actually meet until two hours or so before the flight leaves. It is interesting trying to pick them out and put a face to a name as the team slowly assembles. It is at this point, working with Andy Rockall, the BTCV team leader, that we start to put together the smaller teams so that, when we reach the Holy Mountain, we can split into three groups.

The 11 September events in the United States had an influence even on our small project. The group insurance scheme we had used the previous year was withdrawn very shortly before we were due to leave. After we had unsuccessfully cast around the UK both by telephone and on the Internet, a local broker just four miles away came to the rescue and provided suitable cover for each of the volunteers.

This year the Prince of Wales and his party, which included Professor David Cadman, a member of the Friends' Executive Committee, again joined us. They spent a day meeting members of the team and working alongside them clearing a wonderful arch on a pathway leading to a skete outside Karyes.

The task: In our first year, 2001, we had cleared some five kilometres of footpath and surveyed a further twenty-six kilometres. The focus of our clearance efforts had been the paths from Vatopedi to Esphigmenou and to Chera and we had surveyed paths from Chera and Zografou towards Esphigmenou as well as several paths from Vatopedi in the direction of Karyes. The main path from Vatopedi to Karyes is one of the more important links and we made this a prime target for our efforts in 2002. With a team of six based at Vatopedi we spent several days working towards Karyes, whilst a smaller team based in

Koutloumousiou worked towards them from Karyes. Part way along this path we came across a small fountain, set into a stone wall, well back from the path. It was no longer functioning, trees had fallen across the path, and the water was now making the path a quagmire. We cleared away the fallen trees, made a sensible gully for the water, and managed to clear things up somewhat. However, the restoration of the fountain remains as a task for the future. This is a wonderful long walk and has been well used in the past.

During the latter part of the work, towards Karyes, we could see the skete of St Andrew with its large church but now with many of the buildings and surroundings in a very poor state of repair. We made a cursory survey to see if there was any specific short-term clearance work that we might be able to undertake, but the magnitude of the task was well beyond the capabilities of our small team. We did clear a section of path northeast of St Andrew's, to meet up with the road, then in the direction of Pantokrator where the path again left the road, thus making a walk from Karyes to Pantokrator at least partially on footpath.

In the second week we changed around the membership of the three teams, and by then the monasteries of Pantokrator and Koutloumousiou had gained more understanding of the sort of work we were capable of. With the considerable enthusiasm of the Abbot, the team of six at Koutloumousiou were able to clear a very overgrown section of path, thereby re-establishing the route between that monastery and its arsanas. This walk, passing the skete of Koutloumousiou, goes directly to the arsanas and links then to the footpath between Iviron and Stavronikita. The Abbot was able to help us find the path where it had become so completely overgrown as to be indistinguishable from the surrounding undergrowth. In one section it now forms a tunnel through this undergrowth.

We met a very badly scratched and bruised pilgrim who had attempted the walk between Pantokrator and Vatopedi and completely lost the path. With the encouragement of the monastery, our small team working from Pantokrator set about the task. Initially they too had great difficulty in locating the path and found the work of clearing it very demanding. With considerable effort, however, it was satisfactorily completed and we hope it will be well marked so that pilgrims can take advantage of this footpath to Vatopedi.

Surveying: This year we were equipped with two GPS devices, one generously donated by a member of the team. These enable a position to be established from satellites; and, with the help of a small computer, maps can be produced of the paths. The mapping company Epsilon SA based in Athens provided further GPS equipment and radios that were a great help in facilitating communications between groups, but only over short distances. Communication between the three teams was a difficulty and we resorted to text messages on mobile telephones via the UK. This was both expensive and unreliable but was the best method we could find.

Plans for 2003

With the help of the GPS equipment, computer, and mapping software loaned to us by Easy GPS, we were able to map the paths as they were cleared, to survey other paths, and to plot the forest roads, thus distinguishing on the map between footpaths and forest roads. Most days we were able to send out two people together to walk, survey, and thus map footpaths, as well as to record their condition to add to our file of information. We hope this work will contribute towards a new map of the Holy Mountain and we are encouraging efforts in this direction. Whilst the most accurate map is without doubt that produced by Reinhold Zwerger, the far less detailed map recently produced by Road Editions SA is more readily available and is now the map used by most pilgrims. We would like to see the accuracy and detail of this map improved and have been discussing with the company ways in which this might be achieved. We now have our sights set on 2003 and a further visit is scheduled.

The website of the society (www.athosfriends.org), maintained by Professor Robert Allison, has been expanded to include a simple spreadsheet that details the best information we have been able to collect on the current state of the footpaths. This information comes partly from our own efforts but also from others who have walked the paths and recorded their condition, sending the information to me by e-mail so that it can be entered on the website. We have established a scale that can be used to describe the condition of the footpaths and this is entered on the chart together with estimates of the time taken to walk between monasteries. We hope that this information will prove of value to future pilgrims and will help us to monitor the overall condition of the paths. Any further detail that can be added to this information would be greatly appreciated.

In total we estimate we cleared a further fifteen kilometres of footpath, surveyed a further forty kilometres, and mapped some fifty kilometres of forest track. We are making progress but it is a big task. A particular path that we have surveyed and that is in a very poor condition is the ridgeway going south-east from Chera. We would like to connect this with the footpaths between Vatopedi and Konstamonitou where we have already done some preliminary work. There is no easy approach to this path and it is going to represent a considerable (but worthwhile) challenge for the future. There are also the paths from Chera and Zografou to Esphigmenou that we surveyed in 2001 and that we should like to see re-established if circumstances permit.

Readers of last year's Annual Report may recall the encounter we had with a lone pilgrim from Khabarovsk in the far east of Russia who joined us for lunch and was surprised to be introduced to the Prince of Wales. This year, whilst waiting at Thessaloniki for our return flight home, we came across the same Russian pilgrim, also waiting for his return flight – a remarkable coincidence! Though we now have a full team for this visit, I should always be pleased to hear from anyone who has any suggestions or comments or who might wish to join us in the future. If you are making a pilgrimage to the Holy Mountain this year, please also visit the website, familiarize yourself with the information we have posted there, and contribute your findings when you return.

The continuing enthusiasm of the Prince of Wales for this project has ensured its future. We were able to demonstrate what had so far been achieved at the seminar at Highgrove in June and to raise funds at the reception at Bridgewater House in December. In his address at Bridgewater House, His Royal Highness spoke of the importance of the Holy Mountain as both refuge and inspiration in today's changing world. He also spoke of the need to encourage pilgrims to use the footpaths as an alternative to a bumpy ride over a dusty road.

We are most grateful to the Latsis Foundation which has borne the considerable costs of travel and accommodation en route and to its staff who have always been most helpful. One member of the team had to be flown home to the UK at very short notice due to a family bereavement. The staff of the Latsis Foundation made this possible without any difficulty. They should also be commended for getting a bus driver out of bed at 6 a.m. on a Sunday when arrangements had become confused.

The British Trust for Conservation Volunteers provide the experience, the training, and the templates necessary for organizing other aspects of the project such as risk assessment. They also provide tools and equipment at a discount, and we are very grateful for this support and assistance.

The monasteries of Vatopedi, Koutloumousiou, and Pantokrator were most hospitable and enthusiastic about the work we were doing. The gratitude of the abbots and monks is an instant reward for our footpath-clearing efforts; but each member of the team gains in his own way from exposure to the monastic life and from the spirituality of the Holy Mountain.

JOHN ARNELL, Bishop's Stortford

Footpaths Project 2003–2018

Since John's 2002 report, the footpaths project has gone from strength to strength, with FoMA members being kept informed of developments via the FoMA Annual Reports. What follows is a summary of what appeared in the FoMA Annual Reports for 2003 to 2018. Until 2010, the reports were all produced by John (who led the groups), sometimes with the help of others. After that, they were produced by different hands.

2003. This year saw eighteen people from various countries in Europe and North America staying in three monasteries; Vatopedi, Pantokrator and Koutloumousiou. It was found that the path between Esphigmenou and Vatopedi, cleared only two years previously, already needed work to bring it back to the desired standard. More progress was made on the long ridge path that runs along the spine of the peninsula, forming a major artery down the middle of Athos. Paths around Pantokrator and Koutloumousiou were opened up, and contact was made with the monastery of Simonopetra with an eye to doing work there in the future.

2004. Once again there was a group of eighteen, and this year some were based in Filotheou for the first time. More of the ridge path was opened up towards Chilandar, and an old path from Vatopedi to the nearby settlement of Kolitsou was made passable again.

2005. Only seventeen in the group this year, and a number were struck down by an unpleasant bug during their time on the Holy Mountain. The 'usual' monasteries of Vatopedi, Pantokrator and Koutloumousiou were joined by Simonopetra this year.

2006. Once again there were seventeen path-clearing pilgrims, based in the same monasteries as 2005, but with the addition of Zografou. Recognition of the fact that some people may be wary of using the paths because of inadequate maps, signage or directions has opened up a new dimension for the project.

2007. Seventeen in the group again this year with yet another new monastery, Konstamonitou, participating, so that the path between there and Zografou could be worked on from both ends. Descriptions of twenty-seven paths were produced and posted on the FoMA website.

2008. The number setting off from the UK was down to sixteen, but they were joined in Greece by three more pilgrims from Belgium. A lot of the work done consisted of keeping paths that have already been cleared up to standard, but the path from Zografou to Konstamonitou was finally reopened in its entirety. More work was done on path descriptions, and some new signposts were erected to help walkers find their way.

2009. This year's work mainly involved consolidation. Since its inception in 2001, the footpaths project has opened and continues to maintain over thirty miles of paths, no mean feat for fewer than twenty people working for only two weeks a year! More signposts and constantly revised and improved path descriptions help to encourage their use.

2010. Twenty-one people in the group this year, with Andrew Buchanan now taking on many of the organisational responsibilities. A team was based at Chilandar for the first time, and the ridge path from that monastery to Karyes was finally cleared in its entirety, a distance of around fourteen miles.

2011. This year the main report was written by a first-time member of the group, and, indeed, a first-time visitor to the Holy Mountain, David Holloway. David Bayne, who had taken on responsibility for the path descriptions, also reported on that aspect of the project. After a couple of false starts in that direction, a fresh beginning on a project to map the footpaths was made by another new group member Peter Howorth. The aim is eventually to map not only the paths, but the whole of the Holy Mountain itself. With the help of the monastery of Koutloumousiou, more signs were erected to guide walkers.

2012. Andrew Buchanan (who wrote his first of many reports this year) led a group of twenty to continue the work, with some old paths around Pantokrator being brought back into use. An important development was the translation of a number of the path descriptions into Greek by Dimitris Bakalis in order to make them accessible to more pilgrims. Peter Howorth's work on the map project continues apace.

2013. Andrew Buchanan led nineteen people back to the Holy Mountain this year. The number of path descriptions on the FoMA website is now fifty-five, with David Bayne regularly updating them, where required. Peter Howorth's mapping project is now moving into the checking stage. Group members were heartened to see ample evidence on the ground that the paths are being used.

2014. David Stothard led a group of 25 pilgrims this year, the first time that neither John Arnell nor Andrew Buchanan had been in the party. A group was based in Dionysiou for the first time. Not only were some paths around the

FIG. 43 *The Team 2002*

FIG. 44 *HRH with Father G (centre) and Father M*

monastery itself cleared, but it also formed a useful base for surveying other paths along the southern side of the Holy Mountain. Descriptions of over a hundred paths now appear on the FoMA website, and the mapping project is nearing completion.

2015. Andrew Buchanan returned to lead another group of twenty pilgrims. Described paths on the FoMA website now cover an impressive 150 miles. With the limited resources available, it is clear that some routes that are used less will have to receive less attention and be maintained to a lower standard, although still kept passable. There is a clear emerging demand for descriptions to be available in Serbian, Bulgarian and Russian as well as English and Greek. The mapping project was brought to completion, and a copy of the new map was presented to the Holy Epistasia.

2016. Twenty-two pilgrims led by Andrew Buchanan spread themselves over eleven monasteries, including the Great Lavra. This indicates the level of interest shown in the project by the monasteries of the Holy Mountain, and the level of support they provide. For the first time it was made possible for volunteers to work for only one week rather than two, thereby making it possible for more people to participate in the project. The new map is being well received.

2017. David Stothard took charge again, this time with a group of twenty-eight which included a larger number of Greek FoMA members than usual. The weather on Athos is not always kind, and path-clearers had to deal with many of the effects of a harsh winter, including many fallen trees.

2018. Andrew Buchanan led a team of thirty-two pilgrims who were hosted by a full fourteen monasteries and two sketes. Checking and maintenance continues, and evidence of monks and pilgrims using the paths continues to grow.

And finally... two anecdotes from John Arnell's collection

Prince Charles meets Father G

A hermit monk, Father G, lives some miles from Vatopedi, well into the hills. We arranged to take the Prince of Wales and his party to meet Father G, who seems pleased to have visitors. There was an interesting conversation between His Royal Highness and Father G with Father M acting as interpreter. Having learnt that he had become a monk on the Holy Mountain at about the age of eighteen, the Prince asked why he had become a monk. 'To escape the girls who would not leave me alone', was his immediate reply.

Who needs enemies?

We had been clearing an area well away from Vatopedi, a path that for some considerable distance went along the beach. The beach itself was a mess of plastic so we put a number of the team to the task of clearing the beach. Sitting on the balcony outside the monastery long after the doors had been locked for the evening, we noticed a glow in the distance, on the beach. We managed with some difficulty to find a monk still awake and raised the alarm. Soon the fire brigade arrived and we all chased off to the beach and the fire was quickly put out. At this point a monk was heard to ask: 'Who needs enemies when you have the Friends of Mount Athos?'

FIG.45 *Who needs enemies!*

Not on My Shift

DIMITRIS BAKALIS

I first set foot on Mount Athos in August 1987. With a bunch of friends, 'luck' brought me to spend the first night with the brotherhood at the kellion of Evangelismos at New Skete, which would later revive Vatopedi and accept the blessing of Elder Joseph. And I walked the Athonite footpaths for the first time. From New Skete to Great Lavra and from Konstamonitou to Zografou and back.

Meeting that 'place' marked me. And then I came and came again, improving my knowledge of the place, its tradition and its people. Born in a country where history is measured in millennia, time and tradition are reckoned differently in Greece from the rest of the world. But even for us, to return to the Byzantine way of life can only be awe-inspiring.

I was lucky because I met a different Athos from the one pilgrims encounter today. Dilapidated monasteries, without electricity or amenities like hot showers, fewer pilgrims, and especially fewer roads and cars. So, I got to know the footpaths and walked almost everywhere. Dozens of visits, thousands of kilometres. I walked with friends, I walked alone with the company of birds, during all seasons, rain and snow. Many times, I lost my way, looking for information from rusty signs, outdated maps and elderly monks. And I have found that this is the ideal way to 'reach' that particular 'place'. Panting uphill, slamming my feet onto the kalderimi, wet by the rain, without the unnecessary luxuries that will burden my backpack. This is how a pilgrim can control his ego, prepare himself for the wonderful Athonite hospitality and participation in worship and the spiritual life of the monasteries that always comes as an 'antidoron' at the end of the day.

This was a time of great change on Athos. New monks and more pilgrims began to arrive and the new brotherhoods were struggling to revive the monasteries and restore their lost glamour. This has also led to the need for new roads to facilitate the movement of people and goods. And unfortunately, this led to the abandonment of the footpaths. They were destroyed or crossed by the roads, and the monks and pilgrims abandoned them for the convenience of UNIMOGS.

I, of course, also changed … I grew up, had a family, acquired more obligations. But I kept walking on Athos, not as often as I used to, but I kept going, refusing to lose what I knew, what filled my life and my soul. And with bitterness I saw abandoned footpaths obstructed by vegetation and destroyed by the roads. As a Greek, as a citizen of the country blessed to host this 'holy place' and as an Orthodox, I felt some responsibility for the fact that this architectural wealth inherited from many generations of our ancestors might be lost forever, and that this would happen during my 'shift'. And I also knew that this loss was not just material.

I was looking for a way to help. But I didn't know what I could do. I felt too small for the work needed. But at the end of the first decade of the twenty-first century, I noticed that there were some improvements on some of the paths I was walking. Something was changing for the better. The vegetation had been removed and new signs had been installed on the historic footpaths.

During a pilgrimage at that time, walking from Karyes to Vatopedi, I met a Belgian. We walked for quite some time together and Roland told to me about the Prince who initiated the footpaths project and about some strange foreigners coming to Athos every year, struggling to keep the footpaths open to pilgrims. After that I kept a watch on their work, the paths they had reopened, the new signs they had placed, the footpath descriptions they had issued. And soon I decided that I was eager to become one of them.

Unfortunately, terrible things happened during the same period. The 'scandal' concerning Vatopedi shocked Mount Athos and Greek society in general. And the economic and social crisis had begun to slowly spread its tentacles and affect all the areas of social life in my country.

PL. 60 *Courtyard, Agia Anna*

The consequences were dramatic. People lost their jobs, their fortunes and their hopes. Thousands of our fellow citizens suddenly found themselves unable to obtain access to basic goods crucial to their livelihoods such as food, clothes or heating. Others – and especially the young and educated – left the country looking for a better life abroad. Everything around us was changing. And most of all, our collective psyche had changed. The fear of tomorrow, the uncertainty, the aggression, had nested in our souls.

Most Greeks suffered from depression during that period. You would pray, begging for the sad stories that you heard every day to stop, but they never ended. You would pray to no longer see your brother, your neighbours and your friends suffering and your country slowly collapsing.

This was the time when I decided to actively participate in the FoMA programme. I was accepted onto the footpaths project in 2012 and worked in Chilandar and Zografou. I was the only Greek on the team. Joining it gave me the opportunity to do what I had been looking to do for many years: to help maintain the paths I loved so much, to meet new friends and work with them for a common cause.

But it also helped me to escape the reality around me. Since then I have participated every year up to the present. My involvement in the project gradually increased. Cutting and carrying heavy branches under the hot sun or working the nights in front of my computer to produce the footpath descriptions in Greek became a point for me to hold on to. And I think the project made a lot of progress.

The number of volunteers involved in the project was increasing, giving us the opportunity to expand the areas we covered. We got in touch with more monasteries, offering to work in their areas and more of them met and then recognized FoMA's work on footpath maintenance. Our teams now cover almost all of the Athonite peninsula and we have been hosted at sixteen monasteries and some sketes. Our missions are now very welcome in the monasteries and the hospitality we enjoy is always excellent. But this is something that we have gradually gained through a lot of work, love and respect for Athos, its people and traditions.

We have tried to expand the network of path descriptions we have written and made available through our website. Our goal is to provide detailed descriptions for all pilgrims who wish to hike on Athos, whether they are members of our society or not, and keep them safe. Our footpath descriptions cover routes to all twenty Athonite monasteries and are regularly reviewed so that they remain accurate. Now all of the routes on our site are also accompanied by GPS files, and are available in both English and Greek.

At the same time, we have adopted a new way of constructing and placing signs on the trails. Our signposts are now cheaper, lighter (so easier to transport) and made on the spot. This has made it possible to set up hundreds of signs, making the footpaths safer.

And I left the map for the end. I feel extremely proud that I had the pleasure to assist my friend Peter Howorth, who has put tremendous effort and resources into producing that fantastic result. In all that we have accomplished as a team, I have tried my best to contribute. As a native Greek speaker I have been able to help in many areas, from communicating with monasteries to translating footpath descriptions into Greek. And as my involvement with the project grew, so did my reward (the 'antidoron') from it. And now despite the crisis, I have been able to become rich. But my wealth is not material, it is the relationships I have built with the 'warriors' working on the programme, and with the monks of Mount Athos. Those relationships have marked my life and will last a lifetime. Through the programme I have also had the honour to meet HRH Prince Charles. But mostly I met Dimitris, and I think I managed to make myself a little better.

I hope the programme will continue for many more years as an offering to Athos and to help more pilgrims experience the peace and beauty of the Garden of the Holy Mother of God by walking along the ancient paths. And also giving more volunteer path-clearers from all around the world the opportunity to encounter this special 'place', its people, traditions but mainly its spiritual life. And may God bless me to participate in many more path-clearing pilgrimages in the future.

Πλούσιοι ἐπτώχευσαν καὶ ἐπείνασαν, οἱ δὲ ἐκζητοῦντες τὸν Κύριον οὐκ ἐλαττωθήσονται παντὸς ἀγαθοῦ (Rich men were needy, and were hungry; but men that seek the Lord shall not fail of all good).

The First Lopper?

DOMINIC SOLLY

FoMA is properly taking pride in their thirty years of service on the Holy Mountain but I believe that we can show that our endeavours as loppers can be traced back to the fifth century and that we have an imperial pedigree.

The monastery of Vatopedi claims that the future emperor, Arcadius, visited the Holy Mountain as a child, based on a reference in a seventeenth-century manuscript, as I was told by Father Philippos, the monastery librarian, in May 2019. Arcadius succeeded Theodosius as emperor in the East in 395; he was born in 377. Recent archaeological research carried out in 2000/01 reportedly shows that remains of an early Christian basilica are to be found next to the church, although I have not been able to examine the evidence. A visit by a future Roman emperor would be spectacular, suggesting a very early Christian presence on the Holy Mountain. It is, I believe, possible but I think that the monastic traditions stand in need of correction: I write to suggest that a more likely candidate for the first Christian visitor was the eastern emperor's younger brother, Honorius. I should add that my suggestion was roundly rebuffed by the monks at Vatopedi but I think I can explain their mistake.

John Malalas was the first of the Byzantine chronographers, writing during the later years of Justinian, so around 560. He reports that Arcadius was in Rome to visit a sick Honorius in 395, the year of Theodosius's death and was not in Milan when his father died. This visit cannot have occurred: we know that Honorius's second visit to Rome took place in late 403, following a visit as a child in 389. Claudian, the poet who served as the emperor's panegyrist, is crystal clear on this point. The poem was delivered in Rome in front of the emperor in January 404 and the poet asked 'Do you recognize, revered emperor, your home that you once admired as a boy in your early childhood when your loving father showed it to you?' The visit to Rome took place when Honorius was four. Claudian goes on to add that Honorius was accompanied on a later journey from Constantinople to Milan in 394-95 by his aunt Serena; the latter served as his surrogate mother after the death of his own mother, Flaccilla, in 386. 'Serena herself, not frightened by any risk, left the East and accompanied you through the cities of Illyricum, cherishing you with a mother's care'. This later journey, just before Theodosius's death in January, 395, is a less likely candidate. The purported etymology of Vatopedi, the child in the bramble bush, is unsuitable for a nine-year-old boy.

It is probable that Malalas, whose chronicle is more targeted at monastic improvement rather than historical accuracy, intended to portray the western emperors as ensconced in Rome as their counterparts were in Constantinople.

The young Honorius, even at the age of seven, begged to be allowed to take part in his father's battles; the latter was the last emperor to rule as the single master of the Roman world and was, with his grandson Theodosius II, largely responsible for the creation of Constantinople. Claudian, in his panegyric on the boy's third consulate (awarded when he was eleven years old!) describes the infant playing with the weapons that were his father's spoils of war. The child was brought up, according to Claudian, surrounded by gifts from Minerva, including weapons. These, I assume, will have included the first loppers. I should add that the poet also suggests that the visit was dangerous, which might suggest a reason for the dedication of a church. Honorius was thoroughly Christian although his panegyrist shows him in a purely pagan environment.

Arcadius was much more feeble: Synesius of Cyrene claimed that he compared the emperor, to his face, to a jellyfish and that he was only interested in pleasures of the body, surrounded by courtiers with small heads and petty minds. We also know, from Gregory of Nyssa's funeral speech on Flaccilla that his mother rarely left the palace, and only to give alms to the poor of the city. The emperor's health was probably poor: he was unable to take part in the procession held some time in 400 or 401 to welcome the relics brought to St

Thomas's chapel in Drypia, nine miles from the city, which John Chrysostom describes in detail. In contrast, he emphasises the very active and unusually visible role that the empress, a rather frightening lady named Eudoxia played, 'she herself wearing the imperial diadem and clothed in the purple'. The laws as collected by Seeck shows that Arcadius is firmly attested as present solely in Constantinople with occasional summer holidays in nearby parts of Anatolia, usually to Ancyra (modern Ankara) for the whole of his reign.

One certain visitor to the Holy Mountain was Stilicho, Honorius's father-in-law, the generalissimo in charge of the armies of the West who has been unfairly blamed for the Sack of Rome in 410. He is said by Claudian to have been on Mount Athos before 400. Claudian describes his visit as follows, '*nivibusque profundum / scandebat cristatus Athon lateque corusco / curvatas glacie silvas umbone ruebat*'.

It may be translated as follows '[Stilicho] wearing a plumed helmet climbed Athos, deep in snow, and forced his way through the trees bent down (curved) by the ice with his gleaming shield-boss'. The boss on a Roman shield was a metal section intended to deflect blows. He clearly was the precursor of all path clearers on the Mountain, although I hope we do not share his fate; he was beheaded on 22 August 408 on the orders of his son-in-law following a palace conspiracy. Remarkably, he forbade both his bodyguards, who were Huns, and his soldiers to come to his defence. Zosimus wrote 'The Barbarians who attended him, with his servants and other friends and relations, of whom there was a vast number, preparing and resolving to rescue him from the stroke, Stilicho deterred them from the attempt by all imaginable menaces, and calmly submitted his neck to the sword'. He continues 'He was the most moderate and just of all the men who possessed great authority in his time. For although he was married to the niece of the first Theodosius, entrusted with the empires of both his sons, and had been a commander twenty-three years, yet he never conferred military rank for money, or converted the stipend of the soldiers to his own use'. Clearly all loppers should take him as their model.

Brotherhood on the Holy Mountain

ANDREW BUCHANAN

'Seek to know an inward stillness, even amid the activities of daily life.'
'Cherish your friendships so they grow in depth, understanding and mutual respect.'
—*Advices and Queries*, Religious Society of Friends

In May this year (2006) I spent two weeks in Greece with a team of volunteers. It was my third visit to Mount Athos, the Holy Mountain which is home to 20 Greek Orthodox monasteries.

The idea of staying in a monastery and working to clear overgrown footpaths seems to fascinate and bemuse in roughly equal measure, so I'm often asked why I spend time on Mount Athos. My answer usually includes phrases like 'a chance to reflect' and 'sharing in the life of the monastery' plus the words architecture, art, and scenery. However, after my path-clearing trip this year, I realise that I've now added another word to this list – brotherhood. I also realise that this is, for me, the most important of them all.

Clearing paths on Athos is a fascinating mix of the practical and the spiritual. Until recently, the way from one monastery to another was along cobbled paths that are hundreds of years old. Now most people travel along dusty tracks in 4x4s or minibuses, but there are still those who prefer to get closer to the spirit of the Holy Mountain by walking. However, if a path isn't used enough, in less than five years much of it can become completely blocked by undergrowth. So our job is to work along the paths and, using hand-tools only, cut back the bushes and trees that have grown across them. It's a great pleasure to be out in the open, surrounded by beautiful scenery, as part of a team that is slowly and quietly cutting its way across the landscape.

The experience of working together like this is very special, and is an excellent example of how individuals can work together. There's no competition between us, rather an understanding that each has his own pace and style. We spread out along the path, the distance between us determined by the thickness of the vegetation that needs to be cleared. Much of the time we work on our own, but with a constant awareness of what others are up to. So when you get to a difficult section, or to a job that needs two people, someone else will materialise unbidden to lend a hand.

The choice of path is rarely ours. The Abbot, or one of the senior monks, will have decided which footpaths should be cleared. Usually it will be a path linking one monastery to another, but occasionally we'll be asked to clear a way to a ruined building which one of the monks wishes to turn into a monastic cell. We don't often see people using the paths, so sometimes, particularly when faced with a steep or difficult section in the full heat of mid-day, we might wonder why we're doing this.

I think it's all about learning obedience, and the importance of putting yourself at the service of others. The monks themselves serve as a good example of this; they submit to the discipline of the monastery – eight hours prayer, eight hours work, and eight hours rest each day. The Abbot allocates tasks, and monks are often assigned to one particular job for twelve months or more. There's no dissent, since they know that the smooth running of the community, both spiritually and practically, depends on each member accepting his role and willingly making his contribution to the common good.

Our days aren't as closely regulated as the monks', but there's a clear pattern. Up early, breakfast, work from 7 a.m. to 3 p.m., then join the 4.30 p.m. service and the shared meal in the refectory. The evening is usually free;

PL.62 *Youthful, keen, and energetic*

sometimes there's a tour of the monastery, or there's a chance for a quiet conversation with one of the monks; most often we spend the time talking with other members of the team. Topics vary widely depending on the interests and experiences of those present. Theological differences, pension arrangements for priests, major life-changing events, bizarre occurrences while travelling, how relationships work and many other subjects are explored in detail. There's also time for laughter, with a mix of quick wit and dry humour often highlighting the unusual situation we're in or gently pointing out our foibles and weaknesses.

In these circumstances, it really isn't surprising that a close companionship develops very quickly. We have a common task, we're sharing accommodation, and we're away from our usual lives. Our surroundings play a vital part in this, as we're constantly seeing how the monastery works as a brotherhood, each monk willingly doing his bit for the benefit of all. For those of us who aren't orthodox, or whose Greek can't cope with the liturgical details, services provide time for reflection. So there's every opportunity, and every reason, for us to be open and truthful with each other, building a strong and trusting relationship between our band of path-clearing brothers.

A visit to the Holy Mountain is very special, a great privilege and full of wonderful insights. There are times of deep peace and tranquillity, brought about by the seemingly unchanging nature of the landscape and the monasteries. There are also times of great hilarity, when a chance remark is taken and spun into an ever more ridiculous fantasy. For me, it's this mix of inner stillness born of beautiful surroundings and close relationships with true friends forged by shared experience which make the fortnight so unforgettable.

And yes, I'll be going again next year.

Reflection

DAVID HOLLOWAY

In May 2011, I visited Mount Athos as a member of the path-clearing group. Now, eight and a half years on, how does the Holy Mountain appear in retrospect? Perhaps the most effective way in which to answer that question is to revisit what I wrote at the time and then to append a current reflection.

Thoughts in May 2011: I had given some thought to this trip in advance, taking careful note of Andrew Buchanan's helpful packing list, attending a first aid course, and obtaining a copy of the Zwerger map from Graham Speake (whose book *Mount Athos: Renewal in Paradise* I re-visited). However, none of this prepared me for the startling contrast of old and new, which was evident from the moment I saw a monk leaning over the rail of the *Agios Panteleimon* intent on texting. Before long we were ashore and surrounded by monks in four-wheel drives named 'Defender' and then we were in a minibus with, to my delight, Byzantine chant blasting from the speakers. As we drove we passed a monk walking through the countryside with a cat obediently trotting behind him and then – a helipad! Perhaps I should not have been so surprised, since I knew that monastic life on the Holy Mountain was experiencing a revival and I had already admired the colourful trucks and cranes as we sailed past Dochiariou and the splendidly restored red and green roofs and cupolas of Agios Panteleimon. On our arrival at Vatopedi, impressively sited on an eminence above the sea, we were offered loukoumi and raki by the very friendly and helpful Father M, an American from Milwaukee, and I began to accept the blending of the old world and the new.

The next morning, after a breakfast of red wine and feta, bread and olives, Father M drove us up into the misty mountains to start work on clearing paths. 'I wondered why things were a little blurry – these are my reading glasses', he remarked cheerfully as we slithered round a muddy bend with a sheer drop down to the sea on one side. It was very quiet, except for the sound of birdsong and the ceaseless drone of insects. We set to, cutting back broom,

bramble, rock-rose and oak, all of which would obliterate the path in a couple of years if left to grow unchecked. The variety of approaches to the task in hand was a joy to behold. For example, Graham O'Neill, the former consul of Montevideo, descended from a great height to snip with languid detachment the heads of his selected blooms; whereas Peter Howorth tackled whole branches of overhanging trees with all the gusto that one might expect of a stocky New Zealand engineer, tossing the limbs down the hillside with irrepressible glee. Each in his own way, of course, obeyed the injunction to 'make his paths straight' (Peter also mapping the paths as we went). Andrew Buchanan had quipped at Heathrow – 'With me it is boot camp!' He was as good as his word, since Peter's GPS showed that we covered eleven miles in the first day, despite being short of sleep.

One of the most memorable places that I saw was near the bottom of the hill opposite Vatopedi, after returning from the shrine / signpost known as 'the hand'. The path down – which had varied from a slightly overgrown grassy track, to little more than a washed-out rocky stream bed and then remarkably good cobble ('kalderimi') – finally emerged into a beautifully restored old olive grove, which was carpeted with wild flowers – the blue of forget-me-not, pink rock-roses, geraniums, yellow and white marguerite daisies, purple vetch, broom and a whole host of other flowers whose names I do not know. The song of a nightingale was accompanied by the gentle lapping of the sea and the whole was bathed by the warm glow of late afternoon sun.

The next day I was ill and was prescribed a day's rest with medicine. Kind companions brought me food and I lay, mildly delirious, moving between dream and nightmare. A Romanian priest kept hurrying past the door muttering 'Nicht!' Was this a statement of apophatic theology and, in any case, what was real in this land of black-clad monks and orange and yellow butterflies? I rose for vespers, where the singing was wonderful, and also attended part of a

PL. 64 On path from Kavsokalyvia to Kerasia

service in the tiny and mysterious Chapel of the Paramythia, which contains the Icon of the Restraining Hand. The compassionate eyes of the Panaghia impressed me deeply.

Nevertheless, I had to spend a second day in bed, which was in a way fortunate as it poured with rain. The men working on the fishpond below cried out in Greek and Russian. The wind was stirring the leaves of the eucalyptus tree outside the window with its dusty blue-painted frame and battered mosquito net. I contemplated the early fourteenth-century image of the 'Guiding' Mother of God on the wall and thought of Seferis – 'the wind forgets always forgets / but the flame doesn't change'. The monks seem to shift from western time to Athos time effortlessly, perhaps regulated by a kind of musical time that transcends history.

That evening as we approached the katholikon for the service of the Eve of St George's Day the bells were ringing in different patterns and a monk was scurrying across the courtyard clutching an umbrella. Within the church the antiphonal chanting was beautiful, the gold and crimson vestments were splendid and the many candles illuminated the darkness with powerful symbolism – *ΚΥΡΙΟΣ φωτισμός μου*! (Christ my light!) Breakfast was a feast which concluded with joyful singing and the rhythmic clashing of censors under a dance of swaying lights.

I have many memories of Vatopedi – the treasures of the old Sacristry (including a variety of royal gifts), the blue of the Aegean (so blue that it was hard to tell where sea and sky met), a visit to Simonos Petras (seemingly only a stone's throw from the snowy ravines of Agion Oros) and to the Skete of St Andrew – but perhaps the most haunting memory is the image of the Pantokrator high in the apse of the katholikon. The eyes are focused on the far distance and the mouth is sad. It is the image of one who is infinitely removed and yet endlessly present.

It was to the Monastery of Pantokrator that we went next – a short walk to a very different spirit of place. Father V told us that their concern there was for spirituality, not deeds. A benefactor is prayed for at least five times a day and our work would be regarded as a benefaction, no matter how little we did. Indeed, he would not mind if we did not do any! Nothing is obligatory in the Orthodox Church. I thought that this was an admirable attitude, although we felt that we owed it to our sponsors, as well as to the monastic community, to remember the dictum, *laborare est orare*. In the event, we had time to

clear paths, attend services and also visit other places. One such place was the Bogoriditsa Skete, where Father S, an engaging Russian physicist, regaled us with fresh oranges, excellent local honey and photos of his hometown. The gardens were astonishingly well terraced and tended. On the way back down to Pantokrator we visited the Prophet Elijah Skete, eating lunch en route on a stone bridge that Clive Strutt had cleared on a previous occasion, and then negotiating kalderimi that had suffered from the ravages of wild boar. Where the kalderimi ended we found the Skete, whose impressive architecture is largely the result of Imperial Russian funding during the nineteenth century. The katholikon, graced by a magnificent gold iconostasis, is wonderfully light and airy, and the monks were most hospitable.

The katholikon of Pantokrator (mother house of the Prophet Elijah Skete) is smaller and darker – smaller, since the Monastery is built on the edge of the sea, and darker since it is in the style of an earlier age, dating from before the fall of the Byzantine Empire. These characteristics combine to create an atmosphere of mysteriously intense spirituality, which is enhanced by the wall paintings and by the beautiful chanting of the monks. If one wanders out of the church into the courtyard, one meets with orange trees and finely restored buildings, decorated with indigo and terracotta paint. The whole effect is very different from Vatopedi but no less inspiring. I found myself parodying W.J. Turner – 'Pantokrator, Vatopedi / Had stolen me away'.

As with Vatopedi, there is too much to recount in full – our visit to Stavronikita and to the kellion of Father G, the marvellous icons in the Museum, Dru Brooke-Taylor's most helpful identification of a range of birds including a purple heron, and finally the view from the gatehouse – Mount Athos standing clear in the evening light, a waxing moon, the sky fading from blue to pink above the silvery sea, swifts swooping low with a falcon gliding above them and, as ever, the frogs croaking interminably.

Do I have any regrets? Only that I was often too tired to combine work and contemplation in the way that I would have wished. However, I am very grateful for all the organization that went into this trip, for the companionship and for the patience and good humour of the monks. I would not have missed it for the world.

Reflections in November 2019: It is tempting to think of the Holy Mountain as 'at the still point of the turning world'. Yet how unchanging is it? As Heraclitus has it, '*τὰ πάντα ῥεῖ καὶ οὐδὲν μένει* (everything stays the same)'. Shortly after I left in May 2011 Dmitry Medvedev established (in September 2011) a fund to restore and preserve the cultural and spiritual heritage of the Monastery of St Panteleimon. Russia has given many millions to this end and the buildings and infrastructure of Mount Athos have benefited substantially. However, this has raised fears that Russia may be seeking to have too much power on the Holy Mountain. Taken in conjunction with the Russian annexation of Crimea and the consequent war between Russia and Ukraine, as of 2018 there is a schism between Moscow and Constantinople, which inevitably complicates life on Mount Athos.

The European Union (which one faction in Ukraine would like to join) has also given Athos funds for historic preservation. If one bears in mind that China is upgrading the Port of Piraeus (with the result that the number of Chinese tourists to Greece has doubled over the last year) and that the US signed a Mutual Defence Cooperation Agreement with Greece last month, it would seem that Mount Athos, notwithstanding its status as a UNESCO World Heritage site, is at the centre of a web of geopolitical tensions.

If further indication of cultural flux were needed, one might point to the law passed by the Greek parliament in 2017, which permits Greeks over the age of fifteen to declare that they have changed gender – which might mean that women could claim the right to travel to Mount Athos, thereby overturning the tradition of a thousand years that the Mother of God is the only female allowed there.

However, it may be that some changes (unlike global warming) should be embraced as positive. For example, a Chinese monk in Simonos Petras converted from Buddhism to Orthodoxy on the grounds that one has more hope of facing the vicissitudes of life if one believes in a personal God, to whom one can speak.

As I write this in the month before Christmas, the season of peace and goodwill, I recollect the moment when, in an Athonite monastery, my eyes were drawn to an icon of the Pantokrator – ruler of all – a face both fully God and fully human, and I recall the words from *Malachi*: 'I am the Lord, I change not'.

FIG.46 *Forest road near Karyes*

Surprise, Grace and Serenity

DAVID STOTHARD

The spiritual, mental and physical benefit that comes from working together on the footpaths and in the sharing of monastic life, adds a profound and highly important dimension to clearing paths on the Holy Mountain. The grace encountered on the holy mountain never ceases to surprise, perhaps none more so than in 2014. The pilgrimage got off to an inauspicious start when the team found that the pilgrims' office in Ouranoupoli was not expecting them and there were no diamonitiria to collect. Things were compounded by the fact that two members were driving from Sofia and not expected to arrive until Monday. The idea of a day on the beach followed by dinner in a taverna was beginning to look attractive when Dimitris Bakalis managed to contact the Holy Epistasia, despite it being Sunday morning and his contact was, not unexpectedly, in church. By God's grace our diamonitiria were issued fifteen minutes before the ferry sailed.

The privilege of sharing the life and worship of the communities on the mountain never diminishes. In 2014, the team at Vatopedi were doubly blessed by being present when the Patriarch of Alexandria visited the monastery with a host of bishops and abbots and, being invited to the Patriarch's reception, were treated as honoured guests. What a blessing that was. Yet, on every returning there are monks who welcome team members by name with a smile that would melt the heart of the most irascible, and on leaving there are gifts, farewells and words of wisdom from the Abbot in person.

On a secular level, over the years the number of pilgrims and monks met when out working has increased dramatically and the gratitude of travellers for the work is never ceasing. The offer of a path-side drink from a raki bottle is occasionally difficult to resist! However, the increased use of footpaths has its downside and pilgrims do get lost. Consequently, to reduce the number of rescue call-outs the police stationed on the Holy Mountain have recruited the path clearers to provide signposting at locations where pilgrims frequently go astray. Team members have also enjoyed the company of individual policemen assisting with path-clearing during the day and, on at least one occasion, a few team members spent a convivial evening in a police station watching football on television.

Much of the path-clearing in the northern half of the peninsula now involves maintaining paths previously opened and putting right damage caused by winter weather and forestry enterprise. This is perhaps less satisfying than reopening 'lost' footways, but is just as important because, without the regular clearing that FoMA does, the vegetation would take over again. The work continues due to the verdant nature of the Holy Mountain and in 2017 the effects of exceptionally heavy snowfall during the winter presented conditions similar to those found in the early days of path-clearing. Parts of the footpaths around Great Lavra and between Pantokrator and Vatopedi were a particularly dense mass of vegetation, fallen trees and vines and in many places large trees lay across the footpaths. Oh, for a chain saw on occasions!

Finding and clearing lost paths was an art the team quickly mastered in the early years. Often, Roland Baetens (Ephrem) was called on to investigate. He would disappear into a bush and reappear sometime later in another part of the forest or, occasionally, during the evening meal back in the monastery. The technique of crawling on hands and knees to find the lost path resulted in some 'interesting' sights with backsides emerging from the undergrowth, pairs of boots protruding, apparently unattached to any legs, or a call for help with extraction.

At the other end of the 'difficulty' scale, on one occasion the team of three at Koutloumousiou were sent to assist the monastery's forester. Having breakfasted at the monastery the team were taken by vehicle to the forester's house in the woods where the working day began with Greek coffee brewed on his stove. A little light work, mainly removing dead branches from dry gully paths,

PL. 65 *Bridge on path to Esphigmenou*

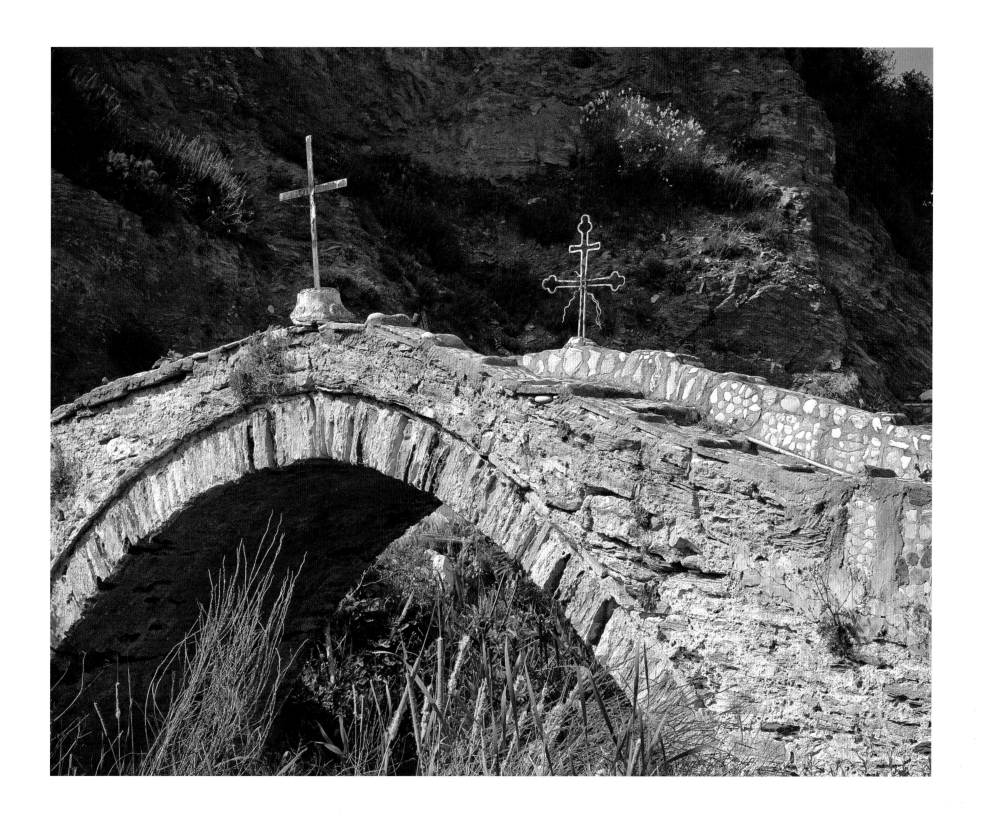

was followed by a retreat to the cottage for more Greek coffee accompanied by raki and then a return trip to the monastery for lunch in the kitchen. We managed two very happy days along these lines.

Of course, those people who return year after year often find themselves covering ground seen previously. There is a doubtful pleasure in clearing the same thicket of brambles each year, but once through that intimidating field of 2.5 metre high intertwined thorn onto the shady path leading up the sunny hillside where the wild thyme fills the air and rock-rose is the biggest burden, life seems complete.

Over the years the range of tasks done by the team has increased. Gone are the days where the task was limited to tracing the route of a long-lost footpath through densely wooded uplands and opening it up once more. First to be added were written descriptions of the newly opened routes, describing features by which to navigate and pacing out distances using short bits of stick to keep tally, which developed into the use of GPS tracking and even to maps that show where paths and tracks really are. Signposts with the FoMA symbol abound and monasteries have begun to put up their own signs of similar design. Instead of keeping us at a respectful distance, monks now give the teams information and ask for help on areas where work is particularly needed, which is as likely to be in an overgrown olive grove or area damaged by forestry operations, as overgrown kalderimi.

Better still, as well as transport to work locations at a distance from the monastery the monks occasionally offer one or two lay workers to help with difficult areas or come to visit us themselves. One of the most welcome sights halfway through a hot dusty day's work is Father M striding up from Vatopedi with bottles of his home-made lemonade in the bag over his shoulder.

The beauty and peace to be found on Athos is beyond measure. It is a wilderness that is almost tamed but leaves us wanting more of the wild. The lack of domesticated animals allows grass and foliage to grow high. Once the paths we work on were kept open by mules carrying provisions between monasteries but motor vehicles on forest tracks can carry far more at one time. Mules may still be found in some places pulling timber and carrying a few packs, but other animals are always close by. Wild pigs dig up our newly restored paths. At Chilandar, we hear wild dogs calling in the night, sending shivers down the spine as we try to sleep in a dormitory shared with 12 pilgrims, where the calling of the dogs competes with the music of snoring companions. On hot days, snakes and lizards bask on the dusty tracks until we come along, scorpions hide under rocks about to be sat on, cats abound at kitchen doors, and nightingales call out their songs of joy.

Athos is a place to return to again and again, whether as part of a path-clearing team or as a simple pilgrim seeking tranquillity and hospitality, a place to gently reflect on life.

A Lopper's Diary

JOHN MOLE

3 a.m. Talanton. Talanton. Talan-talan-talanton. The call for matins hammered out on a plank. On days when we are not working, for example when we leave or change monasteries, I get up. We are working today so I roll over and go back to sleep.

6 a.m. Ease protesting limbs out of bed. Wash and dress. Long sleeve shirt, hiking trousers, boots, elastic socks and knee bandages supplemented by Ibuprofen and trekking poles, the rambler's Zimmer frame. Drink two litres of water for all-day hydration and put another three in the pack. Sun hat. Trail mix. Goggles. Work gloves. Loppers. I've also bagged the new shears, Britneys we call them, after Ms Spears, the pop singer. I have a Red Cross certificate that qualifies me to carry the first aid kit.

7 a.m. The three of us breakfast at the workers' table. Monday, Wednesday and Friday are fasting days so we start the day with a sugar high on nutty halva and dark chestnut honey with yesterday's bread. Other days we get fried eggs or an omelette. A friendly monk gives us a plastic bag with a generous picnic. The monks' breakfast is about 9.30 a.m., too late for us as we start early to get back in time for vespers.

Illustrations in a Book of Hours, we plod through massive nail-studded gates with shouldered loppers to muffled chanting from the katholikon. A glorious morning, porcelain blue sky and the crystal light of Greece. Today we are making a thousand foot descent from Karyes to seaside Iviron. Other days we go uphill, a morning slog but easier to stagger home.

The first stretch is past fields of shimmering polytunnels. We are in the Garden of the Virgin – To Perivoli Tis Panagias. There are two Greek words for garden. Kipo is the land round the house with lawns and flowers and shady places for a barbie. Perivoli is a more utilitarian plot away from the house for growing fruit and vegetables, like an allotment.

8 a.m. We follow the FoMA sign with its striding pilgrim logo onto a kalder-imi path of massive stone slabs. I'm the designated fool to proof the FoMA path descriptions that can be downloaded from our website in English and Greek. We also note changes for the cartographers responsible for the FoMA map, a coveted resource for pilgrims, police, fire service, monastery administrators and the governing council.

The path is overgrown by rock rose, tree heather, strawberry tree, Spanish broom, brambles, various thorns and the persistent smilax creeper that knits the rest into impenetrable tangles and climbs trees ten metres tall. The first man puts his pack down twenty metres on and works backwards. The second puts his down another twenty metres ahead. And so on. We should keep in sight of each other, in case someone gets injured or lost.

9 a.m. We've done two hundred yards. Mostly back-breaking ground level work. We stop for a water break before a stunning view of the forested valley, cells and sketes among the green, and the sea beyond.

10 a.m. Work is now at eye level under a luscious canopy of trees. We attack with our saws a dead specimen toppled across the path by the winter snow. As we heave the final bit of trunk into the undergrowth we break into Monty Python's lumberjack song.

11 a.m. We stop at the kelli of the famous Elder, now Saint, Paisios. After Turkish Delight and a draught of spring water the resident monk shows us the moving little chapel where Paisios spent most of his nights. And the long string from his balcony to the front gate on which he let down the key to visitors.

A wide kalderimi under a tall tunnel of trees with little to do but trudge on. I loiter behind the others, enjoying solitude in the sound scape of birdsong and distant machinery. The rhythm of the Jesus Prayer sets the pace.

12 noon. Lunch. In the shade with a stunning view of the coast, a monastery beside the cobalt sea and the white marble peak of the Holy Mountain, for

once without its tonsure of cloud. We delve into the bag and bring out what we had for breakfast with the addition of a tomato salad. Our conversation ranges from the theological (the uncertain meaning of 'daily' in the Lords Prayer) to the secular (Arsenal's chances of winning the Premiership).

1 p.m. Traffic noise gets louder. The path crosses a main road. Careful not to get run over we put up signs to help pilgrims navigate a hundred yards of dispiriting concrete. It is not the Athos we come for but one we must get used to. Our Team Leader takes GPS readings.

2 p.m. We are back on a beautiful woodland path, lopping and hacking. We are encouraged by passing walkers, speaking mainly Russian or Greek interspersed with other Balkan languages. A cheerful Serbian monk says he walks the paths in a struggle with his waistline. He slaps the offending part and we exchange commiserations on the subject. I suggest he takes over my Britneys for the exercise but he thinks I am joking and stomps off with a laugh.

3 p.m. Many find path-clearing a spiritual exercise. Chopping a rock rose is a chore or a prayer, depending on your outlook. Ora et Labora, pray and work, as Benedictines say – not so inappropriate since one of the first monasteries on Athos was Italian Benedictine. It lasted three hundred years and its ruined tower is nearby. Right now I am too tired and hot to meditate on anything but a cold shower and a beer.

I limp into Iviron behind the others. They can walk back up the mountain if they like, I'm calling a cab. Several monks run taxis and I ask the guest-master if he has any of their numbers. He says there is a bus back to Karyes in fifteen minutes. We have just time to venerate the wonderworking icon of Our Lady the Gatekeeper, not forgetting a word of thanks for laying on transport, before scuttling to the stop. It takes twenty minutes to whizz back to where we started that morning. Isn't the concrete road wonderful?

4 p.m. The shower has two temperatures, agonisingly cold in the morning and deliciously cold in the afternoon. The quiet hour before vespers is the time to make a cup of tea and relax with an improving book. Or in my case collapse on the bed in a stupor.

5 p.m. Vespers. The katholikon and the narthex are packed with monks and pilgrims. Four members of a motorcycle gang make their presence felt, big men in every direction with shaven heads and scars, their affiliation advertised on bulging T-shirts. One has to be turfed out of the abbot's seat. They cannot spoil the numinous of chanting, the glorious Psalm 103, incense, jingling censer, icons and frescoes alive in the light and shadow of late afternoon.

6 p.m. We troop into the trapeza. At first the non-Orthodox were seated in a side room. The kindly abbot noticed this on the third day and invited us into the refectory. After grace and the first bell we scoff quickly in silence, listening to the reading and gazing at the spectacular frescoes. At the second bell we may drink but no wine on a fast day, alas. On the third bell we stand for grace and file out between the abbot's blessing and the cooks bent double in apology. We go back into church for compline and veneration of the relics.

7 p.m. Monks and pilgrims mill around in the courtyard. I chat with a genial Cypriot monk about this and that, the Apocalypse mainly, until one of the team comes over in search of a sharpening stone. They go to the workshop discussing the merits of Chinese tools.

8 p.m. I join other pilgrims in the kiosk outside, taking pictures of the Holy Mountain, phoning home and catching up with the BBC news, the more fatuous the longer one stays here.

9 p.m. Nightfall. Time to break out the tsipouro. The noisy bikers on the floor below keep themselves to themselves and their vodka. We sit on the balcony gossiping with the guest-house warden, an elderly Greek and a trio of Cypriots. They ply us with a meze of feta and tomatoes, which we reciprocate with crisps. The existence of footpaths is a surprise to the Greek. He thought we were here to keep the roadside verges tidy. One day perhaps we shall be tasked with this.

10 p.m. Bedtime. Drift off to the sound of nightingales, jackals and bikers. Tomorrow will be another beautiful day on The Allotment.

Brotherhood of the Lopper

JOHN MOLE

The Athos peninsula is about 50 km long and 10 km wide. A central spine of mountain ridge runs down the middle and rises to the Mountain at the end. Water courses, ravines and valleys run down like ribs on either side. In the west and on plateaus is cultivable land for market garden crops, orchards, bee keeping, vineyards and olive groves. The rest is bare mountain or thick forest, a source of wild food to forage and home to boar, foxes, jackals, wolves, reptiles and birds.

Paths follow the spine, the valleys down to the sea and the perimeter shore. Until the 1960s they were conduits for food, fuel, forest products, building materials, exports and imports. They were channels of communication, messengers, mail, books, newspapers, ideas. Monks, rulers, governors, soldiers, police, workers, craftsmen, artists, refugees from hardship and the law passed along them. And, dear to our own hearts, pilgrims. There were only two ways to use the paths – on two or four legs. Each monastery had hundreds of mules. The rule was that if you borrowed one you could take it only as far as the next monastery. If you wanted to go further you had to change steed like the American pony express. There are still a few around in the east, mainly for going up the steep paths from the ports. There is still a police mule stationed at Great Lavra, the only mule in Greece registered as a vehicle with its own number plates. According to the records it is over seventy years old. This is because, when an incumbent dies, a replacement quietly takes its place without the need for tiresome paperwork. One senses a legend in the making.

The motor vehicle first came to Athos in 1952 when the monks of Agios Pavlos built a road and invested in a truck to bring logs from the forest down to their port. No longer would they have to be hauled down by mules. For the first time in history animal and human muscle on the paths was supplanted by machine. The foundation of motorised Athos was the millennium celebration of 1963. It was thought beneath the dignity and comfort of the Ecumenical Patriarch, King Paul, Prince Constantine and other dignitaries to ride up from Daphne to Karyes on mules. A road was bulldozed and vehicles imported. In 1967 the road was opened from Karyes to Iviron on the north coast. Over the years that followed roads took over from paths, vehicles took over from bipeds and quadrupeds. Agriculture, construction, human transportation, communication, all the functions of the paths were usurped by the motor and the bulldozed road.

Before vehicles pilgrimage was for the relatively young and fit. Now it is open to the sedentary, elderly, ailing and idle. There has been an explosion of the pilgrim business. We should not be over-sentimental about this. Nostalgic perhaps but not depressed. Monasteries are primarily centres of prayer and salvation. They also have a mission to bear witness to the faith and one of the ways they do this is to open their doors. At the same time they have to make a living. For agriculture and forestry, exports and imports, roads are indispensable.

With their main functions lost to roads and vehicles, footpaths became overgrown and impassable. Was this the end of the traditional walking pilgrimage? In 2000 a Greek friend of the Mountain wrote to the Prince of Wales asking for his help in saving the footpaths. At his instigation a small group of FoMA members launched the first Path-Clearing Pilgrimage in 2002. The path clearers have gone from strength to strength. We now keep clear 50 km of footpath. In the early days it was hard and slow physical labour to clear away twenty years of undergrowth, fallen trees and deteriorated fabric. Much of the work is now maintenance rather than clearing but winter snows and storms still create challenges. If roads do not eliminate paths altogether, piles of rock and debris created by their construction block the paths that cross them. And there are still plenty of wild stretches to reconquer bit by bit.

The project is meticulously planned and managed. Thirty or more men from half a dozen countries are recruited, accommodated, provided with air-

PL. 69 *Athonite parking warden*

line tickets, ferry tickets and a diamonitirion. They come with different backgrounds, faiths, and motivations but united by mutual kindness and a love of the Holy Mountain. Teams are based in a dozen different monasteries. Each has nine days' work to be allocated to over fifty stretches of path identified as needing attention. Tools are bought and distributed. Signs are stencilled, photographed and identified with GPS co-ordinates. A kind donor has even provided us with a lapel badge, crossed loppers under the FoMA logo, the crest of the Brotherhood of the Lopper.

So why do we do it?

Hiking and working in beautiful landscape is physical and spiritual re-creation. The paths are captivating, each one distinctive in character, in plants and trees, in scenery bathed in light and shade and birdsong. If this sounds self-serving, by keeping the paths alive we are serving others too. The gratitude of pilgrims we meet is a great encouragement. Some have the excellent FoMA map and downloaded path descriptions. Our work is a tangible and charitable service to them.

Every year a few unfortunate pilgrims get lost on the Mountain and the police have to search for them. From time to time they are unsuccessful. Bodies may lie months or years undiscovered. The police are keen to have the paths cleared and mapped and signposted. Their knowledge and experience of the paths is unsurpassed and they advise and occasionally join us. The fire service too values the FoMA map.

The experience of living in a monastery for a week in the company of genial colleagues and generous monks instead of the single day of a normal pilgrimage is unique. The monks seem to appreciate our sharing their life and work, if only in a symbolic way. Part of their vocation is to welcome pilgrims, which they do tirelessly and generously and we are able to give a token demonstration of thanks for their hospitality.

Maintaining and mapping the paths makes a contribution to the conservation of the Holy Mountain. Nothing can stop road building and mechanisation. You are almost as likely to hear a bulldozer as a bullfinch. Busier stretches of dirt roads give way to asphalt and concrete and in places you have to be careful crossing the road. But fit pilgrims who now walk will go by minibus if the paths are lost. By keeping them open we can at least provide an alternative to roads and slow down their development.

In places we clear paths made of massive stone slabs called kalderimi. Some were laid in the expansions of the eighteenth and nineteenth centuries. Others are much older, perhaps the oldest man-made artefacts on Athos dating from pre-Christian times. As we work and walk we preserve a priceless element of the living history of the Mountain. We have the privilege of preserving and experiencing first hand highways of reflection, meditation and prayer, keeping alive the physical and spiritual presence of ancient ways thousands of years old.

PL. 70 *Kalderimi from Pantokrator to Profitis Ilias*

Mount Athos over Fifty Years

DAVID BAYNE

I first visited the Holy Mountain in 1966, the year England won the World Cup. At the time, given the shrinking numbers of mostly elderly monks, the pundits were predicting that the Athonite communities were in terminal decline and that within ten years or so the peninsula would be either a museum or a holiday destination, or both. How wrong they were!

A fellow student and I were spending the summer exploring Greece and Turkey by car. Having failed to find any way of getting to Albania, we decided that visiting Mount Athos would be an alternative and intriguing challenge. So started an association of over 50 years.

Our first step was to obtain the necessary permissions. On reaching Thessaloniki, therefore, we visited the British Consulate where, without question, we were given the required letter of recommendation. This we took to the Civil Administration who promised that if we returned the following morning we could collect the necessary 'letters of introduction'. So far so good – and indeed the letters were ready as promised. But, by the time we had then taken one of them to the local Police HQ to exchange it for another permit, it was already late morning when we set off for the Athonite peninsular.

As the road left the plain and began to climb, it became increasingly narrow and winding and abounded in blind corners. We passed through Arnea and then Stagira, the home of Aristotle, but then the metalled road ran out. This scuppered any chance of catching a boat that day as we had hoped. We stopped at Tripiti, the small hamlet where the road across the foot of the peninsular reaches the western shore, just short of Ouranoupolis and the place from which the boat to Mount Athos was to start – and where the out-of-service ferries still moor today. Why we didn't continue the few miles to Ouranoupolis I remember not. At Tripiti we spent the rest of the day swimming and sunbathing, had a meal at the local 'hotel' and spent the night on the shore just above the beach. I vividly remember waking in the night to see what appeared to be a row of street lights, but were in reality the twin flood-lamps on the backs of a string of fishing boats off shore.

At 5.30 a.m. we boarded a 25-foot open caique which set off first to Ouranoupolis to collect more passengers and thence to the Holy Mountain. I made no note of how many others made the voyage but it was fewer than a dozen and included at least one monk and a cat. We called, and collected more passengers, at the arsanas along the way until around midday we docked at Daphne. There it was with considerable surprise we found a bus, registration number A 001, waiting to take everyone to Karyes. It was just three years after the 1963 millennium celebrations for which the road from Daphne to Karyes had been built. I like to think the same bus had been used to convey the visiting dignitaries. At Daphne we presented the relevant permit to the Greek police for ratification. But the Holy Epistasia from which we needed to obtain our diamoniteria was firmly closed until 4 p.m. We had a meal in the small café and waited. At 3 p.m. the Protaton opened so that we were able to marvel at its magnificent frescoes. At last we could present our documents plus 100 drachma each to receive diamoniteria. Then we set off on foot in what we were told was the direction of Pantokrator accompanied by a French pilgrim.

Even in those days there were few direction signs and we lost our way, so it was late by the time we reached Pantokrator. We were warmly greeted in the guest-house with the familiar refreshments and then given space in a six-bed room. The monastery was buzzing and it was evidently a major feast day. There were many monks and quite a few lay people at trapeza, there was fish to eat and the meal ended with extensive chanting. Next morning we attended a fine celebratory Divine Liturgy during which the central chandelier and corona were swung. Afterwards everyone assembled in a reception room for coffee, local brandy, loukoumi and what I now know to be kollyva.

PL. 71 *Kalderimi from Karyes to Agiou Nikolaos Bourazeri*

Sadly, this was to be our only experience of collective monastic celebration and hospitality. Unlike today, practically every monastery then was idiorrhythmic so that, apart from on feast days, there was little corporate activity. While we were everywhere made most welcome with generous hospitality, apart from at Pantokrator this was always in the guest-house. And while we were welcomed at other services, none we attended were on the same scale.

Leaving Pantokrator we walked via Stavronikita, where we admired the fine katholikon and its miraculous Icon of St Nicolas, to Iviron, where we were given a meal and a place to rest. In the afternoon, we boarded a smaller caique which took us as far as Megisti Lavra where, again to our surprise, a truck was waiting at the arsanas to transport the passengers up to the Monastery. After the usual welcome, all who wished were given a tour of the Monastery Library, Sacristy, the beautifully decorated trapeza with its marble tables and the fine katholikon before the now-familiar meal of butter beans. There were some 20 visitors staying at Megisti Lavra, many more than anywhere else we went, all sleeping in a large dormitory. Altogether it seemed more 'commercial' – in those days I believe male groups from cruise ships were allowed to visit – and there was even a small shop from which we bought welcome chocolate to supplement our diet.

Next morning, once services ended, the entire Monastery was closed up. We explored it, inside and out, but couldn't get into any buildings apart from the guest-house. After another meal (more beans) we lay on our beds and then went down to the arsanas to wait for the next boat. This eventually appeared in the mid-afternoon, an even smaller caique than the last, very noisy and extremely uncomfortable. But the journey round the head of the peninsula made up for it. It was, as many will know, an incredibly beautiful and moving voyage, where Mount Athos comes steeply down to the sea, the cliffs dotted with hermit cells, until after some 2½ hours we reached Agia Anna. The boat was supposed to stop there, but the boatman generously took us on to Agios Pavlos. Here as everywhere we were well received but told to change into long-sleeved shirts. We had stewed aubergines and rough retsina and were given a small guest room with straw mattresses on wooden boards. I think we were the only visitors.

Next morning, not even a cup of coffee was available after the services so we left early, back to the shore and north along the coastal path. In an hour or so we reached Dionysiou, perched above the sea, where we were shown the

FIG. 47 *Bridge below Filotheou Monastery*

finely-painted katholikon and trapeza. Then on along the coast path to Grigoriou where again we were shown the katholikon and trapeza, once more finely decorated, given a meal – fried potatoes this time – and shown to a guest room to rest. We set off again a couple of hours later, now in the heat of the August sun. On the shore below Simonos Petras, a monk fishing in a small cove greeted us. He suggested we have a swim, but to be sure to stay out of sight of the Monastery above. Reluctantly, we declined. Then he gave us some figs, nuts and a cucumber, which were extremely welcome. Then he offered us a fish from his pocket and to share his ouzo.

The final tiring climb up to Simonos Petras was soon forgotten as, after a meal of lentils and aubergines, we sat on the balcony of the guest-house – then on the top floor of the Monastery – watching the sun set over the sea. Next morning we left early to catch the boat north to Daphne and thence back to the mainland and to another way of life.

It was 40 years before my next pilgrimage, yet the draw of Mount Athos remained. I joined the Friends as soon as I heard of them in the early 1990s and read each annual report with fascination. These reports soon began to contain information about the project to clear the footpaths, which started in 2000. 'That', I resolved, 'is something I shall do when I retire'. And so, in the early hours of one Saturday in May 2006, with considerable trepidation I arrived at Gatwick airport to meet John Arnell and a motley selection of like-minded path-clearers, a mixture of old hands and new faces like me. There followed a thoroughly enjoyable and rewarding two weeks, first at Vatopedi, new to me, and then at Pantokrator, to which I had been before. Indeed the guest room at Pantokrator looked just the same as it must have done 1966.

Needless to say I found huge changes – the numbers of pilgrims, the roads, the motor transport, the modern ferries – but in other respects much appeared exactly the same. The ever-present feeling, however, was one of renaissance and regeneration, most evident in the numbers and the ages of the monks and in the multitudinous building renovation projects under way – almost every monastery was dominated by a tower crane. And in the course of the preceding 40 years all the formerly idiorrhythmic monasteries had changed to become cenobitic resulting in huge differences to the conduct of monastic life.

The whole experience was and continued to be so compelling that I took part in every footpath-clearing expedition since then, bar one, until 2018. And I soon became involved with the project's planning.

From that first year, 2006, I was immediately struck, as others have been, by how few pilgrims seemed to walk the paths that we so lovingly and labouriously cleared. This was not surprising since the Athonite topography is challenging: it takes a brave (or foolhardy) soul with a lot of faith to follow an unsigned path through a rugged and isolated landscape in the hope that in several hours it will lead you to the place you aim to be. What was needed were two things: first proper signage (to replace historic wooden signs which had now almost all disappeared) and second some kind of straightforward directions that pilgrims could use. In the years since 2006 both have been introduced.

My particular contribution has been the creation, in English, of 'path descriptions' which describe, in both directions, each of the many walking routes between monasteries, a number of sketes and of course Karyes. Each one comprises a set of specific directions, together with the distance to the next direction, from the point of departure to the point of arrival.

We made a modest start in 2007, my second year, when in between clearing footpaths a few of us, armed with GPS handsets, documented and measured a handful of routes. The results were then made available via the Friends' website. Since then the library of footpath descriptions has grown progressively: it now extends over the whole peninsular and numbers over 70. It has become part of the task of the annual footpath expedition to check as many of these descriptions as practicable for accuracy and recommending changes.

An important step forward took place when Dimitris Bakalis joined the group. Not only has he added significantly to the library of descriptions but he has generated versions of every description in Greek. Between us, we ensure that the latest versions of all these descriptions, both in English and in Greek, are available to all via the Friends' website, together with the associated GPS tracking data for each route which may be downloaded.

It has been a real privilege, and a joy, to be involved with the footpath-clearing project and its organisation, even though I have not taken a direct part in an expedition since 2017. But I continue to make pilgrimages to the Holy Mountain and, with Dimitris and with Peter Desmond, to maintain the footpath descriptions on the Friends' website.

An Orthodox Pathclearer

JOHN ANDREWS

I first went on a FoMA Footpaths Expedition in 2006. I had read John Arnell's article about it in the yearly journal published for members, and having been there many times on my own, I volunteered to go. I would go many times after as well.

Going on these expeditions was a great experience on many levels. Being able to go to Athos in a capacity to be able to do something useful for the monks and pilgrims, and perhaps for the future preservation of the place, was a great joy. The comradery shared with the other participants was a wonderful thing, and has led to many lasting friendships. And being Orthodox, I had long wanted to go to Athos for longer periods, so being able to go for a full two weeks was a great privilege.

Most of the monks we encountered were very enthusiastic about our work, although some were sceptical, and concerned about our welfare. But as we opened more and more paths and they saw them being used, they were always extremely grateful. Although the work was often hard and the weather hot, no one ever complained. Being outside and enjoying the beauty of Athos was its own reward. The barely touched dark forests, deep ravines and stunning coastline are hardly rivalled in much of Europe, and led to a constant desire to help in the preservation of the natural wonders of the peninsula.

Working together for a common goal, and sharing the spiritual nature of Athos as we all attended services, was a great bonding experience among the participants. Indeed, many who came for the first time soon became regulars joining every year. It was always a pleasure to meet old friends, as well as make new ones, every year. This program attracts people of many different interests and faiths, and they are always extremely interesting people. Some are attracted to the beautiful nature that abounds on Athos, some to the traditional techniques employed by the monks in their daily work, some to the priceless icons and frescoes in the churches, and others to the spirituality of the place.

As an Orthodox Christian, it is hard to overestimate the value and joy of time spent on Athos. It is the true spiritual home of the religion, with treasures beyond description; the fact that it has changed little since Byzantine times, not only in appearance but also in the liturgical rites, makes it all the more compelling. In addition, it was interesting to observe the non-Orthodox members of the teams, especially how respectful they were, and interested to learn more about Athos and its traditions. I believe many left with a new outlook on life, as it is difficult to go there and not be affected in so many ways. As the monks often say, no one comes to Athos by accident!

There have been many wonderful recollections. My first trip found me at Koutloumousiou and Pantokrator, two monasteries I had visited many years before. The changes were striking, especially in the case of Pantokrator, which had been an idiorrhythmic house when I had last visited it and had now become cenobitic; in fact, the last monastery on the Mountain to do so. I also visited Vatopedi for the first time on that trip, and had the great pleasure of meeting Father M, who would be our contact on many subsequent trips.

After that first trip I went many more times, and either stayed at or visited a number of monasteries, including Konstamonitou, Chilandar, Zografou and Simonos Petras. The differences between the monasteries are striking. As working visitors, we were always assured of nice accommodations, and our work was the subject of much interest among the monks! The level of hospitality was hard to overestimate. It was very special to have our meals with monks, and personally I find monastic fare to be excellent: fresh, healthy Mediterranean vegetarian cooking, including vegetables grown on the monastery grounds. In addition to a wealth of wonderful memories, these trips provided the satisfaction of seeing the footpaths we were opening starting to be used, by both the monks and the pilgrims. The positive changes these teams have made has been very striking. These footpaths have not only opened up won-

derful routes to the monasteries, but are surely also among the world's most fabulous hiking experiences.

One wonderful aspect of being on the Footpaths team has been the opportunity to meet (and often work together with) the monks, many of whom I have had the pleasure of remaining in contact with over the years. These have included Fathers V and T at Pantokrator, Fathers G and C at Koutloumousiou, Father P at Prophet Elijah, and Father E at Nea Skete. Their wise counsel has always been very helpful. In addition, I have had the pleasure of being able to assist Father C in proofreading some of his manuscripts.

I have continued to go to Athos on separate trips with friends, as work commitments have regularly seemed to prevent me from joining the Footpaths teams in recent years. However, I am looking forward to hopefully joining a team again soon. The beauty of the Holy Mountain is such that it is difficult to stay away for very long. In addition to its spiritual nature, it is also a place of tremendous natural beauty, rare to see in our time, and I always look forward to returning.

FIGS. 48–51 (clockwise)

Beehives, Hilandar

Scree, Agios Neilos

Outside Zografou

Path, Dionysiou to Grigoriou

Part Four

Back Matter

Food: Mount Athos May 2019

LESLIE CURRIE

Visit as part of the Friends of Mount Athos Path-Clearing Group

In the past, some people have found accounts of the diet on Mount Athos interesting so I'm doing that again this year, together with some observations.

I still can't quite understand which are fast days, which non-fast and which feast – it depends on the monastery, and the season of the year. One point that I had forgotten was that on Mount Athos the monasteries keep 'Byzantine time' – the day begins at sunset one day and finishes at sunset the next and the intervening period is divided into twenty-four hours – with times varying depending on the season. So, for example, if Friday is a fast day, the fasting meals are from the last meal of Thursday to the mid-day meal on the Friday.

However, more correctly an Orthodox friend advises that the situation is as follows: 'On Athos (possibly uniquely but there may be other monasteries elsewhere who follow the Athonite typikon), Monday is also a fast day, in addition to Wednesday and Friday. This is different from most other places (it certainly isn't a regular fast day in 'the world'). If I have read you correctly, I am not so sure as a general point – and allowing for the fact that there are inevitably minor variations across Athos – that the last meal post-vespers before a fast day is actually a fasting meal (i.e. supper on Sunday, Tuesday and Thursday evenings), despite the fact that liturgically, the new (fast) day begins mid-way through vespers that evening'.

Contrary to what I may have thought in the past, 'red meat'– including chicken etc. – is never eaten on Mount Athos. It appears to me that fish generally tends to be eaten about twice a week.

Karyes is the capital of Mount Athos. It is slightly curious, like a normal small Greek village, but with about half its population being monks. The various monasteries keep houses there (sort of embassies) and it is the seat of the Greek Governor and the Holy Epistasia – the administrative body of the Mountain, plus the Police HQ, the Post Office, etc. It is also the main transport hub for the Mountain – which has the effect of leaving groups of people there to await buses and taxis – leading to varied and 'different' conversations over coffee in the two little cafes. At Karyes is also found the Athonite Academy, a boarding school following the Greek school curriculum. It has about eighty students – forty from Greece, the rest from Poland, Romania, Armenia etc.

It seems that the large numbers of visitors are causing real problems, both practical, in terms of feeding and accommodating them, and also in the disturbance to the peace and silence which is, after all, the monasteries' reason for being there.

The first week was spent in Koutloumousiou, a small and relatively poor monastery that is very close (ten minutes) to Karyes. It is quite a sophisticated and 'cultured' monastery. The food there is good and nicely flavoured. They provide relatively little wine there as the Abbot decided that because they did not themselves possess any vineyards, and that wine was expensive, and that it wasn't particularly beneficial to people, they should not have it with most meals.

Sunday 12 May 2019. Dinner: cold spaghetti and vegetables, yoghurt, oranges, olives, bread, water. Two of our fellow diners were introduced to us as 'a Romanian prince' and his companion. I wonder if in this context this was someone whose family had been supporting the monastery since the fourteenth century (or similar) and who had just dropped in to see how things were getting on. But also he may be a member of the more recent royal family. Both are in beautiful suits – not so suitable for walking the Mountain's paths! – though he was very complimentary about how useful the FoMA pathway signs had been (but then I'm sure he was very polished and complimentary in most situations). He also had brought some liqueur which we were treated to later in our visit.

FIGS. 52–55 (clockwise)

Two views of Karyes

Formal tea, Koutloumousiou

Koutloumousiou Monastery

Monday 13 May 2019. Breakfast: two fried eggs, bread, butter, jam, oranges, mountain tea. Lunch: stew of potatoes, peppers and carrots, bread, olives, water. Dinner: bean soup with pasta pieces, olives, oranges, bread, water. We were told before dinner, 'We will have something quite simple if you would like to join us. But of course, if you would like something more…'. We were more than happy with the above meal.

During a visit to the coffee shop that afternoon we were greeted by a passing monk with a cheery 'Christos anesti, gentlemen!' 'Christos anesti' is the 'Christ is risen' greeting after Easter, but the addition of 'gentlemen' rather intrigued us.

Vespers (the service before the evening meal) that day ended with the Orthodox in the congregation being sprinkled with water using a bunch of rosemary.

Tuesday 14 May 2019. Breakfast: two fried eggs, cheese rusks, feta, bread, butter, jam, honey, mountain tea and lemon juice. Lunch: sea bream in oil, beetroot and garlic, feta, oranges, bread, red wine and water. Dinner: feta soup, red-dyed boiled eggs (from Easter), apples, bread, water. It was a wet morning so we were told that, 'It is better that this morning you go to your room and pray' rather than work – it is, after all, a monastery.

A bishop from the Ukraine visited that evening – interesting as this was the first visit from a Ukrainian bishop since the split between the Ukrainian and Russian churches which has radically affected Orthodoxy – including Mount Athos (Russian Orthodox are not supposed to communicate in churches owing allegiance to the Ecumenical Patriarch in Istanbul).

Wednesday 15 May 2019. Breakfast: halva, tahini, bread, butter, sweet brioche-type bread, jam, honey, cheese rusks, feta, mountain tea and lemon juice. Lunch: vegetable stew, bread, olives, oranges, wine and water. There were chocolates at the end (given by a visitor). Dinner: vegetable stew, olives, spinach puffs, apples, bread, water.

Thursday 16 May 2019. Breakfast: two fried eggs, Edam-type cheese, bread, butter, sweet brioche-type bread, jam, honey, mountain tea and lemon juice. Lunch: small fish (like sardines) fried, salad of beetroot and greens, feta, apples, bread, wine and water. Dinner: pasta with Parmesan-type cheese, cheese rusks, red-dyed boiled eggs (from Easter), water, apples.

In the evening we saw the – very magnificent – collection of manuscripts and early printed books. Father C, who showed it to us, mentioned his recent visit to an Oxford or Cambridge College where the young (and perhaps slightly naive) librarian brightly told him 'Oh, we have some manuscripts from Koutloumousiou'. And he thought to himself, 'Yes, indeed, I know you have!' Koutloumousiou was a place from which manuscripts 'disappeared' to end up in Western libraries.

Friday 17 May 2019. Breakfast: halva, apples, bread, mountain tea and lemon juice. Lunch: bean soup, halva, spring onion, olives, apples, bread, wine and water. Dinner: bean soup, pickled peppers, olives, apples, bread, water.

In the coffee shop we chatted to a monk from a small kellion who talked of the problems the world was facing. He was particularly concerned by those of 'extremism' and 'pan-religionism' (the idea that all religions are the same, for which there appears to be a Greek word). He was also worried by freemasonry (as many Orthodox in the East are).

Saturday 18 May 2019. Breakfast: fried eggs, sweet brioche-type bread, honey, jam, butter, mountain tea and lemon juice. Lunch: potato stew, mushrooms (fried in garlic), cheese, apples, bread, wine and water. Dinner: bean soup and pasta, olives, apples, bread, water. After dinner we were invited to a 'social time' with Father G, the acting Abbot.

Sunday 19 May 2019. Breakfast: spaghetti, mushrooms, tomato sauce, salad, bread, wine and water, and then kollyva (spiced, sweetened, wheat kernels eaten in commemoration of the dead) served to all from one common bowl. Finally, a piece of bread blessed at liturgy was handed round for each to take one small piece. Morning social time, all (monks, workers, visitors) go to the general monastery 'lounge' where each person has: ouzo, water, coffee, a pastry and a chocolate cake/biscuit. One monk observed to us that this time was important to the monastery and it was noted that monks who did not participate in this had difficulty in fitting in to monastic life.

The second week was spent at Pantokrator. It was the last monastery to become cenobitic (i.e. functioning as an organized community) having previously been idiorrhythmic (i.e. functioning as a collection of, in effect, individual hermits).

The food was plain and simple to the extent that I think they have taken the decision that no spices – including salt and pepper – are necessary or desirable. There was very little flavour in any of the food. All of the bread at Pantokrator was very dry; I think they bake only once each week. Their welcome to pilgrims is in a 'Pilgrims' Lounge' where there is a coffee machine, water and a large bowl of loukoumi (Turkish delight). After the evening meal there is mountain tea and a selection of dried fruit and little biscuits! All slightly surprising!

Sunday 19 May 2019. Dinner: pasta and Parmesan-type cheese, olives, apples, bread, wine and water.

Monday 20 May 2019. Breakfast: lentil soup with carrots and peppers, olives and peppers, apples, bread, water. Dinner: lentil soup, small olives, peppers, bread, jam, water. Dinner was very informal – no grace or reading, conversation allowed.

At the Karyes coffee shop I had a nice chat (in French) with Father J, who had originally been a teacher in France – and who had visited the UK and had studied in Rome. On hearing that I was Scottish he was intrigued (as everyone in Greece is) by the reality of the kilt and told his 'kilt' story. While studying in Rome he and a friend were in a café filled with kilted Scotland supporters during a Italy/Scotland rugby match. He remarked to his pal that he had never seen people in kilts before – but why were they looking at them? To which his friend replied that perhaps they had not seen many people dressed in a long black robe with an enormous beard. He saw the point.

FIG.56 *Pantokrator*

On the path to the neighbouring Stavronikita monastery a hermit (a very amiable and friendly German gentleman) popped out of the undergrowth and asked us not to clear the way off the main path onto the path to his hermitage – though he thanked us for clearing the main path itself. Stavronikita is pretty, but one of the smallest monasteries.

Tuesday 21 May 2019. Breakfast: moussaka with pasta, olives, apples, bread, wine and water. Dinner: 'soup' (dairy stock, possibly with chicory and fish?), rice with vegetables (and fish?), olives, apples, bread, wine and water.

During the day we visited Pantokrator's skete of Prophet Elijah. Now with a small number of Greek monks and a magnificent Russian building founded by a Russian Grand Duchess, Alexandra Petrovna, who sat offshore on her yacht and watched it being built.

Wednesday 22 May 2019. Breakfast: fish and roast potatoes, salad, bread, water. Dinner: rice and fish, salad, apples, bread, wine and water.

We cleared a path to the Romanian kellion of St George, Kolitsou. It is a small kellion that constantly receives visitors (mainly Romanian and Moldavian). Their news was that an almost abandoned skete nearby was going to be occupied by a group of thirty monks from Hamatoura (a monastery in Lebanon). This is clearly very exciting – and there was much discussion of how lovely Arabic chant is.

Thursday 23 May 2019. Breakfast: tomatoes stuffed with rice, plus rice, olives, apples, bread, water. Dinner: there were alternatives depending on where you sat (either rice and vegetables or beans, cooked with their pods, and mushrooms), olives, apples, bread, water.

In monastery gift shops it is notable that people spend hundreds of euros on icons, bracelets etc. – I think often for everyone in their church back home. Also – how difficult it is for an Orthodox priest to go through a religious artefacts shop when he must cross himself in front of every icon.

Friday 24 May 2019. Breakfast: chickpea and vegetable soup, olives, peppers, apples, bread, water. Dinner: chickpea soup, peppers, olives, jam, apples, bread, water. We had an interesting discussion with a Western European Orthodox priest about the difficulty of walking rough mountain trails in a full-length cassock and clerical hat (which priests must wear on the Mountain). He described it as 'unbelievably hot'.

And on Saturday 25 May 2019, we took the ferry to Ouranoupolis and then the coach on to Thessaloniki.

Athonite Iconography and the Patriarch

PETER BRIAN DESMOND

My first pilgrimage to Mount Athos came as the result of encouragement by my Spiritual Father, the late Archimandrite John Maitland Moir. Every year after Pascha, he would make his own pilgrimage to the place where he was received into the Orthodox Church: the Holy Monastery of Simonos Petras. He would stay there for a week or two, before resuming his pastoral role as principal priest of the community of St Andrew in Edinburgh. It was perhaps only natural that my first visit to the Holy Mountain would be to his own Athonite spiritual home, a place of immense beauty and prayer. Many people reading this will perhaps have seen the monastery in photographs or in TV documentaries. It is an enduring image or indeed icon of Mount Athos, familiar across the world to those who have been able to travel there and the many who cannot.

Later on during that pilgrimage, a chance encounter with a FoMA footpath-clearing team at Vatopedi monastery sowed the seed for three further pilgrimages as part of that group whose shared experiences, hard work and camaraderie is well attested elsewhere in this publication. The path-clearing pilgrimages and the people I have been privileged to encounter – with their myriad, multi-layered expertise, humour and unabashed willingness to offer advice and critique to one's lopping inadequacies – truly helped me to find my bearings in this most special of places. So where, if anywhere, would this lead?

In the autumn of 2017, I was working on ideas for completing the final piece of a Master of Theology degree in Orthodox Theology. The 20,000 word piece was primarily going to be about the 'Iconographic Renewal' that happened over the course of the twentieth century – in particular, looking at the legacy of the great icon painter, writer and philosopher Photios Kontoglou (1895-1965) and the generation that succeeded him. Kontoglou is widely credited with 'opening the door' back to a form of traditional Byzantine iconography that had long been neglected in both Greece and Russia. I wanted to explore whether the legacy that he inspired, which had been shaped by contemporary artistic influences, had been filtered through to Mount Athos – a sort of 'Modern Athonite Iconography'. In other words, something that did not simply copy older models but was conscious of a wider artistic expression, albeit within the bounds of Holy Tradition. A chance conversation with a monk at Vatopedi while admiring some of their frescoes, led to my first solo pilgrimage to the Holy Mountain in October 2017. What follows is something of a brief summary of 'lessons learned', 'mea culpas' and unforgettable experiences.

My first solo pilgrimage did not quite get off to a flying start. I found myself alone, standing by the roadside at Ierissos, the point of departure for ferries to monasteries along the Athonite peninsula's eastern coastline. Despite my prompt arrival, the ferry had gone without me and I watched mournfully as it disappeared into the distance around the headland. Oh dear. An hour before, all seemed well. The ferry arrived at 8 a.m. and weather conditions were good for October. The dozen or so passengers presented themselves to the man with the clipboard and would be issued with a diamonitirion – the three night prerequisite 'visa' for entry to the Holy Mountain – and then board the ferry. Job done. Alas not – at least in my case. For reasons unknown and unknowable to me, I was not on the list. I had a ticket reservation number, but no diamonitirion, no ferry! Prior to leaving the UK, it was suggested that my host monastery would issue me with the document (rather than the Pilgrim Bureau), so making things 'simpler'. Yet despite showing copies of emails from the monastery, my clipboard interlocutor – who in all probability had encountered this sort of pilgrim incompetence many times before – was understandably unmoved. When I enquired what I might do next, I was told to go to Ouranoupoli. 'How?' was greeted with 'I don't know'. I knew there was a ferry at 9.45 a.m. but it was too far to walk with a large pack. Meanwhile, back at the roadside 'bus stop', another half an hour had passed with no sign of a bus (that stopped) or any other means of getting to my new destination.

At the precise moment I was about to give up, my clipboard friend pulled up opposite me in his car. 'What are you doing?' he shouted. 'Get in!' was his reply to my rather lame 'Waiting for a bus'. Twenty minutes later, I stood in

Dionysiou

Grigoriou

front of the main man in the Pilgrim Bureau in Ouranoupolis, who politely but simply said 'No' to most things I had asked of him on the understandably sound basis that they had no record of my diamonitirion either. My final plaintive move was to unearth the previously unsuccessful pile of email correspondence from the monastery and try to persuade him of my bona fides. Success! The diamonitirion was printed. I ran to the ticket office and managed to tunnel through the scrummage of large Russian gentlemen to the front of the queue, secure my tickets and scramble aboard the ferry to Daphne just as it was about to leave.

'Before you come to Mount Athos, you must have a plan. But, when you arrive here, you must be prepared to change, disregard or tear it up completely. Things will happen according to God's will, not yours. It is important to let go of your 'worldly' mindset and embrace what might seem like obstacles or difficulties. You must not worry. Pray. The Panaghia will guide you!'

This wise counsel was given to me on arrival at Vatopedi on my solo pilgrimage to carry out doctoral research for two weeks in February 2019. It was given by Father E, a monk I had got to know while completing a Master's degree the previous year. His advice and guidance – and that of many other Fathers – was helpfully direct and always rooted in prayer and humility. His words have become a guiding light on my journeys to the Holy Mountain ever since, serving as a sort of spiritual compass to help navigate the inevitable spiritual and emotional ups and downs.

At the time I received these words, I had just arrived back on the Holy Mountain to start my research and I was still carrying my worldly preoccupations along with my rucksack. I had spent considerable time planning this 'expedition': booking travel and diamonitirion, contacting the half dozen monasteries I wanted to visit and working out in what sequence to visit each one. Of critical importance was ensuring that I could identify monastic houses where there was someone familiar with my topic and who would agree to be interviewed. There is no central record or census of monastic houses where iconography is practised today and that remained firmly the first significant challenge. Secondly, and perhaps as a consequence of the first point, was that very little has been written about contemporary Athonite iconography. This meant that fragments of information needed to be knitted together from monks I met or pilgrims I encountered in order to work out those monasteries where hospitality might be sought. Any small change to these logistics, arranged at some considerable distance from the Holy Mountain, could, so I thought, have significant consequences.

My research topic concerns how the rediscovery of the icon that took place across the Orthodox world during the twentieth century has impacted upon Mount Athos, given its unique place as the pre-eminent conservator of Orthodox Tradition. 'Rediscovery' in this context does not imply that icons were wholly neglected prior to this period. On the contrary, the icon, unlike religious or other art forms derived from the Western tradition, is par excellence a liturgical art. Its purpose primarily is to engage with the beholder in a way that mediates the space between the here and now and the heavenly kingdom. In so doing, the icon facilitates prayerful encounter between the worshipper and the person or festal scene depicted, in a dynamic relationship of mutual love. To quote St Basil's famous words: 'The adoration of the icon passes to the prototype, that is to say the holy person represented'. The icon transcends time and opens a door to the nearness and otherness of eternity. For this reason it is an essential feature of Orthodox worship. Indeed, it is no overstatement to say, that for the monks of Mount Athos, icons are among the things they treasure the most and for which they have greatest reverence.

Returning now to my conversation at Vatopedi and the monk's very good advice to the effect that you need a Plan, but do not despair if you need to change, adapt or junk it completely. I took him through my programme and he seemed to think it was coherent. It covered a period of two weeks on the Mountain, starting and ending at Vatopedi. Only one monastic house, a slightly remote cell, had not replied to my request for hospitality prior to my arrival. The master iconographer at Vatopedi knew this monk well and so offered to give him a call. There was a lot of encouraging sounding talk in Romanian and hopes were high until the call ended: 'He is in Romania and will not be back for a while'. The only others at that cell were novices and it would not be appropriate to go and speak to them and try to cover the same ground without his supervisory presence. At a stroke, there was a two-night hole in my programme. Some improvisation would be needed and I was assured that in the worst case scenario of having nowhere to stay, monasteries would find a way to take me in as a lone pilgrim, despite not having a reservation. It was February after all and pilgrim numbers were relatively low.

Having completed my two-night stay at Vatopedi, the following morning I waited for the minibus to Karyes, as I was expected for two nights at Koutloumousiou. At that point, I heard a monk I knew from path-clearing enquiring loudly and repeatedly of the assembled pilgrims 'Has anyone here seen Peter?' I acknowledged his calls and went over to speak with him. The second adjustment to my Plan was about to take place, although I did not know it. The monk said: 'The Fathers have agreed that our catechumen W should be baptised on Saturday morning and they have said they would like you to be his Godfather. So can you stay another few nights?' Naturally I was delighted, humbled and honoured to be asked, but I had already spent two nights at Vatopedi and really needed to make progress elsewhere. So we agreed a compromise. I would go as planned to Koutloumousiou but return the following afternoon (Friday) in time for the first part of the Baptism to be performed that evening, then stay overnight and be primed for the Baptism proper on the Saturday morning.

On arriving at Koutloumousiou I met the charming Archontaris and using my modest Greek, explained the situation which was, in effect, yes I was staying two nights, but just not necessarily the ones I had anticipated. When I explained the situation further, he was delighted and said: 'You must go back – it is a great honour. We will keep your room here for when you return'. How wonderful.

When I arrived back in the Vatopedi katholikon for vespers on Friday, several iconographers and other monastic friends approached me and said: 'You're back already?' and before I could explain, they had put two and two together and asked: 'Are you going to be the Godfather tomorrow?' They appeared delighted. I spent time with W that evening, doing my best to answer his many questions. This was the Plan going awry for all the right reasons! The following morning, the baptism took place in a small chapel with a full walk-in-walk-out immersion pool. Given the weather, it was deemed a little too precarious to conduct the baptism by the rocks and the sea, which in winter seemed fairly lively. All went well and it was an absolute privilege to be there; a somewhat dreamlike experience. At one point, when the monastery photographer arrived in the chapel, W, a splendidly dry-humoured Bostonian, said to me sotto voce: 'I had no idea the paparazzi were gonna be here!' Along with another friend I had met, an Orthodox pilgrim from Turin with whom I have also remained in touch, we had a special place set aside for a marvellous festive meal in the trapeza and everybody was buzzing with the drama and excitement of the day.

The remainder of that research pilgrimage was a joy and the flaws in my original plan opened up opportunities that I could not have anticipated. I was told by many monks that as I was travelling alone and during a relatively quiet time of year, there would be little likelihood of my being refused a night's hospitality if I were to arrive somewhere unexpected for the night. One such place I considered was Stavronikita, a small, beautiful and quite traditional monastery, which was known to be rather difficult to gain access to. Buoyed by this advice and simultaneously trying to let go of a British reluctance to do the 'wrong thing' in not having booked ahead, I arrived unexpected at the entrance. I explained my purpose to a young monk with an intelligent and somewhat piercing gaze, and duly presented him with my paper – translated into Greek – that explained my research into contemporary Athonite iconography. Oh, and could you put me up for the night as I had been let down elsewhere and I have nowhere to stay this evening? He mused over the paper, then said: 'Ah, so you are interested in new iconography?' 'Yes', I replied, thinking this was all going rather well. He continued: 'Well, hmm, I should explain. The most recent iconography that we have in our monastery is around five hundred years old'. Ah. I had one other card to play. Stavronikita is also renowned for having some of the finest frescoes on the Holy Mountain, painted by the pre-eminent artist of the post-Byzantine School and dating from the sixteenth century, Theophanes the Cretan. A number of the monasteries I had visited cited the Cretan School as a primary influence in their contemporary iconography and so, with some small sense of justification, I explained that it would be a great privilege to study them first hand in the Stavronikita katholikon. The monk then excused himself to consult the monastery Secretary and five minutes later he returned, smiled and said that I had permission to stay for one night. 'The services tomorrow start at 2 a.m. for the feast of The Three Holy Hierarchs and will finish at about 7.30 a.m. After trapeza, you may rest but if it would be possible for you to vacate your room by 8.30 a.m., it would be very much appreciated'. He smiled and I smiled, too. I may be limited to an hour's sleep before setting off again but I was delighted to be there. My host also appeared happy to have been able to help, which he most certainly did.

During the beautiful All Night Vigil, the marvellous frescoes of Theophanes – a contemporary of Henry VIII, so not quite as contemporary as I would have liked for my research – were suddenly illuminated by a thunder and lightning storm that raged outside and continued violently through the night. It never ceases to amaze me that Athonite liturgical services that are complex and elaborate, finish almost always on the dot – in this case precisely 7.30 a.m. The chance to spend the night in the company of these beautiful paintings in their proper liturgical context was a joy unconfined. A quick repose after a delicious meal and a cup of red wine, and I was once again walking the monopati, fully loaded with my 65 litre rucksack and camera/valuables bag (must pack lighter, must pack lighter!). I walked to the skete of Prophet Elijah, built and occupied originally by Russian monks on and off until the effects of the Russian Revolution in 1917 led to a period of decrease and decline. On the advice of my gatekeeper friend from yesterday, I would be stopping for coffee at Pantokrator for

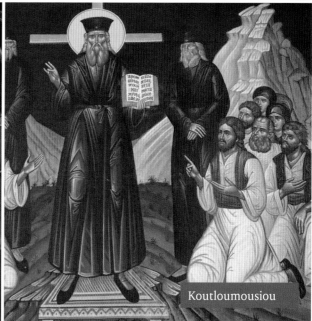

Koutloumousiou

Konstamonitou

a brief respite before the steady 30 minute climb to my destination. I reached Pantokrator after about 50 minutes, having slid over backwards and sideways a couple of times on sections of smooth rock that had been washed glass-like to an unwalkable slippery state by the night's storm. It may have been worse but for one of my Stavronikita roommates' insistence on giving me his walking pole for stability before setting off. He and his friend were heading home to mainland Greece and he no longer needed it. I tried to refuse but in hindsight, and having reached Pantokrator unscathed, I was delighted that he had insisted.

Pantokrator was silent when I arrived at about 9 a.m., so I waited and drank some water. Presently, a young monk appeared and asked if I was staying the night ('no') and if I wanted trapeza (also a polite 'no thank you'). He then kindly showed me around the katholikon, including the opportunity to venerate the miracle-working icons of the Mother of God 'Gerondissa' in the nave and St George the Phaneromenos in a chapel on the north side. The former is distinctive in depicting the Mother of God in full length and without holding the infant Christ. It represents the Mother of God as 'Elder' and protector of the Holy Mountain. This theme is very important to the monks, who pay her great reverence. The theme can also be seen in the very popular modern icon (originally from Bourazeri skete) depicting the Mother of God as 'Ephor' (overseer). In it, she stands large on the Holy Mountain itself holding the elder's staff of office, flanked in heaven by Athonite saints and surrounded at her feet by her monasteries. This icon illustrates a very important point: that the Holy Mountain itself is the Garden of the Panaghia, where the spiritual life will grow and flourish, whose monks and pilgrims she will guide and protect, and on whose behalf she will intercede.

Also in the katholikon, I noticed two portable icons that reminded me of similar examples I had seen in Bourazeri skete and at Vatopedi, painted in a traditional but unmistakeably contemporary style. When I asked who had painted them, I was told it was Father K and that to my surprise he was a monk of this monastery. He had been a pupil of one of the best-known iconographers on Mount Athos. This unexpected news was indeed another blessing. As a quid pro quo for helping me, the young monk in return asked whether I knew anything about Samsung dryers. The conversation tailed off fairly quickly as I was plainly out of my depth. A few days later I returned and, after waiting, was able to meet Father K in his studios situated high above the crashing waves. After explaining what I was doing, Father K invited me to return to Pantokrator to speak in greater depth and to stay at the monastery in October, as part of a second research pilgrimage.

I reached the skete of Prophet Elijah shortly afterwards. It is a spectacular place, set high above Pantokrator, of which it is a dependency. It can be seen very clearly from miles around, including from ferries out at sea. On the face of it, it belies description as a skete, which traditionally comprise smaller monastic settlements centred on a kyriakon or church. As mentioned earlier, it is constructed in the Russian style. The church, once one of the largest in the Balkans, is sixty metres in length and can accommodate two thousand people. The iconostasis is vast at twelve metres high and is reputedly gilded with ten tonnes of gold. The icons and others in the principal (but much smaller) chapel of St Nicholas are of the later Russian ('Western') style and, seen in their proper context, they have their own, albeit less familiar, beauty. However, the main surprise on arriving at such a vast space was to learn that there were only eight monks, several of whom came from Thessaloniki in 1992 to regenerate the ostensibly abandoned skete. Yet what they lack for the moment in numbers, they more than compensate in energy, enthusiasm and joyous hospitality, ably abetted by a dedicated group of lay workers. The views from the concourse at the east end of the church facing out to sea and Pantokrator monastery below are remarkable. I had arranged to stay for two nights to speak with Father P, who had in earlier years painted icons, and, moments after I arrived, had taken possession through the post of a series of original watercolour paintings of Athonite monasteries painted between 1924 and 1929 by the celebrated artist Spyros Papaloukas. It was an intriguing start to my putative two-night stay.

On the afternoon of Friday 18 October 2019, I had arrived at the Archondaríki at Pantokrator and was waiting to be shown to my room. I had travelled from Koutloumousiou to the cell of Axion Estin, back to Karyes, and then down to Pantokrator. At various points on this small journey, rumours abounded that the Ecumenical Patriarch of Constantinople was on the Holy Mountain and would be visiting a number of monasteries during his short sojourn. Police would be cordoning off roads or sections thereof to facilitate the Patriarch's smooth vehicular passage to his various destinations, so travel by road would be a little less predictable than usual. Walking the footpaths seemed – and probably was – the safest and, as ever, most rewarding option and all had passed off well without cordon or diversion. This was my return visit to Pantokrator that had its origins in my brief encounter with the monastery back in February and the promise of an opportunity to carry out research in the icon studios.

During vespers I spotted Father K, the principal iconographer, and was pleased that I had the next three nights to find opportunities to meet and discuss all things iconographic with him. So after trapeza, I set about trying to

Pantokrator

find him only to discover that he and perhaps fifty per cent of the brotherhood had just left for Xenophontos, their sister monastery on the West coast, to help with preparations for the Patriarch's visit there and the correspondingly huge influx of pilgrims. Oh dear. A senior monk then explained that he may be back on Sunday, or perhaps later, and that they would be happy for me to stay over an extra night on Monday, when the Patriarch would be in Vatopedi – which is where I was also supposed to be, although travel might not be easy with my heavy pack. I was reminded of the good advice I was given from Vatopedi about my Plan when the senior monk also said that I would be free to experience the many spiritual benefits of staying at the monastery and still visit the icon studios, take photographs and speak with the Apprentice Iconographer and so forth at my leisure. This is where pilgrimage proper takes over from pilgrimage as research. Just let go. In the meantime he asked about me, my research, whether I was Orthodox, married, children, (all answers were yes), and then 'Perhaps you will become a priest then', which I took to be a way of letting me down gently from the realisation that I could not become a monk! After blushing somewhat, I thanked him for his kind words and for reminding me why we make pilgrimage to the Holy Mountain, the pre-eminence of prayer, of bowing down (proskynesis) and opening one's heart to God. Research could wait.

The following morning I woke at 2.30 in time for matins and the Divine Liturgy from 3 to 6.20. The Apprentice Iconographer I had met the night before was also the second chanter. He had a beautiful voice and indeed a number of different jobs or obediences around the monastery. A short rest period of an hour and a half followed before the paraklesis, a short service of petition and intercession to the Mother of God that preceded trapeza. I had heard that the frescoes in the trapeza had been painted by a well-known iconographer from Pantokrator's sister monastery and that they had not been completely finished, evinced by outline line drawings on the walls near where we were sitting that had not been fully transformed into vibrant coloured frescoes. Later in my stay, I was given a blessing to photograph these unfinished sections whose temporary monochrome potential reflects the high demand in which the painter is held, such that time has yet to allow for the completion of this final section.

I decided to take a walk up the hill to Prophet Elijah, which stood out majestically in the autumn sunshine and where – according to further rumour – the Patriarch would be hosted for lunch on Tuesday after his visit to Pantokrator. I was beckoned to sit with a gentleman who had been staying at Prophet Elijah for a few days, having found it a very convenient base from which to travel and explore the Holy Mountain. He was well travelled and, in his time, had been acquainted with John Julius Norwich and Steven Runciman. The gentleman was considering a visit to Esphigmenou, which has been somewhat isolated in the Orthodox milieu in recent years, principally on account of its stance on what it perceived as a worrying drift towards 'ecumenism'. By other accounts, it has been most welcoming to visiting pilgrims. A monk of that monastery wanted him to look at a piece of canvas that was being used as a cover or adornment for icons in procession. The monks' understanding was that its provenance was Napoleonic, deriving from the Egyptian campaign. However, a historian friend thought its origin was more likely to be from the reign of Louis XV and that it had later been stored in 'gare de meubles' – vast warehouses used to store Royal furniture no longer required – and which later made its way to Egypt with Napoleon's forces. Either way, it was likely taken, along with other possessions of conquest, by the British and in this case given to the Ottoman Sultan in Constantinople, who, for reasons unknown, gave it to the monks of Esphigmenou. The gentleman was charming and erudite and I wanted to go with him to Esphigmenou to see how the story unfolded, if ever it were possible to know. We were then treated to some wonderful figs preserved in syrup and a small glass of mastic liqueur, before taking the half-hour hike down the hill, having bade farewell to my generous hosts.

In the evening I spent time with the Apprentice Iconographer Father I, who showed me some of his work in progress. He was painting an icon of St Theodore, a bishop who had worked miracles in his home region, and also of the Archangel Gabriel for his Abbot and namesake. Father I was very interested (as were many monks) in why people from a 'western' background or heritage had decided to become Orthodox and was curious to learn of the numbers and the fact that they continue (albeit from a relatively small base) to grow. There were noticeably fewer pilgrims today than when I arrived the day before, but that was about to change. A monk bustled in to the icon studios to say that a group of pilgrims was being sent by bus from Xenophontos to Pantokrator to stay the night, due to the fact that there were about 700 pilgrims at Xenophontos and the monastery could not cope and risked being overwhelmed. The Apprentice Iconographer – who had been assigned temporarily to the Archondaríki – would need to assist with their reception and room allocation before they were bussed back to Xenophontos in the morning. I returned to my room of seven beds, occupied only by myself, a Russian and a Georgian, and hunkered down waiting for an influx that never came our way.

On the morning of Sunday 20 October 2019, the first talanton came and went without my noticing, but I somehow reached the katholikon twenty minutes after the start at 4.50. Matins this morning was three hours long followed immediately by the Divine Liturgy, which finished at exactly 9. After a hectic night and a busy early morning in church, the Apprentice Iconographer told me that the Abbot's deputy would like to meet with me to discuss my research after trapeza. Given that it had now been confirmed that the Patriarch's arrival would be in 48 hours' time, it transpired that the Abbot's deputy was otherwise engaged with more pressing and important work after trapeza. The Apprentice Iconographer was likewise re-reassigned to the Archondaríki, the worldly hub of the monastic engine. So many pilgrims, so many beds, so many changeovers, so much trapeza and so forth. The fact that as pilgrims, we rarely notice what happens below the surface is a testament to the organisation and endeavour that is itself a physical manifestation of the monastic life of prayer for the world. At a similarly prosaic level, I was quietly pleased at locating two large sinks with hot water that had been outside my room. It meant I could wash some clothes and hang them in the dusty fortified alcove with a narrow open-to-the-elements window, situated in the corner of our quite large (for three people) room. With luck, everything might be dry by the morning.

It was a 'calm before the storm' kind of day. Reading a book on 'iconography as pedagogy', a gracious and unexpected gift from the Abbot of Dionysiou a few days earlier, and sitting on a small balcony overlooking the gently wind-stirred sea, I had still not decided whether to keep to the Plan of going to Vatopedi on Monday, as the Patriarchal visit there would be in full swing, or stay and wait for him to come to us here at Pantokrator. I decided I would wait until the Iconographer returned from Xenophontos. After all, I had met him briefly by chance in February and he was my principal reason for being here now. On Athos, things have a way of happening like this but immediately after evening trapeza, I was told that the Iconographer had returned. Later that evening I encountered him and we arranged to meet the next day at 12 noon in the icon studios. This was a good moment to phone home for a catch up, from the vantage of a turreted low wall, down from the pilgrims' smoking kiosk and above the fishermen's rocks with a view southward to photogenic Stavronikita set against the dramatic backdrop of the Holy Mountain. And yes, in contrast to this idyllic vista, it was of course dank, raining and cold at home in rural Leicestershire, but it was nevertheless good to hear a familiar and reassuring voice. I decided that I would stay at Pantokrator on Monday night and see what unfolded on Tuesday morning, which was now confirmed as the date of the Patriarchal visit.

Monday 21 October 2019 followed a similar pattern to the previous day. The obvious exception was the amount of Athonite and Greek flags adorning the tower and katholikon entrance, along with washing and sweeping of the monastery paths, inner courtyards and external stairs. Also, the relaying and resurfacing of a substantial area of flagstones and cobbles at the entrance to the monastery, that lay workers had been doing since I arrived on Friday – and probably before. The brotherhood that had travelled to Xenophontos had now returned and was also fully engaged in the preparations. My meeting was arranged for 12 noon, so I simply needed to go over thoughts and questions and previous interviews, making sure I would cover the most pertinent areas first and fill in any gaps in case our time might be cut short by much weightier priorities. At a remarkably mundane but fundamental level, I also had new batteries for the digital Dictaphone, generously provided after some essential explanation of 'what I was doing here' by the monk in charge of stores – once again, the Greek translation of the nature of my research on Mount Athos saved the day. Without his help, any further interviews would have been so much more difficult.

At 12 noon I climbed the stairs to the icon studios and waited for Father K. He had already had a busy morning. First as the celebrant priest at Matins, Divine Liturgy and the Paraklesis (I did not know he was a priest!), then, either side of our interview, choreographing the forces of the monastery choir in rehearsing music to be sung especially for the Patriarchal visit, which I had been listening to while waiting on the steps above the katholikon. It sounded quite magnificent – in fact, the best I had heard. In addition to the Apprentice Iconographer mentioned earlier, there was the protos, or 'principal' of the first antiphonal choir, who sang solo parts at various times in the services. Although very obviously singing Byzantine chant, nevertheless it sounded unmistakably 'eastern', reminiscent of fusion of almost operatic 'high-synagogue rabbinic' combined with the soaring elisions and changing dynamics of a muezzin's call to prayer. At the same time, it was first and foremost unmistakeably Orthodox, Athonite, and Christian. In addition, at Sunday's Divine Liturgy, I had heard a layman sing the most beautiful rendition of the Cherubikon – the solemn hymn that precedes the Great Entrance – that I had ever heard. No words can do it justice other than to say it was devastatingly beautiful. Perhaps it was no coincidence that he was there at this time to join the other solo talents and the amassed tannic backbone of the antiphonal choirs in full spate.

Father K, the Iconographer, arrived just as the rehearsals were taking a break. He was softly spoken, gentle, helpful, and showed no outward signs of nervous anticipation regarding the next day's guest and festivities. The interview was delightful and we covered much ground in a relatively short time, he being comfortable with the recording device in the background and with me taking

Xenophontos

Vatopedi

photographs in the studios. At one point, an older lay gentleman came in with plates of sliced apples and some olives. I happily accepted this hospitality while Father K politely declined and continued to explain more about his work with the attendant modesty that all iconographers appear to possess. During a brief interlude, he mentioned that his brother was also a monk at the monastery. Indeed, another member of the community had three sisters, all of whom were nuns in a metochion of the monastery on the mainland. And lastly he said: 'The old man who came in with the apples … that is my father … he is a novice here'. Nothing can fully prepare you for such unexpected examples of Christian commitment, modesty and piety (in its fullest sense). It simply leaves you without words. As we concluded, conscious of the need to continue rehearsals, he invited me to return to Pantokrator for a longer conversation in 2020.

On Tuesday 22 October 2019, after the morning services, it became apparent that there was no prospect of transport into or out of the monastery for some time that day. In spite of my earlier thinking that I might be able to have my interview with Father K and then smoothly progress to Vatopedi, waving discretely to the Patriarch's entourage as it passed me on the road, that had always been a pipe-dream. For one reason or another I would not be going anywhere and the Patriarch was on his way, expected at around 9.30 a.m. Surely this must be a blessing? In the meantime, there was further sweeping and last-minute snagging to be done. Earlier, I had received Holy Communion from the priest and iconographer that I had waited so long to speak to the previous day. Another blessing. There was no customary trapeza in the morning, but the coffee machine that had been the putative reason for my Pantokrator pitstop back in February, was still working and in much demand. Meanwhile, I had packed my bags ready for a prompt, if unknown, departure time to Vatopedi for my last night on the Holy Mountain.

The previous evening, my two roommates were watching something on a mobile device. It was footage from two days ago of the Patriarch's visit to Karyes to meet Athonite dignitaries and to visit the historic church of the Protaton. A great throng of people filled the narrow streets, jostling for position and all on foot. Then I noticed someone walking backwards immediately in front of the Patriarch, almost anticipating where he was going to step, all the time filming him at close range with a very smart mobile device, lighting and a sizeable portable battery, all hand-held. My Georgian friend smiled at me. Suddenly I realised that it was he that was doing the close-range filming. 'What, why, how … did he get that sort of access to the Patriarch?' 'Oh, I know him. He is a friend of mine. I used to live in Istanbul. I told him I was on the Holy Mountain and

he asked me to come along. Sometimes I help with security'. It was only then that I realised he was built like a marine as he showed me a rather neat way of disabling a combatant, if circumstances required – all rather slow-motion so as to accommodate my struggle to assimilate what I was hearing and seeing. He explained, seemingly reluctantly: 'I learned this technique which is used by the Israeli Defence Force, but I have other full-contact martial art training also'. Goodness! I became slightly worried that I may have moved his socks from the improvised washing line yesterday in my haste to dry my clothes. Nothing to worry about here. He was on our side so that was fine. I slept well.

As 9.30 a.m. approached, I found a vantage point at the top of an external staircase facing the entrance to the internal courtyard. Small groups of monks were gathering, readying themselves – as we all were – for the Patriarch's arrival at any minute. As I watched, a man with a dog appeared (which is unusual on Athos, where cats predominate), the latter on a lead venturing here and there around fire buckets and plants and doorways sniffing around. A sniffer dog, here in the monastery? After a more few cursory sniffs, the dog and its handler withdrew. I could not decide whether I was reassured or not. Such thoughts were immediately dispelled by the sound of a multitude of bells, large and small, announcing the Patriarch's arrival in celebratory and festive ringing. A monastic choir with music gathered below me at the entrance and made ready, while all of the priests and deacons, wearing matching white vestments adorned with rose-crimson crosses and black monastic hats and cowls, also gathered. Great anticipation mingled with underlying nervous energy everywhere. Pilgrims, likewise, were poised with phones and cameras at the ready.

The choir started to sing. The first glimpse was of armed, riot-style police emerging purposefully through the arch, together with local police and plain clothes officers, many of whom were listening to and speaking into earpieces and radio microphones. Then all of a sudden there he was: Bartholomew I, Ecumenical Patriarch of Constantinople, the 'primus inter pares' of the Orthodox hierarchical world, accompanied by his erstwhile host, Abbot Ephraim of Vatopedi. They were welcomed by Abbot Gabriel as the choir sang and walked across a carpet of welcoming bay leaves scattered on the ground between the entrance and the katholikon. As the bells continued to ring joyfully, I made my way up to another vantage point outside the katholikon, looking down the slope at the approaching entourage. The Patriarch was in the middle of it all, wearing his distinctive crimson mantle and carrying the patriarchal staff. The matching attired priests led the way, followed by police, uniformed officers from the Greek Navy, Army, and Air Force, high ranking police officials, dignitaries in civilian dress and the monks, shadowed by photographers, both professional and pilgrims.

As we entered the katholikon, anyone joining the throng was simply swept along with it, reminiscent of the different eddies and currents of a river. The singing was in full force and overhead the chandeliers and the great suspended crown, all illuminated with candles, were swaying excitedly in celebration, having been set in motion by the monks. Somehow, with a little bit of minor jostling, I had been deposited immediately to the left of the Patriarch, who was standing at his throne, staff in hand, within easy touching distance. There was a slight feeling of being overwhelmed by the realisation I was mere inches away from a man I had only ever seen in photographs and who occupied such a position in the Orthodox Church. I was closer than any of the bodyguards and next to the gentleman who carried his black staff topped with beautifully crafted gold filigree. It was one of the most remarkable moments in my life, yet only the day before I had been enquiring into how I might get to my next monastery, without having to get caught up in all of the pomp and ceremony. How embarrassing to have even held that thought. Yet again, the Plan went awry. Yet again, for all the right reasons. It was time to abandon the selfish ego and embrace the Divine will. This was the greatest of privileges and a truly humbling experience.

The priests and deacons were all assembled in front facing him, with their backs to the iconostasis and singing with the choirs. During the (relatively) short service of blessings and prayers, words from Abbot Gabriel and a response from the Patriarch, gifts were exchanged. The monastery presented the Patriarch with a highly decorated and beautiful icon of Christ the High Priest in a distinctive gold mosaic style. The Patriarch presented a slim and elegant silver jug and salver, which was passed right in front of me by an assistant to the Patriarch and then to the Abbot. Throughout the service, the singing was of the highest order – a combination of enormous talent and dedication with the music soaring up to the magnificent dome of the Pantokrator above and the acoustics resonating around the katholikon. The spirit could not be held from being moved.

Afterwards there was a brief 'blessing of the waters' service and the ceremonial planting of a cypress tree outside in the courtyard, following which the dignitaries went inside for private discussions until midday. After trapeza, which spilled out into overflow areas on the first floor balcony, the Patriarch, after pausing for photographs, gave an interview in Turkish to Hakan Celik, CNN's man in Istanbul. It was filmed in high-resolution video at close range by my Turkish-speaking Georgian roommate, with kit that could cope with the consumption of vast amount of gigabytes. Afterwards, Mr Celik, in answer to several questions, said that he would look to put English subtitles to the finished piece and that it would be made widely available online. The Georgian had earlier showed me his extensive and exclusive close range filming of the Patriarch's visit to Vatopedi the previous night. A man of many talents!

In the immediate aftermath of the interview, the police mini-cordon had relaxed a little and I managed to receive the Patriarch's blessing, the consummation of an extraordinary day. The whole of the brotherhood and the pilgrims at Pantokrator seemed moved and uplifted by this joyous occasion and the atmosphere was truly celebratory. Another reason for joy was the Patriarch's announcement, two days ago in Karyes, of the Glorification of four widely revered Athonite Elders: Joseph the Hesychast, his disciple Ephraim and Elders Daniel and Ieronimos of Simonos Petras. After some final farewells, the entourage moved out through the monastery gates and into a cavalcade of police and other 4x4 vehicles, and sped off along the dirt road towards another reception – somewhat later than anticipated – at Prophet Elijah.

I left very shortly afterwards and made my way to Vatopedi, my final destination, where I was reunited with the iconographers who had been so generous in sharing their ascetic wisdom, time, and expertise during my various research pilgrimages. One of the first things they asked was: 'How was the Plan?' They appeared to notice that some of the more worldly logistical preoccupations of earlier visits were no longer evident. I was reminded briefly of Christ's words to Nicodemos, which seemed to echo the sentiments of the Vatopedi fathers in guiding me: 'The wind bloweth where it listeth, and thou hearest the sound thereof, but canst not tell whence it cometh, and whither it goeth: so is every one that is born of the Spirit' (Jn 3:8). Yes, a Plan and a structure are important but it can also become a burden. On the Holy Mountain, which is far from 'The World', priorities and expectations are guided by prayer and living the life of Christ. To embrace these ideals is not easy, but experience suggests that it would seem to be the right approach to pilgrimage and to the research that may flow from it. The foreshortened time at Vatopedi passed all too quickly before it was time to leave for the UK. I had spent exactly three weeks on the Holy Mountain, travelling alone but meeting many remarkable people for which I give thanks. By the time I reached home at 1.30 a.m. the following morning, I had completed a journey that comprised eight monasteries and two sketes, two planes, two hotels, three trains, three taxis, three coaches, three minibuses, three army trucks and six ferries. And a bit of walking too!

I am looking forward already to my next research pilgrimage.

Profitis Ilias

Our Lady's Garden:
The Historical Ecology of the Holy Mountain

OLIVER RACKHAM

The Holy Orthodox Church has a well-developed theology of the Creation. As I understand it, humanity forms a link between God and the material world. Mankind is made in God's image and shares in God's creativity. Christ's redemption of the world applies to the whole of creation and not just the human species. God intends a particular relationship between humanity and the natural world. Although an Anglican and no theologian, I have much sympathy with such a positive doctrine, very different from the view that one encounters in other quarters, that Christians have no particular duty to care for the natural world because it will shortly be melted down at the Judgement.

In my scientific work I take the line that most of the world's ecosystems are in fact cultural ecosystems, the product not just of environment and of the natural behaviour of plant and animal species, but of their interactions with human activity as well. By 1,500 years ago human influence had reached to virtually all parts of the world's land area. It was not merely destructive but was often creative as well. Without people, Whittlesey Mere would still exist but the Norfolk Broads would not have been formed.

The infrastructure of meadows, woodland, and hedges has been altered and partly created by people; people also, for good or ill, have brought plants and animals from distant parts of the world, like rabbits and horse-chestnuts, and have even created new species like wheat. Many of these human influences are inadvertent, and they are still taking place. Creation is an ongoing process, and the human species has become part of how it happens.

Although I pay tribute to the Orthodox Church in developing a positive theology of Creation, I doubt whether there is universal agreement on any one form of it. I suspect a range of opinion among Athonite monasteries themselves. At one extreme there is a monastery that has no truck with mo-

tors and relies on mules, which the monks treat as honoured friends; and there is another that greets the pilgrim with piles of rubbish and defunct vehicles.

Athos is a very peculiar place: a range of rounded granite mountains, ending in a soaring pinnacle of limestone. It has attracted botanists since Belon, the Frenchman, went there in around 1550. Grisebach, the Austrian, had an adventurous visit in 1839, when pirates were added to the other difficulties of access. My knowledge of it derives from long discussions with Philip Oswald, also a botanist, and from three pilgrimages which he and I have made together. (I am grateful to him also for comments on this article.)

The story goes that on the Holy Mountain no female, animal or human, has been allowed for more than a thousand years. In consequence the vegetation has been allowed to develop largely unaffected by human activities; in particular it has been free from the multitudes of sheep and goats which have 'devastated' the rest of the Mediterranean. This interpretation may have been in Grisebach's mind; it was expounded by Turrill, the English botanist of the 1930s, who called the Holy Mountain 'a unique botanical paradise in an almost primitive condition, thanks to the lack of grazing animals', and likened it to an ecologist's exclusion experiment. This interpretation is true up to a point. The monks (with minor historic exceptions) never eat meat and keep no sheep or goats. But monks have to eat, like the rest of us; they have built majestic and wonderful buildings to the glory of God; and they have had to pay architects and craftsmen and boatbuilders and to provide transport. The Holy Mountain has an economic history; and it had a history before it became Our Lady's.

The Holy Mountain has always had forests, which have lately increased to the point that there is now not much else. It presents what in history has been rare in Europe, a region so densely and extensively forested that trees are quite

a constraint on its animal and plant life. Wolves are extinct and roe-deer almost so. Roe, although the most forest-adapted of deer, need some non-woodland to feed in. On the Mountain there is little for a deer to eat, and not enough deer to sustain a wolf. The animals that can squeeze or crash through the forest are wild pig and jackal. Pigs break into hermits' gardens and eat their vegetables; jackals seem to feed mainly on beetles.

I was once inadvertently benighted and had to spend the night in the bush. It was warm and I had plenty to eat, but some large animal came snuffling round in the dark. I awoke to a dawn chorus of nightingales and made my way to my destination, where the monks welcomed me as one who had escaped great dangers. They made me give special thanks to our blessed Lady, at whose intercession I had been delivered from the mouths of jackals.

Most of the Greek flora, and especially the endemics, the plants limited to Greece or some part of it, will not grow in shade. Athos is so very forested that such plants are restricted too. The glorious yellow Spanish Broom, for instance, is restricted to the edges of paths: probably it is a relict from when there was less forest.

Athos is the most forested part of Greece; and forests have always made up much of its economy. As in the rest of Europe there is a distinction between timber (produced from big trees) and underwood (poles and faggots produced by periodic felling of coppice-woods). Although there was some timber production the monks went in more for underwood and charcoal, less difficult to transport by mule.

Underwood was (and still is) used by the monks for heating and cooking: the numerous chimneys of monasteries give an idea of its importance. The monks got (and still get) much of their external income from sales of timber, wood, pine resin, etc., for which there were excellent markets in Thessaloniki and Constantinople. Even in the tenth century the emperor rebuked them for taking too much time off prayer and meditation for selling planks and charcoal. Repeated felling and regrowth keep some trees alive for many centuries: they form huge multi-stemmed stools. An example are the gigantic sweet-chestnut stools on the south face of the Mountain.

Chestnut coppice is a speciality of Athos and is managed to produce huge poles: straight poles for ordinary construction and curved ones for balconies. The timbers of monastic buildings seem to be mainly chestnut since the eighteenth century and oak or pine before that. Athos may be the main source of the chestnut poles that are widely used all over Greece. The tree has been introduced widely over Europe: whether it is native on Athos is impossible to say.

Athos has had periods of prosperity and recession. Travellers tended to write about it at times of recession: they underestimated the human activities at times of prosperity. In the eighteenth century, Athos made a brave attempt to start a university, of which the sad ruins still stand. In the nineteenth century, Vatopedi and the Great Lavra built second courts; the vast extensions of the Russian establishments were never finished after the events of 1917 overtook them. The number of monks probably never exceeded 10,000, but there were countless builders, servants, soldiers, and assistants to be fed and paid.

The monasteries had estates outside Athos, now mostly taken over by communists and imitators of Henry VIII, but they cultivated as much of the Mountain itself as they could. They may not have had cows, but they had bulls to draw the plough: there are place-names like Tavrokalyva ('Bull-shed'). There are still hundreds of mules, and there once were several thousand, feeding mainly on wild vegetation.

Some of the recent forest has grown up on old cultivation as the monasteries declined in the twentieth century. Olive-groves became infilled with wild trees; some of them, which had not gone too far, have recently been recovered. Near Vatopedi is a wonderful evergreen forest. Everything is evergreen: trees, vines, and undershrubs such as a giant butcher's-broom. Here, one might think, is the Mediterranean rain forest, or (to look at it another way) a survivor of the laurisylvan forests of the Tertiary era before glaciations ruined the flora of Europe. However, much of that forest is on old cultivation terraces; and it contains the ruin of a water-mill – which must have ground something – and an aqueduct.

Recent forest has arisen in a second way, through the infilling of savanna: of what had been scattered trees in grassland or heath. Some of the Vatopedi forest contains huge spreading pollard plane-trees which were once free-standing. In the south of Athos are ancient oaks, which grew up when they had plenty of room, embedded in what are now dense woods. These too are reminders of when there were grasslands grazed by thousands of mules.

Ancient trees are a special feature of Athos and are likely to be internationally significant as a habitat for very specific plants and animals, especially lichens and insects. Here is another aspect of mankind as an agent in the process of Creation. Most of the world's ancient trees are not forest trees: they occur in grassland where animals have been kept, and many are pollards, repeatedly cut at about four metres above ground level, to prevent livestock from eating the young shoots. Pollarding prolongs the life of a tree and turns it into an ancient tree.

All over Athos there are constructed mule-tracks and ancient holloways, many of them still in use, though damaged in the 1980s and 90s by road-building of a perfunctory kind. As reported year by year in their Report, the Friends of Mount Athos, and their Patron the Prince of Wales in person, have put much effort into recovering the many disused paths.

In 1990, a huge forest fire burnt tens of square kilometres of vegetation; it would have consumed Simonos Petras but for the intercession of Our Lady and St Simon the Hermit. This was regarded as a terrible disaster, and Philip Oswald was sent out by the World Wildlife Fund (now World-Wide Fund for Nature) to investigate and to advise about rehabilitation. He reported, in effect, that this was a normal, if infrequent, event in that kind of vegetation, that no drastic measures were called for, and if left to itself the landscape would recover.

Within weeks, the burnt trees had begun to sprout from the base. Within months, there was a profusion of wildflowers. As often in the Mediterranean, the places richest in flowering plants are those that have been recently burnt. When Philip Oswald returned on the eleventh anniversary of the 1990 fire he took me with him. We concluded that the vegetation had progressed about two-thirds of the way back to what it had been. The fire exposed many remains of mule-tracks and gardens. At Simonos Petras, very sensibly, the monks have restored and extended the gardens to create a firebreak between the bush and the monastery.

Mediterranean plants are flammable, not by misfortune but by adaptation. Bay laurel makes laurel oil, which when heated evaporates and produces a fuel-air bomb, a fireball which burns up laurel's competitors. The burnt laurel quickly sprouts and recovers. Fire is part of the life cycle of such trees. It is hardly reasonable to complain of fire, but it is most unreasonable, as Mediterranean foresters do, to plant pines and eucalyptuses which are even more fire-adapted than laurel, and then complain when they catch fire before they get big enough to harvest.

Fires are repeatable events. In 2001 we found remains of a previous fire close to the area that burnt in 1990. Traces of other fires can be found in places where the forest is now too dense to burn easily. There have been many fires on Athos, but so long ago that the present generation of monks do not remember them. Most of the wildflowers come up from seed laid down after a previous fire.

Early in 2002 there was a huge avalanche on the south face of Athos. A mass of accumulated snow detached itself during a sudden thaw, went roaring down through the forest into the Gorge of St Nilos, and presumably crashed into the sea, with 1,500-metres'-worth of kinetic energy behind it, to cause a small tsunami. This forest is a unique mixture of holly and aspen. Over a track about 400 metres wide every tree was sheared off at ground level. Avalanches are repeatable events. The Gorge of St Nilos – a sinister place, where Grisebach told a nasty little story about pirates – evidently gets scoured by an avalanche once every half-century or so.

You may say that avalanches are God's way of coppicing. Vegetation responds much as it does to human coppicing. Aspen sprouts from its root system, and holly sprouts from the stump. Wildflowers flourish, just as in an English coppice-wood: wood-spurge, for example, germinates from buried seed shed after the last felling or avalanche. *Aristolochia pallida* and *Lamium garganicum* are among the many plants that are there all the time but rush into blossom when the canopy has disappeared. The part of a forest that has the most plant life is usually the area that has just been felled. We found evidence of other avalanche tracks on Athos. Icons of the eighteenth and nineteenth centuries depict the Holy Mountain divided by an avalanche.

The flora of Athos is difficult to study and is still not fully known. Most of the Mountain is inaccessible, and botanists tend to stick to well-frequented paths. Then there are the problems of what constitutes a species? Do different botanists record the same plant under different names? Many travellers fail to give localities or even to say on which side of the frontier wall they found a plant. Philip Oswald and I, on our modest visits, have added nearly a hundred species, bringing the total number of native plants to about 1,000. This is less than I would expect for the area. Possibly there is too much forest: the dry shade of uncut Mediterranean forest is a harsh environment which does not have many species.

Many species are endemic to the Balkans (found nowhere else). About twenty-eight have some claim to be endemic to Athos only. Only three are woodland plants: in Europe there are very few woodland endemics. Two are coastal, including the special Athonite sea-thrift. There are few cliff endemics, compared to most of Greece and especially Crete. The peak, however, houses twenty of the twenty-eight endemics.

The peak of Athos is 2,000 metres high. It is not a difficult climb by the south face, but there is a lot of it: pilgrims who worshipped on the summit used to call themselves 'Haji', as though they had been to Jerusalem or Mecca. The west and north faces are tremendous, headlong, unstable cliffs: have they ever been climbed? On the way up one passes from the scented thickets of the Mediterranean maquis into the zone of chestnut and deciduous oak, with patches of open ground with colourful broomrapes and magnificent thistles. Next comes a belt of firs and black pines. The firs are the mysterious *Abies borisii-regis*, somewhat of a speciality of Athos, thought to be a hybrid between the silver fir of the Alps and its Greek counterpart. Above 1,500 metres come the last huge, old, surrealist, weather-beaten firs and pines, and at last the alpine zone. This is a 'rock-garden' of mainly endemic plants; a kind of woad *Isatis athoa*, Athos harebell *Campanula sancta*, intensely spiny hedgehog-plants, Our Lady's everlasting (*Helichrysum sibthorpii*), and many others. These have been sitting on those few acres of marble and have seen the ice ages come and go.

On the summit is a little chapel almost buried in scree. On rocks is the spectacular long-spurred violet *Viola delphinantha*, and in a hollow where snow persists is a special, tiny forget-me-not. As on other Greek peaks there are surprising numbers of beetles: what can they live on? The pilgrim looks out over the emerald chestnut woods, is surprised to see so many roads, wonders what treasures may lurk in the inaccessible nooks of forest far below – and tries, with the eye of faith, to imagine the fabled dome of Constantinople shimmering on the horizon.

In the 1930s the boundary wall of Athos marked an impressive division between the Holy Mountain and the World. The Mountain was populated by a declining band of monks, and that part of the World was overcrowded with refugees and their livestock. Things are very different now. The Mountain has not changed much: it has got rather more forested; but the World has changed drastically and has got much more forested. The wall is buried in trees and invisible from a distance.

The Mountain is not isolated from the World. The bulldozing of roads in the 1980s and 1990s began to bring it into line with the rest of Greece. It has added to the list some of the universal roadside plants of Greece, such as the mustard-like *Hirschfeldia incana*.

Sithonia, the neighbouring secular peninsula, is a possible comparison with Athos. It is much lower and probably drier. It too is now very forested by Greek standards, but with Aleppo Pine, which is rather local on the Holy Mountain. A more striking contrast is between Athos and Lemnos, the nearest island. Only fifty kilometres away, this is the most desert-like of the bigger Greek islands. Even in the mountains and even on cliffs, a tree is a rarity.

What would have happened had Our Lady been stranded on Lemnos instead of Athos? There would now be the Holy Island instead of the Holy Mountain. How much difference would this have made? I doubt whether monasticism could have converted Lemnos into Athos. The peculiarities of Athos are partly due to its position on the fringe of the Mediterranean. Its high mountains make their own rainfall; the screes and rotten granite retain moisture. Lemnos is not high enough to attract rainfall; its dense hard volcanic rocks are impenetrable by roots and do not absorb moisture. Lemnos must always remain arid, as indeed the holy island of Patmos is arid.

Athos became monastic around the tenth century: how is not known, nor what became of the secular population. What happened before it was the Holy Mountain? In Classical times it seems to have been a normal region, though mountainous and thinly populated. Athos, being very vegetated, does not lend itself to the archaeological survey that has been so productive in Crete or England, but at least five small 'cities' are known from documents. Classical Athens is known to have got much of its timber from Macedonia: I have speculated whether this means Athos, but such scraps of evidence as survive point to places further north in Chalkidiki.

Sacred groves – of various religions – are often claimed to be remnants of untouched wildwood carefully preserved. This is not always so. Those of the two religions of Japan, Buddhism and Shinto, are curious and wonderful places, but they are not wildwood: they are cultural landscapes with histories of their own. A Shinto shrine may be set in what looks like a tropical forest of giant evergreen tabu and shii trees – but these are infilled with planted trees of sugi: they did not escape the tree-planting fashions of nineteenth-century Japan. A more extensive woodland belonging to a shrine may have ancient pollard trees embedded in it: this cultural landscape tells a story not unlike parts of Athos. Even England has sacred trees – the ancient yews of churchyards – but few would claim that they are relics of wildwood.

The pilgrim may think of Athos as an enclave of Paradise on earth. We had the good fortune to visit Simonos Petras when the katholikon was being repaired. The liturgy was celebrated in one of the cavernous vaults of the skyscraper monastery, and the guests were privileged to sit in the overflow stalls outside. We looked up at the peak of Athos and the heavens, and down through the cracks in the balcony floor at the sea a thousand feet below; and it was easy to imagine the 'six-winged Seraphim' and the 'Cherubim full of eyes' swooping down to praise the Lord in the likeness of swifts and house-martins.

Athos is a Paradise, not only spiritually, but also in the botanical sense in which it impressed Turrill. (It has serpents, and creatures worse than serpents: fierce vivid biting flies – or was it the Devil in such likeness?) But it is not a prelapsarian Paradise withdrawn from the corrupting effects of human activities. It is a cultural landscape but formed in a peculiar way. To quote Father M of Simonos Petras: 'Nature is used to satisfy needs, with the facilities provided by technology; but all monks have deep and personal reasons for limiting this exploitation to what is strictly necessary, and not using nature for profit, ease or pleasure'.

This, in general, is how the inhabitants have used the Holy Mountain and formed its cultural landscape down the centuries. By the grace of God, it is no longer in danger of dying out through recession and neglect. Even endemic plants partake of this interaction. One of the most beautiful, Campanula lavrensis, displays its glorious blue flowers and grey foliage on the ancient masonry, not only of the Great Lavra but of nearly all the monasteries. What did it do before there were monasteries? Its original home was probably on the marble rocks of the peak, whence it has spread on to the artificial cliffs provided by the monks – but not on to natural cliffs at low altitudes. Another wonderful endemic, Viola athois, grows on the peak but has spread also into open areas in the forest created by monastic woodmen.

This symbiosis may have begun to break down with the recent phase of prosperity in the Mountain, and with the influx of new monks who have yet to learn the ways of Athos and how to live in harmony with its vegetation and environment. This may be a problem, but it is also an opportunity, because some of the newcomers bring with them a knowledge of ecology and of ecological problems derived from the countries that they come from. In paying tribute to the monks, I do not disparage secular traditions of living in harmony with the environment and vegetation. Old-fashioned Greeks made a better job of this than most ecologists will allow. But that is another story.

Previously published as: Rackham, Oliver (2004), 'Our Lady's Garden: the historical ecology of the Holy Mountain', Annual Report of the Friends of Mount Athos *(2004), pp. 48–57.* © Jennifer Moody <hogwildjam@mac.com>

From the Shore to the Summit: The Vegetation and Flora of the Holy Mountain

PHILIP H. OSWALD

The vegetation of the Holy Mountain is not 'virgin forest' (as is often stated). Like most of the world's surface, its natural state has been modified by human beings, in this case by a millennium of God-centred monkish activity. A major influence has been the absence of the grazing by goats and sheep that has created more typical Greek landscapes, but the woods were always cut for timber and firewood, the numerous domestic animals had to be fed, olive trees and vines were planted, and substantial areas were ploughed for crops.

A Introduction to the photographs

I shall illustrate the various types of vegetation and some of the characteristic trees, shrubs and herbaceous flowering plants of each. Starting with the soft shores and then cliffs, banks and walls, I shall next illustrate the major cover of the peninsula, evergreen broadleaves, which may form woodland (*maquis*) or low scrub (*garrigue* or φρύγανα); this section will include photographs showing the effects of a major forest fire in August 1990 which burned much of Simonopetra's land and threatened the monastery itself. (Sometimes evergreen broadleaves are replaced by Aleppo Pine, especially after forest fires.) Then I shall show the cultivated areas and the roads and paths, followed by the deciduous woodlands of higher altitudes, some of which have been converted to chestnut coppice stands (an important source of income for some of the monasteries); these areas often include the special fir tree of Athos. Next come streams (which often support Oriental Planes) and springs, followed by an area on the south flank of Mount Athos that was devastated by an avalanche during the winter of 2001/02. Finally – since I have never managed it myself – we shall ascend to the summit as if on 18 June 2002 with my late

friend and fellow pilgrim, Professor Oliver Rackham, and on 1 June 2013 with the Chairman of the Friends of Mount Athos, Dr Graham Speake, and his Serb friend, Radoman Matovic. To them and to two of my other fellow pilgrims, the late Dr Duncan Poore and my son Christopher, I am grateful for some of the photographs presented here.

B Soft shores

- B001: The coast below St Paul's, looking south (21 May 2001)
- B003: Coastal flora near the Great Lavra (1 May 2003)
- B004: *Armeria sancta* (Holy Thrift), a Macedonian endemic, near Iviron (2 May 1991)
- B007: *Matthiola incana* (Hoary Stock), a coastal species long grown in gardens, near the Great Lavra (1 May 2003)
- B009: *Ophrys cornuta* (a relative of the well-known *Ophrys apifera*, Bee Orchid, by some botanists treated as a subspecies of *Ophrys scolopax*, Woodcock Orchid) by the sea at Xenophontos (30 April 1991); one of seven species of orchids that I have seen on the peninsula; see also H018.

C Cliffs, banks and walls

- C001: Simonopetra from the sea from the west, with scrub on the cliffs (17 June 2002)
- C002: Sea-cliffs of 'the Desert' just north-west of Katounakia, close to the south-west corner of the peninsula (17 June 2002)
- C004: *Ptilostemon chamaepeuce*, a non-spiny knapweed-like shrub related to

thistles, near Dionysiou (16 June 1993); a characteristic chasmophyte (a plant that grows in the crevices of rocks) in Crete and elsewhere; χαμαιπεύκη (*chamaepeuce*) means 'ground-pine'.

- C005: *Papaver dubium* (Long-headed Poppy, a variety with a central cross in the flower as in *Papaver rhoeas*, Common Poppy) on cliffs by St Athanasios' cave (20 May 2001)
- C007: *Arabis turrita*, now *Pseudoturritis turrita* (Tower Cress), on a steep bank by the path between Hilandar and Chera (15 February 2011)
- C010: *Euphorbia acanthothamnus* (Greek Spiny Spurge) near the Skete of Ayios Nilos on the south coast of the peninsula (20 May 2001); ἀκανθόθαμνος (*acanthothamnus*) means 'spiny bush'.
- C020: *Campanula lavrensis* (Great Lavra Bellflower), a perennial species endemic to the Holy Mountain (growing on the walls of most of the monasteries) and to the neighbouring peninsula, Sythonia, by a tap in Karyes (17 May 2001)
- C021: *Campanula ramosissima* ('Very branched' Bellflower), an annual species, also in Karyes (17 May 2001)

D *Evergeen broadleaves (maquis and garrigue or φρύγανα)*

- D002: Simonopetra from high above it, with *Spartium junceum* (Spanish Broom, Σπάρτο) in the foreground (23 May 2001)
- D003: Simonopetra almost engulfed by flames as a result of the volatilisation of the oils in the trees of *Laurus nobilis* (Laurel or Bay-tree, Δάφνη) growing higher up the hill above a major forest fire (end of August 1990)
- D004: Simonopetra from the sea 12 years later (17 June 2002), showing the gulley with inflammable *Laurus nobilis* and the speed of its recovery after the fire
- D005: Aftermath of the fire below Simonopetra, from the west (end of August 1990)
- D006: Regeneration of *Laurus nobilis* below Simonopetra (6 December 1990, three months after the fire)
- D007: Regeneration of *Quercus coccifera* (Kermes Oak, Πουρνάρι or Πρίνος) below Simonopetra (6 December 1990)
- D009: Burnt area south-west of Xeropotamou from near Daphne

(8 December 1990, three months after the fire); note the unburned area by the sea at the bottom right of the monastery.
- D011: The same two and a half years later (19 June 1993), a little closer in; the unburned area is still distinct.
- D012: The same nearly ten years later (30 April 2003), twelve and a half years after the fire, slightly closer still, so with the unburned area off to the right
- D015: *Quercus coccifera* colouring spectacularly (30 May 2013, photo by Radoman Matovic)
- D020: Flush of colourful flowers near Simonopetra in the spring after the fire: *Verbascum phoeniceum* (orange-flowered variant of Purple Mullein) (29 April 1991)
- D021: Flush of colourful flowers near Simonopetra in the spring after the fire: *Pisum sativum* subspecies *elatius* (a wild variant of Garden Pea, Μπιζελιά) (29 April 1991)
- D022: Flush of colourful flowers near Simonopetra in the spring after the fire: *Vicia ?cassubica*, a handsome vetch (29 April 1991)
- D030: Evergreen broadleaves between Dionysiou and Grigoriou (22 May 2001)
- D031: *Jasione heldreichii* (a sheep's-bit related to the British *Jasione montana*) between Dionysiou and Grigoriou (22 May 2001)
- D034: *Dianthus deltoides* (Maiden Pink), between Dionysiou and Grigoriou (22 May 2001)
- D035: *Euphorbia rigida* (synonym *Euphorbia biglandulosa*, Narrow-leaved Glaucous Spurge) with *Quercus coccifera* behind, below Simonopetra (17 February 2011)
- D036: *Ruta chalepensis* (Fringed Rue, related to *Ruta graveolens*, the rue grown as an ornamental plant and herb), below Simonopetra (17 February 2011)
- D037: *Romulea bulbocodium* (related to the extremely rare English *Romulea columnae* and to *Crocus* species), below Simonopetra (17 February 2011)
- D040: *Arbutus unedo* (Strawberry-tree) in flower at Xeropotamou (8 December 1990)
- D041: *Arbutus unedo* (Strawberry-tree) in fruit at Xeropotamou (8 December 1990)
- D042: *Rhamnus alaternus* (Mediterranean Buckthorn), a food-plant of Brimstone and Cleopatra butterflies, coming into flower near Esphigmenou

(14 February 2011), an evergreen shrub of the evergreen broadleaves zone; see also D073 and G010.

- D043: *Pistacia lentiscus* (Lentisc or Mastic-tree, *Μαστίχα*) at the same place (14 February 2011), another evergreen shrub of the evergreen broadleaves zone, related to the deciduous *Pistacia vera* (Pistachio)
- D050: The path (*καλντερίμι*) between Hilandar and Chera, at a higher altitude and so including some deciduous broadleaved species (15 February 2011)
- D051: *Erica arborea* (Tree Heather, one of several species called *Ρείκι*), on the path between Hilandar and Chera (15 February 2011)
- D052: *Crocus flavus* (Yellow Crocus), on the path between Hilandar and Chera (15 February 2011)
- D053: *Crocus sieberi* (formerly distinguished as *Crocus athous* from this species found in mountains from the southern part of the former Yugoslavia to Crete), growing very close to the sea at the Simonopetra Arsanas (25 January 1992), but also found on the path between Hilandar and Chera on 15 February 2011
- D062: *Ruscus hypoglossum* (Large Butcher's-broom, related to the British *Ruscus aculeatus*) in high forest at Vatopedi (8 May 2001), where even the 'herb layer' is evergreen
- D071: Coast near the Great Lavra, with flowering *Cercis siliquastrum* (Judas-tree, *Κουτσουπιά*) and *Fraxinus ornus* (Manna or so-called 'Flowering' Ash, *Φράξο*), two deciduous trees – the former with bright pink flowers and the latter with creamy white flowers – growing in the generally evergreen broadleaves zone (1 May 2003)
- D073: *Cercis siliquastrum* in flower, with a Brimstone butterfly (*Gonepteryx rhamni*), near the Great Lavra (1 May 2003)
- D075: Flowering branch of *Fraxinus ornus* (May 2003)

E Lowland pine forest (replacing evergreen broadleaves especially as a result of fires)

- E001: *Pinus halepensis* (Aleppo Pine, *Πεύκο* like other species of pines) on both sides of the dividing wall near Ouranoupolis, seen from the sea (19 June 1993), showing how, with the present lack of grazing on the Ouranoupolis side as well as on the Holy Mountain, the previous contrast in the vegetation on the two sides no longer exists.

- E002: A closer view of the same (18 February 2011), probably burnt since then on 8 August 2012 in a fire that caused the evacuation of some hotels in Ouranoupolis

F Cultivated fields, gardens and trees

- F001: One of the huge trees of *Cupressus sempervirens* 'Pyramidalis' (Funeral or Italian Cypress, *Κυπαρίσσι το κοινό ορθόκλαδο* or *Κυπάρισσος η αειθαλής*) at the Great Lavra, reputedly over 1,000 years old (15 June 1993)
- F003: A vineyard near Esphigmenou, with a grove of *Olea europaea* (Olive, *Ελιά*) beyond (14 February 2011), demonstrating a combination of old and new technology
- F005: *Veronica cymbalaria* (Pale Speedwell), a southern European agricultural weed of this vineyard (14 February 2011)
- F006: Olive trees and garden at St Anne's Skete on the west coast near the end of the peninsula (21 May 2001)
- F007: Iviron, with *Asphodelus aestivus* (Summer Asphodel, *Ασφοδίλι*) in the foreground by the track and with the forest behind (2 May 1991)
- F008: *Asphodelus aestivus* below Simonopetra, often an indicator of overgrazing and fires, and therefore rare on the Holy Mountain (unlike over much of Greece) (17 February 2011)
- F009: The abandoned Skete of Ayios Dimitrios south of Vatopedi, with trees of *Olea europaea* and *Cupressus sempervirens* 'Pyramidalis' (27 May 2013, photo by Dr Graham Speake)
- F010: A new olive grove in the pine forest on the south-facing coast near Giovanitsa, seen from the sea (19 June 1993)
- F011: *Cupressus sempervirens* 'Pyramidalis' and (on the right) probably *Populus nigra* 'Italica' (Lombardy Poplar, *Λεύκα της Λομβαρδίας*) in an olive grove at Koutloumousiou, with the summit of Mount Athos directly behind the tower (1 May 1991)
- F012: *Lamium garganicum* (Large Red Deadnettle) in an olive grove at Koutloumousiou (1 May 1991)
- F013: An olive grove and pasture at Hilandar, with *Cupressus sempervirens* 'Pyramidalis' and flowering *Anemone pavonina* (Peacock Anemone, *Ανεμώνη*) and *Muscari commutatum* (Dark Grape-hyacinth) (13 February 2011)
- F014: *Anemone pavonina* at Hilandar (13 February 2011)

- F015: Close-up of *Anemone pavonina* at Hilandar (13 February 2011)
- F016: *Muscari commutatum* (Dark Grape-hyacinth) at Hilandar (13 February 2011)
- F017: *Ranunculus ficaria* or *Ficaria verna* (Lesser Celandine, *Ζωχαδόχορτο*) at Hilandar (13 February 2011)
- F018: *Cerinthe major* (Honeywort) near Esphigmenou (13 February 2011)
- F020: *Arisarum vulgare* (Monk's-cowl) below Simonopetra (17 February 2011)
- F021: *Myosotis incrassata* (a forget-me-not, *μη με λησμόνει*) below Simonopetra (17 February 2011)
- F030: *Onopordum bracteatum* ('Bracted' Cotton Thistle, related to the species found in Britain, *Onopordum acanthium*), near the Zografou Arsanas (18 June 1993); *Onopordum* is latinised from the Greek for 'donkey's fart', *ὀνόπορδον* – from the effect that the plant has when eaten by a donkey!
- F031: *Carduus ?taygeteus* (one of the *Carduus nutans* group, Musk Thistle) with a Hummingbird Hawk-moth (*Macroglossum stellatarum*), on the way to the summit (31 May 2013, photo by Radoman Matovic)
- F032: *Allium ampeloprasum* (Wild Leek), near the Zografou Arsanas (18 June 1993)
- F040: *Asphodeline lutea* (Yellow Asphodel or King's Spear), high above Simonopetra (6 May 2003)

G Pathsides and roadsides

- G001: Roadside above Xenophontos with *Hirschfeldia incana* (Hoary Mustard, a recent colonist of roads) and *Spartium junceum* (Spanish Broom, *Σπάρτο*, rarely occurring far from a path, track or road), looking north-west (30 April 1991)
- G002: Professor Oliver Rackham on an overgrown mule-track (*καλντερίμι*) near Prodromou, with *Spartium junceum* and *Cistus creticus* (the pink-flowered cistus, *Λαδανιά, Αλαδανιά, Λάβδανος* or *Κουνούκλα*, characteristic of Greek garrigue or *φρύγανα* and the principal source of ladanum) (20 May 2001)
- G010: *Centranthus ruber* (Red or Spur Valerian) with a Brimstone butterfly (*Gonepteryx rhamni*) by a forest track near the end of the peninsula (20 May 2001)
- G011: *Convolvulus althaeoides* (Mallow-leaved Bindweed), on a trackside near the end of the peninsula (20 May 2001)
- G016: *Papaver rhoeas* (Common Poppy), *Psoralea bituminosa* (Pitch Trefoil), etc., on a trackside near the end of the peninsula (20 May 2001)
- G017: *Alcea rosea* (Hollyhock) and wild oats, by the road to the Great Lavra above Prodromou (20 June 2002)
- G020: *Phytolacca americana* (American Pokeweed), by the road to the Great Lavra above Prodromou (20 June 2002): a rare example on Mount Athos of a widely established alien species, probably because of its former use to give a better colour to red wine
- G021: An *Orobanche* probably related to *Orobanche minor* (Common Broomrape), parasitic on an unidentified host plant, on a roadside in Simonopetra's forest (6 May 2003)

H Deciduous woodlands (mainly of oak)

- H001: View from Simonopetra's deciduous woodlands, looking towards the north-east coast, with *Quercus* (three deciduous species of oaks, *βελανιδιές*, including *Quercus frainetto*, Hungarian Oak), *Castanea sativa* (Sweet or Spanish Chestnut, *Καστανιά*), *Fagus sylvatica* or *Fagus orientalis* (Beech, *Οξιά*), *Carpinus betulus* or *Carpinus orientalis* (Hornbeam, *Γαύρος*), *Acer monspessulanum* (Montpellier Maple) and *Acer platanoides* (Norway Maple) (two kinds of *σφενδάμια*) (23 May 2001)
- H002: Woodland above the Great Lavra, with storm debris in the stream bed, looking towards the summit (15 June 1993)
- H003: *Tilia platyphyllos* (Broad-leaved Lime, *Φλαμουριά* like other species of limes) in flower in woodland above the Great Lavra, with a *Rumex* species (almost certainly *Rumex cristatus*, Greek Dock) and *Malva sylvestris* (Common Mallow, *Αγριομολόχα*) (15 June 1993)
- H005: Summit of Mount Athos seen from its south-east flank, with deciduous woodland (2 May 2003)
- H010: An ancient oak (*Quercus* species) in Dendrogalia on the south-east flank of Mount Athos (2 May 2003)
- H013: Multiple trunks of an ancient oak (*Quercus* species) regrown around the site of the original trunk, in Dendrogalia on the south-east flank of Mount Athos (2 May 2003)
- H016: *Anemone blanda* (Balkan Anemone) by the high-level track in

Dendrogalia south-east of the summit (2 May 2003)

- H017: *Digitalis lanata* (Woolly or Grecian Foxglove) by the high-level track east of Kerasia (18 June 2002)
- H018: *Cephalanthera rubra* (Red Helleborine, a woodland orchid which is extremely rare in England) near Kerasia on the south-east flank of Mount Athos (21 May 2001)
- H019: *Silene compacta* (Umbel-flowered Catchfly), with a skipper butterfly, probably *Thymelicus sylvestris* (Small Skipper) or *Ochlodes venatus* (Large Skipper), and a bush-cricket, probably an immature female *Tettigonia viridissima* (Great Green Bush-cricket), near the coast between Vatopedi and Kolitsou tower (28 May 2013, photo by Dr Graham Speake)
- H020: *Linum elegans* (Elegant Flax, a Balkan endemic) by the high-level track in Dendrogalia south-east of the summit (2 May 2003)
- H031: *Fritillaria pontica* (Black Sea Fritillary) by the high-level track in Dendrogalia south-east of the summit (2 May 2003)
- H032: *Muscari tenuiflorum* (a Balkan grape-hyacinth) by the high-level track in Dendrogalia south-east of the summit (2 May 2003)
- H035: Tree Frog (*Hyla arborea*) in Simonopetra's forest (23 May 2001)
- H040: An ancient oak (*Quercus* species) in another area of deciduous woodland near Konstamonitou (18 June 1993)
- H041: *Hypericum olympicum* (Mount Olympus St John's-wort, a large-flowered species now grown in British gardens) near Konstamonitou (18 June 1993)

J *Deciduous woodlands including coppiced Sweet or Spanish Chestnut* (*Castanea sativa*) **and the special fir of the Holy Mountain** (*Abies borisii-regis*)

- J001: Summit of Mount Athos seen from its south flank, with deciduous woodland with *Abies borisii-regis* (King Boris's Fir, *Ελάτη* like other species of firs) in the foreground (4 July 1976, photo by Dr Chris Preston)
- J004: *Doronicum orientale* (a Balkan leopard's-bane), carpeting one of Simonopetra's *Castanea sativa* coppice stands (29 April 1991)
- J006: Simonopetra's forest, looking north, principally of *Castanea sativa* (still leafless), some *Abies borisii-regis*, *Fagus sylvatica* or *Fagus orientalis* (Beech, coming into leaf) and *Populus tremula* (Aspen, *Λεύκη η τρέμουσα*, still leafless) (29 April 1991)

- J010: *Iris reichbachii* (Reichbach's Iris, *Αγριόκρινος* like other wild irises), a Balkan species, in Simonopetra's forest (6 May 2003)
- J013: *Ornithogalum nutans* (Drooping Star-of-Bethlehem) in Simonopetra's forest above Dontas farm (29 April 1991)
- J016: *Viola athois* (Mount Athos Pansy, a plant characteristically growing on the peak which seems to have colonised lower altitudes), in Simonopetra's forest (23 May 2001); see also M008.
- J020: Cutting harvested chestnut poles at Vatopedi (17 June 1993)

K *Streams and springs*

- K001: Kalamitsi, a stream by the road from Daphne to Simonopetra (30 April 1991)
- K003: Megalos Lakkos, a well-vegetated ravine, just south-east of Simonopetra, seen from the sea (17 June 1993)
- K008: *Platanus orientalis* (Oriental Plane, *Πλατάνι*) with its characteristic spherical pendent clusters of fruits
- K009: Previously coppiced *Platanus orientalis*, by a stream above Vatopedi, with a derelict aqueduct behind it (18 May 2001)
- K020: St Athenasios' spring, by the road north-west of the Great Lavra, with *Adiantum capillus-veneris* (Maidenhair Fern) (15 June 1993)

L *The site of an avalanche during the winter of 2001/02, on the south flank of Mount Athos*

A cataclysmic cyclical event rarely witnessed by anyone owing to the remoteness of the site and the time of year when it occurs; the avalanches are followed by periods of regeneration beginning with flushes of herbaceous species just as after coppicing.

- L001: General view in the first summer after the avalanche, looking uphill, including the summit of Mount Athos (18 June 2002)
- L010: View towards the sea, where the avalanche must have plunged over a cliff (2 May 2003)
- L012: View southwards, showing the forest beyond the damaged area unaffected by the avalanche (2 May 2003)
- L016: Trees (*Abies borisii-regis* and probably *Populus tremula*) untouched by the avalanche, behind second-year saplings (2 May 2003)

- L017: *Euphorbia amygdaloides* (Wood Spurge), a 'coppice plant' common in British woods (2 May 2003)
- L018: *Viola riviniana* (Common Dog-violet), another 'coppice plant' common in British woods (2 May 2003)

M *Ascent to the summit of Mount Athos*

- M001: *Pinus nigra* subspecies *pallasiana* (Black Pine, Πεύκο like other species of pines), with the sea beyond, on the path to the summit (1 June 2013)
- M002: Bare rocky tops, with scattered bushes of *Sorbus umbellata* subspecies *umbellata* (a whitebeam) and Black Pines just above the refuge of Panayia at 1,500 m (1 June 2013)
- M003: View southwards from the summit (2,030 m) down towards the refuge of Panayia at 1,500 m and the sea beyond (1 June 2013)
- M004: *Berberis cretica* (Cretan Barberry, Λουτσιά), a low spiny shrub of high mountains in Greece, Crete and Cyprus (18 June 2002)
- M005: *Isatis tinctoria* subspecies *athoa* (Mount Athos Woad, similar to the well-known dye-plant but endemic to the peak) (1 June 2013)

- M006: *Viola delphinantha* (a violet which is a chasmophyte almost confined to northern Greece) (18 June 2002)
- M007: *Anthyllis montana* subspecies *jacquinii* (Mountain Kidney-vetch) (1 June 2013)
- M008: *Viola athois* (Mount Athos Pansy), probably endemic, though similar plants occur on Mount Ossa (1 June 2013); see also J016.
- M009: *Campanula orphanidea* (an alpine bellflower confined to southern Bulgaria and north-east Greece) (1 June 2013)
- M010: Flowery patchwork including *Valeriana italica* (Italian Valerian, with pink flowers on tall stems and pinnate basal leaves), *Thymus boisseri* (a thyme endemic to the Balkan peninsula, carpeting with pink flowers) and *Veronica austriaca* subspecies *austriaca* (a speedwell, with spikes of bright blue flowers) (1 June 2013)

Given as a lecture by the author to FoMA members in London, 13 November 2013.

Two SYNDESMOS *Sagas*

DIMITRI CONOMOS

Founded in 1953, SYNDESMOS, the Worldwide Fellowship of Orthodox Youth, aims at encouraging cooperation, communication and exchange among Orthodox youth groups, theological faculties and schools, as well as promoting a deeper reflection and understanding of themes of importance to the whole Church. One aspect is to encourage an awareness in the Orthodox Church of the ecological crisis; to this end I began a programme of Spiritual Ecology Camps on Mount Athos in 1994. I estimate that between 1994 and 2019 around 350 young men, representing official Orthodox youth groups from about forty-five countries, have participated in and benefited from the camps. For the majority it was their first visit to the Athonite peninsula; and for most of these, it constituted their only possible means of entry. Aided by the generosity of FoMA, SYNDESMOS has, through these Spiritual Ecology Camps, provided golden opportunities for countless youth to enter fully into the life of the monasteries and sketes on Mount Athos. I say 'golden' precisely because participants from underprivileged and post-communist countries were afforded the unique occasion to embark upon this adventure – one which otherwise would have been beyond their every expectation.

I

Forest fire at Filotheou: 30 July 1998

At 3 a.m. on Thursday 30 July 1998 the SYNDESMOS contingent was roused from deep slumber, not by the clap of the talanton, but by the frantic door-knocking of the fathers summoning unexpected action. A fire had flared up high in the forested mountains behind the monastery, precisely at the Filotheou-Simonos Petras frontier. The alarm had gone off. Monks from both monasteries, together with a fire-fighting force of soldiers and firemen, fifty

men in all, had begun to ascent the slopes from all angles. An alert issued to Thessaloniki's airport also brought water-carrying planes. Would SYNDESMOS lend a hand? There was scarcely time to repeat the appeal – after all, preservation was our mandate.

In a matter of moments, the team members donned work clothes, armed themselves with tools and boarded a lorry that carried them to the site of the flames. Our party arrived at 3.50 a.m. Apparently, the fire had first been spotted at 1.28 a.m, by then it was raging in different locations. Its direction and its speed were constantly changing. The flames, propelled by the wind down the gorge, had to be extinguished before ascending the opposite face which was totally inaccessible. All of the volunteers were paired off. Working close to the blaze, the couples were required to clear the ground (of dry leaves especially) in order to impede its progress, clear fire-breaking paths, cut trees and chop down protruding branches. The planes began dropping water at 6 a.m. With workers on the ground it was dangerous to do so before daybreak.

Sixteen hours later, the SYNDESMOS contingent returned to Filotheou, charred, sweating, exhausted, but victorious and exhilarated by the experience. One thing was that we were not hungry. If anything, we were overfed for the simple reason that word, swifter even than the flames, had spread far and wide that young Orthodox from foreign lands were waging a holy battle for the survival of the monasteries. This prompted the Simonos Petras, Xeropotamou, Filotheou, Iviron Monasteries, as well as the fire brigade, to send abundant supplies and provisions: bread, olives, cheese, fruit, sweets, endless coffee (not that anyone was feeling sleepy), vegetables and holy water. Athonite hospitality knows no limits.

Ultimately, four square kilometres of mainly chestnut forest were consumed by the fire, a statistic generally considered by the monks to be trifling. They had seen much worse than this. The wind indeed died down dramatically during the early morning hours. I was later to discover that the fathers at Simonos Petras, mindful of the monastery's impending feast of St Mary Magdalene (4 August by the old calendar), had prayed fervently to their holy patroness to bridle the wind. Experience had educated them in the ways of nature; they knew that without the rampancy of a bluster, any blaze could be held in check. They also knew that safe fires were indeed a necessity and inevitable gift of nature to the forest. The saint was quick to respond to their supplications.

But was this incident one of nature or of man? Recriminations arose between the lay forest workers accused of taking revenge for government-imposed salary cuts and smoking visitors accused of negligence. The increasing frequency of forest fires is a matter of considerable sensitivity since the monasteries largely depend on the woodlands' proper exploitation for economic survival.

As a tribute to the heroic response and manly effort of the SYNDESMOS team, a number of dispensations were speedily put into effect. Filotheou's puritanical prohibition of head-to-toe bathing was thankfully annulled and on the following day, Friday 31 July, we were granted an exemption from work. Fr L, wearing his characteristic grin, was quick to add that this did not indicate a 'long weekend'.

Messages of commendation and thanks were also expressed in writing by the Holy Community in an official letter dated 28 July/10 August 1998 and by the Monastery of Simonos Petras on 1/14 August 1998. The former made reference to the courage, high sense of responsibility, and indispensable assistance of the SYNDESMOS volunteers and the latter to the 'syndesmos of unity and love' that exists between the Youth Fellowship and the Holy Mountain.

II

Mountain Music and Protestant Partners:
From St Paul's to Dionysiou, 2006

From 26 July until 1 August the SYNDESMOS squad had been working very industrially at St Paul's Monastery. The feast of Prophet Elijah, which fell on the next day, is marked all over the Mountain by an all-night vigil. The service at St Paul's began at 8 p.m. on the night before and terminated at 3 a.m. for a rest period of four hours before the Divine Liturgy. By about 11 a.m. the celebrations were over and, since it was a holiday, most of the group caught the boat to Dionysiou.

A few Slavic adventurers (five Poles and one Belarusian) decided to keep the vigil by climbing up to the peak of Athos. It took them nine hours of hard walking at the end of which they collapsed in a heap inside the chapel. It was bitterly cold outside (around −1°C) but their photos displayed breathtaking (literally) views from the peak. Scarcely had they rested an hour when there was a resounding knock at the door. The unexpected intruder was none other than a wandering hieromonk from the Holy Trinity/St Sergius Lavra near Moscow who stood timidly outside. He was with two Russian seminarians who had made the torturous ascent to Athos's summit in order to celebrate a Transfiguration Liturgy (somewhat early, but this is the chapel's dedication) in Slavonic – the very liturgical language of our SYNDESMOS alpinists. An opportunity not to be missed! According to trustworthy reports, never before had the Athonite apex resounded with such mellifluous sonority as at that dawn chorus when an octave of Slavs rendered liturgical responses in music reminiscent of Boris Godunov.

Meanwhile, the rest of us, at Dionysiou, were in for another unexpected encounter. Entering the Archondaríki (guest hall), we noticed six fair-haired, blue-eyed young men dressed in grey fatigues energetically sweeping, mopping, washing, dusting, scrubbing and polishing everything in sight. Their zeal and motivation were more than enviable. Who were they? Orthodox from Karelia? No. Evangelical Lutherans from Hamburg! They were on an officially organised two-week work programme that involved visits to a few monasteries at which they participated in the liturgical and diaconical life. And they seemed very much at home. After one day at Dionysiou they had virtually taken over the running of the Archondaríki: greeting the newcomers (ensuring that each signed the visitors' book), serving raki, loukoumi, and coffee, showing guests their sleeping quarters (which the team had earlier cleaned and prepared) and offering important details about services and meal times. When the SYNDESMOS party arrived, we noticed that the fathers at Dionysiou had been lavishing a lot of attention on these young Nordic heterodox – indeed spoiling them. For there, on the kitchen table, where they were supposed to have been polishing silver and brass, were mouth-watering distractions: flagons of juice, fresh figs, assorted sweets, bowls of nuts, cakes, biscuits, a device to make frappé and chocolate.

The temptation was too great: in earnest we offered to be their partners.

The Map

PETER HOWORTH

In 1999, I think it was, I was approached by Sandy Thomas, a first cousin of my father-in-law. He had a reputation in the family as being quite the man, having been a General in the British Army.

He used to come over and visit the family in New Zealand several times a year from Australia, and he would put himself up at a rather large hotel, bringing his pewter brandy goblet, where he ensured that he purloined enough bacon and bread at breakfast to make himself lunch every day. The staff thought he was wonderful and always referred to him as 'The General'. At one of these times Sandy had an urge to make a little bit of extra money, and decided to republish his bestselling book, *Dare to be Free*. To do this as cheaply as possible he engaged some of my wife's family to be the publishers. He then decided to approach me, because I was an engineer and had a familiarity with computer systems and other things, to draw some maps for this book.

At this stage I had not read the book, but I sort of nodded knowledgeably whenever it was referred to. I thought a map would just involve a little bit of tracing off some standard maps and certainly that's how it started, but then I found out I had to dig quite a lot deeper to get accurate information, particularly when Sandy was quite vague about where he actually had been on the Holy Mountain.

One of the limiting factors was that I had never drawn a map before, so I cast around to get help and information. At this stage I had prepared small outline maps for the book, and had eventually had Sandy's acceptance of them, but I wanted to know more about the Holy Mountain.

The idea of Mount Athos percolated around after this, and then I learnt that Sandy's grandson, Tyson, was going on an expedition, in 2009, led by Chris Paul, to retrace Sandy's route. I saw the book Chris Paul had written, and also some Greek TV footage that had been broadcast of the endeavour. I was jealous!

I needed to find a way to visit the Holy Mountain, but I had no Greek and was not Orthodox. After a little bit of trawling around the Internet, I discovered the Friends of Mount Athos and their path-clearing programme. Without consulting my wife, I enrolled for the 2011 programme, and was delighted to be accepted.

We then planned a trip to the UK. My backpack was hopelessly overburdened, it was like walking around with a wardrobe strapped to my back. I had included a GPS because I thought it might be quite fun to see how it all fitted with the scruffy little maps that I had drawn. I had a wonderful time on the trip – it rained dreadfully, and we all got terribly, terribly wet. Father M and the experienced path-clearers made us all feel very welcome and at home. It was hard work, but the hard regime and the diet ensured that we lost quite a lot of weight!

As I was wandering around one day, David Bayne, one of the team members, came up to me and said, 'Why did you come all the way from New Zealand for this?'

I said 'Well, I drew a map for a book'.

He looked at me and said 'Good', and gave me a CD which he said was full of GPS tracks.

'Could you draw a map please?'

I replied 'Certainly!' I thought at that stage it would take about six weeks.

When I got home to New Zealand and looked at things, I realised that I was a little out of my depth. I had quite a bit of work to do! I found some software and I started drawing, but the GPS tracks of that era were not terribly useful, so I determined to learn about this stuff called cartography.

I rang the New Zealand Cartographic Association and sought some help. Their response was 'We've got a conference coming up in three months. Would you like to come and give a paper?' Like an idiot, I said 'Yes'.

I assumed that proper maps were printed on big bits of paper, so I managed to procure three wide-format printers that had been damaged in the Christchurch earthquake. By some miracle I was able to make one work, and, in between making life-size photo prints of friends' children, was able to print some big maps. (After a dump of magenta ink on my shoes, I moved to newer, and much more reliable printers!)

I don't think I did very well at the conference, but the big lesson to me was how generous those at the top of their professions can be! I was welcomed and nurtured. I have been welcomed as a participant in the International Cartographic Association Mountain Cartography Group, and have attended and spoken at conferences around the world. I like to introduce myself as 'the world's oldest and least experienced cartographer'.

Owing to the generosity and enthusiasm of the Friends, in particular Roland Baetens of Belgium, and Dimitris Bakalis of Greece, the map has been under continuous development. It has been a long haul. I will never forget sitting on the beach at Dionysiou, talking to a monk friend, wondering about the air-miles I had clocked up in the project. His comment: 'When you are in the hands of the Living God, it can all get a little scary'.

Yeah, right. It is!

I print the maps at home, and have now sold them to 44 countries, and made countless friends in the process.

In the moments when I am not fighting with complex software and printers, my interests have developed into the specifics of maps for pilgrims.

A successful pilgrimage (or, dare I say it, 'adventure') embodies 'liminality' – the idea of being in a threshold state where change can happen. This really only happens when the participant fully engages with his surroundings. This does not happen only in 'religious' situations!

Thus, my efforts during the last years have been to create a new map to assist these pilgrims in their way-finding. I now realise that at the outset of the work I had forgotten a lesson I learnt early in my career – (I was writing up the instruction manuals for a power station) that I was making this map from a position of privilege – that is, I could easily read and understand a map. The users, I should have assumed, cannot.

Recently, however, I have become aware that this cartographic incompetence is not an isolated, singular phenomenon, but an increasing one. I am concerned that the type of map I am producing, using classical practices, is now not as useful as it could be. This could well be in part because of the rise of photorealism, Google Earth, and other devices that make us more 'observers' of our world rather than direct participants in it.

Traditionally, way-finding was a mode of travel made possible by intimate social and cultural knowledge of the geography of a region. This knowledge was not originally written down, but rather transferred from generation to generation by experience, for example, during hunting expeditions. Cartography developed as a means of encoding this information, more or less, through a series of rules and conventions.

The cartographer 'encoded' his impression of the landscape, according to conventions and rules that were gradually developed. The user then decoded this map within that landscape. There was intellectual effort involved by the user in this practice but the interpretation was the user's own. People now depend on GPS – few know the traditional navigation skills.

In the world of cartography, GPS technology has certainly increased convenience, but this technology, like that of Google Earth, has in fact forced us back from direct engagement, and made us all dispassionate observers, rather than the mud-encrusted hunters we like to pretend we are!

What started out as a tool has become (like much of technology), a crutch. A keyboard has removed the need for effective handwriting, and television has removed the need for creative entertainment. What social and cultural losses are incurred when traditional methods and ways of life are altered by the use of modern technologies?

What I would like to hear discussed is whether there is a way, a format, or a manner of creating or presenting a map that will encourage proper engagement with the surroundings by people who have no experience or expectation. What we have is the decoding of the map by the user. In doing that, the user owns the image he has created for himself from the map. This then helps him engage with the landscape. (It also reflects the skills of the cartographer in encoding that landscape onto a printed map.) This is similar to the way a good writer, by prose alone, can get us to create an image in our heads.

When it comes to my interest, which is the pilgrimage or transformational journey, this engagement with the landscape is absolutely vital for the endeavour to obtain the outcome the pilgrim desires. Engagement can only happen when the user makes sense of the landscape by relating the map that they have studied and the landscape features.

The most important outcome is that when you engage with landscape, you cannot, thereafter, be indifferent to that landscape. When I was learning map-reading, I was taught that one must first study the landscape and then the map. If you do it the other way around, you can easily convince yourself (wrongly) that the landscape matches what you see on the map. It is harder to convince yourself (wrongly) that the map matches what you see in the landscape. I heard one instructor explain this, somewhat tongue-in-cheek, to students by saying, 'The land is God and the map is the Bible. You want to study God and then try to find him in the Bible, not the other way around'.

One idea I have is that engagement with place occurs when one deviates from the plan. In other words, it is not until something unexpected catches the eye that discovery begins. From this point of view, the more you know about what you will see (or think you will see) the more you are insulated from what you really might see.

Something I would like to try (but have not had the courage yet) is to go to a place completely new to me, never having looked at a guidebook, but carrying only a collection of maps. My sense is that where a guidebook acts to structure your expectations and create a to-do list, a map invites you to explore in a less directed way. The guidebook in effect gives you blinders (because you think you know what is valuable before you go) whereas the map generally presents all locales equally. (Some tourist maps are the exception, with top ten sites picked out on them and so on.)

Where does all this lead us? A pilgrimage, or transformational journey, has three distinct phases. The preparatory phase, includes physical and mental preparation, study, and purchase of all manner of aids and devices. The second phase is the actual journey, which may be of quite limited duration. The nature of the undertaking means that it will be physical, and in unfamiliar surroundings – not the sort of environment where one can be a dispassionate observer or armchair traveller. The pilgrim must engage with the environment. It is this engagement, added to the cognitive map (and the expectations that form part of this) that will provide the background for the catharsis that will occur during the third, reflective phase after the journey.

So, here I am now – a geriatric wanna-be cartographer, with far more questions than answers, a renewed sense of wonder of and for mankind, and an ever-increasing sense of awe of creation and the intricacies of the provision of the Almighty.

I went to the Holy Mountain the first time to gaze at the buildings – now I go for the love and the joy that is as much a part of the landscape as the rocks. The only regret? That Sandy is no longer with us.

He died, aged 98 in 2017. Until then I so enjoyed ringing him in Brisbane from the Holy Mountain. It grounded him.

Monastic Medicine

PETER HOWORTH

Σώπα παραπονιάρικο μα ο κόσμος δεν εχάθει, και με τα βότανα της γης γιατρεύονται τα πάθη.
Be quiet, grumbler, for the world hasn't come to an end, and sufferings are healed with the plants of the earth.
—A Matinada in the Cretan dialect

In the early Middle Ages there was significant illness, and this encouraged the development of medical practice and care. The growth of cities created poor living conditions with a lack of sanitation and clean water, so disease was a constant issue and controlled the lives of many people. There were epidemics of diseases such as leprosy, influenza, the plague, as well as problems of infection and the problems of congenital disorders. Societies began searching for ways to deal with this, and medicine expanded into quite an important occupation. This included many professional people; folk practices, religious practices, herbalism, and magic were also used. Within this environment monastic health care became significant as monks tended to be some of the better educated people in society, were very good record keepers, and had the tradition of hospitality.

They were in a situation to offer treatment to other monks, pilgrims, poor people and even the wealthy. Monks tended to focus on natural physical medical practices such as cleanliness and care for the sick, bloodletting, and herbalism. Quite often these treatments were seen as an extension of religious or spiritual work.

The available literature demonstrates vividly that monasteries and doctors in ancient Greece, the Roman Empire and their successors, knew and valued both wild and cultivated plants being employed as drugs, and this is fully shown in the works of many Byzantine physicians and pharmacologists. Byzantine concepts of what was herbal medicine were fundamental in the teaching of herbal pharmacology in the medical schools of Europe, and many of these teaching institutions boasted of their own teaching gardens that incorporated the traditionally cultivated herbs.

Medical botany was quite prominent, and Byzantine medicine and early Byzantine pharmacy occupied a central and a main role in how the doctor treated disease. The texts we have, including that of Paul of Egina, show how the Byzantine philosopher-physicians – those known as iatrosophists – reworked, streamlined and clarified the medical texts of the Greco-Roman era. It is actually Galen of Pergamon who became the absolute authority on all facets of medicine, with extensive publications (159 volumes!) in about AD 850. These were not translated into Greek until 1525. Ancient compendia of formulas for medicines are unique witnesses to the daily life of practitioners: they report data collected during medical consultations, the preparations administered to patients, occasionally their therapeutic successes and failures, and at times may contain the traditional wisdom of Elders about collecting plants in the field. Greek iatrosophia, that is books of therapeutics which are usually – and questionably – assumed to date back through the Early Modern to the Ottoman period of the Greek world, are no exceptions. In spite of their interest to modern practitioners, iatrosophia have not, thus far, been much studied.

In 2015 the scientific world was astonished when a recipe for eye infections from the tenth century was prepared and tested – a remedy made from onions and garlic. What two microbiologists and a historian from the University of Nottingham found out when brewing it was that it was extremely effective even against the dangerous methicillin – resistant Staphylococcus aureus, also known as the super-germ MRSA. (Since first emerging in the 1960s, as many as 50 million people are now believed to carry MRSA worldwide, that now is resistant to methicillin. In the US, more people died in 2005 from MRSA infections [approximately 18,000] than from HIV/AIDS [approximately 17,000].) Dr Christina Lee, the historian, came across the "eye ointment" in Bald's Leechbook, a collection of old recipes for various ailments from the first half of the tenth century. There it is written on sheet twelve: "Take equal amounts of leek and garlic, crush them well, take equal amounts of wine and ox gall, mix them with the leek, put everything in a brass kettle, leave the mixture for nine days rest, then press it through a cloth, clarify it well and put it in a horn." Following the instructions, microbiologist Dr Freye Harrison and her team tried to recreate the age-old ointment as faithfully as possible. They tested the eye ointment on a large MRSA culture – with astonishing results.

According to the researchers, the special combination of leek, wine, ox gall and brass killed up to 90 percent of the resistant staphylococci.

Researchers from the United States had already examined the ointment formulation of the old English manuscript ten years ago. But they had – for hygienic reasons – made the experiments with modern pots. The results were sobering. It was not until the scientists in Nottingham last year that a real effort was made to fully mimic the recipe requirements, so copper strips were inserted into the mixture because the brass or copper pot was expressly required in the recipe!

Nottingham University is not the only institution in the western world studying these historical documents now – realisation of their effectiveness (as shown above) is encouraging this!

In 2019, therefore, I was surprised and delighted, on a visit to Koutloumousiou, to see extensive new plantings of medical herbs, and an enthusiastic group of monks experimenting with ancient recipes, and investigating wild herbs growing on the Holy Mountain. The Holy Mountain has a history of no chemical sprays, no browsing animals, and a pristine environment. Monasteries have been making their own remedies for at least 1,200 years, and it is an ideal place to re-start this activity.

Since that visit, they have installed and commissioned a new still for making the base for the tinctures, and have developed an initial range of medications:

FIG. 57 *New garden under development*

FIG. 58 *New still under installation*

- *σπαθόλαδο* – St John's wort oil (100 ml). St John's wort from Mount Athos in pure olive oil, ideal for burns, tissue regeneration, cures mouth ulcers and several mouth illnesses (as a mouthwash). It helps in the detoxification of the peptic system, helps to cure gastric ulcers and psoriasis. Dosage for internal use: 3 tablespoons/day.

- *αναπλαστικό – φυσική αποκατάσταση.* Oil for natural regeneration (100 ml) – Extract of nettle, rosemary, and wild olive tree leaves, in pure olive oil. Anti-inflammatory, for skin cracks in feet and heels, hair loss, inflammation of the eyelashes, wound healing.

- *φυσική αντιβίωση – αναπνευστικό* – natural antibiotic – respiration (100 ml). Oregano, thyme and sage tincture with pure honey. Powerful antibiotic, antimicrobial, antiviral, releases the respiratory tracts. Dosage: suggestively 3 teaspoons/day.

- *χωνευτικό* – digestive (100 ml). Mint and peppermint tincture. Suggestive dosage: 1 tablespoon.

- *προστάτης* – prostate (100 ml). Cypress and equisetum tincture. For benign prostate hyperplasia. Dosage: suggestively 3 teaspoons/day for 2–3 weeks.

- *αναλγητικό μυών και οστών* – analgesic for muscles and bones (100 ml). Eucalyptus, oregano, cypress and rosemary tincture, for all muscle-and-bones/rheumatic pains, due to intense body exercise, or advanced age or injuries. ONLY external use, up to 6 times/day. Shake well before use.

- *φυσική κρέμα επούλωσης* – ointment for natural healing (50ml). Regenerative ointment with pure beeswax, St John's wort oil, tinctures of equisetum, nettle, rosemary and propolis, and chestnut tree honey from Koutloumousiou monastery.

- Gel with Athonite seaweed tincture (50 ml) – against swellings and cellulite, increases blood circulation, helps to eliminate bruises from ruptured veins, promotes cure of varicose veins.

FIG. 59 *Sample medicines*

A Brief Introduction to the Monasteries of Mount Athos

TREVOR CURNOW

No one knows when the first Christian hermits made their way to Mount Athos. Some chose to live in isolation, while some came to form themselves into loose communities of various sizes. However, 963 is recognised as the year of the foundation of the first recognizable monastery on the Holy Mountain. Today, twenty monasteries and their associated lands and dependencies, great and small, occupy the whole of the Holy Mountain. While many monks continue to live outside monasteries, some still in eremitic isolation, the twenty monasteries collectively and individually dominate and govern the Holy Mountain.

The main aim of this brief introduction is to provide some very basic facts about each of the twenty monasteries. A secondary aim is to introduce the reader to the way in which Greek place names are treated in this book. There are various ways of presenting Greek names within an English text, and one such approach is to stay as close to the original as possible, to transliterate rather than translate. This is also the approach taken in the 'filathonites' map of Mount Athos, another FoMA spin-off. However, mindful that readers are likely to encounter different spellings of place names elsewhere (and also here in contributions taken from the works of those now deceased), the main alternatives are also indicated. Note that the abbreviation 'I.M.' that appears before the names of all monasteries stands for 'Holy Monastery'. Some monasteries add a second 'M' meaning 'Great'. The monasteries are presented in their traditional order of precedence. Dates are sometimes speculative. The monasteries have always been Greek unless otherwise noted. However, 'being Greek' in this context does not mean being exclusively Greek. Athonite monasteries house monks from all around the world.

The monastery that was founded in 963 is known as I.M. MEGISTIS LAVRAS, and still exists. It is the most southerly of the monasteries. Also known in English simply as (the) GREAT LAVRA, its feast day is 5 July, the date of the dormition of St Athanasios the Athonite, its founder.

Second in precedence comes I.M.M. VATOPEDIOU (or VATOPEDI). The exact date of its foundation is unknown, but it was somewhere around 980. Its feast day celebrates the Annunciation (25 March).

Third comes I.M. IVIRON. It was also founded in around 980, and its name reflects the fact that it was founded by Iberians, a name once given to those who came from what is now Georgia. It remained a Georgian monastery until 1357 when it became Greek, reflecting a shift in its monastic population. Its feast day falls on 15 August, celebrating the Dormition of the Mother of God.

Fourth in precedence is I.M. CHILANDARIOU, also known as CHILANDAR, CHELANDARI, HILANDAR, and other variations. It was founded by Serbians in 1197 and remains Serbian today, although Bulgarians formed the majority of the monks there for a period during the eighteenth and nineteenth centuries. It is dedicated to the Presentation of the Mother of God, with its feast day on 21 November. It is the most northerly of the monasteries. Collectively, these first four monasteries enjoy a special prestige on the Holy Mountain.

I.M. DIONYSIOU was founded by St Dionysios, a monk from near Kastoria in northern Greece, in around 1375. It is dedicated to St John the Baptist, with its feast day on 24 June.

I.M. KOUTLOUMOUSIOU is the monastery that lies closest to Karyes, the modest capital of the Holy Mountain. It was founded in the eleventh century, but later went into such a steep decline that it was effectively refounded in the fourteenth. It is dedicated to the Transfiguration, with a feast day of 6 August.

I.M. PANTOKRATOROS (or PANTOKRATOR) is also dedicated to the Transfiguration. It was founded in the middle of the fourteenth century, but, as with many Athonite establishments, perhaps on the site of an older monastic settlement.

I.M. XEROPOTAMOU is the monastery that lies closest to Daphne, the principal port of Athos. It may have been founded as early as 971. It is dedicated to the Forty Martyrs, whose feast day is 9 March.

I.M. ZOGRAFOU (or ZOGRAPHOU) is the only Bulgarian monastery on Athos today. Founded by Bulgarians, it is dedicated to St George, the patron saint of Bulgaria (feast day 23 April). It also may have been founded as early as the tenth century, but little is known of its history until the thirteenth.

I.M. DOCHIARIOU is familiar to visitors to Athos as the first monastery to appear on its shores on the boat journey to Daphne. It may have been another tenth-century foundation, or originally founded elsewhere and then refounded later at its present location. It is dedicated to the Archangels Michael and Gabriel, with a feast day of 8 November.

I.M. KARAKALLOU is dedicated to Sts Peter and Paul (feast day 29 June). Accounts of its foundation vary widely, with different traditions assigning it to anywhere between the third and eleventh centuries. Such conflicting traditions are not uncommon on Athos.

I.M. FILOTHEOU (or PHILOTHEOU) was probably founded in the tenth century and is dedicated to the Annunciation (25 March).

I.M. SIMONOS PETRAS occupies one of the most dramatic sites on the Holy Mountain, perched atop a high cliff. Its name sometimes appears as Simonopetra and it is dedicated to the Nativity (25 December). Its foundation is reliably established to around 1360.

I.M. AGIOU PAVLOU (or ST PAUL'S) has a confusing history, such as can be ascertained. It seems that it may have been a monastery only intermittently for a significant period, reverting to being a dependency of I.M. Xeropotamou from time to time. It finally achieved full and permanent status as a monastery at the end of the fourteenth century.

I.M. STAVRONIKITA has had an even more chequered history, even being totally abandoned on occasions. It has been a full and permanent Athonite monastery only since the middle of the sixteenth century. Dedicated to St Nicholas (feast day 6 December) it is the smallest monastery on the Holy Mountain.

I.M. XENOPHONTOS (or XENOFONTOS) was founded in the tenth or eleventh century. It is dedicated to St George (feast day 23 April).

I.M. GRIGORIOU (or GREGORIOU) was founded in the fourteenth century and is dedicated to St Nicholas (feast day 6 December).

I.M. ESPHIGMENOU (or ESFIGMENOU) was probably founded in the early eleventh century. It is dedicated to the Ascension, so its feast day moves in line with Easter.

I.M. AGIOU PANTELEIMONOS (or ST PANTELEIMON) is often simply referred to as the Russian monastery. It was built on its present site only in the late eighteenth century, replacing a much older and dilapidated foundation located further inland. Although the Russians have always been associated with the monastery, and entirely dominate it today, for parts of its history it was substantially Greek. It is dedicated to St Panteleimon (feast day 27 July).

I.M. KONSTAMONITOU comes last in the Athonite hierarchy. Dedicated to St Stephen (feast day 27 December), it was probably founded in the eleventh century.

The Diamonitirion

TREVOR CURNOW & CHRIS THOMAS

The diamonitirion is an intrinsic feature of every visit to the Holy Mountain. Although sometimes referred to as an Athonite 'visa', technically it is something quite different. The distinction was clearer in the days when a diamonitirion had to be obtained in Karyes, well after entry to the Holy Mountain had been effected. Now it is obtained before entry, and so it is easily confused with an entry permit.

The standard diamonitirion for visitors (there is a slightly different kind for invited guests) is essentially a letter of introduction from the Holy Epistasia in Karyes that is addressed to the twenty monasteries. It identifies the bearer of the letter as a pilgrim who has come to the Holy Mountain in order to visit the monasteries and venerate their holy objects (icons and relics). Any monastery receiving the letter is asked to welcome the bearer and provide him with the hospitality required for his pilgrimage. The diamonitirion is normally valid for a period of four days, and it is expected that no more than one night will be spent in any one monastery.

The reverse side of the diamonitirion now contains a brief code of conduct to guide the visitor on the Holy Mountain. In the past it was blank, and at one time listed monastery telephone numbers. These have become ever more important as most monasteries now require pilgrims to make reservations for their stays in advance. It has to be said that the code of conduct is patchily observed and patchily enforced.

A diamonitirion has to be arranged well in advance (the whole process is described in detail on the FoMA website: https://athosfriends.org/pilgrims-guide/), and presently costs thirty euros.

Visiting the Holy Mountain requires pilgrims to respect a number of basic rules which are beautifully listed on the back of the visa or diamonitirion essential for entry. Most rules are common sense, others require minor adaptations from everyday behaviour but all are critically important because they are designed to maintain the peace, tranquillity, holiness and beauty that together contribute to the mountain's unique landscape and atmosphere.

1. Your clothes and behaviour should be decent and fit for a sacred place. Never wear shorts, short sleeve shirts or sandals – colours should be muted – see below for behaviour.
2. Your mobile phones should be turned off in church, in the trapeza and generally inside the boundaries of the holy monasteries or other sacred buildings such as sketes and cells.
3. Do not enter parts of monasteries not associated with hospitality unless invited.
4. In church and at trapeza, you should be silent and noiseless, and you must observe the order and special rules of each monastery. The guest-master at each monastery will make you aware of what's expected of you. You should obviously be quiet and focused during services – trapeza is an extension of the service so you must continue to be silent and to follow the example set by your hosts.
5. The use of television, radio and music playback devices is prohibited.
6. Smoking is prohibited. See 7.
7. Be especially careful to avoid the causes of fires. It is strictly forbidden to camp out in the open. The Holy Mountain does not have a fire service so fires anywhere on the mountain can be especially devastating. And please do not even think of camping or sleeping anywhere other than a monastery or skete – animals including snakes, wolves, jackals and wild boar consider the mountain to be their patch, particularly at night.

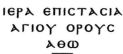

ΙΕΡΑ ΕΠΙΣΤΑΣΙΑ
ΑΓΙΟΥ ΟΡΟΥΣ
ΑΘΩ

ΤΙΜΗΣ ΕΝΕΚΕΝ
ΚΑΡΥΑΙ ΤΗ: 1/14-6-2014
ΛΗΓΕΙ ΤΗ: 17/30-6-2015
ΑΑ-16024/1

01798

ΕΤΗΣΙΟΝ
ΔΙΑΜΟΝΗΤΗΡΙΟΝ

ΠΡΟΣ ΤΑΣ ΕΙΚΟΣΙΝ ΙΕΡΑΣ ΚΑΙ ΣΕΒΑΣΜΙΑΣ ΜΟΝΑΣ
ΤΟΥ ΑΓΙΟΥ ΟΡΟΥΣ
ΑΘΩ
—

Ὁ κομιστὴς τοῦ παρόντος ιεροκοινοσφραγίστου καὶ ἐνυπογράφου γράμματος ἡμῶν

κύριος ....

τοῦ .... θρήσκευμα: ....

ἰδιότης: ....

ἀρ. Δ.Α.Τ.: .... LH528571\ .... ἀρ. Διαβ.: ....

πόλις ἢ χώρα: ....ΕΛΛΑΔΑ............ ἔλαβε τὴν ἡμετέραν ἄδειαν πρὸς ἐπίσκεψιν τῶν

ἱερῶν σκηνωμάτων καὶ προσκύνησιν τῶν ἐν αὐτοῖς ἀποκειμένων ἱερῶν καὶ ὁσίων τῆς

Πίστεως ἡμῶν καὶ δύναται κατὰ τὴν διάρκειαν τοῦ Ἐπιστασιακοῦ ἔτους 2013-2014 νὰ

εἰσέρχεται εἰς τὸ Ἅγιον Ὄρος, πέραν τοῦ προβλεπομένου ἡμερησίου ἀριθμοῦ εἰσερχομένων.

Παρακαλεῖσθε ὅθεν, ὅπως παράσχητε αὐτῷ πᾶσαν δυνατὴν φιλοξενίαν καὶ περιποίησιν.

Ἐφ᾽ ᾧ διατελοῦμεν λίαν φιλαδέλφως ἐν Χριστῷ ἀδελφοὶ

ΟΙ ΕΠΙΣΤΑΤΑΙ ΤΗΣ ΙΕΡΑΣ ΚΟΙΝΟΤΗΤΟΣ ΤΟΥ ΑΓΙΟΥ ΟΡΟΥΣ ΑΘΩ

Ο ΔΙΟΝΥΣΙΟΥ	ΠΡΩΤΕΠΙΣΤΑΤΗΣ	Γέρων Συμεών
Ο ΖΩΓΡΑΦΟΥ	ΕΠΙΣΤΑΤΗΣ	Μόναχ Ευθυμιος
Ο ΡΩΣΣΙΚΟΥ	ΕΠΙΣΤΑΤΗΣ	ιερομ. Κυριων
Ο ΚΩΝΣΤΑΜΟΝΙΤΟΥ	ΕΠΙΣΤΑΤΗΣ	Γέρων Εφραίμ

1393246

FIG. 60 *Diamonitirion*

8 Hunting is prohibited as is the importation of weapons and dogs.

9 Cinematographic/video equipment and filming are strictly prohibited. Filming anywhere on the Holy Mountain requires the permission of the Holy Epistasia.

10 Photographing of monks and the interior of monasteries is forbidden without prior permission. Common courtesy is required in both instances.

11 The duration of your stay shall be 4 days in all and no more than 1 day in each monastery or skete. Be sure to make a reservation in advance. Exceptions are only possible if you are engaged in work to support the Holy Mountain such as clearing footpaths with the annual FoMA pilgrimage – see 12.

12 Even if you have a special diamonitirion, issued by a particular monastery or skete, it does not entitle you to stay anywhere other than the issuing institution.

In all instances, you should fully plan your pilgrimage. The monasteries are not hotels and they are not really geared up to accept last minute guests – and nor should they be.

The Friends of Mount Athos website should give you all the information you need to plan your pilgrimage. By the time you receive your diamonitirion the only part of your trip that should be unplanned is the wonder you will feel so many times in the days ahead – as you depart the 'world' at Ouranoupolis, as you glimpse your first monastery when the boat rounds a headland, as you disembark at Daphne, and as you enter a monastery, speak to a father, share prayers and trapeza for the first time.

Author Biographies

ALLISON, ROBERT Bob earned his BA from Brown University in Religious Studies and his PhD from the University of Chicago in New Testament and Early Christian Studies. Supported by a series of National Endowment for the Humanities grants, as a research fellow of the Patriarchal Institute for Patristic Studies in Thessaloniki, he undertook a long-term project describing the manuscripts and studying the history of Filotheou monastery on Mount Athos. He moved to Bates College to teach in Religion and Classical and Medieval Studies. His manuscript studies led to a decade of work on the study of paper as evidence for the productions of manuscripts. Professor Allison is also widely known for his role in organizing and leading the branch of the Friends of Mount Athos in the Americas.

ARNELL, JOHN John Arnell worked in the computing industry for many years. Since taking early retirement he has thrown himself into a variety of projects, most notably the FoMA footpaths project. He is also a keen saxophonist.

ANDREWS, JOHN John calls Chapel Hill, North Carolina his home. He has studied and taught English and History, worked on a tobacco farm, brewed beer, directed and produced documentary films, and created general mischief throughout the world. However, his favourite destination is Mount Athos, which he has visited many times, both as a pilgrim as well as with the Footpaths Expeditions. He is currently a lecturer at a university in Riyadh, Saudi Arabia, where he lives with his wife Jill.

AVERITT, NEIL After studying at Harvard and the LSE, Neil spent many years at the Federal Trade Commission, and had a long and varied career at the agency, helping to shape both anti-trust and consumer protection laws, and becoming the person most familiar with the relationships between these two parts of the agency statute. He wrote the book *The Single Gospel*, which was published by Wipf and Stock in 2015. This edits the four accounts of Matthew, Mark, Luke and John into a single narrative in chronological order.

AVRAMOV, ROUMEN Roumen is an economist with interests in economic history, the history of economic ideas and monetary economics. He has been working at the Institute of Economics of the Bulgarian Academy of Sciences (1976–1990); as Vice-President of the Agency for Economic Coordination and Development of the Bulgarian Government (1991–1994); Member of the Board of Governors of the Bulgarian National Bank (1997–2002); Program Director at the Centre for Liberal Strategies, Sofia (1995–2012). Since 2013 he has been Permanent Fellow at the Centre for Advanced Studies Sofia (CAS).

BAETENS, ROLAND (EFREM) Roland is Belgian and became attracted to the Holy Mountain after becoming Orthodox. He has a passion for the landscape of Athos, the footpaths and the cats. He has been a very significant contributor to the Footpaths Team, and to the creation of the map. Quite often the only glimpse you will have of him are shoes poking out of a dense bush.

BAKALIS, DIMITRIOS Dimitris studied aeronautical engineering at the Hellenic Air Force (HAF) Academy and currently holds the rank of HAF Colonel. He first visited Athos in 1987 and he was attracted by the nature, people, traditions and the spiritual life of that special place. As he loves to hike in the Greek mountains, he was also enticed by the ancient footpaths of the Athonite peninsula. Since his first visit to Athos, he comes back frequently, steadily improving his knowledge about the footpaths and also, witnessing their dereliction in favour of modern roads and tracks. He has completed more than 100 pilgrimages with a total stay of over a year in Athos. In order to help pilgrims experience the peace and beauty of the Garden of the Holy Mother of God by walking along the ancient paths, he joined the FoMA footpath project, and has participated in all missions since 2012.

BAYNE, DAVID David studied chemistry at Oxford University before starting his career in the UK civil service. During his student days he developed an interest in classical and Mediterranean history, in particular in Byzantine architecture and culture, which has never left him. His visit to Mount Athos in 1966 was a manifestation of this. Since his retirement in 2004 he has been closely involved with the project to clear and maintain the footpaths of the Holy Mountain, in particular the provision of footpath descriptions as an aid and encouragement to walking pilgrims.

BRUCE, MICHAEL ROBERT (1909-1973) A barrister in the North of Ireland, Michael was educated at Winchester and Oxford. After service in the Army during World War II, he returned to Co. Down, where he was a lay reader in the Church of Ireland, for whom he was also on its governing committee, the Representative Church Body. After his first pilgrimage in 1957 he introduced himself to Emmanuel Arnand de Mendieta and became his translator.

BUCHANAN, ANDREW After working in theatre, feature films, and TV drama, Andrew moved into wildlife documentaries and produced many successful programmes for international broadcasters such as Animal Planet, Discovery, and National Geographic. His passions include sustainability and conservation. His free time is spent working in a wood, scuba diving, cider making, and trying to become a better archaeologist.

BYRON, ROBERT (1905-1941) Robert visited Mount Athos with two Oxford friends at the age of twenty-two and wrote *The Station*, a classic account of its treasures and its men. One of the most remarkable figures of his generation, throughout his life he was a lover of Byzantine civilization, and his reverence for antiquity glows from every page of this book. His life was cut tragically short when he was killed at the age of thirty-six, during World War II, when the ship on which he was travelling was torpedoed by a U-boat off Cape Wrath, Scotland, en route to Egypt. He travelled to widely different places; Mount Athos, India, the Soviet Union, and Tibet.

CAIRNS, SCOTT Scott was born in Tacoma, Washington. He earned a BA from Western Washington University, an MA from Hollins College, an MFA. from Bowling Green State University, and a PhD from the University of Utah. He is the author of eight books of poetry, including *The Theology of Doubt* (1985), *The Translation of Babel* (1990), *Philokalia* (2002), *Idiot Psalms* (2014), and *Slow Pilgrim: The Collected Poems* (2015). Besides writing poetry, he has also written a spiritual memoir, *Short Trip to the Edge* (2007). He has received fellowships from the Guggenheim Foundation and the National Endowment for the Humanities. He has taught at numerous universities including the University of North Texas and the University of Missouri.

CAMPBELL, JOHN M   Born in 1930 in Detroit, Michigan to an auto engineer and a librarian, John was raised to be an engineer. He graduated from Bowdoin College in 1952 with a major in Physics and was shortly drafted into the Army. He then attended Harvard Graduate School of Architecture for a long intermittent period. The Architect's Collaborative, Charles W. Moore and Skidmore, Owings and Merrill each contributed something to his education. He successfully entered a competition to design 120 units of housing but a delay in financing offered an opportunity to visit the Holy Mountain. In 1983, a slump allowed him to leave commuting behind and move to Orcas Island, Washington, in the woods. He is now a very retired very old architect.

CASO, DJ   DJ is an aspiring jack of all trades and an accomplished master of none who learned all he really needed to know by walking in the mountains. His love of hilly terrains led him to the Holy Mountain, where he bumped into Peter Howorth and FoMA, which in turn allowed him to discover just how truly special a mountain it was, and to join the FoMA path-clearing team. Currently, DJ is busy discovering the joys of fatherhood while aging more or less gracefully in the middle of France, which happens to offer some of the finest massifs and mountaintops this side of the big drink, and perhaps anywhere on the blue planet.

CHRYSANTHOU, ANDREAS   Andreas is married to Rena, and they have three young children. He is the chairman of an amazing not-for-profit Greek language school, where he teaches the next generation the Greek language, Greek and Cypriot traditions, and the fundamentals of the Greek Orthodox faith. He works as a technology services consultant in London, and enjoys cooking, barbequing with friends, red wine and spending quality time with his children.

CONOMOS, ANNA   Performance Storyteller and Author, Anna Conomos is of Greek-Australian origin. She was born in Canada and spent her early life in Sydney and Greece before moving to the UK. Anna graduated with a Joint Honours Degree in Performing Arts and Modern Greek Literature. While a student, Anna worked in galleries and museums bringing to life paintings and exhibitions through live performance. She now works internationally as a storyteller,

script-writer and trainer. Her performances include World War I and World War II narratives, extraordinary biographies and lives of influential saints as well as mythical tales. Anna has a great love for singing and Byzantine chanting which she uses in performance. Her most recent show was at Buckingham Palace. Anna is married to Emmanuel Wedlock, a Cretan, and he is her greatest fan.

CONOMOS, DIMITRI   Dimitri holds a doctorate in musicology from Oxford University and has lectured widely in music history, hymnography, and ecology. He has published on Byzantine and Slavonic chant, hymnography, Orthodoxy and the environment, and mythology.

CURNOW, TREVOR   Originally from Cornwall, Trevor was the first Professor of Philosophy at the University of Cumbria. He previously taught philosophy at all levels at various institutions, both in the UK and elsewhere. His research interests include wisdom, oracles and ancient philosophy. He has travelled widely and is a regular visitor to Mount Athos. His book *Pantokrator: An Introduction to Orthodoxy* (CSP, 2007) was largely written during stays there.

CURRIE, LESLIE   Leslie grew up in Scotland and studied history at Glasgow University, where his interest in the Orthodox Church and the world of 'East Rome' started. He worked in banking in Cyprus, Bahrain, Hong Kong and London before moving to Bath in 1988 to set up the International Office at Bath University and finally worked on a national admissions project based in Cheltenham. His involvement with FoMA started in 2016 and he has visited the Mountain in 2017, 2018 and 2019. He now helps with the administration of the path-clearing pilgrimage and, on the Holy Mountain acts as a first-aider.

DALES, DOUGLAS   Douglas was Chaplain of Marlborough College from 1984 until 2012, and is now an Anglican parish priest working in the diocese of Oxford. He is the author of a number of books on Anglo-Saxon church history and Anglican theology. He goes each year on retreat to the Holy Mountain, and also has close connections with the Orthodox monastery in Essex and the Camaldolese Benedictines in Rome.

DELISO, CHRISTOPHER   Christopher is an American travel writer and journalist who was awarded an MPhil. in Byzantine Studies by Oxford University (1999). He has published travel essays on Mount Athos in travel media and magazines such as The Tablet, and covered the Holy Mountain in contributing to four volumes of the Lonely Planet travel guide to Greece.

A long-time member of the Friends of Mount Athos, he is also a board member of the Mount Athos Foundation of America.

DELLA DORA, VERONICA, FBA   Veronica was born in 1976, and is a distinguished Italian cultural geographer. She is Professor of Human Geography at Royal Holloway, University of London. She comes from Venice and grew up living on the Lido. She gained a PhD from the University of California, Los Angeles (UCLA) in 2005, with the thesis 'Geographies of the Holy Mountain: Post-Byzantine and western representations of the Monastic Republic of Mount Athos'. She joined Royal Holloway, University of London as professor in September 2013. In 2018, she was elected a Fellow of the British Academy.

DESMOND, PETER BRIAN   Peter is a post-graduate doctoral candidate at the University of Winchester, undertaking primary research into contemporary iconography that is being painted today on Mount Athos. In 2018, he was awarded a Master of Theology degree in Orthodox Theology with Distinction, also at Winchester. Before taking (very) early retirement, Peter was Director of Human Resources at the University of Stirling and represented Scottish universities on a number of regional and national committees. Peter tries to provide help of sorts to the small group behind the organisation of the FoMA Pathclearing project, as well as being a participant over the last four years.

DUNNE, JONATHAN   Jonathan graduated in Classics from Oxford University. He directs the publishing house Small Stations Press. He translates literature from the Bulgarian, Catalan, Galician and Spanish languages. He has written books on language, translation, and the environment including The DNA of the English Language, and Stones of Ithaca. He lives with his family in Sofia, Bulgaria, and serves as a subdeacon in the Bulgarian Orthodox Church.

EDWARDS, RICHARD   Richard was born and raised in London. After school, he studied mechanical engineering, then studied business and moved into supply management, working in England, Australia and Zambia. Married to Jill, he has three adult children and three grandchildren. He studied theology and Christian education in Brisbane and was ordained an Anglican deacon and priest in 1985. As a parish priest he worked in Australia and the UK and now lives in rural Southern Tasmania. He has a deep interest in the links between Eastern Orthodoxy and Celtic Christianity.

ERIKSEN, DANIEL   Daniel was raised in New England, was awarded a BA in Philosophy, and apprenticed as a luthier; had multiple jobs in many States; finally found Orthodoxy, which meant God found him; graduated MA in theology from St Vladimir's Seminary and a graduate fellowship at Duke University in counselling. He married late in life, has a 12-year-old son, and loves living now in Western Colorado where he designed and built his own solar house. No more world travel. Family is most important!

HOLLOWAY, DAVID   David taught at the Universities of Bristol and Oxford (mainly American literature and linguistics) and Charterhouse School (chiefly English and Russian language and literature), where he also worked as the museum curator and lieutenant in charge of naval cadets. After retiring, he lectured for a few years in Russian history. He is married with two grown-up sons and is a member of the Friends of Mount Athos, the Johnson Club and the Athenaeum Club.

HOWORTH, PETER   Peter is a retired professional engineer. His career involved managing major projects in food processing, ship repair, and other construction, in New Zealand, Chile, Burma, and the Pacific Islands. As projects got bigger and clients got more demanding, he retired and began building keyboard instruments. A relationship with Sandy Thomas (a relative of his wife) resulted in the drawing of maps for the re-publication of *Dare to be Free*, and joining the path-clearing team. The map for the Holy Mountain then emerged as an abiding passion. Now he continues, as always, to offer to do things that he knows nothing about. It keeps life interesting, if not challenging.

JANSSENS, BART   Bart studied Classics and Byzantine Studies at the universities of Antwerp, Leuven and Thessaloniki. He earned a PhD (2000) in Classical Languages and Literatures from Leuven University with a critical edition of two Christological works by St Maximus the Confessor. As a publishing manager with Brepols Publishers (Turnhout, Belgium) he is responsible for the Latin and Greek titles in the *Corpus Christianorum* series.

LEAVEY, SHAUN, OBE   Shaun served in the British army (Germany, South Arabia, Persian Gulf, and Northern Ireland). After agricultural college and farm work he took up a post in Skiathos to establish a beef farm there for the Konialides family. Later he developed another farm near Aliartos. He left there in 1971 to work for National Farmers' Union (NFU) in the UK and was NFU Regional Director for SE England until 2004. He was appointed chairman of Defra's Sustainable Farming and Food Board for SE England. He retired in 2014.

LOCH, JOICE NANKIVELL, MBE (1887-1982)   Joice was an Australian author, journalist and humanitarian worker who worked with refugees in Poland, Greece, and Romania after World War I and World War II. The Lochs worked in a Quaker-run refugee camp on the outskirts of Thessaloniki for two years before being given a peppercorn rent on a Byzantine tower by the sea in the refugee village of Ouranoupolis, the last settlement before Mount Athos. To help the villagers, Loch purchased looms so that the women could work as rug weavers; she used Byzantine designs for the rugs. For their work in Greece the couple were awarded medals by the King of the Hellenes.

LOCH, SYDNEY (1888-1955)   Sydney was a Gallipoli veteran and a humanitarian worker. He was born in London, raised in Scotland, and sailed to Australia in 1905, aged 17, working first as a jackaroo. He joined the Australian forces at the outbreak of the World War I and served in Gallipoli until being discharged because of wounds and illness. He later became a journalist and writer. He and Joice NanKivell wed in 1919. They sailed for England and secured a contract to write a book on Ireland, which was published as *Ireland in Travail*. In later years he and his wife settled in the tower at Ouranoupolis, and he formed a deep relationship with the people of the Holy Mountain.

MCCORMACK, JOHN   John escaped to Guernsey in 1961, after reading English with Kingsley Amis as tutor in Swansea. After a few years' teaching, he became seduced by old buildings and set about restoring fourteen houses at various times, two of them containing the oldest interiors in St Peter Port, dating to the seventeenth century. He decided to research all buildings shown on the 1787 Richmond Map of Guernsey and eventually produced *The Guernsey House* in 1980, followed by *Channel Island Churches* in 1986. He was elected a Fellow of the Society of Antiquaries of London. He has been a member of FoMA since its inception.

MCINTYRE, PETER (1910-1995)   Peter was born in Dunedin, New Zealand. He abandoned his studies and travelled to England, where he was awarded a BA in Fine Arts at the Slade School of Fine Art. He achieved notable success, graduating with prizes in composition and figure drawing in his final year. In January 1941 he was appointed New Zealand's official war artist, and his work from this period belongs to the collection of war art at National Archives in Wellington. In December 1970 he was made an OBE.

MARTIN, BEN   Ben is an Hellenophile, now retired and living in England. He first went to Greece in 1948, stepping ashore in Piraeus with his mother. That was the first of many visits, and for the last nearly fifty years he has had a small house in the Mani between Mount Taygetos and the sea.

MOLE, JOHN   John has been on three FoMA path-clearing teams and several private pilgrimages. After modern languages at Oxford and an MBA from INSEAD he had a succession of jobs from selling stencil duplicators in Eastern Europe to banking in the Middle East. He wrote the best-selling *It's All Greek To Me!* about life in his village on Evia. Travels in the Aegean have inspired *The Sultan's Organ*, a modern English transcription of the diary of an Elizabethan musician taking a self-playing organ to Constantinople; *Martoni's Pilgrimage*, a translation from Latin of an Italian lawyer's diary of 1393; and *The Hero of Negropont*, a novel.

OSWALD, PHILIP H.   Philip took his degree at King's College, Cambridge, in Classics and Theology, but, having been a keen amateur botanist since his childhood, he worked for 30 years in nature conservation. He first visited Mount Athos in December 1990 on behalf of WWF to report on the ecological consequences of a devastating forest fire. He was one of a three-man team which in three visits in 1991–1993 went to 17 of the 20 ruling monasteries to discuss their environmental and conservation issues, and he has made four further visits to the Holy Mountain, combining botanical investigations with pilgrimage. He became a member of FoMA in 1994 and has taken part in six of its overseas pilgrimages.

PATTERSON, DOUG   Doug trained originally at the Royal College of Art, London, graduating with an MA. He then studied architecture at the Architectural Association, graduating in 1974, formed his own design practice and spent the next twenty-five years designing on a wide variety of projects, ranging from film sets to a private twenty-eight-suite yacht. During the past five years he has been retracing the journeys of three eighteenth- and nineteenth-century travelling artists who recorded the three great world faiths – Islam, Buddhism and Orthodox Christianity. This has involved sketching and painting Islamic mosques and monuments in North Africa and India, Buddhist dzongs in Bhutan and the Christian orthodox monasteries of Mount Athos and Meteora in Greece.

PRICE, ROBIN   Robin is a retired librarian, having served for seven years as Assistant Librarian in the House of Lords and thirty years as Deputy Librarian of the Wellcome Institute for the History of Medicine. He first visited the Holy Mountain in 1963 and has returned many times since.

RACKHAM, OLIVER, OBE, FBA (1939-2015)   In 1958 he won a scholarship to Corpus Christi College, Cambridge, graduating in Natural Sciences in 1961 and subsequently gaining a PhD. He was appointed Honorary Professor of Historical Ecology in the Department of Plant Sciences in 2006 and Honorary Director of the Cambridge Centre for Landscape and People in 2010. Rackham also worked as a tutor in the Kingcombe Centre in Dorset, teaching about the history of woodlands, and studying the ecology, management and development of the British countryside, especially trees, woodlands and wood pasture. His books included *Ancient Woodland* (1980) and *The History of the Countryside* (1986).

SAWDAY, ALASTAIR   Alastair was born in a wooden shack 9,000 feet up the mountains of Kashmir, India, to a lawyer. He boarded at Charterhouse, and after this he read law at Trinity College, Oxford. Over the years he has been involved in development and relief work. In 1994 he published his first travel book on France, and is the founder of Sawdays Travel. The business was for a decade operated from barns near Long Ashton. In 2012, he was granted an honorary Doctor of Letters by Bristol University.

SCHOLTES, ARTUR   Artur was born on the 2 April 1952. His parents later told him that luckily he had been born twenty minutes too late to start his life as an April fool. After leaving school, he studied dentistry at the University of Saarbrücken. During his time there he made his first visit to the Holy Mountain in 1975. In 1982 he opened his own dental practice in a medium-sized town close to the borders of France and Luxembourg. Since 2015 his son, Frederic, has accompanied him on his regular pilgrimages to the Holy Mountain.

SHAKESPEARE, NICHOLAS   Nicholas was born in Worcester and grew up in France, Cambodia, and South America. Translated into more than twenty languages, his prize-winning novels include *The Vision of Elena Silves* (winner of the Somerset

Maugham Award and Betty Trask Award). His non-fiction includes the critically acclaimed authorized biography of Bruce Chatwin, and *In Tasmania*, winner of the 2007 Tasmania Book Prize. He is chief book reviewer of the Daily Telegraph and a Fellow of the Royal Society of Literature.

SIMONS, DEREK   Derek is a retired art lecturer. As an artist, he has painted in various media including egg tempera on icons. Many of his works have been inspired by Mount Athos. He is a trustee of the Monastery of St Antony and St Cuthbert, and a member of FoMA since about 1991. He worships at the Orthodox Church in Shrewsbury.

SOLLY, DOMINIC   Dominic worked for nineteen years as a merchant/investment banker in London until moving to New York. The first nineteen years there were the worst! He then taught high school for seventeen years, for nine years in a tough public school in New York City teaching English to non-native speakers, and then Latin in a prosperous suburb on Long Island. He is currently studying for a doctorate at the Open University on the subject of 'How did Claudian reshape epic to praise Stilicho?'

SPEAKE, GRAHAM   Graham studied classics at Trinity College, Cambridge, and wrote a doctoral thesis at Christ Church, Oxford, on the Byzantine transmission of ancient Greek literature. He is founder and Secretary of the Friends of Mount Athos, author of *Mount Athos: Renewal in Paradise* (Yale University Press 2002, Denise Harvey 2014), a Fellow of the Society of Antiquaries, and Peter Lang's publisher in the UK.

STOOR, THOMAS   Thomas was born in 1955 and is a priest in the Church of Sweden. He was formerly the seamen's priest at the Scandinavian seamen's church in Piraeus, Greece. Revd Dr Stoor has been a member of FoMA since 1991, and is a member of the Lutheran-Orthodox Dialogue in Sweden.

STOTHARD, DAVID   David is a professional town planner who spent most of his working life in central London, managing a team specialising in conservation and development. He retired to the English Lake District in 2016 and now spends his time walking in the mountains, cycling, doing voluntary work and campaigning for the protection of the environment. David visited Mount Athos with the FoMA path-clearing team seven times between 2009 and 2017, leading the team in 2014 and 2017.

SWEHLA, TERRY   Terry lives in Modesto, California, with his wife, Karen. Born and raised in California, he was educated at the University of California, Berkeley, where he received his BA in Religious Studies. He was ordained a Lutheran minister after receiving his seminary training at Pacific Lutheran Theological Seminary, Berkeley. After ten years, he resigned from the Lutheran church. He and his wife were chrismated into the Orthodox Church in 1995, along with their three sons. He is now retired.

TALBOT RICE, NICHOLAS   Nicholas was born in June 1944, the son of David and Tamara Talbot Rice, both noted art historians. Educated at Eton College and Christ Church Oxford, he is married with two children and two grandchildren. He worked in finance in the City of London and in Birmingham and now lives and farms in the Cotswolds.

THOMAS, CHRIS   Chris is the managing director of a successful sports technology business. He is a member of Mensa, Fellow of the Royal Geographical Society, Fellow of the Royal Society of Arts and rather more impressively, a member of the FoMA footpaths team as well as a FoMA trustee. He is the proud father of three adult children, he loves Arsenal FC and football in general and is proud to have coined the slogan for EURO 96 'Football Comes Home', which has since become part of common parlance.

THOMAS, WALTER BABINGTON 'SANDY', CB, DSO, MC & BAR, ED SILVER STAR USA (1919–2017)   Sandy was a New Zealand-born British Army officer. He was commissioned into the New Zealand Military Forces at the outbreak of World War II. During his service in the Middle East, he was wounded, became a prisoner of war in Crete, escaped from a prison hospital, fled to Syria, and was awarded the Military Cross and Bar. As a temporary major he received the Distinguished Service Order in 1943, and rose to command the 23rd Battalion in Italy to become, at age 24, the youngest New Zealand battalion commander in the war. After the war he obtained a commission in the Royal Hampshire Regiment and served in Kenya. He was appointed General Officer Commanding 5th Division in 1968, and Chief of Staff at Headquarters Far East Land Forces in April 1970, before becoming General Officer Commanding Far East Land Forces in October. He was appointed a Companion of the Order of the Bath in 1971, and retired in 1972.

WARE, KALLISTOS Metropolitan Kallistos holds a doctorate in theology from the University of Oxford where from 1966 to 2001 he was Fellow of Pembroke College and Spalding Lecturer in Eastern Orthodox Studies. He is a monk of the monastery of St John the Theologian, Patmos, and was ordained to the priesthood in 1966. Since 1982 (as Bishop Kallistos of Diokleia) he has been assistant bishop to the Greek Orthodox Archdiocese of Thyateira and Great Britain. His publications include *The Orthodox Church* (Penguin, 1963, 1993, 2015) and *The Orthodox Way* (Mowbray, 1979), and he is co-translator of the five-volume *Philokalia* (Faber and Faber, 1979–1999). He is currently President of the Friends of Mount Athos.

WARRACK, JOHN John was born in London in 1928 and is an English music critic, writer on music, and oboist. He is the son of Scottish conductor and composer Guy Warrack. From 1954 until 1961 he was music critic for The Daily Telegraph, and from 1961 until 1972 he was music critic for The Sunday Telegraph. From 1978 until 1983 he served as the Artistic Director of the Leeds Festival. From 1984 until 1993 he taught on the music faculty at the University of Oxford. He is the author of *Carl Maria von Weber* (1968, 2nd ed. 1976), the standard study of Weber in English; *German Opera: From the Beginnings to Wagner* (2001) and the co-author of *The Concise Oxford Dictionary of Opera* (1964, with Harold Rosenthal) and *The Oxford Dictionary of Opera* (1992, with Ewan West).

WHORLOW, COLIN Colin left Oxford with a maths degree to join the civil service. Both his job and his leisure time include plenty of international travel. He is a member of FoMA and visited Mount Athos in 1998 with his friend Michael, who was subsequently best man at his wedding. Colin spends much time setting and solving puzzles, and is pleased to have survived appearing on 'Only Connect' without doing anything embarrassing.

Book List

A much longer list of valuable books for further reading could be produced here – one only has to consult the book review section in the FoMA annual reports or see the list of Publications by the Friends of Mount Athos printed in front of the present volume. The selective list of English titles given below came into existence rather randomly during the compilation of this book and does not claim to be complete in any way. Its main aim is to inform and excite readers, both present and future.

Archimandrite Sophrony, *St Silouan the Athonite*, St Vladimir's Seminary Press.

Averitt, Neil, *The Single Gospel: Matthew, Mark, Luke and John Consolidated into a Single Narrative*, Wipf and Stock, 2015.

Bryer, Anthony, and Mary Cunningham (eds), *Mount Athos and Byzantine Monasticism. Papers from the Twenty-eighth Spring Symposium of Byzantine Studies, Birmingham, March 1994*, Aldershot: Variorum, 1996.

Byron, Robert, *The Station: Athos: Treasures and Men*, London: Duckworth, 1928; Phoenix Press, 2000.

Cairns, Scott, *Short Trip to the Edge: A Pilgrimage to Prayer*, HarperOne, 2007.

Conomos, Dimitri, and Graham Speake (eds), *Mount Athos the Sacred Bridge*, Oxford: Peter Lang, 2005.

Curnow, Trevor, *Pantokrator: An Introduction to Orthodoxy*, Cambridge Scholars Publishing, 2007.

Curzon, Robert, Jr., *Ancient Monasteries of the East, Or: Visits to Monasteries in the Levant*, London, 1849; reprint Piscataway, NJ: Gorgias Press, 2001.

Dalrymple, William, *From the Holy Mountain. A Journey in the Shadow of Byzantium*, HarperCollins, 1997.

Dawkins, R. M., *The Monks of Athos*, London: George Allen & Unwin, 1936.

della Dora, Veronica, *Imagining Mount Athos: Visions of a Holy Place, from Homer to World War II*, Charlottesville and London: University of Virginia Press, 2011.

Elder Aimilianos, *The Way of the Spirit: Reflections on Life in God*, Athens: Indiktos, 2009.

——, *The Authentic Seal: Spiritual Instruction and Discourses*, Ormylia, 1999.

Elder Joseph, *Monastic Wisdom*, St Antony's.

——, *Elder Joseph the Hesychast*, Vatopaidi.

Elder Paisios, *The Epistles*, St John the Theologian.

——, *Spiritual Counsels*, St John the Theologian.

——, *Saint Arsenios the Cappadocian*, St John the Theologian.

Elder Porphyrios, *Wounded by Love: The Life and Wisdom of Saint Porphyrios*, Limni (Evia, Greece): Denise Harvey, 2005.

Golitzin, Alexander, *The Living Witness of the Holy Mountain: Contemporary Voices from Mount Athos*, South Canaan, PA: St Tikhon's Seminary Press, 1996.

Gothóni, René, and Graham Speake (eds), *The Monastic Magnet: Roads to and from Mount Athos*, Oxford: Peter Lang, 2008.

Hieromonk Christodoulos, *Elder Paisios of the Holy Mountain*, Holy Mountain, 1998.

Kefalopoulou, Eleni, *Mount Athos Wines. The History of Winemaking on the Holy Mountain*, Athens, 2018.

Konidaris, Ioannis M., *The Mount Athos Avaton*, Athens: Sakkoulas, 2003.

——, *The Status of Mount Athos*, Mount Athos, 2019.

Loch, Sydney, *Athos: The Holy Mountain*, London: Lutterworth Press, 1957.

Loch, Joice NanKivell, *A Fringe of Blue: An Autobiography*, London: John Murray, 1968.

Mathewes-Greene, Frederica, *The Jesus Prayer: The Ancient Desert Prayer that Tunes the Heart to God*, Paraclete Press, 2009.

Merrill, Christopher, *Journey to the Holy Mountain*, HarperCollins, 2004.

Metropolitan Hierotheos, *A Night in the Desert of the Holy Mountain: Discussion with a Hermit on the Jesus Prayer*, Birth of the Theotokos Monastery.

Monk Epiphanios of Mylopotamos, *The Cuisine of the Holy Mountain Athos*, Synchronoi Orizontes, 2010.

Mylonas, Paul M., *Atlas of the Twenty Sovereign Monasteries: Topography and Historical Architecture*, Tübingen, Wasmuth, 2000.

Norwich, John Julius, and Reresby Sitwell, with photographs by the authors and A. Costa, *Mount Athos*, London: Hutchinson, 1966.

Palmer, G. E. H., Philip Sherrard, and Kallistos Ware (transl.), *The Philokalia: The Complete Text compiled by St Nikodimos of the Holy Mountain and St Makarios of Corinth*, London: Faber & Faber.

Pennington, M. Basil, *The Monks of Athos: A Western Monk's Extraordinary Spiritual Journey on Eastern Holy Ground*, 2003.

Sherrard, Philip, *Athos: The Holy Mountain*, London: Sidgwick & Jackson, 1982.

Speake, Graham, *Mount Athos: Renewal in Paradise*, New Haven: Yale University Press, 2002; 2nd ed., Limni (Evia, Greece): Denise Harvey, 2014.

Speake, Graham, and Kallistos Ware (eds), *Mount Athos: Microcosm of the Christian East*, Oxford: Peter Lang, 2012.

——, *Spiritual Guidance on Mount Athos*, Oxford, Peter Lang, 2015.

St Ephraim, *Elder Ephraim of Katounakia*, Katounaikia.

The Way of a Pilgrim (anon.), translated by R. M. French, Harper.

Thomas, W. B. 'Sandy', *Dare to be Free: One of the Greatest True Stories of World War II*, Cassell Military Paperbacks.

Ware, Kallistos, *The Inner Kingdom*, St Vladimir's Seminary Press, 2000.

Ware, Timothy (Kallistos), *The Orthodox Church: An Introduction to Eastern Christianity*.

Glossary

Abaton the traditional principle, common to all monasteries, that enables monks and nuns to close their doors to members of the opposite sex.

Arsanas port.

Asceterion a single dwelling for an ascetic.

Archontariki guest-house.

Archontaris guest-master.

Axion Estin ('It is meet') a hymn to the Virgin sung at the Divine Liturgy and other services; also the title of the holiest icon on Athos, preserved in the sanctuary of the church of the Protaton in Karyes.

Bematoris the monk in charge of the sanctuary.

Cenobitic system the system by which monks live a common life in spiritual obedience to an abbot, worshipping and eating together, and contributing any wealth they may have to the Common purse; cf. idiorrhythmic system.

Cenobium a house in which monks live according to the cenobitic system (q.v.).

Chrysobull a document or charter bearing the emperor's gold seal.

Corona a large brass candelabrum suspended in the nave of the church.

De-esis a visual representation of Christ flanked by the Virgin and St John the Baptist in which the Virgin and St John intercede with Christ on behalf of the world.

Deification the doctrine by which mankind shares in the divine nature – 'God became human that we might become divine', according to Byzantine theology.

Diamonitirion the official permit or visa that permits a pilgrim to enter Athos and to enjoy hospitality at the monasteries.

Diakonima the work or duty allotted to a monk.

Dikaios the prior of a skete.

Docheiaris the monk in charge of provisions.

Dokimos a novice.

Enkolpion a pendant bearing a sacred image that is worn 'on the breast'.

Epistasia the governing body of the Holy Community on Athos.

Epitropos the representative of a monastery.

Exonarthex the antechamber to the narthex (q.v.) in an Orthodox church.

Filioque the doctrine stating that the Holy Spirit proceeds from the Father and the Son.

FoMA the Friends of Mount Athos.

Gerontas Charismatic Elder.

Hegoumenos the abbot of a cenobitic monastery.

Hesychasm a spiritual tradition developed by St John Klimakos (seventh century) for whom hesychia ('tranquillity') was a state of inner silence and vigilance, closely associated with the name of Jesus and the repetition of short prayers.

Hesychasterion a remote hermitage.

Hieromonk Priest-monk.

Iconostasis the stand, separating the altar from the nave, on which icons are displayed.

Idiorrhythmic system the system by which monks were permitted to set their own pattern, were not bound by the vow of poverty or of obedience to an abbot, and lived in separate apartments, often with their own servants and their own worldly goods, neither eating together nor contributing to a common purse; cf. cenobitic system.

Kalderimi cobblestone-paved track or path.

Kalyve a cottage-sized monastic dwelling containing a small chapel and no land.

Kathisma a cell with a chapel next door, close to the parent monastery.

Katholikon the main church of a monastery.

Kellion a monk's cell; also a separate monastic house with a chapel and several rooms, perhaps inhabited by three or four monks.

Kenosis the emptying of the self to let God work through you.

Konaki a monastery's residence in Karyes, inhabited by that monastery's representative to the Holy Community.

Kopanos a wooden blade hung from a pair of chains or an omega-shaped piece of iron, struck with a mallet to call the faithful to services.

Ktitor the founder of a monastery; also used to refer to a major benefactor.

Kyriakon the main church of a skete, used for worship on Sunday (Kyriaki).

Lavra an assembly of anchorites.

Loukoumi Turkish delight, served to pilgrims on a guest tray, along with coffee, water, and either raki or ouzo.

Metanoia to repent; to turn toward God; to make the sign of the Cross.

Metochion a dependency of a ruling monastery.

Narthex the antechapel or vestibule at the west end of an Orthodox church.

Orthros matins.

Panaghia immaculate or all-holy, an adjective used to describe the Virgin Mary.

Panegyri the annual celebration of a monastery or skete for the feast of its dedication.

Parousia the Second Coming of Christ.

Phiale a basin for holy water.

Prohegoumenos the principal of an idiorrhythmic monastery.

Prosmonarios the monk responsible for the icon of the Axion Estin.

Proskynitis a pilgrim.

Protos hesychastes the 'first hesychast', subsequently shortened to Protos (first), as the primate of Athos is still known.

Rason a loose-cut gown with billowing sleeves, part of the monastic habit.

Schema the monastic habit the small schema (now rarely conferred) is the first grade; the great schema (or great habit) denotes the highest rank to which a monk may be promoted.

Semantron a kind of double-bladed oar struck with a mallet to call the faithful to services.

Skete one of twelve monastery-like settlements on Athos: a monastic village or group of houses gathered around a central church (or kyriakon, *q.v.*), dependent upon a ruling monastery.

Starets a Russian holy man.

Stasidia the wooden chairs lining the walls of the church.

Stylite an ascetic who lives atop a pillar.

Synaxis a meeting of the brotherhood of a monastery or of the representatives to the Holy Community in Karyes.

Talanton a wooden plank used instead of a bell to summon the fathers to prayer.

Theoria the vision by which hesychasts are initiated into spiritual knowledge.

Theosis deification, the mystical union between God and man.

Theotokos the Virgin Mary or Mother of God, as she is known to the Orthodox.

Trapeza the refectory of a monastery.

Typikon the rule or charter by which a monastery or group of monasteries is governed.

List of Illustrations